OPEN WOUNDS

VICKEN CHETERIAN

Open Wounds

*Armenians, Turks and a Century
of Genocide*

OXFORD
UNIVERSITY PRESS

Oxford University Press is a department of the
University of Oxford. It furthers the University's objective
of excellence in research, scholarship, and education
by publishing worldwide.

Oxford   New York

Auckland   Cape Town   Dar es Salaam   Hong Kong   Karachi
Kuala Lumpur   Madrid   Melbourne   Mexico City   Nairobi
New Delhi   Shanghai   Taipei   Toronto

With offices in

Argentina   Austria   Brazil   Chile   Czech Republic   France   Greece
Guatemala   Hungary   Italy   Japan   Poland   Portugal   Singapore
South Korea   Switzerland   Thailand   Turkey   Ukraine   Vietnam

Oxford is a registered trade mark of Oxford University Press
in the UK and certain other countries.

Published in the United States of America by
Oxford University Press
198 Madison Avenue, New York, NY 10016,
United States of America

Published in the United Kingdom in 2015
by C. Hurst & Co. (Publishers) Ltd.

Library of Congress Cataloging-in-Publication Data
is available for this title.

ISBN 978-0-19-026350-8

1 3 5 7 9 8 6 4 2
Printed in the United States of America
on acid-free paper

To Varoujan and Siruni
who have witnessed

CONTENTS

ACKNOWLEDGEMENTS

I never thought I would write a book on the Armenian Genocide. Simply reading about this history was unbearably painful. As a kid, while growing up in a country in war, I did not want to be associated with survivors of massacres. As an adult, even if I worked in conflict zones reporting and analysing wars and revolutions, I tried as much as possible to avoid reading and writing about the Genocide. So I was surprised at my spontaneous answer to the suggestion of my publisher Michael Dwyer to write a book on the occasion of the centenary of the Armenian Genocide: I will not write about the Genocide itself I said, since there are some excellent books that were published recently about the subject, but I suggest instead to write about the political history of the Genocide since then and the consequences of denialism.

Later, as I was wondering what made me answer positively to write this book, I realised it was the changes taking place in Turkey over the last few years. The politics of absolute denialism, next to the massive destruction that the Genocide itself had caused, erected an unsurpassable barrier between the survivors on the one hand, and modern Turks and Turkey on the other. It was this growing awareness inside Turkey that alleviated the pain to a degree that made the work bearable. It also made the research on the consequences of the Genocide possible. In the past few years, the memory of the vanished Armenians has made a strong comeback. People in Turkey want to learn the truth about the conditions in which one part of their population, the Armenians, suddenly vanished. Others are searching for the stories of their ancestors, acknowledging their victimhood, or even confessing to being grandchildren of the perpetrators. Some want to apologize for what happened, for the killings itself and for the one hundred years of indifference. I was genuinely curious to know why, after suppressing the memory of this great crime for nine decades, did the debate return to Turkey? At the same time, I was continuously frustrated to think that for nine long decades there was dead silence in Turkey, reinforced by international indifference to this silence. How could so many intellectuals, scholars, and artists be so oblivious to the enormity of the crime that happened on their land and in their names? How could they remain indifferent to the continuous suffering, keep their silence for so long? This book, therefore, is the product of the tension between hope that truth cannot be repressed and will eventually prevail, hope in the possibility of justice even after one hundred years, and on the other hand the frustration that human beings can accommodate living in darkness for so long.

It was a handful of courageous men, and women, who made this change possible. They challenged those in power and their deep-rooted lies, by risking their lives, and at times by paying the ultimate price. Their choice of struggle was writing: articles, letters, and mostly books. As I was researching, many of the people I interviewed were either authors, or themselves working on books. But there are also the others, those who egotistically used their position of intellectual authority, their freedom of expression to serve power, to serve denialist silence, or even to justify the criminal enterprise. Still, when we are in need of truth, we first turn to books.

It continues to be important to read and to write books on the Armenian Genocide. Even a hundred years later undoing its mystery is charged with lessons. The first major mass slaughter of the twentieth century provides a unique case study to social scientists to see what is the price we have collectively paid, and the consequences for providing impunity in a crime of such magnitude. Armenian survivors have always said that impunity encourages mass murder and genocide. In this book I tried to show that this impunity and the shroud of denialism provided the necessary cover to continue the

ACKNOWLEDGEMENTS

crime for nearly a century: Armenian as well as other minority communities such as Greeks and Assyrians, continued to be targeted: their property was confiscated again and again, their cultural heritage destroyed, and pogroms threatened their physical security. I also show that the continuity is also on the side of the perpetrators. Impunity allowed the criminal structures that were responsible for organizing and committing the crime to continue to survive at the heart of the Turkish state, sometimes visible, and often not, popularly known as the Deep State. Minority and majority being a relative conception I also discuss how Kurds who once were instrumental in destroying their Armenian neighbours fell victims to the same mechanisms of denialism, of suppression and massacres. I have also shown how future perpetrators, from Nazi Germany to Azerbaijani nationalism, looked at the Armenian Genocide for inspiration; their conclusion was that mass murder is an efficient and accepted means to resolve conflicts, as long as one emerges militarily victorious in the end. The curse of the victims has remained with us, as we see again today in the Middle East, where entire civilian populations, ethnic and religious groups, minorities and majorities become targets of mass murder, rape and forced conversion as if the region that once was ruled by the Ottomans is unable to overcome its dark violence.

While working on this book I have accumulated enormous debt towards many who have helped generously my efforts to finish on time. I am especially grateful to Calouste Gulbenkian Foundation for a generous and timely grant, without which I could not have realized several visits to Armenia, Lebanon and Turkey, which thereby enabled me to complete my narration. I also thank the support of several of the Armenian foundations in Geneva including Hagop Topalian Foundation, Diran and Charles Philippossian Foundation, Fonds Hayastan, as well as the National Association for Armenian Studies and Research, and my colleagues at Webster University Geneva. Several people read parts of the manuscript and made valuable comments, and I would like to thank Hovann Simonian, Ozcan Yilmaz, and Razmik Panossian for that. I would also like to thank the anonymous peer reviewers for their helpful remarks and suggestions. In Istanbul I would

ACKNOWLEDGEMENTS

like to thank Ardashes Margosyan from Aras, Karin Karakaşli, Rober Koptaş and Fatih Gökhan Diler from Agos for their continuous support, Timur and Sakip Erdoğdu for their hospitality in Istanbul and Malatya, and Engin Pişkin for sharing with me his passion for the Armenian culture from Van to Ani. I also want to thank Bariş Alen, Vahé Gabrache, Raymond Kévorkian, Meda Khachatourian, Giro Manoyan, Ara Sanjian, Paul Sarkissian, Ronald Grigor Suny, Amaduni Virabyan. Special thanks to Michael Dwyer for his continuous support for this as well as other projects, as well as to Tim Page and Georgie Williams for copy editing. Their efforts not only eliminated mistakes but also made this book more readable. I would like to thank them for their efforts. Lastly, many people gave me their time to answer to my questions, some are quoted in this book but many others are not. I remain appreciative to their time and efforts.

This work took me long hours away from my family, travelling for interviews, or spending long nights in front of books or the screen. I could not have managed the stress without the love and continuous support of Carine, and the patience of Varoujan, Jivan, and Noé. I express my affection and gratitude to them.

I would like to dedicate this book to Varoujan and Siruni, two persons "who have witnessed".

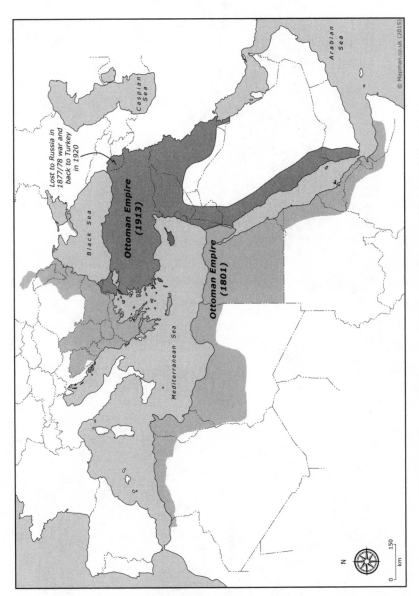

Map 1: Collapse of an empire. Ottoman territorial losses 1801–1914.

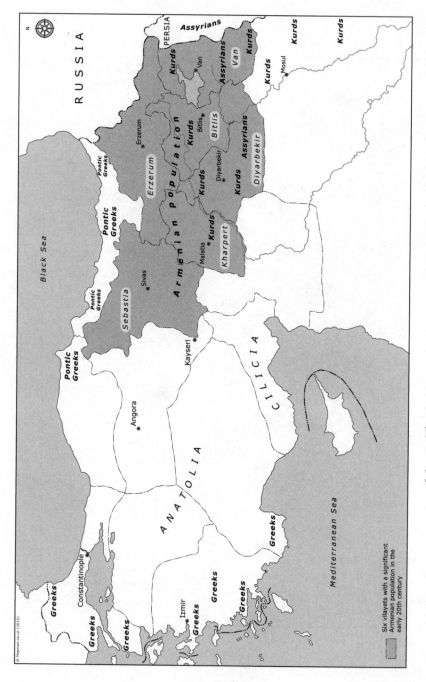

Map 2: The Six Armenian provinces, before 1914.

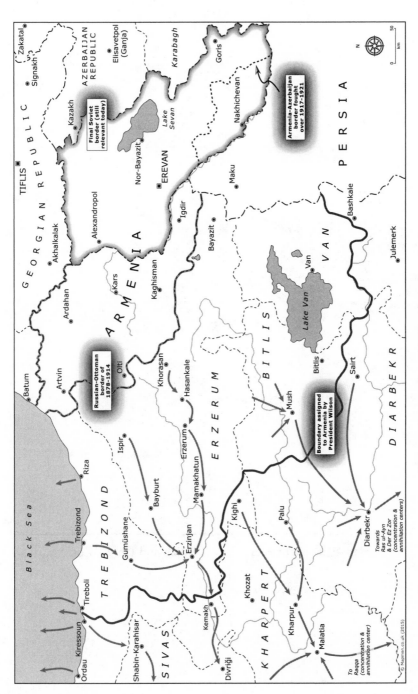

Map 3: Genocide and Wilsonian Armenia.

Map 4: Sanjak of Alexandretta, Anjar, and Der Ez-Zor.

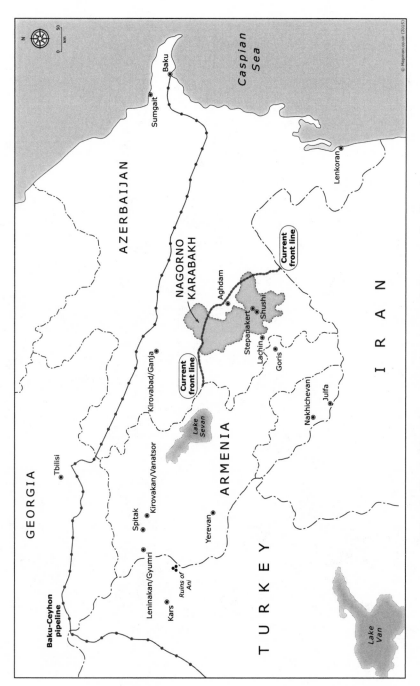

Map 5: Karabakh autonomous borders and the cease-fire frontline.

1

'WE ARE ALL HRANT DINK,
WE ARE ALL ARMENIAN'

THE SACRIFICE

Hrant Dink had just left his office at 192 Halaskargazi Street, in the Osmanbey district of Istanbul, when someone approached him. He had been anxious the whole day, and had felt the same way the entire week. A student from Ankara had asked to meet Dink, the editor-in-chief of *Agos*. But the receptionist had refused to let the unknown youth enter the editorial offices as he did not have an appointment. The young man hovered nearby. Video cameras positioned on the bank next-door and the shops nearby show him waiting in the neighbourhood streets. A couple of hours later Hrant Dink left the *Agos* offices and went out on to the street—it was then that the young man approached him, took a handgun from his jacket and fired three bullets at point-blank range into the back of Dink's head. He was killed instantly. Upon hearing the gunshots, Dink's friends and colleagues from the newspaper immediately went to see what had happened. When the photojournalists arrived, he was lying face-down in front of the entrance to the office, his lifeless body covered by large sheets of newspaper and blood flowing on the pavement. Within a few hours pictures had begun to circulate in the Turkish and global media. In the images, the soles of Dink's shoes were visible, a large hole discernible in the left one. It was Friday, 19 January 2007.

The news quickly spread throughout the city. Within minutes a crowd had gathered at the site—friends, journalists and political activists rushed to *Agos* in disbelief: 'We are all Hrant Dink. We are all Armenians,' they shouted. There was a sense of defiance in their gaze, as if they were saying 'Come on bastards, come kill us too.' In the evening the crowd walked to Taksim Square, less than 3 kilometres away. There, the crowd kept growing in size. People were standing in silence, holding candles together with portraits of the slain journalist.

Three days later, on the day of Hrant Dink's funeral, something happened that no one could have expected: tens of thousands of people marched behind his coffin. One participant wrote on his blog that the mourners were like waves filling a six-lane road packed with people for more than 4 kilometres. They first gathered in front of the offices of *Agos*, and from there they marched 8 kilometres through the streets of Istanbul until they reached Balikli cemetery. Many people had travelled from distant provinces and cities to attend the funeral. Thousands more gathered in major Turkish cities such as Ankara, Izmir, Diyarbakir, Bodrum and in Dink's birthplace, Malatya, to protest the killing. They were Armenians, Turks, Kurds, foreigners, Islamists, human rights activists and leftist militants. They were citizens of Turkey. As the funeral procession advanced through the streets of Istanbul, thousands more leaned from their office windows and gathered on balconies to wave their hands or throw flowers. Many wept as they marched. As the mourners crossed Fatih district, demonstrators saw armed men wearing black ski masks standing on rooftops and elevated positions. Were they positioned there to protect the marchers? Or were they there to shoot the protestors if orders were issued to do so? Although the Dink family had asked for a silent procession without any political sloganeering, thousands of people were shouting slogans calling for solidarity and brotherhood between nations, as well as anti-fascist slogans. The funeral marchers were carrying red carnations distributed to them by the municipality, while many others were holding round, black posters, with the words:

'Hepimiz Hrant Dink'iz' and 'Hepimiz Ermeniyiz'—'We are all Hrant Dink. We are all Armenian.'

Turkish society had clearly come a long way since the press conference thirteen years earlier in which Hrant Dink first became active in engaging Turkish public opinion with the aim of telling the story of his people; yet what a price he had been forced to pay.

The funeral was even attended by Turkish officials. During his lifetime, Hrant Dink had been subject to almost constant state harassment, defending himself in one court case after another in order to protect his reputation against seemingly endless legal attacks. For a man persecuted by the Turkish justice system and attacked by the Turkish nationalist media as a 'traitor', the presence of high-level officials at his funeral—including Deputy Prime Minister Mehmet Ali Sahin and the Interior Minister Abdulkadir Aksu (both representing the ruling AK Party)—was utterly surreal.[1]

One of the most astonishing aspects in the drama of Hrant Dink's murder was the reaction of the public, the way in which it catalysed a deep change in Turkish society, a process that began with the thousands of people who mobilised to attend the funeral and express their opposition to the racist murder. 'We never imagined that such a thing, that thousands of people could go down the streets, to take part in the funeral,' said Karin Karakaşli, a colleague of Hrant Dink at *Agos*. 'When I was walking in the procession I did not realise its size, how huge it was. Our pain and grief overtook us all. Then, at a certain moment, I could see the sea of people marching, the thousands walking around me with us, and I thought: "My God, something is happening here, but what is it?"'[2]

An entire country had changed. The thousands of people who expressed their grief, their repugnance at the assassination, saw Hrant Dink as embodying yet another victim of the state repression committed in the name of the Turkish nation. It was the largest public demonstration in Turkey for three decades, and those attending had reason to be nervous. During the last mass public demonstration, on Labour Day 1977, up to half a million people had gathered at Taksim Square to listen to trade union leaders, when gunfire suddenly rained

3

down on them from the surrounding buildings and from the trucks parked on the edge of the square. Around thirty-five demonstrators were killed and hundreds more wounded; when the police cars arrived, they arrested the demonstrators rather than the killers.

In the period since the 1980 military coup, large numbers of journalists, human rights activists and intellectuals have been arrested, tortured or assassinated in Turkey. Indeed, Hrant Dink was the sixty-second journalist to have been killed in Turkey since the 1908 revolution and the demise of Sultan Abdul Hamid II's (r. 1876–1909) regime.[3] Long before that date, many Armenians—as well as Greeks, Assyrians, Alevis and Yezidis—had been killed in silence, with their families often failing to file a complaint to the police, such was their lack of faith in the Turkish justice system.

For decades, calling someone 'Armenian' in Turkey was the worst kind of insult—yet, at Dink's funeral, thousands of people sought to demonstrate their defiance by saying 'we are all Armenians'. Why did so many people come together to attend Hrant Dink's funeral? What were the changes taking place in the country that led thousands of people to raise their voices against a political murder? Moreover, who was Hrant Dink, and how did he come to exert this kind of influence?

Dink became a public figure in Turkey as the editor of the bi-lingual Armenian–Turkish weekly paper *Agos* (meaning 'furrow' in Armenian), which was founded in 1996 and published in Istanbul. In its eleven years under his direction, *Agos* succeeded in creating a bridge between the secluded Armenian community of Istanbul and various currents of Turkish public opinion. He himself crossed that bridge to become a symbol of the struggle for human and minority rights, and of the struggle for democracy and European integration. He had become a close friend of leading intellectual figures in Istanbul including writers, journalists, professors and human rights activists. His remarks condemning restrictions on freedom of speech were often quoted in the foreign media along with his stinging critiques of governmental censorship.[4] As Hrant Dink grew in popularity he increasingly irritated the Turkish authorities by writing editorials on minority rights, which touched on topics long considered taboo, and for reminding the Turkish public about the previous existence of a vast Armenian community in that country, a community that had suddenly vanished during the dark days of the First World War, with silence reigning as to their fate ever since.

'Jesus Christ was the First Socialist'

Hrant Dink was fifty-three years old when he was assassinated. He was born in 1954 in the south-eastern town of Malatya, the capital of Turkish apricot production. Sarkis, his father, was a tailor who had been born in the Sivas district, while his mother, Gülvart, was from Gürün. Like many Armenians in Anatolia, Sarkis Dink had a second, Turkish name: Haşim Kalfa. This in itself indicates the persecution faced by Anatolian Armenians—decades after the genocide, living in republican Turkey, they were forced to conceal their ethnic and religious identity and take a Turkish name in order to survive while simultaneously living in the midst of people who knew their real origins and would remind them of this whenever they felt it necessary to do so.

Hrant Dink was six years old when the family moved to Istanbul; his parents divorced a year later, and Dink, along with his brother, was sent to the Armenian Evangelical Church of Gedik-Pasha, where Pastor Hrant Guzelian had created a boarding school for children from the Anatolian provinces. He later went to the Sourp Khach Tbrevank (Holy Cross) secondary school in Uskudar.

Two encounters were to prove decisive in these formative years of Dink's life, encounters which provided the spiritual references that nourished his soul and laid the basis for his worldview. The first was a meeting with Rakel Yağbasan, a young Armenian girl originally from Silopi (on the border with Syria and Iraq). They first met at the Gedik-Pasha boarding school, and some years later Dink would express his love for her. Rakel belongs to the once-large Vartan clan, known as Varto in Turkey, and was originally from Mush. Yet during the genocide the family escaped to the mountainous regions of southern Turkey before establishing themselves in the Jezire region near the Iraqi border, close to the town of Silopi. For decades the few hundred surviving clan members thought they were 'the only Armenians left in the world', and tried to preserve their identity through inter-marriage, despite the practice being prohibited in the Armenian tradition.[5] Hrant Dink and Rakel married in 1977.

The young couple soon became very involved with the Protestant Armenian Church, and especially the summer camp of the Gedik-Pasha boarding school, known as the Tuzla camp. In 1979 the Turkish police arrested Pastor Guzelian on the spurious grounds that he had abducted children from the provinces and had been involved in training extremists in his church. Guzelian was tortured extensively while in captivity, a punishment he was forced to endure simply for bringing Armenian children to Istanbul and providing them with an Armenian education. After his arrest, Dink and Rakel took over the responsibilities of the church as well as the Tuzla camp.

But the authorities did not leave them in peace. The Turkish government launched a court case against the Tuzla camp on the grounds that it had been purchased illegally, just one example of the ongoing state repression of non-Muslim minorities and in particular the campaign to confiscate their capital and property. The Tuzla case stretches back to 1936, when the government ordered all non-Muslim minorities to prepare a list of their real estate properties. In the 1970s, in the context of Turkish–Greek tension over Cyprus, the Turkish state decided to unleash yet another wave of repression against its own religious minorities: the government now declared that any property acquired by minority foundations in Turkey that was not on the 1936 list was unlawful and would be confiscated. The Tuzla camp was finally confiscated in 1984 after a long court battle. The state returned it back to the previous owner of the land, without paying any compensation to the church. Hrant Dink and Rakel Dink were devastated. He reflected on this event years later:

> I went to Tuzla when I was eight. I worked there very hard for 20 years. I met my wife Rakel there. We grew up together. We married there. Our children were born there … One day, they gave us a paper from a court …

'You, minority institutions are not entitled to buy any property! It turns out that we made a mistake when we permitted you to do so back then. Now, this place will be returned to its previous owner.' We lost after fighting for five years ... Unfortunately, we were opposed by the state. Hear my cry humanity! ... They threw us away from the civilization we created. They took away the labor of one thousand and five hundred children who were raised there. They took away our labor, children's labor. If they had made there an orphanage for poor children, if they had used it as a camp for poor or handicapped children of whatever identity, I would have given my blessing. But I do not give now ...[6]

The other formative influence to have acted on Hrant Dink during his youth came from his fellow students at Tbrevank, one of the five Armenian secondary schools in Istanbul. Tbrevank was a boarding school, primarily for Armenian boys from various towns in Anatolia; the only pupils who had been born in Istanbul were orphans. As a number of the teachers at the school had leftist sympathies, it became something of a hotbed of socialist ideas and secret Communist societies. In the words of Zakarya Mildanoglu, a former student, 'Tbrevank was a laboratory of leftist organisations.'[7] One such person was Garbis Altinoglu, one of the earliest converts to Maoism in Turkey. Even before the translation of Maoist classics into Turkish, Altinoglu used to hold an English version of Mao's Little Red Book and simultaneously translate it into Turkish in front of an audience composed of captivated young idealists.

Dink often attended such meetings and was influenced by the discussions about the coming revolution. But the individual who left the deepest impression on him was his classmate Armenak Bakirçiyan, who later changed his name to the more Turkish-sounding Orhan Bakir. This former student of Tbrevank later became an icon of Turkish leftist activism, known for his role within the Maoist guerrilla movement, the Workers' and Peasants' Liberation Army of Turkey (Türkiye İşci ve Köylü Kurtuluş Ordusu, TIKKO). This organisation was the armed wing of the Maoist Turkish organisation, the Communist Party of Turkey/Marxist–Leninist (Türkiye Komünist Partisi/Marksist–Leninist, TKP/ML). TKP/ML was founded by Ibrahim Kaypakkaya on 24 April 1972, the same day on which the Armenian Genocide is commemorated.[8] Dink and Bakirçiyan were close friends, part of a larger group of idealistic leftist revolutionaries. As Bakirçiyan become increasingly involved in the Turkish revolutionary movement, he told Dink: 'You found the love of your heart, go and make a family. From now on our relationship should remain within limits.' The Maoist activists believed that the revolution should start in the provinces before advancing towards the cities. It was for this reason that many young militants left for the mountains with the aim of launching a guerrilla war against the 'fascist state', thereby emulating Mao Tse-tung's experience and the Long March, or later the disembarking of Fidel Castro and Ernesto Che Guevara on Cuba. Bakirçiyan—or Orhan Bakir, who was also known by his nom de guerre 'Ali Daye'—was one of these young, educated and urban men who left Istanbul to go to the remote mountain provinces. He was eventually killed in 1978 in an armed clash with the Turkish security forces in Karakoçan, Elâzığ province. His heroism continues to be celebrated in the eastern high plateaus, where the idea of making the ultimate sacrifice in the asymmetrical struggle against an unjust and foreign state has an enduring popular appeal.

Another member of the group, Hayrabed Hancer, was a year younger than Dink. Hancer was ultimately killed by the security forces in Caesarea (Kayseri).

Although Dink was certainly influenced by the intellectual atmosphere at the school, he did not join any of the radical leftist groups— it seems more than likely that the loss of his friend encouraged him to distance himself from the Maoists and other socialist rebels. Yet this did not prevent him from being arrested—like thousands of others—after the military coup of September 1980, whereupon he was imprisoned for forty-five days and subjected to torture. 'We did not know where he was taken. We walked from prison to prison and finally we found him after a week,' Rakel Dink told me.[9] He would continue to suffer from the trauma of his experience in prison for a long period thereafter. Although the authorities refused to tell him what crime he had actually committed, for many years he was denied a passport and was unable to travel abroad.

When I asked Rakel Dink if socialist ideas had influenced Hrant, she told me there was another important source that influenced his thoughts: Christianity. 'Wasn't Jesus Christ the first socialist?' In addition to the ideas he first encountered in school, Hrant was also heavily influenced by a number of Armenian Christian priests. He had attended schools run by the Armenian Protestant Church ever since he had arrived in Istanbul as a child, later going on to attend the Holy Cross Church Seminary—Tbrevank. As he grew up, he was influenced by Patriarch Shnorhk Kaloustian, and later a close collaborator of Archbishop Mesrob Mutafian. As Rakel Dink put it, 'All three Armenian churches, Apostolic, Catholic and Protestant, have toiled for us.'

According to Tuba Çandar, the author of a biography of Dink, 'Hrant was a leftist, and most of his friends thought that he was an atheist. But he was not.'[10] She remembered how she was first introduced to Dink at a funeral in Istanbul:

Cengiz [Cengiz Çandar, her husband] introduced me to Rakel saying: 'This is the Armenian girl who thought she was Kurdish', and then turned to Hrant and said: 'And this is the secular leader of the Armenians.' Hrant's reaction was: 'Ulan Allahsez [Oh you Godless] why don't you introduce me properly.'

Hrant Dink was a decisive, rebellious person. He was not reckless, however; he used to gauge the risks he was taking by the way the authorities responded to his activities, something which comes instinctively to Armenians who were born in and live in Turkey. Unlike some self-styled revolutionaries, Hrant Dink actively practised what he preached. He was rebellious, disobeying school rules, which often got him into trouble with the school administration. On one occasion a Turkish army officer was trying to deliver a lesson on civil defence, and the topic was what to do in case of a fire. Hrant Dink stood up and said: 'Sir, there is a fire burning in my heart', meaning that he was in love. The class erupted in laughter, and he was promptly suspended from school. He finally left Tbrevank at the age of sixteen when he and some of his classmates were expelled for a violent attack on his English teacher, and he was forced to finish his last school year at a Turkish secondary school in Şişli.

Hrant Dink studied zoology at Istanbul University, and eventually followed courses in philosophy, thanks to a student grant from the Gulbenkian Foundation.[11] After leaving university, he opened a photography shop along with his brothers, before later running a bookshop in Bakirköy called 'Beyaz Adam', or 'White Man'. Yet for all his success as a businessman, Dink's true passion was writing. He was a regular contributor to the Armenian-language newspaper *Marmara*, where he would write reviews of Turkish books on Armenian issues, some of which were so sharply worded that the editors of *Marmara* were apprehensive about publishing them—self-censorship had become second nature for many Armenians.

The period in which Dink was writing was the early 1990s, when the world and all of its previous certitudes were changing. After the Berlin Wall was torn down, the Soviet Union disintegrated and the appeal of socialist ideas as a cohesive, alternative worldview gradually dissipated. The Cold War had ended, and there were many questions about Turkey's role in the emerging post-Soviet international system. For those who had grown up holding internationalist ideas and humanist values, the imposition of communitarian identities on societies and inter-ethnic wars in the aftermath of the Soviet collapse was nothing less than a return to the dark ages. Nationalism was on the rise once again in Turkey, with hopes of Turkish influence expanding from the Balkans to the Chinese Wall in the imagination of the then president, Turgut Özal (r.1989–93).[12] It was also a period in which Turkey was haunted by the ghosts of its past, with the Balkan conflicts and the wars in the Caucasus having important repercussions for Turkey's domestic politics. The violence between the Serbs and Bosnian Muslims in the Balkans brought back memories of the early twentieth century—many Turkish citizens have ancestors who were *muhajirs*, or Muslim refugees who had escaped the Balkan wars of the nineteenth century and early twentieth century, and Turkish public opinion as well as the political elite naturally sympathised with the cause of Bosnians and other Muslim minorities there. In the Caucasus, the Karabakh conflict evolved into a bloody war between Armenians and Azerbaijanis. In this conflict, the Turkish government and public opinion unconditionally supported Azerbaijan against the Armenians. Past ghosts were suddenly coming back.

During this period, Turkish public figures continually blamed the Armenians for Turkey's internal problems. In the Turkish press, not only were the Armenians accused of responsibility for the Kurdish conflict, but even assassinations committed by Hezbollah were attributed to 'converted Armenians'. The very word 'Armenian' had become a curse, a swearword in the Turkish media. When writing about this period twenty years later, Dink described the prevailing atmosphere as one of 'paranoia': 'In this way we covered the real problems, with negative transfer towards the Armenian. Such apprehension, such contempt towards the Armenian can only be caused by a deep paranoia.'[13]

Popular anti-Armenian sentiments regularly erupted into violence. In 1993 nationalists demonstrated in Bakirköy, a mainly Armenian-inhabited neighbourhood in Istanbul, where they chanted anti-Armenian slogans. All of the five Armenian cemeteries in Istanbul were desecrated in 1993 and 1994, and at least twenty attacks were recorded against Armenian churches and community centres. The atmosphere was set for anti-Armenian pogroms.[14]

In an effort to counter the negative stereotypes and blatant defamation campaigns directed against the Armenians in the popular press and elsewhere, Dink established a bookpublishing business along with a number of other Istanbul Armenian intellectuals such as Yetvart Tomasian and Megerdich Margosian. The new venture was called Aras, a name which has symbolic importance: it is the Turkish name of the river that runs along the border between Turkey and Armenia, the Armenian version being Arax. The intention behind creating the publishing house was to put forward and promote ideas that were not available elsewhere. According to a participant in the initial debates that led to the foundation of Aras:

> The Turkish youth did not know who the Armenian was, while books, newspapers and the media continuously presented the Armenian as *the* enemy, ... Two thirds of our publications are in Turkish. Before us, there were Turks who were doing enormous efforts. They put the question of genocide on the public place, people like Ragib Zarakolu and Taner Akçam. They were

11

directly political as they were discussing the genocide. We focused more on Armenian history and culture; we aimed to create background knowledge. And in Turkey there is a difference between an Armenian talking about genocide, or a Turk talking about it.[15]

Agos, a new type of publication

The limitations of bookpublishing soon became apparent to Dink. Scholarly publishing is invariably a long-term project, yet Hrant sought something more immediate: a space in which to publish his articles and opinions, where he could respond to current affairs and engage with others in polemic debates. His personality was far better suited to writing editorials than working in a room surrounded by books and piles of manuscripts. He was never a scholar, and had no desire to work on a single text for many years. He was instead a passionate intellectual, someone who wanted to engage with the broader public in terms ordinary people would understand.

Fortunately, an opportunity soon presented itself for Dink to fulfil this ambition. The Turkish daily newspaper, *Sabah*, had published a photograph of Abdullah Öcalan, the head of the PKK, the Kurdish guerrilla movement, together with a priest. *Sabah* claimed that the priest in question was an Armenian, thereby proving once and for all that the Armenians were behind the Kurdish rebellion and were manipulating the PKK to harm Turkey.[16] But the priest in the photograph was not an Armenian—he was from a different Christian denomination and ethnic group. The Armenian patriarch of Istanbul, Archbishop Mesrob Mutafian, wrote to the editors of *Sabah* in the hope that the mistake would be corrected, but to no avail. The letter was never published.

As a result of this incident the Armenian Patriarchate came to the conclusion that the time had now come to act in order to bring an end to this wave of anti-Armenian sentiment in Turkish society. The patriarch gathered together a number of intellectuals to counter the invidious media campaign. A media council was created, with a press conference scheduled to take place at the Armenian Patriarchate in Kumkapi on 18 October 1994. During the conference, Archbishop

Mutafian explained how the daily lives of the Armenian community had been made difficult, or even untenable, as a result of continuous slander in the Turkish media. Over seventy representatives from Turkish and foreign media outlets attended the conference, marked by a tense atmosphere in which Turkish journalists fielded very aggressive questions. The lawyer, Luiz Bakar, criticised 'anti-Armenian paranoia' and asked: 'Is it another 6 and 7 September that you want? Do some circles wish us to leave our homeland and seek refuge elsewhere?'[17] One of the Turkish journalists kept asking questions about Armenian Secret Army for the Liberation of Armenian (ASALA) and their relationship with the Kurdish guerrilla movement. As his tone became increasingly hostile, Hrant Dink stood up and said: 'As a member of the patriarchate's press office, I would like to answer that question':

> Respectable representatives of the press, we are trying to shake off from our shoulders a discomfort which causes pressure. It is for this reason that we are trying to voice our protest against a false claim. Apart from that, all your questions have been answered many times before. The Armenians of Turkey are not terrorists and they have never provided aid to terrorism, from whichever direction that may come. From now on too, this is the way it is going to be. Armenians will never support terrorism. As citizens of this country, we would like to live in peace and tranquillity. This is the message of this press conference. ... The Armenians, all Armenians in the world, especially Armenians in Turkey, at this moment have only one preoccupation: peace, peace, and peace.[18]

Following the unexpected success of the press conference, which was widely covered in the media, the council continued to operate and hold meetings, and became a structure attached to the church that was dedicated to creating a dialogue with Turkish journalists, academics and public figures thus allowing the voice of Istanbul's Armenians to reach broader Turkish society. The council organised weekly dinners to which four Turkish intellectuals would be invited to discuss issues of concern for the Armenian community. 'Our objective was to start a debate and show transparency,' recalls Luiz Bakar, who became the group's spokesperson.[19]

Hrant Dink was also a member of the group. However, he initially avoided the spotlight because of his leftist credentials, which served as a double handicap: while his views would cause him to come under attack from the Turkish state, he would also be shunned by large sections of the Istanbul Armenian community, which feared both Communists and the attention of the Turkish state. Yet Dink was always present at the meetings and developed very close personal relations with Archbishop Mesrob Mutafian. It was during some of the lengthy discussions Hrant Dink held with the archbishop that the idea for a new media platform was first mooted, with Dink telling Mutafian: 'If only we had a paper, we could have published such and such article.' In their efforts to reach out and explain the community's point of view, the group was regularly confronted by the lack of an adequate platform for communicating their ideas. It was in this way that the idea of launching a weekly paper was finally born.

The initial nucleus of the newspaper was composed of four people: the lawyer Luiz Bakar, the engineer Harutyun Sesetian, Arus Yumul, a former reporter who was the only member of the team with journalistic experience, and Hrant Dink, who was still managing his bookshop at that time. They sometimes met in cafés, while on other occasions they would meet at Luiz's apartment. Before anything could be published, the newspaper needed to be registered with the authorities, yet each had their own reasons for being fearful of putting down their true names. In the event, Diran Bakar, the well-known lawyer and Luiz's brother, volunteered to put down his name, and he subsequently became the formal legal director of the publication.

In 1996 *Agos* was launched as a bi-lingual weekly paper; the first issue was made available on 5 April, coinciding with the Armenian Easter. The weekly initially had a print-run of 700 copies; its reports and articles were spread over eight pages, of which six were in Turkish and two in Armenian. Ten years later, 6,000 copies were being printed each week, while the number of pages had increased to twelve (three in Armenian and nine in Turkish). From the outset, *Agos* sought to convey the reality of the Armenian community to the Turkish public, one which stood in stark contrast to their portrayal in the smear campaigns of the Turkish media, and it also sought to express the problems the community, as well as those of other minorities, experienced on a daily basis. With the launch of *Agos*, the Armenian community finally began reaching out to others, something it had avoided for decades given all of the problems this typically entailed.

In an interview a decade after the launch, Hrant Dink explained the rationale behind creating the newspaper:

> Our newspaper was launched for a number of purposes, which were forced on us on [a] daily basis. First, we wanted to struggle through this newspaper, we wanted to struggle against the state, against its injustice, to demand justice, to demand our history, to struggle to become a democratic country. We also wanted to defend ourselves. In that period, eleven years ago, the word 'Armenian' in Turkey was equated to curse. Every day on televisions and on newspapers we heard insults addressed to Armenians. There was the Kurdish question in Turkey which they turned into Armenian question and insulted the Armenians. And one day we were forced to stand up and say no, we are not the Armenians you are narrating, but we will be the Armenians we will be narrating in a way you understand.[20]

The use of the Turkish language in *Agos* reflected the fact that an increasing number of Turkish and Middle Eastern Armenians were no longer using Western Armenian as their primary means of communication, and were increasingly speaking in Turkish. The Armenian community in Istanbul was growing in size as floods of internal migrants left their villages and provincial towns in Anatolia to search for security and employment in the big city. Most of these recent migrants were unable to speak, read or write in Armenian. In contrast to Istanbul, where Armenian institutions—such as churches, schools and newspapers—continued to exist, in the east there were no such institutions, with the exception of seven churches. *Agos* sought to embrace this growing segment of the modern Istanbulite Armenian community.

Despite his initial reluctance to assume a leading position when *Agos* was created, within the space of a few years Hrant Dink became the newspaper's dominant figure. One of the reasons for this was that the other founders had joined the project while continuing to work in a professional capacity elsewhere and were only able to dedicate their free time to the newspaper. Hrant Dink, on the other hand, made it his principal occupation; his vocation. It became his personal mission. He also fell out with each of the other individuals involved in the project, as personalities gradually clashed during the editorial debates that are part and parcel of running any newspaper.

Dink became the face of *Agos*, expressing the pain silently suffered by the Armenians in the articles he signed, the speeches he made and in the interviews he gave to various Turkish media outlets. He spoke out in defence of an identity that the authorities had sought to erase. But he was not naïve. When he started this work he knew that it would be an uncharted journey. In speaking out, he invited others to treat him as a Turkish citizen; he claimed the right to justice. He wanted to be treated as an equal, and not to be singled out as an Armenian. Was this not the same struggle as his predecessors, those Istanbul Armenian intellectuals who were arrested on 24 April, and the rights they had fought for back then? Did he compare himself with the lawyers, militants and journalists of the past, those who believed in reforming the Ottoman Empire? Hrant Dink saw his cause as part of the fight of many others—Armenians, Turks, Greeks, Kurds, Assyrians, journalists, trade-unionists; in other words, all of those who were struggling for equal rights, justice and the rule of law in Turkey. He hoped that his problems would find a solution in a Turkey that was finally becoming a democracy, the name he and others gave to their hopes, to the coming change.

Why was it possible to launch Aras and *Agos* in the 1990s and not before, when there was clearly a need for such institutions in the decades prior to this?

When Hrant Dink was at Tbrevank, he and his friends were not overly preoccupied with the Armenian cause, although they were certainly aware of the difficulties Armenians faced in Turkey due to their own personal experience. More broadly, the Armenian issue was not a topic of discussion among Turkish leftist movements. 'When we were secret members of the Turkish Communist Party, we never heard a discussion about the Armenians. In the party we adopted *nom de guerre* to hide our identity and these were inevitably Turkish names. So people did not necessarily know that we were Armenians,' recalls Zakarya Mildanoğlu. Nor did the Turkish leftist parties necessarily have a differentiated position on the annihilation of the Ottoman Armenians compared to the official Kemalist narrative. According to Mildanoğlu:

> In 1947 the Turkish Communist Party organised a meeting in Moscow to discuss the Armenian issue, after which they prepared a report about the Armenian Genocide. Their vision is not different from today's official position and one can summarise as: Yes, there was a genocide, but they were rebellious, and it was their fault!

In the mindset of Turkish leftists, there was a struggle between global colonialist forces such as the UK, France and Russia, and third world countries like the Ottoman Empire and later the Turkish Republic. In this struggle, the Armenians (and other Christian minorities like the Greeks and the Assyrians) had chosen the camp of the colonialist powers. In this respect, Kemalist ideology was not that different from Turkish communism.

In the period between the genocide and the 1990s, the Armenians of Istanbul were reduced to silence, while the remaining Armenians of Anatolia were reduced to self-denial. Traditional Armenian institutions, such as churches and the daily papers, were understandably scared of uttering anything that went beyond what was permitted by the Turkish state. The Armenian youth with the courage to engage in critical thinking consequently joined the Turkish leftist parties, such as the Turkish Communist Party, or later the Workers' Party of Turkey. Yet even within these parties, which had limited political influence in any case, the Armenians continued to exercise self-denial. When Aram Pehlivanian, who headed the Turkish Communist Party politburo in East Germany, died in exile in 1979, the communiqué issued by the party announcing the news mentioned neither Pehlivanian's real name nor his Armenian heritage.

This situation changed somewhat with the emergence of the new left in Turkey in the 1970s, and especially the TKP/ML (Communist Party of Turkey/Marxist–Leninist) and its leader Ibrahim Kaypakkaya, who was among the first to put the Armenian question on the agenda. They argued that the Turkish state was fascist and explained the destruction of the Armenians as part of a violent project of that state. Back then, however, Kaypakkaya was the exception and not the rule.

As Zakarya Mildanoğlu puts it:

> these young men, Orhan, Hrant, and the others, when they were young and identified themselves as Communist rebels, in their consciousness the Armenian identity or the significance of April 24 had a different and less important role. It was through the various struggles that [were] fought later that their Armenian political consciousness was shaped.

Hrant Dink and Zakarya Mildanoğlu were part of a new generation of Turkish Armenian intellectuals. They had spent their youth within the Turkish leftist milieu and had risked their lives with their Turkish and Kurdish comrades, as well as those of other ethnic minorities. When the Soviet Union collapsed and they became disillusioned with the prospects for creating a communist utopia in Turkey, these men naturally returned to the struggles of their own ethnic community, and by fighting for the rights of their community they were also fighting for a democratic and modern Turkey. Their aim was to live in a country free from repression, one that respected human rights and freedom of speech, a society worthy of joining the European family of states. What Hrant Dink tried to do, an endeavour in which he largely succeeded, was to create a dialogue with the Turkish intelligentsia in order to emphasise his core message: freedom of expression has no value if it is not exercised, and there will never be freedom of speech in Turkey while the fate of the Ottoman Armenians remains a taboo. He brought courage and a sense of vitality to an Armenian community subdued by decades of violence and state repression. He also brought the Armenian question, the issue of the disappearance of the Ottoman Armenians and its consequences, to the attention of Turkish liberal intellectuals.

The message Hrant Dink conveyed in his weekly *Agos* editorials, or as commentaries in other Turkish newspapers, evolved over time. His starting point was the conscience of the average Turkish citizen. He was aware that most were not aware of the fate of the Armenians, who had been consigned to oblivion by the policy of the Turkish state. It would have been counterproductive in such circumstances to demand that the Turks recognise and apologise for the Armenian Genocide, which was the principal demand of the Armenian diaspora organisations in the Middle East, France and the United States. But he also knew that most Turkish citizens must have been aware that something terrible and unjust had happened to the Armenians who at one time had lived in their towns and villages, filling the churches and schools that were now occupied by others or were simply abandoned ruins.

Dink initially adopted a cautious approach because he believed that progress would be achieved through the incremental reform of the Turkish political system and its liberalisation. As was the case with many of his liberal-minded friends and colleagues, Dink sincerely believed that the promise of Turkey joining the European Union would lead to far-reaching changes inside the country—when the Turkish ruling elite committed themselves to this project, they would implement the requisite legal and political reforms to become part of the EU and enjoy its benefits. As a result, Dink was an opponent of any attempt to push Turkey out of the negotiations process because the prospect of EU membership, in his view, would serve as the primary catalyst for meaningful change. This is why he vehemently opposed making Turkish recognition of the genocide a precondition for Turkey's EU accession, in contrast to the stance adopted by many Armenian groups as well as some European politicians. In a departure from the nationalist position, Dink argued that Turkish recognition of the genocide should take place without any foreign intervention or external pressure—foreign powers would simply use the Armenian Genocide as a political tool to put pressure on Turkey for their own interests, and once these interests had been satisfied they would abandon the Armenians to their fate. His reading of history was such that he refused to accept that foreign powers, whether France or the United States, would place pressure on Turkey simply for the sake of historic justice, or to defend the rights of Armenian or other minorities. By adopting laws or issuing statements demanding Turkish recognition of the genocide, foreign countries were simply creating obstacles in the way of Turkish accession to the EU, yet without this aspiration there would never be any meaningful reform within Turkey and such measures were hence entirely counterproductive.

Dink also opposed the adoption of legal measures criminalising those who denied that the Armenian Genocide had taken place. Part of the rationale for this was his strongly held belief in freedom of expression. Yet while this position certainly reflected his principled beliefs, it was also born, at least in part, from political expediency— the Turkish population was suffering from a collective amnesia with regard to the events of 1915, and ignorance of history should not be considered a crime. The first step that needed to be made prior to any meaningful recognition of the genocide was thus to educate the Turkish public in their own history.

I met Hrant Dink on 20 March 2000. I was on a trip to Istanbul with a friend from Switzerland, Bülent Kaya. At the time I was running a project that sought to encourage dialogue between journalists from the South Caucasus, with a special focus on Armenia–Azerbaijan exchanges with the hope of creating mutual understanding between the two countries. After several discussions with Kaya, we considered setting up a similar exchange between Armenia/Armenians and Turkey. We visited Hrant Dink in the editorial offices of *Agos*. He told us that his newspaper had a similar project, and it had just organised a trip to Armenia with four journalists from leading Turkish newspapers such as *Milliyet*, *Hurriyet* and *Radikal*. Dink had been unable to go as he did not have a passport. After mentioning a number of recent initiatives between the two countries, he said: 'We should create structured cooperation within the civil society, and especially among journalists.' He also suggested 'organising discussions in Istanbul inviting intellectuals and journalists from Armenia and from border regions [of Turkey] to discuss relations between the two sides'.[21]

In 2002 Hrant Dink finally received his passport and was able to travel abroad. His first trip was to the United States in order to take part in the Armenian–Turkish scholars' conference at Ann Arbor, Michigan.

His next flight was to Yerevan, where he planned to attend an Armenia diaspora conference. An entire generation had re-discovered Armenian nationalism when the USSR collapsed and Armenia became an independent state. Hrant, by contrast, only came into contact with Armenia as a state and a people a decade later. He became strongly conscious of this new, powerful reality in global Armenian life, and his editorials increasingly reflected this. He argued for the normalisation of Turkish–Armenian relations and for the opening of the border. His editorials in *Agos* and elsewhere focus on Armenian identity and the events of 1915, the diaspora and the deep trauma the Armenians continued to suffer. He wanted to explain to the Turkish public what it meant to be an Armenian, and why the diaspora had such strong anti-Turkish feelings, why they continually pushed for the genocide to be recognised by nations around the world. His public statements and written work often reflected his belief that both the Armenians and the Turks were sick and in need of healing: 'Armenians suffer from traumatism, and Turks suffer from paranoia,' he once wrote.[22]

Dink was also preoccupied with another issue: the forgotten Armenians of Anatolia. Once, during an interview, he said: 'God. Oh, God. I am happy to live in my country. I go to Van, I go to Kars, I go to Diyarbakir. I go everywhere.' The journalist interjected: 'But when you go there you do not see an Armenian, not a single Armenian.' Dink's response was: 'Oh, I see them, I see them. I see Armenians.'[23] Following the First World War and the genocide, thousands of Armenian orphans, mostly women and children, but also some men, were left behind and forced to face a range of hardships. Some were kidnapped and enslaved; neighbours and villagers saved others from certain death. There may have been as many as 200,000 such people in the early 1920s, and they were forced to convert to Islam in order to survive.[24] They lived in provincial cities and villages, but they were known by their Turkish or Kurdish neighbours as '*dönme*', or converts, and were never treated as equals. They had to remain silent about their suffering. Dink wanted to break their solitude, and he knew that the best way to do this was to open the closed border between Armenia and Turkey, bringing oxygen to the eastern provinces of Turkey in order to lift the oppressive silence there. It was with that purpose in mind that *Agos* gradually developed into something more than a newspaper—it became a kind of social network. Many people with Armenian ancestry—the 'hidden Armenians' of Anatolia—started contacting *Agos* to ask for help in locating their lost relatives in Istanbul. So did Armenians in the diaspora. Dink personally tried to help, to learn each story. 'The mails I receive, the e-mails, the phone enquiries! The people who knock on my door, they contact me every day,' he once said in an interview with the BBC. 'There are so many people from here and from abroad. They learn that they have a past. They're looking for information, wanting history and references, looking for relatives. I am involved in it personally every day. There are stunning examples, so many stories reaching me.'[25]

Hrant Dink was not always well received by the Armenian communities. He was simultaneously challenging both the form of diasporan political activism at the time and the passivity of Turkish Armenians. Tuba Çandar describes Dink as a lonely fighter, one who was stigmatised within Turkey yet was not accepted by the Armenians in Turkey either, nor by the Armenians of the diaspora. In the 1990s, most organised and politically active Armenian diaspora organisations saw the central objective of their struggle as gaining international recognition of the genocide. They thought this was the only means available to force the Turkish state to put an end to decades of state-sponsored denial of the annihilation of the Ottoman Armenians. For traditional Armenian political parties it was difficult, if not impossible, to envisage how this aim, and the success of the Armenian cause more generally, would be achieved from within Turkish society. They did not know how to respond to the Dink phenomenon, and they were equally unsure of the 'agenda' he served. They found his discourse ambiguous and his objectives questionable. On the other hand, many Istanbul Armenians had a different concern, as they 'thought that Hrant spoke too much and too loud'.[26] Dink responded to this by stating that: 'Armenians that parade every 24th of April are Armenians once a year. We're Armenians every day.'[27] In 2001, he wrote an editorial arguing that the Armenian problem would only be resolved when Turkish Armenians were able to take part in the annual ceremonies on 24 April alongside the Armenians elsewhere in the world. This was too much for the Turkish censor, however, who immediately prohibited the article from being published.[28]

In 1992 *Agos* published Reymond Kévorkian's *Les Arméniens dans l'Empire ottoman à la veille du génocide*, an encyclopaedic work on the Ottoman Armenian communities before their destruction. Different chapters were translated individually and published in *Agos* as part of a series entitled 'Once Upon a Time'. The series sought to inform the reader that there had once been a strong and prosperous Armenian community throughout Turkey, a community with shops, factories, churches, schools and hospitals, and that this community no longer existed. The series attracted the attention of the Turkish authorities, who asked the editors at *Agos* to cease publication. However, after a brief pause, the paper continued to publish the series.

Hrant Dink did not use the term 'genocide' in his articles from this period. This was not because he had any doubts as to what had happened to the Ottoman Armenians during the First World War, but was instead because he was simply unable to use this term. When *Agos* was founded in the mid-1990s, the expression 'Armenian Genocide' was still a taboo in Turkey, and anyone found using the term could have been persecuted by the Turkish state. During an interview in 2001 with an Armenian journalist, Hrant Dink was asked when *Agos* had first begun referring to the 'Armenian Genocide':

> What happened in 1915 in Anatolia? What happened with the Armenians? For the Turkish public there is an Armenian question. On this issue for the first time, with a bit of courage *Agos* moved its pens, opened its columns. We started writing about that time, about the events of 1915, of course very carefully. On April 24 I wrote in *Agos* that Armenians all around the world remember their ancestors, come out on the streets, visit cemeteries, the only exception being Armenians living in Turkey. Why? This thing rang a bit sharp, our newspaper was confiscated, I was called to court, but they announced me innocent and released me. Our step did not aim to tear apart our two peoples, but in this way we wanted to try and start a dialogue between Armenian and Turk.

The journalist immediately asked whether he could write in Armenia that *Agos* was covering the genocide. Hrant Dink responded: 'We don't use the word genocide, I do not use it. If I use it then I put it in quotation marks. If I used the word genocide, the next day *Agos* would stop publication.'[29]

Since his murder, Dink has become a legend and a symbol for the Turkish liberal intelligentsia, his actions taken as a benchmark by which to behave. It is often stated that Dink opposed the usage of the term 'genocide' and that he was opposed to the adoption of resolutions condemning the genocide by foreign nations. Some Turkish liberal intellectuals even went so far as to distinguish between good Istanbul Armenians, who follow the model of Hrant Dink, and bad, 'nationalist' diaspora Armenians who are vehemently anti-Turkish and cause problems for Turkish democracy.

The Gökçen Controversy

It did not take long for Hrant's troubles to start. During a public event dedicated to identity and citizenship in Urfa on February 2002, he was asked about his identity and whether he considered himself a Turk. He answered: 'I am not a Turk, but an Armenian of Turkey.' A lawyer, Kemal Kerinçsiz, who headed the Büyük Hukukçular Birliği (Great Union of Jurists), later sued him for 'insulting Turkishness'. This nationalist Turkish lawyer would often be in the headlines in the days that followed as he led attacks not just against Hrant Dink but also Orhan Pamuk and others for insulting 'Turkishness', while simultaneously seeking to oppose any reform of the Turkish legal system proposed by the EU.[30] Kerinçsiz was subsequently arrested for taking part in the alleged Ergenekon conspiracy, revealing his close association with the Deep State, as we will see later.[31] Hrant Dink was prosecuted under Article 159, which was 'taken from Mussolini's Italy', according to Amnesty International.[32] Hrant Dink and Sehmus Ülek, the vice-president of the human rights organisation, Mazlum-Der, which organised the event, were finally acquitted in 2006. He was prosecuted under the same article a second time when a sentence from a piece Dink wrote in 2004 urging the Armenian diaspora to adopt a less aggressive policy towards Turkey and instead pay attention to the democratic struggle taking place was taken out of context and again considered to be insulting to Turkishness. Despite the fact that an expert report presented to the court found no elements of any 'crime' or any intention of insulting Turks or Turkish identity, Hrant received a suspended sentence of six months on 7 October 2005. When he commented on the verdict in the press, a new case was filed against his alleged attempts 'to influence the judiciary'. There was clearly an organised campaign against him. Someone wanted to exhaust him, to bring him down or force him to run. The campaign was initially aimed at intimidating him; it would soon develop into a campaign to break him.

The worst was yet to come. On 6 February 2004 Dink published an article in *Agos* entitled 'The Secret of Madam Sabiha', in which he referred to the Armenian origins of Sabiha Gökçen. According to the article, which was based on an interview with the supposed daughter of Gökçen's sister, Sabiha Gökçen was born in Aintab (now Gaziantep) to the family of Nerses and Maryam Sebilciyan. She was one of nine children, seven boys and two girls. One of the girls was Diruhi, the mother of Hripsime Gazalyan, a citizen of Armenia, according to the account given by the interviewee.

This announcement, which declared that one of the icons of the modern Turkish national pantheon was of Armenian origin, caused outrage in Turkey. According to official Turkish historiography, Gökçen was a twelve-year-old orphan girl when Mustafa Kemal noticed her during a visit to Bursa orphanage, adopted her and took her with him to Ankara. Gökçen became a national hero as she was the first female Turkish pilot to fly military aeroplanes. She flew bombing missions over Dersim in 1938, when the Turkish army launched successive campaigns against the Alevi Kurds and crypto-Armenians. In 2009, one of the two airports of Istanbul—the one located on the Asiatic side—was named after her. The other is named after Mustafa Kemal Atatürk. 'She was the human embodiment of Atatürk's dreams realised for modern Turkey, for the modern Turkish woman, and for "Turkishness" and for Turkish civilization', writes Fatma Ulgen.[33]

Sabiha Gökçen's Armenian ancestry was common knowledge within the Armenian community of Turkey and beyond. Articles discussing this issue had been published in the 1970s in the Armenian weekly *Spyurk* in Beirut.[34] Yet the fact that Hrant Dink had dared to say that Sabiha was an Armenian orphan who had been adopted and Turkified, like so many others, was considered an affront by the Turkish authorities. This article simultaneously broke a taboo and touched a personality that had been elevated to the rank of national hero, yet whose true fate and identity could not be studied or discussed. The article not only provoked discussions, responses and television programmes but also threats and violent attacks.

The issue discussed in *Agos* was brought to the attention of the Turkish public by the mainstream daily paper *Hürriyet*, beginning with an article on 21 February 2004 with the headline 'Sabiha Gökçen or Hatun Sebilciyan?'[35] This article in effect reproduced the original piece. On the following day, *Hürriyet* published a second article entitled 'Sabiha Gökçen's 80-Year-Old Secret',[36] which was based on an interview with the Turkish Armenian historian Pars Tuğlacı, an expert on Ottoman history in general and the Ottoman Armenians in particular. According to Tuğlacı, who was a close friend of Gökçen, she was indeed born in Bursa in 1913 to an Armenian family. Her family had been deported in 1915, but she was left to an orphanage as her parents feared she would not survive the forced marches. Tuğlacı emphasised the fact that she was aware of her Armenian heritage. In the interview Tuğlacı stated that Gökçen had relatives in Beirut and she travelled there to meet them. She did not speak Armenian, he said, as she was only two or three years old when she was left to an orphanage. But he remembers that she once told him 'I love you' in Armenian. The last question in the interview was whether Atatürk knew that Gökçen was an Armenian. Tuğlacı answered, diplomatically, that the question was irrelevant—Atatürk was a great humanist who viewed nationalism as concerned with loving his people, and he understood that by loving his people he would love all the peoples of the planet.

It was like a bomb had been thrown into the established conception of Turkish national identity, the holy 'Turkishness' upheld in Article 301. Gökçen had not only been the first female military pilot in Turkey, but in the whole world; she was a national symbol, the only female heroine of modern Turkey. In the words of Fatma Ulgen, she was the 'most successful of Ataturk's project child[ren]' and a 'proud symbol of the military nation'.[37] By writing about the Armenian background of Gökçen, *Agos* simultaneously brought the annihilation of the Ottoman Armenians and the central founding myths around which Mustafa Kemal Atatürk had built modern Turkish identity to the attention of the public. Moreover, the article clearly touched upon issues relating to the character of Atatürk himself, which remains a taboo in Turkey even today.

The vitriol in the media as a result of the article was summarised in a cable from the US embassy in Ankara:

> Recent claims reported in two Turkish newspapers that the late Sabiha Gokcen—Ataturk's adopted daughter and Turkey's first female pilot—was Armenian have exposed an ugly streak of racism in Turkish society. The reports led a number of prominent figures to make racist remarks 'defending' Gokcen, which in turn prompted criticism from more open-minded columnists. Perhaps the most alarming result, however, has been an intensely personal campaign by die-hard nationalists against the editor of the Armenian weekly newspaper that first broke the story.[38]

Immediately after the two articles appeared in *Hürriyet*, Ulkum Adatepe, who had also been adopted by Atatürk, organised a press conference where she described the articles as scandalous and as being intended to defame Mustafa Kemal Atatürk. This was followed by press releases from the Turkish Aviation League, veteran pilots and even Istanbul University, all of which protested against attempts to 'defame Atatürk', Turkishness and the achievements of Turkish women.

The worst was to take place on pages of the Turkish press and on Turkish talk shows. 'What is the purpose of this allegation now?' asked Celal Şengör in *Cumhuriyt*, adding:

> It is implied that Sabiha's so-called family was slaughtered during the incidents of 1915. Within every society there are historical wounds. Civilized

societies discuss these wounds to completely remove them but they don't scratch them. That Atatürk's adopted daughter was an Armenian ... is news that scratches this social wound. If Sabiha was of Armenian descent why would she hide it?[39]

While Şengör argued that there was no need to open old wounds, another commentator in *Cumhuriyet* cried out against the apparent 'conspiracy'. İlhan Selçuk attacked 'imperialism', saying that the West was on the one hand demanding that Turkey become a multi-cultural state, and on the other hand encouraging the Kurds to build a Kurdish nation-state on Turkish lands. The article then added:

> In the meantime so many bloody dramas have been lived; imperialism was never satisfied with the episodes of revenge during the period [the] Ottoman Empire was being split ... and it keeps heating up those conflicts ... Two words: Exchange [*mubadele*] and *Tehcir* [deportation] ... The deportation was too painful! ... In the Eastern Anatolia, the Ottoman administration had to force the Armenians collaborating with the occupying Russians to deportation; during the process, bloody incidents happened ... But who is to blame? Is this [even] a question? Of course Turks are! ... According to imperialism barbarian Turks hung, butchered, deported, massacred the Christians. European parliaments and also Americans are getting ready to bring us to account; 'genocide resolutions' are passing from the parliaments one by one; what will happen tomorrow is evident from today ... In the meantime, news in the dailies ... in the headlines indeed: 'Atatürk's adopted daughter was an Armenian ...' Now go and open up the old books, 'Armenian genocide, deportation, what happened to Christian children', right or wrong, let all be refreshed ... The more you fuel the animosities between the Armenian, the Kurd, the Greek, the more you grease the wheels for imperialism ... and what our media does, in the name of journalism, is nothing else but this. Who does it harm if one more episode is staged of the scenario written about destroying Turkey.[40]

The Turkish chief of staff reacted by releasing a declaration condemning the original article and implicitly threatening its author: 'opening such a debate, whatever its intention, on such a symbol is a crime against the national integrity and social peace'.[41]

The campaign against *Agos* and Hrant Dink did not escape the attention of foreign diplomats. A US consulate cable to Washington, DC, subsequently released by WikiLeaks, states:

These developments spotlight the racism underlying Turkish nationalism. The outrage by Turkey's secular establishment also reflects its hyper-sensitivity to any perceived attacks on Kemalist ideology. We can expect that any attempt to debate establishment-imposed notions of secularism or the meaning of Turkishness will continue to bring out sentiments incompatible with Turkey's professed adherence to universal norms or EU standards.[42]

Hrant Dink was never brought to trial for his article on the Armenian origins of Sabihe Gökçen, but he was invited by the Istanbul veli, the governor, for a meeting. When he went to attend the meeting he was received by the deputy-governor. There were two other people in the bureau. Without introducing who they were, the Turkish official asked: 'Do you mind that my two friends take part in our meeting?'

They were already there, in the room, sitting in the dark. Their features slowly became visible. Hrant Dink saw their faces. What did they want from him? Hrant thought they were there to warn him, perhaps to threaten him. He was wrong. They had already reached their verdict. It was simply a matter of waiting for an opportune moment to tell him. They had come to see him, to make an appearance and to touch their victim with a final handshake. They belonged to an organisation that acted in the name of the state and ostensibly sought to defend their own nation. But they deeply despised their own people.

'They were two representatives of the secret police,' Rakel Dink said. 'And they told him what will happen later and how. They told him if something happens to him it is going to be in the street, in daylight. And they also told him how the trial will end: it will be considered the act of an individual coming from the street.'

The threat was evident during numerous court hearings, in each of which intimidation and acts of physical violence increased. During one of the hearings, a group of ultranationalists managed to gain entry to the courtroom while a larger group gathered at its entrance. They shouted hostile slogans directed towards Dink, who had to be brought into the court through lines of police officers. As he passed, enraged people tried to attack him, shouting insults, spitting and throwing pens and other objects at him. The lawyers accompanying him were treated in a similar manner. In the same period, the members of the ultranationalist Ülkü Ocakları movement organised demonstrations in front of the *Agos* offices, shouting anti-Armenian slogans: 'Either love the country or leave it,' 'To hell with ASALA.'[43]

The extent of judicial harassment, and that conducted by ultranationalist groups, was now severe. The attacks became so intense that the Turkish Supreme Board of Press Council issued an announcement warning nationalist papers that the continuous use of hate language against Hrant Dink could put his life in danger. On 21 July 2006, Dink signed another column in *Agos* titled 'One Vote against 301', which invited yet another court case against him, as well as his son as acting editor, Arat Dink, and another *Agos* editor, Sarkis Seropian. On this occasion the court case was prompted by an *Agos* article that cited a Reuters' report in which Hrant Dink referred to 1915 and was asked whether the events of that year constituted a genocide: 'Of course this is a genocide because the result reveals and names the act itself. You see that a nation that was living on this land for thousand years vanished after what happened.'[44]

Although the Reuters' report was reproduced in numerous other Turkish media outlets, it was only the editors at *Agos* that faced prosecution, only *Agos* that was found to have insulted 'Turkishness' by publishing the report. This court case continued even after the assassination of Hrant Dink—the Şişli criminal court gave Arat Dink and Sarkis Seropian a suspended sentence of one year each for having 'published news that claimed the Turkish nation was guilty of genocide'.[45]

When talking with members Hrant Dink's family and colleagues at *Agos*, one gets the impression of a golden age between the founding of the weekly publication in 1996, and the Gökçen article and the campaign that followed in 2004. The first period was one of learning, of daring, continuous discussions and a feeling of success. It was a period when they had time to read and discuss, to explore new ideas and publish their work. Then, between 2004 and early 2007, when Hrant Dink was assassinated, there was a period of loneliness. It was like traversing the desert. Dink was alone in his fight against the system. He was isolated, an easy target for hate attacks. 'During the series of court cases we felt very lonely,' said Arat Dink.[46] Many of his friends today feel a sense of responsibility for this. First, as the attack from the state and from nationalist circles increased, the Armenian community was afraid and took its traditional defensive position, which was to hide in order to avoid attracting attention. Hrant Dink himself did not ask for mobilisation around him in order to keep his friends and community members away from harm. It was his instinctive reaction to take the heat of the nationalist anger himself and to protect the rest of the community from aggression.

Similarly, Turkish liberal intellectuals did not realise that Hrant Dink was the subject of a specific campaign; nor were they aware of the danger he was in. During this period, Turkish society was becoming polarised between forces and movements calling for change—whether they were pro-European liberals, minority movements, the Islamists of the AK Party or liberal intellectuals—and Kemalists and nationalists, who were afraid of the changes being made and sought to uphold the status quo. It was in this atmosphere that violent campaigns were directed against writers such as Orhan Pamuk, who won the Nobel Prize in Literature in 2006, as well as another novelist, Elif Shafak. Both were attacked by the same nationalist lawyer who had instigated the campaign against Hrant Dink and others, and were also charged under Article 301 for 'denigrating Turkishness'. Pamuk's 'crime' was an interview he gave to the Zürich-based Swiss–German weekly *Das Magazin*, in which he stated that 'thirty thousand Kurds have been killed here, and a million Armenians. And almost nobody dares mention that.'[47] In the following year, when Elif Shafak's *The Bastard of Istanbul* was published, she was also charged under Article 301 with insulting 'Turkishness'. The novel, which was originally written in English and was published in Turkish in 2006, tells the story of four generations of women from Istanbul. It is the first Turkish novel to have dealt with the fate of the Armenians in Turkey. The reason Shafak was persecuted was because of the words of one of the fictitious characters in the novel: 'I am the grandchild of genocide survivors who lost all their relatives at the hands of Turkish butchers in 1915.' Although the charges against both novelists were later dropped,[48] the case against Hrant Dink and *Agos* continued.

By the end of 2006, Hrant was aware of the dangers he faced, as is clear in his final articles. In the first, published in *Agos* on 10 January 2007 and entitled 'At the Dawn of a Difficult Year',[49] Dink states that he was not concerned when the first prosecution was filed against him after the Urfa conference for 'denigrating Turkishness'; he knew he had done no harm and had 'complete trust' that justice would prevail. Yet when the judge imposed the six-month prison sentence, his hopes were shattered. 'My only weapon was my sincerity, ... But the decision was made and all my hopes were crushed. From then on, I was in the most distressed situation that a person could possibly be in.' Hrant clearly points the finger at the 'deep forces' that had decided to teach him a lesson through the justice system, and had purposely misinterpreted his writing to make him pay for daring to challenge the dominant order.

Hrant Dink expressed a fear that his life was in danger on several occasions; he regularly received death threats, mostly by email. After he had been assassinated, his colleagues at *Agos* opened his inbox and discovered thousands of these emails. 'On average he had three threatening email[s] every single day,' said Karin Karakaşlı, a co-editor at *Agos*.[50] But he received one threat which made him particularly alarmed—it was a letter sent by post from Bursa, the old capital of the Ottomans, but also known for harbouring ultranationalist groups. Not only was the letter highly aggressive, with threats directed at Hrant Dink, but it also threatened the lives of his son Arat and Sarkis Seropian. It stated that he would be made to collect their dead bodies from the outskirts of Ankara. Hrant sent this letter to the Istanbul police asking for protection; but he did not receive a response.

According to Rakel Dink, those close to Hrant were completely unaware of the letter's existence: 'We did not know about the Bursa letter back then, he did not tell us about it.'

At home twice he opened the discussion whether we should leave Turkey. He told us: 'I am going through a difficult trial and I am thinking about leaving this country. But I will never leave without you.' Our son Arat said: 'father we will go wherever you go.' But he did not want to disturb the daily life of his children; he did not go further in this discussion. And me, as if I was not awake, as if I did not see what was happening around us … He knew the danger, the risk he was taking from day one. *Agos* became like a mirror he was holding to their faces, to the state. And for the Armenians it became a source of newly found self-confidence. On the streets grandmothers used to stop him and say: 'Son, we are worried for you pay attention to yourself,' but one also saw how proud they were.[51]

In his final articles, Hrant Dink wrote about his indecision over whether he should stay in Turkey or leave in order to find security in exile. He compared his hypothetical departure with the ordeal of his ancestors leaving their country in 1915. Ultimately, however, he decided to stay at least until his appeal could be heard in the European Court of Human Rights. Dink concludes the article with the following words: 'Yes, I may perceive myself in the spiritual unease of a pigeon, but I do know that in this country people do not harm pigeons.'[52]

Hrant Dink had written an article two days before his assassination in which he explained the reasons why he was being persecuted and why he was in danger. He was clearly aware that 2007 would be a difficult year, although he could hardly have been aware that it was also a year he would not survive. The article—entitled 'Why Am I Taken for a Target?'—was sent to the newspaper *Radikal 2* the day before he died.[53]

According to Pakrad Esdoukian, a long-time friend of Hrant Dink and columnist at *Agos*:

> His last two articles are very expressive, … He felt the danger. His friends told him to leave the country for some time. We were discussing the possibility of going to Armenia. Another option was to leave for Belgium where his wife had a number of relatives. But his answer was: 'Even if I leave, trouble will follow me. I cannot keep silent.'[54]

* * *

With his struggle for the rights of Armenians, Hrant Dink succeeded in opening up a new political space. By framing the issue of the

Armenians as a question of citizenship, Dink succeeded in breaking old antagonistic political camps, allowing a new movement to take shape, bringing together the Kemalists and the Islamists, the Alevi and the Sunni, the Kurds and the Turks. The mobilisation on the day of Dink's funeral was not the end point, but the start of a new tradition. On 19 January each year, thousands of people gather in front of the *Agos* offices to express their support to Dink's family and to ask for justice.

Rakel Dink says that Hrant lived his life as if it was some kind of a mission he was destined to accomplish:

> He became a sacrifice. He was like one person who has to walk in front of thousands, this is the rule of God. He brought to conclusion his mission by becoming a sacrifice himself. But could God only act like this? Was there no other way? … But this is the rule of God since the beginning.[55]

Hrant Dink wanted to speak to the conscience of the simple Turkish person, to his *vijdan*. He knew that the population had been forced to forget, but that somewhere deep inside their soul they still knew the truth. He wanted to stir that conscience, that knowledge. In order to do so he wanted to start a conversation with the Turkish public. He wanted them to know that Armenians and other minorities were being systematically discriminated against in modern-day Turkey. He also wanted to tell them that there was a way to escape the past, that there could be equality once there was justice. And the only way justice would prevail involved returning to the original sin, to the way in which the Republic was created, the conditions in which the empire collapsed. In this quest, his own life story became the exemplar.

2

CRIME WITHOUT PUNISHMENT

There is something unusual about the killing of Hrant Dink. The event that seems to have triggered the murder was his unveiling of the ethnic Armenian background of the Kemalist national hero, Sabiha Gökçen. Whilst Hrant Dink may have run the original story, other journalists added to it and investigated further, and yet they were not subjected to the same persecution. The journalists and chief editor of *Hürriyet*, for example, were not harassed. We see a similar pattern elsewhere: when Pamuk and Shafak were persecuted under the infamous Article 301 they were not condemned but released with the personal intervention of the Prime Minister Recep Tayyip Erdoğan. This was not the case for Hrant Dink. Clearly, Turks were at lower risk when challenging similar taboos.

Hrant Dink was aware that he was persecuted more severely than the others, something which he attributed to the fact that he was an Armenian. All Istanbul Armenians recognise that other Turkish intellectuals are able to challenge the state in ways they would never be allowed to; many Anatolian Armenians, meanwhile, are fearful of talking openly about their Armenian ancestry. Even in the 1990s and the 2000s, when the Turkish intelligentsia began to challenge the dogmas associated with the Kemalist regime, it was not the Armenians in Turkey who dared to confront the issue of the Armenian Genocide, but pioneering Turkish intellectuals. Hrant Dink wrote about the systematic discrimination the Armenians of Turkey suffered in an article referring to his own case, when he had been sentenced to six-months imprisonment for 'insulting Turkishness':

> I have to admit that as someone who has matured by experiencing numerous instances of discrimination, my mind can't stop asking this question: 'Has my being an Armenian played a role in this outcome?' ... Of course when I put the things I know and the things I sense together, I do have an answer to this question. This is how it can be summed up: certain people decided and said, 'This Hrant Dink man has gone too far. He needs to learn a lesson,' and pushed a button. I know this is a claim which puts myself and my Armenian identity at central stage ... The facts I have and my life experience leave me no other explanation. My task now is to tell you everything I have lived and sensed. Then, you decide for yourself.[1]

Hrant Dink was the first Armenian in Turkey to claim a place and a voice in public space since 1915. And that was why his life was ultimately brought to an early end.

* * *

To understand why Hrant Dink was killed, it is important to consider the context in which he developed his arguments. The Armenian had become the quintessential 'other' under three regimes that ruled the Ottoman Empire and later the Turkish Republic: Sultan Abdul Hamid II (r. 1876–1909), the Young Turks or Committee for Union and Progress (CUP, 1909–1918) and the Kemalists (as one-party system: 1923–1945). These three regimes represent both the last decades of the fall of the Ottoman Empire and the construction of the Turkish Republic. It was during this period that the 'Armenian Question' was posed as a major political issue before the Armenians were largely eliminated during the First World War.

In the nineteenth century, the Ottoman Empire had struggled to implement reforms that would modernise state and society, and it was undergoing a process of steady decline while losing considerable amounts of territory. Yet the dominant Ottoman and Turkish elites of the late nineteenth and early twentieth century never recognised the right of their religious minorities to articulate political demands or to participate in the reform and modernisation process. Under the sultan-Caliphs, the most educated and industrious members of society— the urban bourgeoisie, composed of urban Greeks and Armenians— was not supposed to intervene in politics because of their religious affiliation. This would repeat itself elsewhere during the twentieth century—modernising powers would destroy those social forces that carried the potential for social change. By excluding those Christian minorities from the political process, the Ottoman reforms could not but fail under the pressure of conservative, nominally Islamic institutions. The Young Turks changed this equation, seeking collaboration with Armenian revolutionary groups to overthrow the Sultan. But by the time they took power in 1908 their priority was not to reform and modernise, but to save an empire falling apart. This change would lead to catastrophic consequences for the Armenian revolutionaries and the population at large.

Late Ottoman and Turkish nationalist elites took their dominant political and military position, and the subordinate status of the minorities, for granted. The latter did not have the right to become a true political actor, to voice its distinct political identity outside state-defined community boundaries. All of the Armenian political parties that emerged under Abdul Hamid II (r. 1876–1909), and more recently Hrant Dink in the Turkish Republic,[2] had trespassed the boundaries of their own community as dictated by the system. It was this sense of self-entitlement that allowed the Ottoman and then Turkish elites to justify the punishment inflicted on what they considered treacherous and rebellious populations. A small section of the Armenian population was politically active, and their demands included legal equality and protection of life and property. These demands were not outlandish; they had already been promised on several occasions by various Sultans, whether in their drive to reform the Empire, or through international treaties. Yet, for an empire unable to fulfil reforms and failing to modernise, political activity by Armenian organisations was seen as a challenge to the existing political hierarchy. The cornerstone of the crime itself and the continuous policy of denial since follows this prerogative. Even if those ruling circles—politicians, officers, government bureaucrats and members of secret organisations—acknowledge that mass killings took place (as some did during the Turkish Court-Martials of 1919–1920), there was never any remorse in their confessions, no acknowledgement of responsibility.[3]

During the period in which the Ottoman Empire was in terminal decline, the political and social status of the ruling group was being threatened and the empire was on the brink of collapse. Any threats, whether real or perceived, needed to be fought against in order to save the empire first, and later to terminal homogenise it. The CUP and later Kemalists thought the only way to save the state was by creating a new identity in which particularities could either be dissolved or exterminated. They thought populations of Muslim origin, such as Kurds, Albanians, Arabs and Circassians, could be assimilated, but the Christian Armenians, Assyrians and Greeks could not. Minorities were considered a potential danger that would eventually cause further loss of territory. Therefore violent acts against the minority groups, the 'fate' that befell them, were largely deserved from the point of view of Turkish officialdom. In this struggle, the same rules did not apply to both parties: for 100 years what was permitted for one was denied for the other. It is this profound imbalance of power that created the conditions in which the crime could happen—the crime of the genocide itself, as well as the murder of Hrant Dink—the imbalance between ruler and ruled, between perpetrator and victim.

The Armenian Plateau without Armenians

The modern city of Van, which is 5 kilometres away from where the historic Van used to stand, is located between a lake and a fortress. My local guide took me to a jeweller on the main Kazim Karabekir Street to show me some examples of old Armenian silverwork. They had old belts and little boxes made of silver, decorated with local motifs. They had learned their craft from an old Armenian *usta* (master), Hagop. I asked whether any Armenians still lived in Van. The shopkeeper answered: 'No one would tell you he's Armenian, or that his ancestors were Armenians, although we know that there are ten thousand converted families here.'[4]

Their elimination was so complete that any traveller in the Armenian Highlands today would need a highly-trained eye to notice any surviving remnants of an Armenian past. In the entire Van Lake Basin, one would not find a single person saying, 'I am Armenian.' Even those who have Armenian ancestry are very cautious with regard to talking about their family history. Yet Van province (vilayat) had over 450 Armenian towns and villages, and a total Armenian population of 110,897 before the First World War.[5] One of these villages, Narik, as the villagers now call it, used to house the majestic Naregavank monastery, built in the tenth century. Its most famous pupil was Gregory of Nareg (Krikor Naregatsi), a tenth-century monk, poet, philosopher and theologian. The Turkish army destroyed the monastery in 1951, following the earlier expulsion and massacre of the Armenians from the village. Today there are only dirty village streets with open sewage, and only with great care is it possible to see the old stones of the monastery, including the famous Armenian *khachkars* (tombstones decorated with characteristic crosses) in the construction of Kurdish houses. Even the village mosque stands on an old *khachkar*. There is little else that indicates the existence of the monastery. Driving half an hour east of Van, I arrived at Varaka Vank,[6] now known as Yedi Kilise ('Seven Churches'). We entered the main, surviving church, which is protected by Suleiman, an old man and the son of an imam, jealously guarding the ruins of the church. Inside, the walls are dark, decorated with *khachkars* of different forms. On one of the walls there is a copy of an old picture depicting a panoramic view of the church before 1915. The monastery looks large and well built, with buildings on both sides which probably served to house the friars as well as the students. At the fore of the picture there are some forty-five young boys, stood in a line. They were students there, learning how to read and write. This picture was taken in 1910. Now, a century later, the state of the village and its dirt and poverty clearly contrasts with what was there before.

Although there are no Armenians left on this land that was once named after them, the evidence of their earlier presence, and their violent destruction is everywhere. Out of the 2,538 Armenian churches originally in Anatolia, only 7 remain active, and only some 300 ruins remain—mostly used as barns by the local Kurdish population. Importantly, both the ruins and their destruction survive in the memory of the inhabitants. Stories of past violence continue to be told, especially by the Kurdish peasants in eastern Turkey today.[7]

* * *

The Armenians and the Ottomans have a long and complex history spanning some five centuries.[8] Today, most people see this history as one of antagonism, destruction and hatred due to a series of bloody events: the Hamidian massacres of 1894–6; the Adana massacre of 1909; and especially the ethnic cleansing under the CUP during the First World War. The official position of the authorities continued to be that this minority was its archenemy, one which posed an existential danger to the unity and survival of the Turkish Republic created in 1923. For the Armenians, and especially the children and grandchildren of those who survived the death marches and constitute the Armenian diaspora, 'the Turk' has become an abstract concept directly associated with those who massacred their grandparents, stole their homes and land, destroyed life as it had been embodied over centuries, and sought to deny the crime for many decades. The first generation had different, more nuanced memories—a Turkish or Kurdish neighbour with whom they shared bread and salt, a friend who had saved them from the gendarmes. But these memories faded away with time to leave space for the imposing and linear narrative of the Turkish 'enemy'.

One problem facing the Turkish authorities was how to address this thirty-year period in which the Ottoman Armenians were stigmatised as the quintessential other and later eliminated and removed from the vast majority of their ancestral lands. The historiography officially sanctioned in Turkey depicts the Armenians as a loyal people (*millet-i sadika*), whose religious rights were respected; they became affluent under Ottoman rule, and worked as successful merchants, bankers and artisans in the service of the sultans. In this narrative, there seems to be no reason for dissent, and still less to rebel. The relationship between the Ottoman authorities and the Armenians are presented in idyllic terms until the foreign imperial interventions in the affairs of the Ottoman Empire with the aim of weakening the state and occupying its territories. Not only were there Russians in the east and the north, with their menacing armies at the gates of the empire, but there were also European and American missionaries who opened numerous schools. The Armenians eventually succumbed to this foreign temptation, as with other Christian subjects, and sought to establish their own separate state on Ottoman lands. They revolted on several occasions, the last wave following the outbreak of the First World War. It left the authorities with no other choice but to deport the Armenians (*tahcir*) away from sensitive warfronts or communication lines. This official narrative was the one told in the Turkish education system for decades, with no space to challenge its veracity. The Armenians had no voice to articulate what they thought, what they suffered. They were ghosts, just like in *Snow*, Orhan Pamuk's novel about Kars: the Armenians are there, in the background, but they are invisible and absent because they have no voice. The only alternative voices heard came from beyond Turkey's borders.

Increasingly, however, new voices have begun to emerge in the last two decades from within Turkey itself, shattering the silence and challenging the official narrative.[9]

Failure to Reform

Numerous books on Middle Eastern history open by referring to the beginning of the First World War, the Sykes–Picot Agreement (1916). Starting the story of modern Turkey in 1919 is to narrate an epic victory of the Turks against 'imperialism'; a narrative in which the modern-day ills of the Middle East are almost solely attributable to the British and French occupiers. This narrative choice is made at a cost. Attributing responsibility solely to the imperial powers and absolving regional actors of any accountability presents a flawed understanding of the on-going problems in the Middle East—the failure of Turkey to democratise, the sectarian tensions, the problem of political Islam, the constant failure of political reforms. Similarly, if one starts the history of modern Turkey in 1908 with the Young Turk Revolution, then we see that the party that produced Mustafa Kemal willingly entered the First World War and lost it, and with it half the territory of the empire. A locally rooted narration of the modern history of the Middle East should start earlier, with the failure of Ottoman attempts to reform. It starts with the declaration of the Tanzimat in 1839, the Imperial Reform Edict of 1856 and the introduction of the first constitution in 1876. By looking at the three major reform attempts of the Ottoman Empire in the nineteenth century, one puts the axis of the analysis on the internal struggles and failures within the empire, rather than to repeat politically motivated accusations with regard to external forces being responsible for the failures of the region, a narrative that was nurtured by the sultans themselves and continues to be highly popular in the contemporary Middle East.

The Ottoman Empire adopted Islam as a state religion (and more specifically the Sunni-Hanafi school of thought) and declared itself to be a caliphate. Yet at its height, the Ottoman Empire's population was a mixture of various ethnic, religious and tribal elements, and as much as half of its population was comprised of people from various Christian denominations. It nevertheless followed the Arab tradition developed under the Omayyad dynasty in recognising Christians, Sabians and Jews as *ahl ul-kitab* ('people of the book', monotheists) and as *dhimmis*,[10] whose religious freedom was respected. They were permitted to run the civic affairs of their communities and were protected by the state as long as they professed obedience and paid an additional protection tax, known as *jizya*. Nevertheless, *dhimmi* communities did not have some of the rights enjoyed by Muslims (e.g. the right to carry weapons or ride horses or camels). Moreover, while *dhimmis* were encouraged to convert to Islam, the conversion of Muslims to other religions was not tolerated. These rules were imposed to varying degrees depending on the period in question and the political relations and conflicts between the Ottoman Empire and its enemies. During the Ottoman–Safavid wars of the seventeenth century, for example, Christians were considered neutral, while the Kizilbash (now known as Alevis) were treated with suspicion and became victims of a series of massacres.

Contemporary worldviews should not be applied to a pre-modern empire. 'Empire may be defined by its preservation, even enforcement, of heterogeneity', as Ronald Grigor Suny reminds us.[11] In its heyday, when the Ottoman Empire was expanding and had large dominions in the Balkans, it did not emphasise its Islamic identity. There were times when Ottoman sultans underlined their legitimacy by claiming to be the continuation of the Byzantine Empire: Mehmed II, 'the Conqueror' (r. 1444–1446 and 1451–1481), claimed the title Caesar of Rome (Kayser-i rûm) after conquering Constantinople and claiming to be of a Byzantine imperial family. The Ottoman Empire quickly became Islamic after losing the Balkans, where the bulk of the Ottoman Christian subjects lived, and as a consequence it received waves of Muslim refugees. The incoming refugees increased the population density and led to inter-confessional tensions in Ottoman Anatolia. In the second half of the nineteenth century, under Sultan Abdul Hamid II (r. 1876–1909), the Islamic identity of the empire was increasingly emphasised. During the Russo-Turkish war of 1877–8, for instance, the Ottoman authorities refused to use the symbol of a red cross to indicate neutral medical personnel after it had signed the Geneva protocol in 1864. It was argued that the cross was offensive to Muslim soldiers because it reminded them of the crusaders. Instead, the Ottomans adopted a red crescent on a white background—the reverse of the colours used on the flag with the red cross.[12]

The Ottoman Empire, which had now become known as the 'sick man of Europe', lost vast swathes of territory throughout the nineteenth century: Greece became independent in 1829; in the same year, the sultan ceded the principalities of Moldavia and Wallachia to Russia; and Russia also gained the fortresses of Akhalkalaki and Akhaltsikhe in the south Caucasus. In the following year, France invaded and occupied Algeria, which had previously been under Ottoman rule. The Ottomans lost yet another war against Russia in 1878, and signed the San Stefano Treaty, which would have pushed the sultan out of Europe altogether if it had ever been applied by creating a Greater Bulgaria. In the south Caucasus, Russian forces occupied and later annexed Batumi, Ardahan and Kars. They also temporarily occupied Erzurum. Russia was in a position to impose its conditions on the Sultan in the San Stefano Treaty. However, the Ottoman Empire was saved from further partition due to the intervention of Britain and France, which threatened a new war unless the conditions of the Ottoman capitulation were revised and the terms subsequently altered in the Treaty of Berlin (1878).

As the Ottoman Empire was receding, losing ground, population and economic resources, it was also facing another challenge: the construction of modern state institutions. The Ottoman Empire's Western neighbours were going through a simultaneous economic and political transformation, as represented in the industrial and French revolutions. An already declining Ottoman Empire suddenly looked obsolete: it remained a theocracy, the legitimacy of which rested on the Sharia, which was interpreted by a conservative cast of religious institutions that tended to resist anything that was modern and innovative.

The Ottoman Empire began trying to implement reforms in the late eighteenth century. In this initial phase, the empire sought to modernise its military so as to allow it to compete against other nations, but also to liberate the state from the grip of a number of now archaic military orders. Yet when these reforms began to be implemented, it became apparent their success would depend on similar efforts to reform the system of tax collection and hence public administration. The problem the reforms sought to solve was the shortfall in the amount of tax collected and that which was ultimately received by the state—according to some estimates the state received only 2.25 to 4 million pounds sterling out of 20 million collected annually in taxes, with the rest being appropriated by local notables or the *ayan*, and various intermediaries who were in charge of tax farming (*iltizam*).[13]

Three major reforms were launched, which each largely coincided with acute international crises, during which the Ottoman sultans needed European support: the declaration of Tanzimat in 1839 was made when the sultan needed the support of the great powers in the face of the armies of Muhammad Ali of Egypt; the declaration of *Hatt-ı Hümâyûnu* in 1856 coincided with the Crimean War (1853–6), when British, French and Sardinian armies helped the Ottomans who were fighting the Russian armies, and was announced days before the opening of the Paris Conference (which started on 18 February 1856); and the constitution of 1876 was declared again at a time of revolt, with massacres committed by Ottoman armies in Bulgaria followed by war with Russia. The three attempts at modernisation reveal both Ottoman consciousness of the need for radical change and their failure to achieve the desired results. The inability to modernise was largely due to the dual nature of the reforms: the sultans introduced the Tanzimat, for example, largely for foreign policy purposes—to defend the empire from outside threats. Yet any successful reforms had to take place in the internal policy domain: to replace archaic institutions such as Muslim religious brotherhoods and their influence over politics, the administration and education, as well as provincial rulers and tribal arrangements, to unleash the potential of development and productivity of the empire. But such reforms had to question the supremacy of the ruling Muslim *millet* (community) over religious minorities. The sultans failed to confront conservative institutions (largely Muslim) by mobilising urban educated and industrious classes (majority Christian), at a time when the empire was being challenged by external powers, which were European and Christian. The Tanzimat era came to an end when Sultan Abdul Hamid II came to power. Initially, the Sultan introduced significant reforms when he introduced the first Ottoman constitution and parliament in 1876, but these were largely intended to ward off European anger following major massacres in Bulgaria in 1876, and to attract desperately needed British, French and German support following a major defeat against Russian armies. Once the Berlin Treaty neutralised the Russian threat, Abdul Hamid II suspended the constitution and ruled over the empire for three decades as an absolute monarch aided his notorious secret police.[14]

The reforms aimed to establish constitutional rule, to reform the military and establish a conscript army, and to reform the bureaucracy, while providing legal guarantees with regard to the equality of citizens and protection of property rights.[15] The school system under the sultans, the Quranic madrassas, was archaic and unable to rival the private schools of minority communities. The purpose of these reforms was to strengthen the central authorities vis-à-vis the local potentates who dominated tax-collection and had increased their local power bases, to curb corruption in the administration, to establish a modern military machine and to centralise tax collection by eliminating the *ayans*.[16]

The reforms ultimately failed because they were half-hearted political initiatives, imitating those of rising European powers but without a social base: the Ottoman bourgeoisie was weak because it was mainly composed of minorities and therefore isolated in the larger political constellation of the empire. It became increasingly linked to Europe for its economic well-being, and a growing number of this class sought foreign protection by becoming citizens of European nations. The most serious resistance to the reforms came from the ulema the Muslim provincial notables, a large part of the bureaucracy and the military. Broad segments of the public were vehemently against the Tanzimat, 'antagonised by what many Muslims saw as the surrender of a pre-eminence that their forefathers had established sword in hand'.[17] The more advanced parts of the empire, which had already gone through a deep socio-economic transformation under the influence of European capitalism, increasingly broke away from the Ottomans on cultural–religious lines.[18] The model of European institutions failed to blend with the socio-political realities of the Ottoman Empire, although the reforms tried to do exactly that: they were the 'partial modernisation of an area; that is to say, new institutions and concepts were established but essentially the old institutions and concepts were retained'.[19]

The reforms created expectations among some and fear of change among others, thus accentuating inter-confessional tensions. In the provinces, the reforms not only failed to establish any kind of equality between the subjects of the Ottoman Empire but at times served to accelerate repression and assimilatory policies. Following the announcement of the Hatt-ı Hümâyûnu—the imperial reform edict—and the declaration of equality between Muslims and Christians, many local Islamised Armenians and Greeks in Sev-Get, or Kara-Dere near Trabzon, who had still retained their past cultural attachments and were Armenian and Greek speakers, as well as Islamised Armenians of west Hemshin who still spoke Armenian, expressed an intention to return to their previous religious beliefs. As a result, local officials exerted increasing pressure on both, and the communities were prohibited from using their original languages before being forcibly assimilated.[20] Similarly, tensions resulting from the reforms transformed local conflicts into sectarian strife. In 1850, for instance, a Muslim mob attacked the Christian neighbourhood of Judaydeh in Aleppo, killing dozens and setting fire to the houses of the wealthier inhabitants in the process. Syriac Catholic Patriarch Peter VII Jarweh was injured and succumbed to his wounds a year later. In Lebanon and Syria, it added to already simmering tensions between local communities and power struggles among feudal families as well as peasant revolts, transforming local conflicts into open sectarian war. In 1858–9 this led to a violent confrontation between Druze and Maronite which spilled over into Damascus where thousands of Christians were massacred in 1860. Regular Ottoman forces were both unwilling and unable to stop the bloodshed. The conflict on Mount Lebanon led to an outcry in Europe and to the direct intervention of foreign imperial powers. A military coalition of European forces, led by French troops, was sent to establish order and to put an end to the atrocities. The European force stayed in Lebanon until a political solution was found, which resulted in the establishment of the 'Mutassarifate': a semi-autonomous order, ruled by a *mutasarrif* (Arabic translation for the French *plénipotentiaire*), ruled by a non-Lebanese Christian ruler appointed by the sultan after the agreement of powers.

Armenians: Merchants and Peasants

In the early nineteenth century, with rebellion throughout the west and south of the Ottoman Empire, the Armenians were considered the most loyal nation. It was not only the Christian nations in the Balkans that were in open revolt against the sultan but also Muslims, like Muhammad Ali in Egypt, along with a series of rebellions in Yemen, Hijaz and elsewhere. Yet by the end of the nineteenth century, the Armenians were considered a major internal threat. They became the target of a series of state-sponsored massacres, and were subject to a policy of forced conversion before being deported en masse to their death in the Syrian Desert. What happened to cause such a profound change of attitude? What made the Armenians become rebellious? Were all Armenians dangerous revolutionaries who deserved the most severe punishments? The argument concerning the rebellious nature of the Armenians was used in the past, and continues to be used today to justify the crimes committed against them.

The Armenian population of the Ottoman Empire was very diverse from a social and anthropological perspective. There was a sharp difference between city dwellers, mainly to the west of the empire, and the peasantry which lived in historic Armenia to the east. Peasants in the eastern provinces had specific security concerns. While writing about the good conditions of the Armenians under the Ottoman Empire, authors often have in mind the powerful *Amira* classes in the capital and major urban centres, who were merchants, bankers and industrialists. The Amira class rose to prominence in the eighteenth century, were closely associated with the sultan and dominated Armenian social and political life in the Ottoman Empire for over a century. Often of Anatolian migrant origins, they became trusted servants of the sultans. The Momjians, a family belonging to the Amira class, were royal bankers and provided the palace with candles, while Abraham Amira Karakehian was the financial representative of Mehmet Ali of Egypt at the Sublime Porte.[21] The Duzians were in charge of imperial coinage. The Dadian family, starting with Arakel Amira Dad, ran the gunpowder industry for the sultans over several generations, producing guns and ammunition for the Ottoman army.

They were so trusted and respected by the sultans that Mahmud II (r. 1808–39) and his son Sultan Abdulmecid (r. 1839–61) visited the mansion of the Dadian family at Yesilkoy (where Istanbul airport is currently located), staying between two and eight days on several occasions.[22] Artin Dadian Pasha served as the undersecretary at the Ministry of Foreign Affairs, but was effectively the minister, as the suspicious Sultan Abdul Hamid II (r. 1876–1909) trusted him for key missions and negotiations.[23] Mahmud II, when he wanted to build a new imperial palace, commissioned Krikor Amira Balian—the architect of Dolmabahçe Palace (1849–56) and a member of another Armenian dynasty who for generations served as architects of the court—to oversee the project. The Balian dynasty was not an exception, but the continuation of a long tradition of Armenian architects in Istanbul, a tradition starting with the Great Sinan (1490–1588, also known as Mi'mâr Sinan, or Sinan the architect).[24] Hovsep Aznavurian, Mgrdich Charekian, Mihran Azarian, Bedros Nemtse, Hovannes Serverian and Kapriel Mgrdichian are among the other Armenians who were given the title of royal architect.[25]

The rise of the Armenian bourgeoisie resulted from complex developments within and outside the community. In 1814 a secret organisation was founded in Odessa, on the northern shores of the Black Sea: known as the Philiki Etairia, or the 'friendly society', it aimed to liberate the Greeks from Ottoman rule. As soon as their rebellion began, Muslim and Jewish populations in the Peloponnese were massacred. Sultan Mahmud II's reaction was brutal. Greek religious figures in Constantinople were accused of treason and were arrested. Ecumenical Patriarch Gregory V (1746–1821) was hanged at the central gate of the Patriarchate in the Phanar district of the capital, where his body was displayed for three days. The Grand Dragoman (a translator and diplomat in the service of the sultan), Konstantionos Mourouzis, was arrested, beheaded and his body put on public display. Anti-Greek pogroms took hold in the streets of Constantinople; priests were lynched and churches pillaged and destroyed. Comones Kalfa, a Greek architect finishing work on new offices for the Ottoman navy at Galata, was snatched and beheaded.[26] These innocent servants of the sultan had no involvement in any conspiracy, yet they became victims of the anger of an ignorant ruler. The violent acts against Greek community leaders did not help the cause of the Ottomans; on the contrary, more Greeks were alienated and their struggle received much sympathy in Europe. Following the Greek revolt of 1821, the Greek community entered a period of decline, having previously occupied dominant positions within the court, the state administration and in trade. This allowed the Armenian bourgeoisie to progress unchallenged, earning the title *millet-i sadika* (the loyal nation).

The Armenians and other minorities of the empire readily adapted to new educational models and progress was made in science, organisation and technology. Yet the dominant Muslim institutions resisted change and European influence as 'anti-Islamic'. The print industry that had transformed European economies and opened the way to the Industrial Revolution and Reformation, for instance, was greatly resisted: Sultan Bayezid II (r.1481–1512) made printing in Arabic script, the language of the holy Quran, punishable by death. Minorities were not restrained by such edicts as they used non-Arabic alphabets. The first press in the Ottoman Empire was a Hebrew press established in 1494, followed by the establishment of an Armenian press in 1567. A Hungarian convert to Islam, Ibrahim Müteferrika, who was given permission to print non-religious books, established the first Turkish press in 1726.[27] But it was soon closed, and another hundred years passed before a new Turkish press would begin operation.

Muslim institutions also resisted innovation in education and insisted on preserving old religious schools while the minorities were open to pedagogical innovations. By the mid-nineteenth century, there was a serious effort to spread modern education among the empire's Muslim elite, and the numbers enrolled in advanced education increased fourfold from 1867 to 1895, reaching 33,469 students. Yet at the same time, the number of non-Muslims attending secondary school was 76,359. Taking into account the difference in population size, the ratio of minorities in education compared with Muslims was six to one.[28] There were two reasons for this: first, the state, now dominated by the Muslim element of the empire, resisted the introduction of modern Western education which they viewed as 'Christian' rather than 'secular'. Secondly, they refused to enrol in the Western schools that had been opened in various Ottoman towns primarily by Americans but also other Protestant and Catholic missionaries. In addition, the Armenian and Greek communities considered education as the key to social mobility and invested enormous resources in order to open community schools, as well as printing facilities, newspapers and periodicals.

The situation of the Armenian population in the provinces was very different when compared to those living in the capital or urban centres in the west. The peasantry constituted the vast majority of the Ottoman Armenian population, some 70 to 75 per cent of the total.[29] Social, demographic and political transformations were making the position of the Armenians in the eastern provinces untenable. One of the major problems facing them was security. As a Christian *millet* (nation), they did not have the right to bear arms, but lived under the domination of Kurdish overlords, paying them taxes in return for protection. In the early nineteenth century, as a result of Ottoman attempts to create a centralised administration, the Kurdish semi-autonomous emirate was disbanded, and chaos followed in its wake. Smaller units of armed Kurdish clans (*ashiret*) roamed the countryside pillaging, kidnapping young girls and clashing with Armenian or Kurdish villagers. The Ottoman religious courts did not treat Christians and Muslims equally, nor did the Ottoman administration provide protection to the victims. The other problem facing the Armenian peasantry was double taxation, the first imposed by the Ottomans, while the second was the protection tax imposed by Kurdish *aghas*. The taxes imposed by the Ottoman sultans increased dramatically when the empire declared it was bankrupt in 1875, only worsening after the start of direct European supervision over the finances and taxation of the empire from 1881 onwards. This heavy burden was one of the reasons for the uprisings in the Balkans, which led to the Russo-Ottoman wars of 1876–7. Similarly, revolts in Zeitun (1862 and 1894) and Sasoun (1894) were triggered by increased taxation on the Armenian peasantry, as well as repeated raids by Kurdish and Circassian irregulars.

The most acute source of conflict was the struggle over land. In the second half of the nineteenth century, a new problem emerged with the increasing sedentarisation of the nomadic tribes. Modern political science recognises the way in which shifting economic patterns create conflict over scarce resources, which is then packaged and presented as a religious or ethnic conflict. Struggle over rare arable land, and the confiscation of land belonging to Armenian peasants by armed Kurdish tribes, became yet another severe problem. The inflow of Muslim refugees from the Caucasus or the Balkans only accentuated this struggle over land, further polarising religious communities. As a result, violent events caused by struggles over land increased in the second half of the nineteenth century. A commission put together by the Armenian National Assembly of Istanbul to look at 'oppressive acts' in the eastern vilayets examined 320 violent incidents from April 1872 to August 1876. Among them, 308 had taken place in villages, and only 5 in towns and 7 in cities. A total of 272 cases were attributed to 'land usurpations'.[30] It was the 'socioeconomic and interethnic relations in the eastern provinces from 1860s on, and not European diplomacy, [that] are [at] the core of the Armenian Question', according to Stephan Astourian.[31] The land issue that grew in magnitude under Abdul Hamid II remained a major problem in relations between the Committee Union and Progress (CUP) and the Armenian Revolutionary Federation (ARF) after the 1908 revolution. In the summer of 1911, the lack of any progress in addressing the problem of confiscation of Armenian lands and government inaction to resolve it brought ARF–CUP relations almost to a breaking point.[32]

This local conflict took on an international dimension with the Russo-Turkish wars. After the San Stefano and Berlin Treaties of 1878, Russia became a direct actor in the conflict. To counterbalance Russian power—which used the problem of Christian minorities as a rationale for intervention—the Sultan Abdul Hamid II allied himself with the Kurdish tribal forces, created the Hamidiye Cavalry composed of Kurdish tribes and sought to eliminate Armenian political expression. The Russian intervention was in turn counterbalanced by the great powers, mainly Britain and France, and later by Germany, which wanted to avoid a situation where Russian expansion to the south would threaten their own imperial ambitions. They saw the preservation of the Ottoman Empire's territorial integrity as their major objective in the east. Western powers were ready to intervene directly to fight the Russians in support of the Ottomans, as they did in the Crimean War (1853–6) and had again threatened to do so following the San Stefano Treaty. However, the same powers had not hesitated to undermine Ottoman territorial integrity when it was for the profit of their own territorial expansion, as was the case with the British occupation of Cyprus in 1878 or the occupation of Egypt by the British in 1882, then nominally an Ottoman territory.

Internationalisation of the 'Armenian Question'

The ascension to power of the conservative sultan, Abdul Hamid II, in 1876 marked the failure and end of the Tanzimat period. He started his reign as a reformist—after coming to power he had announced the creation of the constitution. But his reformist inclinations only lasted a few months. The empire was in a dire situation: the coffers were empty despite constant increases in taxation, which in turn prompted revolts. The Balkan provinces were soon up in arms in protest against harsh taxation. A rebellion that started in Bosnia–Herzegovina in 1875 spread to Bulgaria in 1876. Ottoman authorities tried to put them down with brutal force, using the regular army as well as irregular forces such as the notorious Bashi Bazouks. 15–20,000 people were massacred at Philippopolis (now Plovdiv) and in the surrounding villages, and these events were reported in European newspapers, leading to public outcry. It was in this context that William Gladstone, at the time an opposition parliamentarian, wrote his pamphlet titled 'Bulgarian Horrors', which immediately became a bestseller in Britain. Another disastrous war with Russia soon erupted (1877–8) and, unlike in the Crimean War, the Ottomans were left alone to face the armies of the tsar; even the British could not intervene to defend the Ottomans from Russian advances. The sultan lost large sections of his Balkan dominions, and with them most of the empire's Christian subjects. An influx of Muslim refugees further aggravated the situation, causing inter-communal relations to deteriorate. The Russian armies reached the gates of the capital and threatened to attack it, forcing the sultan to capitulate.

Writing in 1919 about the massacre of the tens of thousands of Armenians and Assyrians in 1915, one Armenian writer stated that: 'Armenians never had [a] separatist impulse. All that Armenians wished and asked for was a most legitimate request; security for self and property. This innocent and natural wish of the Armenians was considered rebellion by the Turkish authorities … [leading them to take] unforgivable steps against them.'[33] In fact, the first time an international treaty mentioned the creation of an independent Armenian state was the Treaty of Sèvres, signed in 1920, and hence after the First World War. Up to 1914, both the struggle of the Ottoman Armenians and the demands of the great powers were about reforms, or the application of what Tanzimat had already promised: physical security for religious minorities and justice in the Ottoman courts. As the Ottoman state failed to introduce reforms and elementary justice, the Armenian elites increasingly hoped that salvation would come through foreign intervention by European powers. This, in its turn, added to the suspicion of the ruling Ottomans felt towards their Armenian subjects.

On 3 March 1878, the Russo Ottoman war (1877–8) was ended with the signing of the San Stefano Treaty. The treaty established an autonomous Bulgaria with boundaries from the Black Sea to the Aegean, and recognised the independence of Serbia, Romania and Montenegro with expanded boundaries. In the Caucasus, Russia gained new territories including the Kars, Ardahan, Ardvin and Beyazit regions. Its armies were to remain in Erzurum until reforms were introduced in the eastern provinces. The successes of the Russian military and the conditions of the San Stefano Treaty alarmed the other European Powers. Under Prime Minister Benjamin Disraeli, Britain opposed Russian gains, while the Austro-Hungarian Empire was disappointed to see its Balkan ambitions ruined by Russia. A new congress was held in Berlin where the terms of the armistice were revised. Ottoman rule over parts of the Balkans was re-established, although everyone understood that this was a temporary measure.

The San Stefano Treaty and the Berlin Congress that followed marked the internationalisation of the 'Armenian Question'. In Article 16, the San Stefano Treaty linked Russian troop withdrawals from Erzurum with the implementation of the reforms. This was changed in the Berlin Treaty. Article 61 of the Berlin Treaty thus states: 'The Sublime Porte undertakes to carry out, without further delay, the improvements and reforms demanded by local require-ments in the provinces inhabited by Armenians, and to guarantee their security against the Circassians and Kurds. It will periodically make known the steps taken to this effect to the powers, who will superintend their application.'[34] Hence the internationalisation of the Armenian Question did not provide any guarantees or protection to the Armenians of the eastern provinces.

Moreover, following the defeat of his armies in 1877 during a war in which the European powers offered little help in saving the 'sick man', Sultan Abdul Hamid II feared that the Russians would annex vast swathes of territory both in the Balkans and in the Ottoman Empire's Asiatic provinces. At this point, he found it in his interest to raise the idea of autonomous Armenian provinces on the border with the Russian Caucasus as a diplomatic instrument of manoeuvring, or in the worst case as an Armenian buffer state between the Ottoman and tsarist empires. He even encouraged the Armenians to raise such demands for autonomy.[35] But what had seemed attractive in the period leading up to the San Stefano Treaty became less so when the European powers intervened in favour of the sultan in order to limit Russian territorial ambitions. After his volte face on the idea of Armenian autonomy, the sultan became concerned that the Treaty of Berlin and the promises of reform in the eastern provinces would serve as the first step in the creation of an independent Armenia. These fears were shared by Kurdish tribal chiefs; they were concerned that any European-sponsored reforms would lead to a shift in power relations, one that would not be in their interests. In the next four decades, a close alliance emerged between the local Kurdish lords and the central authorities, first under Sultan Abdul Hamid, and later under the leadership of the CUP. This alliance proved resilient despite a number of changes in the political situation, and was largely motivated by the fear of the Kurds with regard to losing their power and influence, as well as the lands they had recently taken from the Armenians.[36] In 1890 Sultan Abdul Hamid II created a Kurdish tribal force known as the Hamidiye Cavalry irregulars, based on the Cossack model, with the aim of centralising Kurdish and other Muslim nomadic tribes into a military force that could be used against the Russians. But unlike the Cossacks, the Hamidiye were not efficient fighters, and the creation of this irregular force caused more destabilisation. It appeared to mark a return to the past practice of encouraging tribal identities which the Ottoman authorities had sought to crush in the early nineteenth century when they had endeavoured to weaken tribal confederations among the Kurds. In addition to this, the Hamidiye became very active in theft and brigandage, and especially in targeting the Armenian peasantry. In fact, they were used as an instrument to bring about demographic change, and played a major role in the anti-Armenian massacres of 1894–6. Each act of self-defence against Kurdish double taxation, as in Zeitun in 1862 and again in 1894–5, or in Sasoun in 1894, was considered to be a revolt against the authority of the state and was suppressed through brutal force and massacres.[37] During the Hamidian massacres (1894–6) that followed, which caused the death of an estimated 200–300,000 Armenians and other Christians, the European signatories to the Berlin Treaty criticised the brutality of the Ottomans, but offered nothing that would aid the victims.

As with the fate of the Armenians in the First World War, the Hamidian massacres and the way they have been interpreted is yet another historiographical battlefield. Some view the events as being 'provoked' by 'Armenian revolutionaries [who] stepped up acts of violence and sabotage in the hope of provoking European intervention. The heavy-handed suppression of these activities by the

Ottoman authorities, and ensuing attacks by mobs on Armenian civilians, played a role in the subsequent formulation of contingency plans for the partition of the Ottoman Empire.'[38] For those who adhere to this view, the blame for the massacre of hundreds of thousands of unarmed civilians is attributed to a handful of Armenian militants—whether nationalist or socialist—whose aim was not to put forward rightful grievances, but to invite acts of violence with the hope of foreign intervention and the creation of an independent nation-state in Ottoman territory. The massacre, in this interpretation, was the result of excesses in the reaction of the authorities to the Armenian provocations.

But the Ottoman sultan and the Kurdish tribal leaders were not passive political victims, simply reacting to the political plans of Armenian revolutionaries. In fact, the 'Red Sultan', so-called on account of the killing that took place during his reign, was using the massacres perpetrated by the tribal forces he himself created to put an end to the Armenian Question. He was addressing political issues within his own state with mass murder. The massacres were one of the instruments the sultan employed to convince the European powers that the Armenians were no longer the majority population in the east, and that further reforms had now become unnecessary. The killing stopped abruptly, showing that these were not spontaneous acts of violence or inter-communal conflict. Just after the massacres in 1897, Abdul Hamid told the British Ambassador Sir Philip Currie that: 'The Armenian Question is finally closed.'[39]

The overthrow of the tyrannical Sultan Abdul Hamid II in 1908 opened a new page of cooperation between the political forces in the empire. The new masters of Istanbul were the Committee of Union and Progress (CUP, also referred to as 'Young Turks'). The CUP was a heteroclite group composed of Ottoman reformists as well as nationalists. They spent years in exile based in Paris where they were in regular contact with Armenian revolutionary parties. Their common goal was to overthrow the tyranny of Abdul Hamid II and return to the 1876 constitution as a way to save the downfall of the empire. The CUP succeeded in gaining influence among military officers based in the Balkans where in 1908 they launched a military rebellion that enabled them to take power. For a very short while, Muslims and Christians were euphoric that their long ordeal was over, and a new age of freedom had finally come. Exiled Armenian and Turkish militants knew each other well, met regularly and tried to cooperate. On many occasions they shared close friendships. The CUP had numerous Armenian members in its ranks. For a long time the Armenian revolutionaries were sceptical about the Young Turks; they viewed them as an intellectual club rather than a committed group of revolutionaries. The Young Turks did not have cells within the Ottoman Empire and did not initiate any revolutionary activity or civil disobedience, nor did they engage in violent attacks against symbols of state repression. For many years both sides had tried to attract the attention of the great powers to their plight in the hope that outside intervention would put an end to Hamidian despotism. But the Armenian revolutionary committees had an advantage over their Turkish counterparts: they had committed revolutionaries who were disciplined and experienced in armed struggle, and a structured organisation present within the Armenian communities of the empire.

The Young Turk movement radically changed when two doctors, Bahaeddin Şakir and Nazım Bey, arrived on the scene. They took control of the organisation from Ahmad Rıza and the old guard, and transformed it in the period between 1905 and 1906 from their safe haven in Paris.[40] The two men imposed strict control over what was a coalition of exiled dissidents, and kept this control until the end of the war in 1918. Their aim was to unify the Ottoman opposition, to reorganise the CUP and to create an effective party. In Salonika, the creation of Osmanlı Hürriyet Perveran (Ottoman Liberty Organisation) in 1906, mostly composed of young army officers, was the first concrete result of the reorganisation. It had two important consequences: the beginning of the creation of revolutionary cells within the empire, and growing influence with army officers, which would pave the way for the 1908 Revolution. In their turn, the young army officers would come to dominate the Young Turk movement, thereby changing the history of the Middle East.

It is impossible to understand the subsequent course of events without noting the sociological differences between the Armenian and Turkish revolutionaries, which belonged to two different classes and had completely different visions for political change. The Armenian revolutionaries were the children of the bourgeoisie, a class that suffered from a lack of legal protection and arbitrary tyrannical rule. In the era of Abdul Hamid II, the Armenian revolutionaries had an additional, existential problem: the physical threat against their community. As intellectuals, they professed a belief in socialism and international solidarity, yet their ideas were simultaneously rooted in nationalism and Armenian national identity.[41] Their continuous attempts to create an alliance with other ethnic groups, such as the Turks, Kurds and Muslims in general, were largely ineffective. In the eastern provinces, much of the Kurdish population remained traditional and was still under the influence of the tribal system. They allied with Abdul Hamid II against the Christian Armenians and against the danger of Russian expansion on the grounds of Islamic solidarity. Turkish revolutionaries, on the other hand, were composed of either court members who had fallen out with the sultan, or, more commonly, young army officers. Their main priority was to save the empire from collapse, not necessarily to bring about rule of law and equal treatment of all citizens.

* * *

A new age of freedom was declared after the 1908 Revolution. There was widespread expectation that there would be extensive and rapid change. The Armenian revolutionaries and other exiles were finally able to return to Istanbul and start operating legally. Yet less than a year later, as reactionary forces attempted to return to power, anti-Armenian pogroms erupted in Adana and the surrounding towns and villages. Between 20,000 and 30,000 Armenians were killed and their property destroyed. In the words of Zabel Yesaian, 'We too gave our sacrifice, our blood this time was spilled with our Turkish compatriots. This will be the last time.'[42] Many Armenian leaders had noted that the army led by CUP officers in Adana had not protected the

Armenians, but had in fact taken an active part in the atrocities. While the Armenian Social-Democrats had distanced themselves from the CUP, the ARF continued to collaborate with the CUP until 1913. There was some hope that reforms would finally begin to be implemented, as the CUP government had agreed to name two European inspector-generals to supervise reforms in the Armenian provinces (a promise that, in fact, failed to materialise).[43] However, according to many historians, the fear among the Ottomans of the possibility of European supervision in these territories—the fear, in essence, that this would lead to the loss of these areas—is what triggered the deportations and the massacres of the Armenians a year later.

In 1912 the Ottoman leadership had come to the conclusion that their state could survive only if it had become a protectorate of a great power. The problem was that the various CUP leading figures did not agree among themselves which European power would be the best choice. Mahmut Şevket Pasha, the Grand Vizir, approached the Germans on 24 April 1913, with the intention of placing the Ottoman army under effective German control. He anticipated protests from the other powers, especially the British, whom he approached in order to ask for assistance in implementing the reforms in the provinces. The Ottomans had hoped that once again traditional rivalry between Russians and the British, each fearing the spread of the influence of the other over Asia Minor, would eventually shelve the reform project in eastern Anatolia.[44] Yet this diplomatic manipulation turned out differently:

> The Porte had thought it was making a clever move with its 24 April proposal, juxtaposing the Russians against the British in Eastern Anatolia. However, by coming to an agreement with the British the Russians had turned the tables on the Ottomans and forced them to accept their move in eastern Anatolia. The Russian–Ottoman treaty of 8 February 1914 removed Eastern Anatolia (called 'Armenia' in Europe) from its status of an inter-European issue as determined by the Congress of Berlin and made this region a bone of contention between Russia and the Ottomans.[45]

The continuous injustice suffered under the Hamidian regime led to the creation of a number of Armenian revolutionary parties. The first among them was the Armenagan, established in Van in 1885, and later renamed as Ramgavar (liberal democratic). Seven Armenian students at the University of Geneva founded the Social-Democrat Hunchagyan Party in 1887. They were inspired by the Marxist ideas they discovered in Europe and believed that the suffering of the Armenian peasantry could only be brought to an end through revolution. They also believed in armed struggle to attain their goals. The Armenian Revolutionary Federation—Tashnagtsutyun (ARF)—was founded in Tbilisi in 1890. The socialist and nationalist ideas of the times equally influenced it, and it rapidly became the most influential of the Armenian organisations. Yet in spite of the efforts of party members, the vast majority of the population remained passive and did not take part in militant activities. Istanbul notables accused groups of young revolutionaries of having prompted Hamidian repression through their militant activities, and public opinion largely supported such interpretations.

It is often forgotten that the CUP leadership and the Armenian intelligentsia had very close relations. Those who were arrested on 24 April 1915 were very often old acquaintances, fellow exiled revolutionaries and even personal friends. The personal friendship between the CUP strongman and the interior minister in 1915, Mehmed Talaat and Krikor Zohrab, the Armenian lawyer from Istanbul, and member of the Ottoman Parliament (1908–15), is only one example.[46] The CUP leadership, especially its nationalist wing, felt inferior not only to the Armenian bourgeoisie—along with the Greeks, the Armenian bourgeoisie dominated commerce and industry in major urban centres, and constituted the majority of the educated classes—but also to the Armenian revolutionary organisations: the Armenian Social-Democrats and the ARF were older, more experienced and more disciplined revolutionaries.

At the dawn of the Great War, the Armenians in the capital were still optimistic about the impending reforms. Hagop Jololian Siruni writes that 'in those days the whole of Bolis [Constantinople] as well as all Armenians were on fire with enthusiasm to celebrate the 1500th anniversary of the invention of the Armenian letters'.[47] Public events and cultural activities were organised that created a false sense of empowerment. At the end of March 1915, Turkish intellectuals organised a musical evening to promote Turkish culture and to impress their European guests. The Armenian musician Soghomon Soghomonian, commonly known as Gomidas, was invited to give a performance to these luminaries, including the CUP interior minister, Talaat Pasha. Hamdullah Suphi, the Turkish writer and the master of ceremony, introduced Gomidas with the following words:

> This son of Anatolia, an Armenian clergyman has, with his dedication and hard work, given wings to Armenian music ... he ignored comfort and luxury and spent his time in the villages collecting folk songs ... and presented those songs as part of the Armenian national heritage ... If only our clergy did the same thing. I wonder what treasures they would find, treasures that could elevate the value of the sensitive heart and the thinking mind of the Turkish nation ... The truth ... is that the Armenian nation remains on the forefront of our cultural life. Wherever you go in Turkey, in any corner of Anatolia, the Armenian mind, the creative Armenian mind and hand will greet you and tell you 'I am here.' If you go to the palaces of the sultans, the architects are Armenians ... The tombstones of our loved ones, which are so finely carved, are the works of Armenian masters ... Armenian masters also make the famous jewellery boxes from Van. The founders of the medical schools and the writers of scientific books are also Armenians ... These are the people with whom we have lived for centuries ... Then [Gomidas] sat at the piano and sang and played ... The hall reverberated with the ovations and applauses ... and you could hear shouting ... 'God save him from evil eyes.'[48]

Three weeks later, on 24 April 1915, Gomidas, along with the leading lights from among the Armenian intelligentsia and the leaders of the Armenian community, would be arrested and sent into exile. The extermination of a nation had commenced.

3

OBLIVION

The Armenian Genocide during the First World War was a unique historical experience: what happens after a crime, when the criminal remains free and everyone pretends that a crime has never taken place? What happens when an entire nation is uprooted from its land, massacred and the survivors are dispersed around the globe, and the world simply turns a blind eye?

The Armenian population, which had a strong presence in the six eastern Ottoman provinces and in the major urban centres, including the capital Istanbul, suddenly disappeared in the dark days of the First World War. What happened to them? How did they simply vanish from their ancestral lands? This question has been answered in two very different ways. One explanation holds that a state-devised plan involving deportations and massacres—with the intention of annihilating the Ottoman Armenians and confiscating their property—explains this disappearence. The alternative narrative, in contrast, holds that the Armenians were never subject to genocide at the hands of the Turkish state; instead, the Anatolian Armenians were expelled as a result of inter-communal conflict between Armenians and Muslims The Armenians revolted during the war, collaborated with foreign troops and the Turkish army was forced to take measures against them. This latter interpretation, which is also the view of a number of academics, is the official position of the contemporary Turkish state.

The Armenians were denied the opportunity to speak of the tragedy they had suffered. First, there was the trauma itself and the destruction of all of life's previous certitudes. On 24 April 1915, leading Armenian intellectuals were arrested before being tortured and eventually executed. The young Armenian forces serving on the frontline for the Ottoman Empire were disbanded, and later assassinated. Their community institutions, from church associations to schools and newspapers, were closed down. Their monasteries and churches, centres of memory and creation for millennia, were destroyed, and their stones used to construct new dwellings. The survivors, mainly orphans, women and children, became refugees in foreign lands, where they sought to forget past suffering in order to begin building a new life. For this first generation of survivors, it was almost impossible to envisage a struggle for justice and recognition from Turkey, as the world simply turned its attention elsewhere.

The ruling Turkish elite subsequently chose to erase any trace of the Armenians from Turkish history. In the period between 1945 and the 1980s, school textbooks in Turkey made no mention of the Armenians in the Ottoman Empire or the deportation of 1915.[1] The Armenians had simply ceased to exist.

As part of this campaign of silence, the Turkish government changed the Armenian names of towns, villages and rivers into Turkish. A village named Karmrik (Karmir means 'red' in East Armenian), for instance, became Kezelja, or Tsaghkadsor ('valley of flowers') when translated into Darachichek. In other cases, the names were corrupted to sound Turkish; the name of the Armenian island and monastery Aghtamar, for example, was changed to the more Turkish-sounding Agtamar, while Karhatavan ('settlement where stone was cut') became Karadivan.[2] This practice of changing place names was consistent with the policy that first started to be implemented under the 'Red Sultan' and was also adopted by the CUP and the Atatürk Republic. Following the 1878 Congress of Berlin, when the 'Armenian Question' began to be discussed internationally, Sultan Abdul Hamid II forbade the use of 'Armenia' in official documents, with the name itself replaced with 'Anatolia' or 'Kurdistan'. On 5 January 1916, Enver Pasha—the CUP's minister of war—issued a decree requiring all Armenian, Bulgarian and Greek place names to be changed into Turkish.[3] This practice of Turkifying toponyms continued in the Republican era, and subsequently expanded to include Arabic and Kurdish names as well, especially after the Kurdish uprising in 1925. This practice also continued after the Second World War: the 1949 Provincial Administrative Law, for instance, contained an article on changing 'foreign' names into Turkish, while in 1957 a 'Specialised Organisation for Renaming Toponyms' was created. After researching the background of some 75,000 names, this organisation changed 28,000 names, including the names of over 12,000 villages.[4]

This effort to eradicate any memory of the Armenians was not confined to Turkish territory. In the 1960s, the Turkish ambassador in Bern forced the Swiss airline Swissair to change the nomenclature used on the maps that were available on their planes as they referred to the '*plateau arménien*'.[5] As a result of policies such as these, the expression Armenian Plateau, which had been used for centuries to denote the mountainous highlands around Lake Van and Lake Sevan, was eliminated and replaced by the expression 'eastern Anatolia'. Archaeological sites, monasteries, churches, school buildings or *khachkars*—the distinctive Armenian cross-stones—were deliberately destroyed and erased, monasteries were razed to the ground or turned into mosques or used as stables. One church in central Kayseri (Gesarya) was turned into a sports centre.[6]

The Official Turkish Thesis on 1915

After 1915, the Turkish state continued to adopt a similar position to that used during the time of Sultan Abdul Hamid II and later the CUP to justify the massacres. At first, the Kemalist regime simply denied that any massacres had taken place. This stance was then replaced by the position that the Armenians were rebellious and deserved their fate as they posed a threat to the security of the state and Turkish society. Some of the proponents of this official narrative have even gone so far as to claim that the Armenians were the real aggressors, and that Muslim losses were greater than those of the Armenians. In other words, the official position of the Turkish state has evolved over time—after initially denying that the state-sponsored massacres took place, the official narrative began to claim that the numbers involved were relatively small, and that those who suffered had brought their fate on themselves.

Another position adopted by the Turkish authorities is the idea that the events of 1915 were a temporary relocation, the intention being to move a population with questionable loyalties away from the front lines of the First World War. According to this narrative, the Ittihadist government provided the deportees with money and land, yet an inefficient bureaucracy, the Kurdish tribes and the conditions of war ultimately led to large number of casualties. Given the absence of an intention to commit genocide, those who argue in this way claim that genocide cannot be used in a legal sense with regard to the deportations and massacres of 1915.

The Turkish government has also questioned the numbers of those involved. This includes the number of Ottoman Armenians at the time of the Congress of Berlin—the trigger that internationalised the 'Armenian Question'—as well as the number of casualties caused by the massacres and the *tehcir* (deportations).

The official Turkish literature, which is often addressed to European or North American states that recognise crimes against humanity, has also sought to draw comparisons between 1915 and the actions of other states during times of war. By extension, the same states have no right to demand that Turkey recognise the crimes it committed during the First World War. One Turkish author, for example, cites the American bombing of Japan to emphasise his point: 'The Armenians were forced to emigrate because they had joined the ranks of the enemy. The fact that they were civilians does not change the situation. Those who were killed in Hiroshima and Nagasaki during the Second World War were also civilians.'[7]

The final part of the official narrative is that there is no consensus that the events of 1915 can be classed as a genocide—there are numerous non-Turkish scholars who remain sceptical about using this term, and the way the debate over the genocide has been represented is one-sided, solely reflecting the Armenian version of events. In this vein, they question the authenticity of certain documents used in arguments to support the genocide thesis, and initiate personal attacks on the authors for being Armenian, or simply for reflecting a biased, Armenian point of view.

There were of course numerous rebellions within the Ottoman Empire. Did this justify the Ottoman massacres of entire nations? There were sporadic anti-Ottoman rebellions against unsustainable tax burdens in Yemen, Hijaz and Hawran.[8] In 1916 Sharif Hussein bin Ali of Mecca declared the Arab Revolt, a rebellion encouraged by the British to fight the Ottomans in the name of the creation of an independent Arab Kingdom in the Middle East. In 1910–11 there were also revolts in Albania and Crete, in Hijaz in southern Syria, in Hawran and East Jordan, Asir, Najd and Yemen.[9] As these populations were never deported, the supposedly rebellious nature of the Armenians can hardly be used to justify the actions of the Ottoman authorities.

The Stalinist regime also deported entire populations on the grounds of their collaboration with external powers, in this case the German enemy. Entire nations were forced to enter cargo carriages before being transported to the Steppes of Siberia or Central Asia. Even men enrolled in the Red Army and fighting on the front against the Nazi forces were arrested, accused of collaboration and exiled, just like the Armenian soldiers serving under the Ottoman flag during the First World War. Yet there are differences between the crimes of the CUP government and those of the Stalinist regime: unlike the former, the USSR did not massacre the civilians involved, and they were at least partially—though not completely—rehabilitated after Khrushchev's secret speech in 1956 and were able to begin returning to their homelands from 1957 onwards. The Armenians are still to be rehabilitated and have yet to return home.

Nutuk—*What Mustafa Kemal said about the Armenians*

To understand the continuity between the position of the CUP and the Turkish Republic on the Armenian Question, it is important to recall the continuity between the CUP regime and Kemal's nationalist movement.[10] Kemal himself was a member of the CUP, and as a Young Turk officer he had played a role in the 1908 Revolution. He had also served in Libya in 1911 during the war against Italy, along with Enver Pasha. But after 1913 he was marginalised from the CUP—Kemal was not liked by Enver, who thought of him as competition—and had little role in making decisions during the war. He nevertheless had close contacts with the Ittihadists, serving as an officer on the Western front in Gallipoli (1915) and later as the head of the XIV Corps of the Second Army on the eastern front in 1916–17. More importantly, most of the active collaborators with Mustafa Kemal during the 'war of independence' not only depended on CUP cadres but also on individuals who were heavily implicated in the Armenian Genocide and were fearful that they might face reprisals for their crimes. This continuity between the CUP regime and the Kemalist state also serves to explain the similarity in their official narratives regarding the fate of the Ottoman Armenians.[11]

Moreover, at that time Kemal was concerned by the possibility of an independent Armenia emerging to the east of Turkey's frontiers and by the territorial demands the Armenians had made at the Paris peace conference pertaining to the lands of historic Armenia, and the Armenian demands for independence in Cilicia (from Adana to Marash in southern Turkey). After the armistice, people also began to mobilise behind the Kemalist movement when the Armenian refugees returned and reclaimed their occupied properties, leading the provincial Muslim middle class to rally to the nationalist cause. The members of this class had in fact appropriated Armenian properties and were fearful of having to return them to their rightful owners.

After the war had come to an end, Mustafa Kemal was consistent in his views about the Armenians. In his speeches, he frequently suggested that the Armenians had taken up arms and had fought against the Turkish army.[12] At various times he stated that the Armenians, as well as the 'Rums' (the Greeks), were no more than pawns in the hands of imperialist forces trying to destroy Turkey. A month after the British forces entered Istanbul, Mustafa Kemal was asked to give a speech at the invitation of the Ottoman Parliament. It was 24 April 1920:

We all know our country. Where in our country did these alleged massacres of Armenians take place? Or where are they taking place? I don't wish to talk about the beginning stages of the World War and what the Allied powers are talking about is certainly not the *shameful act* that belongs to the past. By alleging that this kind of *disaster* is being executed in our country today, they were demanding that we stop doing it.

All the American and European individuals and committees who have been travelling to … various regions of Anatolia always returned to their countries with good impressions about us … And hence, these elements whose political expediency lied in provoking the entire world against us through various pressures, in order to shatter this emerging positive public opinion about us and in order to prevent the entire world from changing their negative opinions of us, they have in the end staged and proclaimed this Armenian massacre forgery, which was consisted of nothing but lies.[13]

In other words, Mustafa Kemal was inviting the Ottoman deputies to brush away the past and to concentrate on the current political situation, while, in the best Ottoman tradition, he was simultaneously portraying the Armenians as responsible for their fate.

The reversal in the roles of victim and perpetrator was also evident in Kemal's famous 1927 speech, the *nutuk*. The speech, which was delivered to the second congress of the ruling Republican People's Party, was delivered over six days (taking thirty-six hours in total). It was published as a 600-page document. The *nutuk* sets out the Kemalist vision of Turkish historiography, covering the period from 1919 to 1923. As Kemal marginalised both friend and foe—establishing the foundations of his one-party system, and laying the basis for his own personality cult which survives in Turkey today—and minimised their role in Turkish history, this speech came to have special importance as it engraved its concepts in the social psychology of modern Turkey not only as the official narration of history, as the founding myth of a new republic, but as history itself.[14]

At the opening of the *nutuk*, Kemal refers to the Armenian deportations and massacres as 'cruelties' and 'mistreatment', before adding the qualifier that the 'people' had not been involved in committing them, and instead attributing responsibility to mysterious 'instigators and agitators'.[15] Yet despite acknowledging the cruelties the Armenians had suffered, in the rest of the speech Kemal presents the Armenians as internal enemies who threatened both the Muslim population and the state. The speech then goes on to claim that those seeking to discuss the Armenian massacres solely aimed to present the Muslims as 'savages' to international public opinion in pursuit of territorial expansion and the creation of a 'new Armenia'. In any case, Kemal goes on to say that it would be impossible to make any territorial concession to Armenia in eastern Anatolia as Armenians were not in a majority there.

After addressing these issues, Kemal moved on to the atrocities committed against Muslims in Marash, and in this part of the speech the Armenians are depicted as an archetypal aggressor against the Turk. This portrayal is largely consistent with the remarks of the Red Sultan and the CUP with regard to Armenian treason, where they were not only guilty of attacking armed men but also defenceless civilians:

The Armenians in the South, armed by foreign troops and encouraged by the protection they enjoyed, persecuted the Mohamedans in their district. Inflamed with the spirit of revenge, they pursued a relentless policy of murder and annihilation everywhere. This was the reason for the tragic incident at Maras. Making common cause with the foreign troops, the Armenians completely destroyed an old Mohamedan town, Maras, with their artillery and machine gun fire. They annihilated 76 thousands of innocent and defenceless women and children. The Armenians were the instigators of this savagery, unique in history. The Mohamedans merely offered resistance and defended themselves in order to save their lives and their honour. The telegram that the Americans, who had remained in the town with the Mohamedans during the five days of the massacres, sent to their representative in Istanbul indicates indisputably who originated this tragedy. Threatened by the bayonets of the Armenians, who were armed to the teeth, the Mohamedans in the vilayet of Adana were in danger of being annihilated at every minute. ... The truth was that our nation had never taken up an aggressive attitude anywhere against any foreigner without good reason.[16]

Historian Fatma Ulgen argues that Kemal was seeking to construct an image of the Turkish national character based on nobility, generosity and innocence, one which contrasted with Armenian aggression and evil.[17]

The Turkish state, in short, was established without properly facing the truth of what had happened in 1915. As the Turkish intellectual Murat Belge remarked: 'We have a very unhealthy relation with our history ... It's basically a collection of lies.'[18]

The Forgotten Genocide

Despite the noise made internationally regarding the Armenian massacres, the international community largely ignored the Armenian cause in the period after the Lausanne Treaty (1923). At the same time, what was gradually becoming an 'iron curtain' separated the surviving Armenian population in the Soviet Union from the outside world.

Yet there were some who remembered the Armenians and their tragedy. One was Raphael Lemkin, a Polish Jew and an expert on international law, who would later formulate the legal definition of genocide, basing his concept on the annihilation of the Christians of the Ottoman Empire. As the world approached the Second World War, the Armenians and their fate were recalled in many different ways. The Austrian writer Franz Werfel published a novel about the resistance of seven Armenian villages in 1915 in Musa Dagh, in today's southern Hatay province in Turkey, adjacent to Syria. The novel, entitled the *Forty Days of Musa Dagh*, was published in German in 1933. Werfel, himself Jewish, was alarmed by the rise of national-socialism in Europe, and the story of the resistance of the Armenian villagers against the Ottoman armies and their eventual rescue by two French warships was a source of hope. The book received positive reviews in German-language publications, but pressure from Ankara and the Nazi government soon led to the book being banned in Germany.

The silence surrounding the Armenian issue became so resounding that the Turkish establishment was taken by surprise when the Armenian Secret Army for the Liberation of Armenia (ASALA) began to launch terrorist attacks in the mid-1970s. ASALA justified its attacks as a form of vengeance in response to the Armenian Genocide of 1915 and the silence of the international community, while demanding the return of historic Armenian territories. In order to counter the accusations levelled against it, the Turkish Foreign Ministry began to use a book written in 1953 by Esat Uras, entitled *Armenian Allegations: Nine Questions, Nine Answers*. As the head of the Second Department of the Security Directorate during the war,[19] Uras had first-hand knowledge of the crimes committed against the Armenians. Unlike many authors in Turkey, Uras was able to read Armenian and his book became a reference work for subsequent writers in Turkey. The book was translated into English and published as *The Armenians in History and the Armenian Question* (1988). As the book runs to over 1,000 pages, the Turkish Foreign Ministry asked one of its leading diplomats to write a more concise and accessible version. The result was Kamran Gürün's *Armenian File*, which was first published in Turkish in 1983, with an English edition following in 1985. Gürün borrowed extensively from Uras in form and content. Gürün's only qualification for writing the book was his career as a Turkish diplomat in the Foreign Ministry, which at that time was the institution most opposed to the Armenians as Turkish diplomats were often targeted by Armenian terrorists seeking revenge and recognition.

The book begins with a conceit that informs the rest of its narrative—Armenia is simply a vague geographic concept: 'it is quite impossible that an organised and continuous Armenian state, recognised by other nations, with definite boundaries and with a specific national outlook, could ever have existed in that part of Anatolia'. The book downplays the historic presence of the Armenians and their cultural achievements. 'Most of the historians who wrote on Armenian history were clergymen, the majority of whom belonged to other nations.' After providing a review of Armenian history, Gürün comes to the following conclusion: 'In view of these historic facts, we see no possibility of talking about an independent Armenia, or the existence of a united Armenian nation.'[20]

Both the original author and the revised publication insist that the Ottoman Armenians had no reason to rebel. Uras claims that the Armenians lived 'tranquil and content[ed] lives in Turkey, mainly engaged in commerce and industry', and they were not obliged to serve in the army.[21] Gürün in turn writes that even in the 1980s, no Armenian community enjoys the kind of freedoms it enjoyed in the nineteenth-century Ottoman Empire, a freedom he describes as 'nothing less than a landless autonomy'.[22] Uras identifies two problems that led to Armenian rebelliousness: first, the introduction of revolutionary European ideas, and second the considerable freedoms granted to the Armenians under the Ottomans. Gürün accuses a range of actors—the Armenian Church, foreign missionaries and the Armenian revolutionary committees—of being responsible for inciting the rebellions.[23] Neither book attempts to explain why the Armenian Church or the revolutionary committees sought to engage in such acts: the Armenians simply had no reason to protest.

In order to obtain their goals, they provoked the Turks and then turned to Europeans as Christian victims hoping for the military intervention of the great powers:

> From the first emergence of the Armenian question the most effective weapon used by the Armenians to arouse the Christian world against the Ottoman State was their exposure, purely because of their Christian faith, to oppression, harassment and massacre. Their own criminal activities and mutinies were always concealed behind this propaganda screen, and yet, as many Christian writers bore witness, of all the various states in the world the Ottoman State was the only one to respect religious freedom.[24]

According to this logic, the Armenians deliberately provoked the massacres as a way to attract foreign intervention in support of their cause.

Kamran Gürün discusses the Hamidian massacres (1894–96) in a chapter entitled 'The Armenian Question'. This chapter describes a series of revolts instigated by the Armenians in which the Armenians are accused of having massacred Kurdish tribesmen and the soldiers they had taken as prisoners: 'even if we are to include the Armenians killed by the bullets of the Armenian rebels as having been killed by Turks, the number of Armenians who died during the rebellions in the 1890s will hardly reach 20,000'. The author then adds: 'the Muslim casualties would approach 25,000 and would be twice the Armenian casualties for the same decade'.[25] No attempt is made to explain how the largely civilian, unarmed Armenian population, supported by a small handful of revolutionary activists, was able to kill much larger numbers of armed Kurdish tribesmen and regular Ottoman army soldiers.

The same logic is used to describe the events of 1915–23. 'The Armenians were forced to emigrate because they had joined the ranks of the enemy. The fact that they were civilians does not change the situation. Those who were killed in Hiroshima and Nagasaki during the Second World War were also civilians.'[26] Why was it necessary to relocate the Ottoman Armenian population? In answering this question, the book points to subsequent Armenian revolts as justification. The author refers to official letters documenting Armenian revolts in Zeitun in August 1915,[27] or which describe the arms they received from the advancing Russian army in Trabzon during October 1915,[28] before stating that a decision was made to relocate the Armenians following the arrest of their 'ringleaders' in Istanbul on 24 April 1915.[29] The author also states that Enver Pasha, the war minister and strongman in the ruling triumvirate during the First World War, which included Cemal and Talaat, wrote a letter to the latter, the interior minister, on 2 May 1915 stating that 'the Armenians always start a rebellion where there are large Armenian communities' and that it was necessary to organise their deportation. After quoting the Supreme Military Command order of 26 May 1915, the chapter concludes: 'In short, Armenians residing in the provinces bordering the area of military operations and in proximity to the Mediterranean sea would be relocated.'[30]

The book then goes on to discuss some of the consequences stemming from the deportation. It quotes a 30 May 1915 Council of Ministers' decision to make the transfers in 'comfortable circumstances', with the aim of ensuring that 'their lives and possessions will be protected. … Possessions and belongings left behind will be returned to them in an appropriate way.'[31]

In essence, the book argues that the state decided to relocate the Ottoman Armenians away from the theatre of military operations, as well as coastal areas and other strategic locations because of their rebellious nature, and that great care was taken to defend them against tribal attacks and massacres. The book claims that only a relatively small number of the deportees died en route: 'As the Armenian population in Turkey in 1914 was approximately 1,300,000, the total number of Armenians who died during the war cannot be more than 300,000.'[32] This idea is also expressed in Uras's book: 'The truth is that, while the number of the Armenians killed were exaggerated to reach 600,000 or 800,000, or even a million, even greater numbers of the Moslem population perished at the hands of Armenian volunteer bands and guerrilla fighters during the Russian invasion.'[33]

After its publication, Kamran Gürün's book became the standard reference work in Turkey with regard to the Armenian issue, one that was distributed by the Turkish government to foreign reporters, diplomats and politicians. It was also used as a reference work by a subsequent generation of Turkish historians, including the members of the Turkish History Society, which also follows the official political line.[34]

Denial by Turkish Intellectuals and Leftists

Under Mustafa Kemal, the Turkish state viewed itself as a modernising, revolutionary enterprise, in league with other top-down social engineering projects led by one-party systems that were typical in the early twentieth century. The one-party system developed an ideology known as 'Kemalism', which formed the worldview of the ruling elite and many within the Turkish intelligentsia whose formative education resulted from the modernisation efforts launched by the Ittihadists, and which took shape under the Republic. As one study reveals, 'among the modernist Turkish elite elements there is adherence to the anti-imperialist, liberal-nationalist, populist, secularist, and republican tenets of [Kemalist ideology]'.[35] Kemalism claimed to represent revolutionary ideas and values, such as anti-colonial struggle, national liberation, as well as progress and modernisation. This left only a narrow field of ideological action for the leftist opposition: to accuse the Kemalist authorities of being unable to realise their programme of national-liberation and independence, and to argue that only a social revolution from below could achieve such ideals.

In the official Turkish historiography, reference to 'National Struggle' or a 'War of Independence' against foreign occupation is taken out of its proper historic context. The discussion of the foreign occupation is separated from the fact that the Ottoman Empire, under the CUP's leadership, entered the First World War of its own free will with the aim of carving a new imperial domain in Central Asia and the Russian Caucasus. The British and French occupations resulted from its defeat in the war, and were not an act of colonial aggression.

As students of Kemalism or Ittihadism, the Turkish left cultivated an image of non-Muslim Ottoman minorities as the 'links between the source of capital and the actual producers whose surpluses were converted into interest payments': 'By the mid-nineteenth century a good proportion of the non-Moslem population of the Empire had developed as a class of compradors, mediating between peasant producers and foreign capital.'[36] In the eyes of the Turkish left then— taking into account this ideological portrayal of Armenians as both national enemies but also 'class enemies'—the necessity of the elimination of the Armenians in order to save the state from decline, create a new nation-state by imposing a national identity based on Turkish language and Sunni Islam, and create a 'national bourgeoisie' was self-evident. Once the property of the Armenian bourgeoisie had been pillaged and a new Turkish bourgeoisie was created, it ceased to be a 'comprador' and became a 'national bourgeoisie'.

While both the Ottoman Armenians and the Greeks were certainly active in mercantile activities prior to the First World War, a large number of Armenians were also employed as industrial workers and as artisans. In the province of Sivas, for instance, while thirty-two of the thirty-seven bankers were Armenians (the remainder being Turks), 14,000 of the 17,700 industrial workers were Armenians, with only 3,500 Turks and 200 Greeks and other nationalities employed in these roles.[37] Yet for many decades, those on the left in Turkey maintained complete silence with regard to the fate of the Ottoman Armenians, as well as the Greeks, Assyrians, Jews and other religious minorities brutalised by the 'modernist' Young Turks.

The absence of the Armenian Genocide in the work of, for example, the prestigious poet Nazim Hikmet, the 'Pablo Neruda of Turkey' and a committed communist party member, is striking. Despite the fact that much of his work focused on freedom, justice and struggle, and, even more significantly, despite the fact that he was close to many Armenians,[38] in the writings of Nazim Hikmet we largely find silence when it comes to this great tragedy. In his poem 'Getting out of prison' we find a brief mention, a single line which arguably only serves to underline the long silence that follows:

This Armenian citizen won't forgive
  His father's slaughter in the Kurdish mountains.
But he likes you...[39]

Similarly surpirising is the absence of the genocide in any of the writings of the Nobel Prize winner Orhan Pamuk. Lebanese writer Elias Khoury, reflecting on Pamuk's Nobel Prize, wrote:

Did Pamuk receive the award in his capacity as an alternative to an Armenian writer? Has the game of doppelgangers and the interlocking of identities now overtaken the novelist himself, turning him into the hero of a novel he did not write? The game of the writer's transformation into the hero of a novel he has not penned fascinates me because it is one of the signs of the text's revenge on the writer who considers that his intelligence allows him to pass over the very chalice he has given to the heroes of his novels to drink. Was this not the fate of Salman Rushdie, Kafka and Emile Habiby, among others?[40]

On the rare occasions when the issue has been raised, those who sought to discuss the fate of the Armenians were silenced, following the Abdul Hamid–CUP line according to which the Armenians were agents of imperial forces plotting to destroy Turkey.

There are a number of reasons why the parties of the left adhered to the official Turkish position with regard to the Ottoman Armenians. The first was their fear that they would be labelled as traitors who were colluding with the West. Many Turks on the left feared that, by raising the issue, they would perpetuate the Western, orientalist stereotype of the 'bloodthirsty Turk'.[41]

The ideology of those on the left in Turkey was informed by Stalinist and Kemalist doctrine regarding the 'national bourgeoisie'.

The Turkish left largely subscribed to the Kemalist 'founding myth' of modern Turkey, according to which the Kemalist nationalist movement had brought modern Turkey into being in a war of liberation against the colonial armies of Britain and France, who were supported by internal enemies, namely the Greeks and the Armenians. Armenian and other non-Muslims were amalgamated with the enemy, with imperialists, with colonialists, with the 'comprador Bourgeoisie'. They were the perfect 'other'.

Hitler Remembers the Armenians

It was August 1939. The German armies were at the height of readiness, determined to change the course of history. Hitler had gathered a choice of his top army officers in his favourite Bavarian vacation house at Obersalzberg. He was preparing to launch the invasion of Poland and gave a long and impassioned speech, outlining the imminent invasion and the planned extermination of Poles.

The 'Obersalzberg Speech', also referred to as the 'second Hitler speech', was secret. No official transcript was taken and there is much debate among historians about what exactly Hitler said. The Nuremberg Trial gathered three different documents, unofficial notes taken on the speech, one of which, identified by the tribunal as 'L-3' contained the following paragraph:

> Our strength is our brutality. Genghis Khan led millions of women and children to slaughter—with premeditation and a happy heart. History sees in him solely the founder of a state. It's a matter of indifference to me what a weak western European civilization will say about me. I have issued a command—and I'll have anybody who utters but one word of criticism executed by a firing squad—that the aim of this war does not consist of reaching certain designated lines, but in the enemy's physical elimination. Thus, for the time being only in the east, I put ready my Death's Head units, with the order to kill without pity or mercy all men, women, and children of Polish race or language. Only thus we gain the living space that we need. Who still talks nowadays of the extermination of the Armenians?[42]

Did the extermination of Armenians, as well as Assyrians and Greeks during the First World War inspire Hitler to destroy European

Jews and other minorities during World War II? Did the impunity given to perpetrators in the genocide encourage future crimes against humanity? For decades a fierce debate has taken place between two polarised positions, one arguing that impunity for the Turkish state for the destruction of its Christian minorities motivated Nazis to commit their crimes undeterred, while others arguing that there is no comparison possible between the two historic events.

The story of the quote itself is highly interesting. Since the speech was held in secret, there is no official surviving transcript. Two documents pertaining to the speech were seized by the allied forces after the end of the war and read as evidence at the Nuremberg Trials, where they were used to prove the premeditated and genocidal intent of Nazi Germany in unleashing the war. Those two documents do not refer to the Armenian quote. The above paragraph is taken from a third version, which was brought forward by American journalist Louis P. Lochner, a Pulitzer Prize winner for his excellent reporting. Lochner claims that he received the document from a source while he was stationed in Berlin as Associated Press bureau chief, and he later included it in a book entitled *What About Germany?* published in 1942. *The Times* of London published an unsigned article 'The War Route of the Nazi Germany' on 24 November 1945, also quoting the Lochner version.

The Nuremberg tribunal itself did not use L-3 as evidence, although it did include it in a list of evidence. In fact, the prosecutor had received the L-3 document first, using it to get acquainted with the topic, and subsequently conducting more research and discovering the two additional ones from among German military documents, identified by the tribunal as 798-PS and 1014-PS. The tribunal did not consider L-3 to be unauthentic, and had it published in the second volume of the compilation of evidence entitled *Nazi Conspiracy and Aggression*.[43] Moreover, a German Foreign Office document published in 1961 similarly included the Lochner paper with the Armenian reference.[44] Nonetheless, the debate as to its authenticity continues.

The authenticity of the L-3 letter came under fire mostly—but not exclusively—from deniers of the Armenian Genocide. Their effort in attacking the document was part of a larger campaign with a specific political objective. For example, in one such study questioning whether the inclusion of the Hitler Armenian quote at the US Holocaust Memorial Museum was a major blunder, the author spends one third of his text denouncing Armenian revolutionaries as propagandists and terrorists, conspiring with western powers and Russia to dismantle the Ottoman Empire.[45] Similarly, Heath W. Lowry, in an article published in 1984, attacks US congressional use of the quote in support of 24 April remembrance of Armenian Martyrs' Day, arguing that it is not historically founded. Lowry argues that the quote is a propaganda instrument used by anti-Turkish 'Armenian Spokesmen'. He then adds: 'Armenian propaganda efforts in recent years have been devoted to establish a linkage between their own historical experiences and those of European Jewry during the Second World War.' The article concludes: history is not the forte of many American Congressmen and Senators so they should mind their own business and 'leave the writing of history to the historians.'[46] Lowry's appeal to Congress not to intervene in writing history is a selective process. He himself welcomed intense intervention by the Turkish foreign ministry in shaping the manipulation of history in contemporary political battles in order to deny the Armenian Genocide.

Kevork Bardakjian prepared a detailed study of the Hitler quote. He scrutinises the transcript of the trials, and concludes two reasons why the prosecutor did not use L-3 as evidence. The first was because of a lack of knowledge about real source of the letter at the time, and the second was the impression of the prosecutor that Hitler gave two speeches on August 22, and that L-3 was a 'slightly garbled merger of the two speeches.'[47]

Lochner himself testified at Nuremberg stating that the notes of the Hitler speech with the Armenian reference in his possession were handed to him by Hermann Maass, who passed him a large number of documents from disgruntled German officers. Maass brought the Hitler speech at the request of General Ludwig Beck, a former Chief of the General Staff.[48] Lochner did not know the identity of the person who had actually taken note of the speech. Bardakjian, by referring to two German sources, suggests that the original note-taker was Admiral Wilhelm Canaris, head of Abwehr or military intelligence.[49]

German scholar Richard Albrecht, a researcher on twentieth century genocides, has dedicated an entire volume to the notorious Hitler quote. His work confirms Bardakjian's conclusions. Albrecht, whose first doctoral dissertation was in cultural studies and a second in political sociology, accuses historians, legal experts and social scientists that have debated the Hitler quote for decades of not having referred to the original texts, and specifically to the German version of the L-3 transcript. In summarising his research, Albrecht underlines the importance of this text for world history, as one of the key documents of the twentieth century. He confirms that the L-3 version was delivered to Louis P. Lochner only a matter of days after the 22 August speech, and insists that 'this version must be regarded as the one which most likely sums up and expresses what Hitler said— for what Hitler really said in his notorious second speech was only written down simultaneously during his speech by one of his auditors: Wilhelm Canaris (1887–1945), at that time chief of the military secret service within the Third Reich.'[50]

There is also evidence that Hitler and key Nazi ideologues had knowledge of the First World War massacres and deportations, and approved of these acts and their outcomes. In an interview in 1932 given to Richard Breiting editor of *Leipziger Neueste Nachrichten*, Hitler said: 'Everywhere there is discontent. Everywhere people are awaiting a new world order. We intend to introduce a great resettlement policy … Think of the biblical deportations and the massacres of the Middle Ages (Rosenberg refers to them) and remember the extermination of the Armenians.'[51] Several German officials, who witnessed the Armenian massacres, later occupied leadership positions in the Nazi apparatus. At their head was Franz von Papen, an officer of the German General Staff of the Ottoman Fourth Army with the rank of major, who later played an important political role in Germany. As Chancellor in 1932 he played key role in the Nazis coming to power in 1932–3. Another example was Lieutenant General Hans von Seeckt who, in 1918, occupied the post of Chief of Staff of Ottoman General

Headquarters. He described the the fate of the Armenians as being out of 'military necessity.' He later played a major role in rebuilding German military forces in the inter-war period.[52]

Again, much of the debate was focused on details. Was the Hitler quote authentic or not? The true relevance, however, is perhaps best summed up by historian Margaret L. Andersen: '[whilst] we have no reason to doubt the remark is genuine, both attack and defense obscure an obvious reality': that the Armenian Genocide achieved 'iconic status ... as the apex of horrors imaginable in 1939,' and that it was held up as evidence before the German military by Hitler that that the perpetrators of genocide would largely be afforded impunity.[53]

The Negation Industry

There is a long history of Turkish state intervention to silence any mention of the Armenian Genocide or to relativise its significance. In the 1930s, for instance, the Hollywood film studio MGM planned to produce a film based on Franz Werfel's novel *Forty Days of Musa Dagh*, having acquired the rights to screen the novel in 1934, before it had even been released in English. The film's producer, David Selznick, contacted the Turkish ambassador out of courtesy and to ensure that the script contained nothing that would be overly offensive. The script itself contained no reference to the broader context of the Armenian massacres—it alleged that one Turkish character was responsible rather than the Turkish state. However, the Turkish ambassador threatened to ban all American films in Turkey unless MGM cancelled the production of *Forty Days of Musa Dagh*. When the novel was published in the United States in 1935, it immediately became a best-seller, and this in turn led to further Turkish pressure to cancel the production of the film. A media operation was launched against the film in Turkey, where it was accused of being contemptuous against an entire people, with 'Armenian propagandists' allegedly the real culprits behind this affair.[54] In order to demonstrate their loyalty to the Turkish regime, Armenians in Istanbul were even forced to burn copies of Werfel's novels in the courtyard of Pangalti

Armenian Church. Although MGM had already invested money in the film, and had announced that it would be released in 1935, it eventually opted to shelve the project.

In 1981 the Holocaust Museum in Washington, DC planned to run an exhibition about the Armenian Genocide. But any references to the Armenians were eventually removed after the museum received strongly worded threats from the Turkish Embassy with regard to the Jewish community in Turkey and the possibility of Turkish withdrawal from NATO in the event that the exhibition went ahead. In the following year, Tel Aviv University was planning a major genocide conference with some 400 participants, in which several papers on the Armenians were scheduled to be presented. The event was cancelled at the last moment. Israel Charny, a psychologist from Philadelphia who teaches at Tel Aviv University, said: 'There was serious pressure to cancel the conference because of Turkish insistence that the Armenian Genocide of 70 years ago [should] not be discussed.' When asked about the pressure, the organisers stated: 'Turkey had warned of reprisals against its 18,000 Jews and a diplomatic rupture with Israel.'[55] The honorary chair of the conference, Elie Wiesel, threatened to resign.[56]

* * *

A letter addressed to a New York-based professor sheds further light on the mechanisms used by the Turkish state to deny the events of 1915, as well as the extent of academic collaboration in this campaign. The psychiatrist Robert Jay Lifton received a letter from the Turkish ambassador to the United States, Nuzhet Kandemir. Lifton is the author of several books on the psychological impact of war, mass violence and the Holocaust. His book, *The Nazi Doctors: Medical Killing and the Psychology of Genocide* (1986), contained several paragraphs comparing the Nazi extermination policies with those of the Ottoman government and the role of doctors in both cases. The Turkish ambassador's letter protested against the references to the Armenians and the comparison between the Jewish Holocaust and the Armenian Genocide.[57]

The letter itself was not particularly surprising. However, two documents inadvertently enclosed in the package with it certainly were. The first of these was a long memorandum written by the Princeton Professor Heath Lowry, who at the time was employed as Executive Director of the Institute of Turkish Studies, based in Washington, DC. Lowry had also written a draft letter for the ambassador to sign, which was to be addressed to the author of *The Nazi Doctors*. This unintentional inclusion provided a singular insight into the collaboration between academics in the West and the Turkish state in denying the horrors of 1915.

Lowry earned his doctoral degree from UCLA in 1977 after spending a number of years working in Turkey. In 1983 he was among the founders of the Institute of Turkish Studies, which was a Turkish government-financed think tank established with the aim of lobbying in favour of Turkish interests and promoting the official position of the Turkish government in the United States. In 1985 Lowry had also played a key role in opposing a US House of Representatives resolution condemning the Armenian Genocide. He was one of sixty-nine specialists in Ottoman and Turkish history who petitioned against the resolution, arguing that what happened in 1915 was caused by 'intercommunal warfare' and 'disease, famine, suffering and massacres'. In 1993 Lowry was appointed Atatürk Professor of Ottoman and Modern Turkish Studies at Princeton University, an appointment that was entirely due to an endowment of 750,000 dollars given by the Turkish government to the university in order to create the position.[58]

In the memorandum, Lowry quoted the seven occasions in which Lifton's book referred to the Armenians, followed by an analysis inviting the attention of the Turkish ambassador to the references used by Lifton. The memorandum concluded by giving some policy advice with regard to countering the arguments made in the book:[59] 'In Summation, what we are faced with here are seven references ... They are based exclusively on the articles by Vahakn Dadrian [a leading historian of the Armenian Genocide] (each of which have been the subject of detailed memos by this writer in the past years).' Lowry argues that writers like Lifton are 'the end of the chain' (by which he means academics who base their work on primary sources compiled by others, such as Dadrian, Fein and Kuper), and that the Turkish government should seek to discredit those involved in primary source research: 'Though this point has been repeatedly stressed both in writing and verbally to I. A. D. A.—Ankara, we have not yet seen as much [as] a single article by any scholar responding to Dadrian (or any of the others as well).' Lowry then suggests that the Turkish ambassador should sign the pre-prepared letter and address it to Lifton.

The Turkish ambassador signed the letter on 2 October 1990 and posted it to Lifton's publisher, Basic Books. In it, the ambassador writes that he 'was shocked by references in your work ... to the so called "Armenian Genocide"'. The letter then attacks some of the sources Lifton uses in the book (Dadrian, Fein and Kuper) on the grounds that the authors are not specialists on the subject and are unfamiliar with the relevant primary sources. The letter then goes on to state: 'It is particularly disturbing to see a major scholar on the Holocaust, a tragedy whose enormity and barbarity must never be forgotten, so careless in his references to a field outside his own area of expertise.' This insistence that the Holocaust should not be equated with the fate of the Armenians is a recurrent theme in the denialist literature. The letter continues: 'To compare a tragic civil war (prepared by misguided Armenian nationalists) and the human suffering it wrought on both Muslim and Christian populations, with the horrors of a premeditated attempt to systematically eradicate a people, is, to anyone familiar with the history in question, simply ludicrous.'

The letter concludes by inviting the author to read two books which were also enclosed in the package. The first was written by Justin McCarthy, and the second by Heath Lowry.

Those who have sought to deny the Armenian Genocide adopt exactly the same mechanisms as those who have sought to deny the Holocaust in claiming that there is a lack of evidence or that the authors of certain works were heavily biased in reaching their conclusions. For those who seek to deny these crimes, victims are presented either as not entirely innocent, or even as the guilty party—roles are reversed, the perpetrator becomes the victim, and its actions are depicted as having been made solely in the interests of self-defence. Yet, there is a major difference in the denialist efforts in the case of the two great genocides of the twentieth century: Holocaust denial stems from marginal circles, while no major international organisation, state or established academic figure denies it. In the case of the Armenian Genocide, we still have key states and university departments actively engaged in its denial.

The work of professors such as Lowry and McCarthy started to be used by those seeking to deny the Armenian Genocide. In 1985, as the US House of Representatives was preparing a resolution on a 'National Day of Remembrance of Man's Inhumanity to Man', an orchestrated campaign was launched with the aim of excluding any reference to the genocide in the document. A letter, sponsored by the Assembly of Turkish American Associations and signed by sixty-nine academics, appeared in the *New York Times* and the *Washington Post*. The letter criticised the resolution on two grounds: first, that genocide should not be used in the case of the Ottoman Armenians; and second, that it was unfair to ascribe responsibility to the modern Turkish state when the events in question took place in the pre-republican period.

The letter reads as follows:

> The undersigned American academicians who specialize in Turkish, Ottoman and Middle Eastern studies are concerned that the current language embodied in House Joint Resolution 192 is misleading and/or inaccurate in several respects. Specifically, while fully supporting the concept of a 'National Day of Remembrance of Man's Inhumanity to Man,' we respectfully take exception to that portion of text which singles out for special recognition: '... the one and one half million people of Armenian ancestry who were victims of genocide perpetrated in Turkey between 1915 and 1923 ...' Our reservation focus[es] on the use of the words 'Turkey' and 'genocide' ...

The letter then goes on to argue that the Turkish Republic cannot be held responsible for events that occurred during the Ottoman era. The letter objects to the use of the term 'genocide' on the basis that the events between 1915 and 1923 resulted from 'inter-communal warfare ... not unlike the tragedy which has gone on in Lebanon for the past decade. The resulting death toll among both Muslim and Christian communities of the region was immense.' As the debate over the real nature of the 'events' was going on, the letter concludes that: 'By passing the resolution Congress will be attempting to determine by legislation which side of a historic question is correct. Such a resolution, based on historically questionable assumptions, can only damage the cause of honest historical enquiry, and damage the credibility of American legislative process.'[60]

The signatories to the letter included Stanford Shaw, who had acted as Lowry's doctoral supervisor, Heath Lowry and Justin McCarthy, but also renowned scholars such as Dankwart Rustow and Bernard Lewis.

The funding provided by the Turkish state for academic positions and institutes in the United States had clear objectives, with those holding them expected to promote the official Turkish position on the fate of the Ottoman Armenians. In 2006, for instance, the chairman of the board of governors of the Institute for Turkish Studies (ITS), Donald Quataert, published a review of Donald Bloxham's *The Great Game of Genocide*.[61] In the review, Quataert claims that discussing the Armenian massacres has become a taboo in Ottoman studies and, while he has some hesitation in using the term 'genocide' to describe the events of 1915 as it might 'provoke anger among some of my Ottomanist colleagues', he ultimately decided to do so, as 'to do otherwise in this essay runs the risk of suggesting denial of the massive and systematic atrocities that the Ottoman state and some of its military and general populace committed against the Armenians.'[62]

As a result of using this term, Quataert was forced to relinquish his membership of the ITS board in December 2006. It later became evident that the pressure to remove Quataert came from the Turkish ambassador, Nabi Sensoy, who stated that the Turkish government would cease funding the institute if he did not publicly retract his revised positions.[63] In response to this pressure, the chair of the Middle East Studies Association, Mervat Hatem, wrote a letter to Prime Minister Erdoğan requesting that Turkey respect the academic freedom of the ITS. The Turkish authorities then reminded the ITS board members that the endowment of 3 million USD was 'a gift that could be revoked by the Turkish government'.[64]

The Quataert scandal also revealed that the scholarly debate about the Armenian Genocide had moved on since the 1970s and 1980s when there were 'two sides' to the debate, one of which represented an Armenian view and the other that of Turkey. Indeed, Quataert was one of the signatories to the 1985 letter objecting to the use of the term genocide—the official Turkish position had clearly begun to lose support from scholars of Ottoman studies.

Perhaps the best commentary on the inefficacy of categorising the two opposing views of the massacre as the 'Armenian view' and the 'Turkish view' is offered by Altuğ Taner Akçam, a Turkish-German historian and sociologist.

He points out that one does not speak of a 'German view' or 'Jewish view' of the Holocaust. What would happen to the field of social sciences, he asks, if we were to label all interpretations according to the (imagined) ethnic identity of the author? What would happen if a member of one ethnic group were to deviate from the interpretation they are supposed to follow based on this pre-conceived idea about the relationship between ethnicity and historic interpretation? Two interpretations of the massacres do exist, he continues, but we should categorise them based on their arguments.

On one hand is the Turkish state's official line on 1915, based mainly, he argues, on 'repressing historical realities and forcing those who oppose it into silence.' With the aid of various ministries and institutes, the state 'supervises and controls the ways and means by which Turkish society acquires the requisite knowledge of history.' On the other are those who consider what happened to the Ottoman Armenians, and other minorities, 'a morally wrong act, a crime that must be condemned accordingly'.[65]

The division is not, therefore, determined by ethnicity. Rather it separates those who choose to serve a state and its policy in their interpretation of an historic event from those who choose to narrate the suffering of the victims.

* * *

The Armenians served as a scapegoat for the failures, losses and defeats of the Ottoman Turks during the First World War. They were not oppressed because of what they had done, but because of the way they were viewed by the ruling elite. The Ottoman Armenians never posed a threat to the territorial unity, progress, modernisation and glory of the empire. The Armenians did not resist the reforms of the Tanzimat era and they were not responsible for the failure of Ottoman forces in the war against Russia in 1878; nor were they responsible for the humiliating defeat against the young armies of the Balkan nations in 1913.

The defeat shattered the dreams of eastern expansion in the Caucasus and Central Asia. There were rumours that Armenians had volunteered to join the Russian army, and the Ittihadist leaders jumped on this Armenian 'treachery'.

The negation of the Armenian Genocide constitutes part of a larger suppression of the past in the Turkish mass psyche: the failure to grasp the decline and fall of the Ottoman Empire, and the suffering it generated. This is best illustrated by the confrontation between members of the Turkish Armenian Reconciliation Commission (TARC), one of the first semi-official attempts at dialogue, which took place in April 2001. In the middle of a tense discussion, one member, Andranik Migranian, told the story of his grandparents from Mush, a town in historic Armenia, of how they were deported and how he dreamt of once visiting his ancestral homeland. Then, another member former diplomat Ozdem Sanberk told a similar story of his grandparents, themselves forced to flee their ancestral village in today's Macedonia. Then, Gündüz Aktan another participant and one of the most radical among the Turkish group, intervened saying: 'Do you know how we feel when you try to embarrass us by introducing resolutions in parliaments around the world? Our feelings are hurt.'[66] Later, Aktan had the following to say: 'We Turks do not look to our past ... We never talk of our sufferings. Instead we look to the future. The Republic was formed upon the amnesia of this pain.'[67]

4

WRITING AS RESISTANCE

Writing was the primary tool of the victims to record the crime and to hope for justice. As events were unfolding during the First World War, there were intensive efforts to document ongoing atrocities. These reports relied on three sets of sources. The first was comprised of the eyewitness accounts of the survivors, written in Armenian and later expanded in autobiographical works. The second set came from foreign citizens who were present at the time of the atrocities— including diplomats from neutral countries and those allied to the Ottoman Empire, as well as foreign missionaries—in the various towns where the deportations and the killings took place. The third is composed of the official Ottoman documents. Although many of the orders given by the CUP leaders were coded and destroyed after delivery—and while most of the CUP party archives were destroyed at the end of the war prior to the flight of key CUP leaders responsible for organising the genocide—the documentation which has survived can be used to corroborate Armenian eyewitness accounts and the reports of foreign nationals.

Armenian intellectuals documented eyewitness accounts and collected evidence in three distinct locations. The first location was eastern Armenia, which was part of Russia until 1917. In 1916 the Baku Committee of the Armenian Revolutionary Federation (ARF) started collecting testimonies from refugees who had survived. In 1915–16, thousands of refugees passed the frontier, among them some 30,000 orphans. International aid workers, such as the American Relief Society, carried out interviews with the survivors with the aim of documenting the losses, both human and material, as well as the conditions in which the massacres took place and identifying those who were responsible. These accounts are currently housed in the National Archives of the Republic of Armenia in Yerevan.

Efforts were also made to document the atrocities in Istanbul. Following Ottoman capitulation in the war, the Armenian Patriarchate of Istanbul was re-established in October 1918, and in March 1919 Patriarch Zaven Der Yeghyaian returned to Istanbul from exile in Iraq. In collaboration with historian Arshag Alboiajian and jurist Garabed Nurian, Patriarch Zaven amassed documentation with the aim of identifying who was responsible for the crimes committed against the Armenians. As Kemalist forces were preparing to enter Istanbul in 1922, Patriarch Yeghyaian sent twenty-four boxes of documents to Bishop Grigoris Balakian in Manchester. This archive of information was then transferred to the Armenian Patriarchate of Jerusalem.[1]

Syria, where most of the survivors of the death marches were dispersed at the end of the war, was the third place where efforts were made to document the atrocities committed against the Armenians. The Armenian journalist and writer Aram Andonian received sensitive documents from a Turkish official, Naim Bey, whom he met for the first time in 1916 in Meskene in the Syrian Desert. Bey had been sent to supervise the elimination of the deportees in the desert region, but after his superiors noticed his reluctance to carry out this task he was called back and replaced by Hakke Bey, who decimated the surviving deportees in a short space of time.[2] Naim Bey passed a number of documents to Andonian, most of which had been sent from the Interior Ministry in Istanbul with the signature of Talaat Pasha to the Aleppo authorities. The Aleppo governor would decipher the telegrams before executing the orders. Andonian published these official documents—two letters and fifty coded telegrams—as well as the memoirs of Naim Bey of the Ras al-Ayn and Der Ez-Zor massacres, and comments by Andonian himself, in 1920–1. The documents and commentaries clearly reveal that the CUP had followed a policy of not only deporting the Armenians but also of systematically eliminating deportees and Turkifying the surviving orphans. Telegram number 52, for instance, which was sent on 3 September 1915 and signed by 'Interior minister TALAT', contains the following order to the Aleppo governor:

> We instruct that the orders concerning the arrangements made towards the menfolk of the known personalities be imposed on the women and children as well, and this should be arranged through trustworthy officials.[3]

Although written in slightly ambiguous, coded language, Talaat was evidently ordering the execution of the civilians who had survived after walking hundreds of miles to the Syrian Desert. The CUP Interior Ministry had previously ordered that all adult male Armenians should be executed, and the new orders in September were to massacre the surviving women and children who had managed to reach Syria.

Andonian also writes about CUP policies towards Armenian children. Towns and cities throughout the Levant—Ankara, Kayseri, Damascus, Ayntura, Beirut and elsewhere—were filled with orphanages where surviving Armenian children were placed under the supervision of the Turkish authorities who sought to convert them to Islam and replace their Armenian identities with Turkic ones. In Andonian's words, 'The Turkification project was accepted with such enthusiasm by Turkish intellectuals that famous Turkish writers, like Khalide Edib Hanem, Nigyar Hanem, and teachers, were voluntarily dedicated to that task and by going to Syria personally took over the training of Turkified orphans.'[4] Other children were taken by Turkish, Kurdish or Arab families.

In the 1980s, a campaign was launched that sought to bring the authenticity of this documentation into question by highlighting some of the inconsistencies in the accounts. Based on minor technical arguments, like precision of dates, or the authenticity of signatures, and errors of grammar and syntax, they alleged that the documents were fabrications, and consequently questioned the entire assertion that a state-sponsored annihilation of Armenians had taken place during the First World War.[5]

A major problem in the debate is that the original documents that Andonian sent to Berlin for the Tehlirian trial were eventually lost. Similarly, the archives of the wartime Ottoman leadership and that of the Special Organisation were most probably destroyed in the aftermath of the war, and if any documents survive in Turkish official archives, they are not available to researchers. What remains are the notes and publications of Andonian himself. An additional problem was the circumstances in which Andonian made his notes. He wrote them mainly in the immediate post-war period, hoping to influence the Paris Peace Conference, and therefore his interpretation of the documents was hastily formed.

In a lengthy article historian Vahakn Dadrian scrupulously studies the papers and responds the criticism of Turkish historians in two ways: first by looking at individual accusations and explaining the source of the errors or discrepancies.[6] He argues that inconsistencies in style or grammar, or the differences in the dates were common mistakes in Ottoman officialdom. Dadrian contests that the authenticity of the Naim-Andonian papers can be verified by cross-checking their content with other bodies of evidence. He compares them with documents collected during the post-World War I Court Martials, found in the official gazette of the Ottoman government *Takvim-i Vekayi*. The Court Martials accused CUP leaders of: 'deportation', 'massacre,' 'expropriation,' 'pillage,' 'destruction of villages and towns,' 'rebellion,' and 'violation of public order.' In comparing the Naim-Andonian papers with other independent sources, Dadrian has corroborated their claims.

The debate around Naim-Andonian documents is only one example of a larger phenomenon: to question that a planned genocide was perpetrated by scrutinising individual evidence and question—rightly or wrongly—their authenticity. To this larger attack, Dadrian has the appropriate answer, by confronting them with the ultimate evidence: 'Were the Ottoman Armenians in fact largely exterminated or not?'[7]

* * *

The sources collected by the Allied powers and neutral observers during the war also provide valuable insights into the nature of the events that took place in this period. During the war, the British historian Arnold Toynbee was working at the Foreign Office under the direction of James Bryce, collecting eyewitness accounts as well as diplomatic reports from the field. This documentation was later used in the report 'The Treatment of the Armenians in the Ottoman Empire',[8] which states that an effort had been made to 'exterminate a whole nation, without distinction of age or sex'.[9] The report goes into extensive detail, on a province-by-province basis, with regard to the deportations and mass slaughter, including regions that were distant from the main fronts of the war, such as the city of Angora (Ankara, pp. 381–8), or along the Anatolian Railway (pp. 407–59). At the time, the publication of the report formed part of the British government's propaganda against the Ottomans during the war. This does not diminish its value, however—as Ara Sarafian has argued, Toynbee was meticulous in his work and only used accounts that he could verify and which could be cross checked with other sources. Moreover, the authors of the document also published a separate guide to the sources that were withheld from the report in order to protect the sources, and these can be used to verify the authenticity of the documents.[10] The latter are now housed in the National Archives in Washington, DC.[11]

Henry Morgenthau, the American ambassador to Constantinople between 1913 and 1916, dedicates the third part of his memoirs to the fate of the Ottoman Armenians. He describes how the CUP had fired the governor of Van, Tahsin Pasha, who had managed to establish positive relations with the Armenians there, replacing him with Djevdet Bey, the brother-in-law of the CUP minister of war, Enver Pasha. 'This act in itself was most disquieting', Morgenthau writes, as the Turkish leadership typically made changes in the local leadership before carrying out massacres, placing people in which it had personal confidence to realise its most horrendous orders. 'There is little question that he [Djevdet] came to Van with definite instructions to exterminate all Armenians in this province.'[12] Turkish gendarmes went from house to house searching for weapons and for young men for military service. When Armenians surrendered their weapons, this was taken as 'proof' of their disobedience and inclination to rebel. Priests would be tortured to death, houses destroyed and Armenian women subjected to sexual abuse. Armenian religious and political leaders tried to stop the community from engaging in retaliatory acts. They were well aware that any violence on the part of the Armenians would only serve to trigger further repression. But this did little to stop the subsequent massacres of the Armenians. According to Morgenthau, by the middle of April, 24,000 Armenians had been killed in eighty villages around Van. Djevdet asked leaders of the Armenian community in Van to intervene to ease tensions between Armenians and Kurds. Yet after touring the Armenian villages to call for restraint, the four leaders were murdered in cold blood when they reached a Kurdish village.[13] Immediately afterwards, Djevdet demanded that Armenian leaders in Van provide him with 5,000 able-bodied men for military purposes. The Armenians were understandably suspicious with regard to the true intentions of the Turkish authorities, and instead agreed to provide only 500 men and to pay the authorities a sum of money in place of the men that had been requested. This in turn led Djevdet to begin talking about an Armenian 'rebellion'. On 20 April regular soldiers began arresting Armenian women entering Van. When local men rushed to their rescue, they were shot at, and the Ottoman army, who considered the locals' actions an act of rebellion, started shelling the Armenian neighbourhoods in Van. This marked the beginning of the notorious Van rebellion, an event that was subsequently used by the CUP to allege that all Armenians of the empire were 'rebellious'. In Morgenthau's words:

> Enver, Talaat, and the rest ... when I appealed to them on behalf of the Armenians, invariably instanced the 'revolutionists' of Van as a sample of Armenian treachery. The famous 'Revolution', as this recital shows, was merely the determination of the Armenians to save their women's honour and their own lives, after the Turks, by massacring thousands of their neighbours, had shown them the fate that awaited them.[14]

As the Russian armies advanced, the Turkish troops retreated and the siege of Van was lifted—the bodies of 55,000 Armenians were then collected and subsequently cremated.[15]

Morgenthau gives a detailed description of how the Armenian soldiers were disbanded before being transferred to labour battalions and ultimately executed in small groups. Once this process had been completed, the Turkish authorities were able to attack 'the weaker part of the population [as] an easy prey', beginning with the deportations of villagers and townspeople in the spring of 1915. Their property was confiscated; the men were the first to be rounded up and killed, while the women and children were left to the mercy of the tribes, many of which attacked the convoys to pillage and rape. 'When the Turkish authorities gave the orders for these deportations, they were merely giving the death warrant to a whole race; they understood this well, and, in conversations with me, they made no particular attempt to conceal the fact', writes Morgenthau.[16]

Morgenthau gives an account of a conversation he had with Talaat, the interior minister, in early August 1915. According to Morgenthau, Talaat was the 'most implacable enemy of this persecuted race', and after Morgenthau had made several attempts to intervene in support of the Armenians, Talaat explained in unequivocal terms why the Armenians were being deported:

In the first place, they have enriched themselves at the expense of the Turks. In the second place, they are determined to domineer over us and to establish a separate state. In the third place, they have openly encouraged our enemies. They have assisted the Russians in the Caucasus and our failure there is largely explained by their actions. We have therefore come to the irrevocable decision that we shall make them powerless before this war is ended.[17]

Economic considerations seem to have been the central rationale for the repression inflicted upon the Armenians. On one occasion related by Morgenthau, Talaat stated: 'I wish that you get American life insurance companies to send us a complete list of their Armenian policy holders. They are practically all dead now and have left no heirs to collect the money. It of course all escheats to the State. The Government is the beneficiary now.'[18] The Turkish authorities were increasingly frank about this as the massacres continued. To the successive pleas of the American ambassador, Talaat gave the following reply: 'It is no use for you to argue, we have already disposed of three quarters of the Armenians; there are none at all left in Bitlis, Van, and Erzurum. The hatred between the Turks and the Armenians is now so intense that we have got to finish with them. If we don't, they will plan their revenge.'[19]

* * *

As with the Holocaust, in which it was not only Jews who were the victims, the 1915 genocide did not affect the Armenians alone—the Young Turks also deported and massacred Assyrians, Greeks and Yezidis. In many provinces, Armenian, Greek or Assyrian populations lived side-by-side and often intermarried. During the First World War, these populations and unique civilisations developed over the course of millennia, were destroyed in a matter of months. The Pontic Greeks living on the south-east of the Black Sea were annihilated in the same way as the Armenians. The Assyrians of the Ottoman Empire were subject to the same policies, being deported and massacred in a systematic way: every second Assyrian perished as a result of the CUP's policies—out of a total population of 500,000, at least 250,000 were killed.[20] Although there are numerous sources and books that discuss the Armenian Genocide, much more work needs to be done to document the history of the Assyrians, Greeks, Pontic Greeks and Yezidis during the war years.

* * *

For those Armenians who survived the deportation and massacres, writing became an important instrument in highlighting their plight. There are countless volumes of eyewitness accounts, including memoirs of rural or community life before, during and after the catastrophe.[21] This is particularly astonishing given that the Armenian intelligentsia was almost entirely decimated during the initial phase of the genocide.

Armenian autobiographies and memoirs flourished in the 1920s and 1930s, both in Soviet Armenia and among writers in the diaspora, the authors of which sought to recreate a life that was now lost forever. Kurken Mahari, who was born in Van and deported when he was only five years old, started publishing his poems when he was fourteen and his first autobiographical work was published when he was twenty-five. Writers such as Totovents, Stephane Zoryan, Mkrtich Armen, Zabel Yesayan and many others also wrote autobiographical works in these years. 'The definitive loss of a world, which had been that of their childhood, and consequently the idealisation of this lost world, explains this phenomenon', writes Marc Nichanian. Only Yeghishe Charents, the great revolutionary poet, resisted this trend.[22]

Sarkis Torossian's memoirs, *From Dardanelles to Palestine*, which were recently translated into Turkish, provoked a heated debate in Turkey. Torossian was born in 1891 in Everek, near Kayseri, a town that had a prosperous Armenian population. He was sent to the Adrianapole state college, where he befriended Muharrem, an Arab and son of the brigadier general of Constantinople. Both boys were subsequently sent to the military college, which at that time excluded Christians from becoming students. Torossian graduated in 1914 with the rank of second lieutenant of artillery, before being sent to Germany to perfect his skills. When war broke out he was appointed the commander of 115 soldiers at Fort Ertogrul, at the end of the Gallipoli peninsula, which guarded the entrance to the Dardanelles.

Rumours about unrest in the provinces of the interior eventually reached the western front lines where Torossian was serving the Ottoman Empire. As he was serving as an officer in the Ottoman army, Torossian believed that his family back home would be safe from the repression suffered by other Armenian families. On 19 February 1915 a combined Allied navy of twenty-four warships approached the shores. After a long day of bombardment, in which the British and French destroyed several forts, Fort Ertogrul began to fire cannons at the warships that had entered the straits, sinking one of the vessels via a direct hit. Torossian received the congratulations of his commander, Jevad Pasha, for this military success, as it was the only enemy warship to be destroyed during the exchanges that day. After the destruction of his fort in another attack, during which he lost most of his men and equipment, Torossian was transferred to the nearby Rum-eli Hamidieh, with a short-range battery. On 18 March another seaborne attack was launched, in which the Ottoman forts were destroyed as a result of Allied fire. A French ship approached the Asiatic shores, within range of Torossian's artillery: he ordered fire and the enemy ship was sunk. A British vessel sank after hitting a mine. The fort came under sustained bombardment, during which Torossian received a head wound from shrapnel. After being transferred to a nearby military hospital, he was visited by none other than the minister of war, Enver Pasha, who promoted him to the rank of captain in recognition of his heroism.[23]

According to Torossian, in March 1915 the morale of the Ottoman officers was at a low ebb, and they were fearful that Allied warships would soon capture the capital. 'Turkish military and naval officials had every reason to believe that the high command of the Allied Fleet was fully aware of the very dire circumstances of the Turks. ... All the elements for Allied victory were at hand; practically all Turkish guns silenced and her fortresses in ruins, a shortage of ammunition.'[24] The Turkish military leadership was making preparations to evacuate the capital. But the Allied powers did not return. Writing decades later, Torossian argued that this failure on the part of the Allied powers to launch a sustained attack and bring an end to the Ottoman war efforts proved fateful for the Armenians. In the spring, as he returned to service, rumours about the deportations of entire Armenian villages and the disarming of Armenian servicemen started to reach the Dardanelles. When his superior summoned him to inform him that he was ordered to report to the office of Enver Pasha, Torossian feared his end was near. Instead, Enver received Torossian as a 'hero'; the order to disarm Armenian servicemen and send them to labour battalions did not apply to him. As Captain Torossian was dispatched to lead a battery of artillery in the Battle of Gallipoli in July 1915 the deportations of the Armenian inhabitants of Everek had begun. Able-bodied men were escorted out of town and shot, while the women and children were forced to march southwards towards the Syrian Desert. Torossian met his sister in a refugee camp in Iraq near Tal ul-Halif, who told him about the deportations, during which their parents had died. Torossian deserted the Ottoman army to join the Allied forces shortly afterwards.

In the 1920s and 1930s many memoires, like Torossian's, were published by Armenian survivors. Yet, when Torossian's book was translated into Turkish and published with a lengthy introduction by Ayhan Aktar in 2012, it caused a heated media debate. Some, like Sabanci University professor Hakan Erdem, claimed that Torossian's entire story was a fabrication, that he never went to Ottoman military school, never took part in the Battle of Gallipoli, and that he migrated to the US in 1916 not 1920. The tension surrounding the Torossian narrative also reveals a deeper malaise over a different issue: the fact that the accounts of Toroassian and others negate the Turkish myth that the Battle of Gallipoli was purely a Turkish national victory against European powers. The presence of a Christian-Armenian officer—or the fact that most of the Ottoman troops who fought and died in Gallipoli were Arab recruits from Syrian provinces—contrasts with the exclusively Turkish national narrative, upsetting its proponents even today.

Fifty Years of Silence

On 30 October 1918, the war in the Middle East came to an end with the Ottoman–Allied Murdos Armistice, which also led to the Ottoman army being disbanded. In the years that followed, the Armenian Question was subject to intense political discussion in international fora. The new authorities in Istanbul, composed of rivals to the CUP, distanced themselves from the crimes committed against the minorities of the empire and, under the pressure of the British occupation forces, sought to bring those responsible for the horrendous massacres to justice.[25] At an international level, the Armenians' plight was also the subject of much public debate, particularly as the Armenians killed in the earlier Hamidian massacres had also come to public recognition in Europe and the United States.

Popular mobilisation in support of the Armenians had already started to gather pace during the First World War. In the United

States—which had a long tradition of Christian missionary work in the Ottoman Empire, having established a large number of schools and other charities serving the minorities—massive amounts of money and other assistance were provided, and this continued after the war: from 1915 to 1930, 116 million dollars were collected in the United States alone to support humanitarian relief work.[26]

When the First World War came to an end, this Western mobilisation in support of the Armenians took on an increasingly political hue—the empires of the past had collapsed or were disintegrating, and the right to national self-determination was now the order of the day. The Russian Empire had already disintegrated following the 1917 revolution, leading to a power vacuum in the trans-Caucasus. In the following year, three independent republics emerged: Georgia, Azerbaijan and Armenia. The Ottoman Empire was on the verge of collapse.

It was in this context that in 1917 the idea of uniting the Armenian populated provinces began to be discussed, both by Armenians themselves and within Western diplomatic circles. The most pressing problem during this period concerned the fate of the hundreds of thousands of refugees, the survivors of the death marches, who were now dispersed in towns, cities and camps throughout the Middle East. One of the solutions to this problem mooted at the time would have involved uniting the Armenian provinces of the former Ottoman Empire, the famous six vilayets, and creating an independent Armenian republic to which the refugees would be able to return. During the 1919 Paris Peace Conference, the Armenian delegation demanded an Armenia 'from sea to sea' (i.e. from the Black Sea to the Mediterranean), including the provinces of Yerevan and Kars of the Russian Empire, the six eastern Ottoman provinces, as well as Adana province on the Mediterranean. The Treaty of Sèvres, signed on 20 August 1920, which aimed to establish a framework for relations between the victorious Allies and the defeated Ottomans, stipulated that President Woodrow Wilson would define the future boundaries of an independent Armenia. Although the Armenia map, or the 'Wilsonian Armenia', was never implemented in practice, it remained a source of hope for Armenians over many generations.

In the post-war period, large numbers of refugees tried to return to their homes only to find that they were now occupied by Muslim refugees, perpetuating a general atmosphere of communal violence. In 1917 some 150,000 Armenians returned to the six provinces, which at that time were occupied by the Russian armies.

With the rise of Mustafa Kemal's nationalist movement, the political and military situation in the former Ottoman territories began to change. In 1921 the Greek army, which in 1919 had invaded Ottoman lands as part of a deal made with the allies, was defeated. Kemalist forces also drove French units stationed in Cilician towns to retreat, which preceded a second wave of massacres and expulsions of the Armenian refugees who had returned to their homes in 1919.

In the early 1920s, the Armenians found themselves cut off from their historic land and dispersed throughout the world—in the Caucasus and the Middle East, as well as in Europe and North America. Out of the two million Ottoman Armenians, some 300,000, two-thirds of them kidnapped women and children, were now left in Turkey; 100,000 were in Istanbul while the remainder were scattered throughout the provinces. The newly independent Republic of Armenia found itself in a similarly desperate situation. Nearly half of its population of 720,000 people were refugees.[27] During the war 295,000 Armenians had left the Ottoman Empire and entered lands controlled by Russia, the vast majority of whom became refugees in the Republic of Armenia,[28] which faced constant military pressure from the west, first from the Ottoman and later the Kemalist armies. The Turkish attacks aimed not only to reach the 1914 borders between the Ottoman and tsarist empires but also to advance towards Kars and Yerevan provinces before finally reaching Baku. To the east, the Republic of Armenia was engaged in the war with Azerbaijan over the provinces of Nakhichevan, Zankezour and Karabakh. On each occasion the republic lost territory, the civilian population left behind in these areas was subject to pogroms. It was unclear if the republic would be able to survive. It was in this context that the Red Army entered Armenia, having previously established Soviet Azerbaijan, and brought an end to ARF rule and Armenia's independence. In the Soviet–

Turkish Kars Treaty (1921), the provinces of Kars, Igdir and Ardahan passed to Turkish sovereignty. The final blow came with the Lausanne Treaty (1923), which defined the borders of the Turkish Republic, and put an end to the notion of a unified Armenia.

Once the optimism of the initial post-war period had dissipated, and the new borders of the world had been drawn, the Armenians found themselves in three different places. In Kemalist Turkey, those left behind in Istanbul were able to retain their Armenian identity, despite facing discrimination socially and from the state, whereas those in the provinces were forced to assimilate by converting to Islam. The second place with an Armenian community was Soviet Armenia. Finally, there were the survivors who had found refuge in the new countries of the Middle East, many of whom migrated to the rest of the world and came to constitute the diaspora. In the 1920s, those of the diaspora living in the Middle East, the vast majority being survivors of the death marches, were estimated to total 200,000 people.[29] They mainly lived among Arabs, although they did not speak the language and hence had difficulties in communicating and integrating in their new environment. The majority were orphans who had survived the marches and the massacres before spending several years in Turkish orphanages where they were forced to convert and become Turks. Communication between the three sites where the Armenians were now based was difficult and in some cases utterly impossible.

The majority of the Armenians in Syria and Lebanon were originally from Cilicia, from towns such as Aintab, Marash, Hajin and Adana, and most of them were unable to speak or read Arabic. They were cut-off from the Ottoman-Armenian intelligentsia, which had been decimated on 24 April 1915; the Armenian intellectuals who had remained in Istanbul largely migrated to France and other European and North American destinations after the 1920s.

The priority of the dispersed communities was to construct a new society. A campaign was launched with the aim of saving the wives, mothers, daughters and young boys that various Muslim tribes had kidnapped in Anatolia or the Syrian Desert. Groups were organised in Syria and Lebanon to rescue kidnapped Armenian women and children. Many others had travelled in the immediate post-war period to their towns or villages of origin in order to search for lost relatives. The large number of young girls and women who had been kidnapped and were now living with their Turkish, Kurdish or Arab captors posed a serious dilemma:

> children and girls were often traded as if they were commodities, in order to obtain food for the simple purpose of prolonging the lives of the rest of the family. In other words, the great anxiety and profound despair of the refugees were factors enabling the local population to take children and young girls with relative ease. On the other hand, a majority of the women had lost their husbands and other family members; many had been raped, and all their possessions had been stolen from them during the deportations. They had endured famine and occasionally given birth to illegitimate children. The group of women who had undergone these terrible experiences were often shunned by the other refugees as well. This was one reason that, simply in order to survive, some of them became prostitutes in large towns such as Aleppo, Damascus, Baghdad or Mosul. Others, kidnapped by Muslims and forcibly married, had given birth to children; after the War, they continued to live in their new homes.[30]

In a conservative society dominated by traditional values, it proved difficult to reintegrate such women back into the Armenian community, although many were given the opportunity to do so on the condition that they abandoned any children they bore from Muslim men. A process of re-Armenisation had to take place: turning names back to their original form, teaching the Armenian language to orphans who were raised only speaking Turkish or Kurdish and returning to the Church.

The next priority was *azkabahbanum*, the preservation of the Armenian identity in exile. In the words of Meguerditch Meguerditchian, a member of the ARF Bureau:

> In the inter-war period the problem of refugees was how to survive, and how to organize a communal life … [as] most of the leadership were annihilated … [it was] only after the Second World War when the community was organized that the question of recognition [of the genocide] and the issue of reminding the world what had happened became possible.[31]

This meant creating new community institutions, founding new churches and schools and raising thousands of orphans. Cities like

Aleppo and Beirut became new centres replacing Constantinople, Adana or Aintab. Armenian intellectuals from western cities such as Istanbul or Izmir had gathered in Paris, a city in which the Armenian intelligentsia flourished in the 1920s and 1930s, as well as Cairo, which became another Armenian cultural centre. But Paris ultimately failed to produce a subsequent generation of Armenian intellectuals who were able to speak on behalf of Armenian national interests and give new life to the Armenian cause. Instead, Beirut soon became the capital of the diaspora.

In the meantime, Armenians and other Christians continued to face deportation in the Turkish Republic, despite the provisions of the Lausanne Treaty, which supposedly guaranteed the security of the minorities. In November 1929, for instance, the British consul in Syria reported that there had been a continuous flow of refugees into Aleppo over a period of six months from Kharput (Kharpert), Diyarbekir and Mardin. The refugees reported that bombs had been thrown into the churches and that the Armenian bishop of Diyarbakir had been murdered. The total number of refugees in 1929–30 was put at 30,000.[32] In 1924, Armenians, Assyrians, Jacobites and Arab Christians began to be deported once again from Adana, Urfa, Diyarbakir and Mardin, and all of their property was confiscated. Hence the remaining Armenians, who had managed to survive the CUP death marches because the local feudal lords needed them as skilled labourers and artisans, were finally 'cleansed' once and for all. Children from the age of five years upwards were forced to pay taxes for exemption from military service. The wave of refugees continued throughout the 1930s and 1940s.[33] The Armenians of Sanjak in Alexandretta did not fare any better. After resisting deportations in 1915, when they had been saved by the French navy and transported to Port Said, the inhabitants of the seven villages of Musa Dagh returned to their homes at the end of the war. In the inter-war period, the area was considered a part of Syria and was under the French mandate. In 1938, the French authorities returned the region to Turkey, as a result of which most of the 23,000 Armenian inhabitants of the Sanjak left for Syria. Only 600 Armenians remained.

The new communities had to live through the un-ending upheavals of the Middle East. The initial challenge was to find a balance between the French authorities in Syria and Lebanon and the Arab communities. While the Armenian refugees resented the French for having promised that an Armenian homeland would be created in Cilicia, which they later abandoned to the Kemalists, and for surrendering the region of Iskenderun to Turkey, they were nevertheless forced to rely on the French in Syria and Lebanon to create conditions for a new life in the lands of refuge. At the same time, the Armenians were viewed with apprehension by the Arab populations, with whom they had limited contact. They were poor, competing with the local workforce as cheap labour, and were viewed as a source of disease and criminality.

This first generation of refugees in Arab lands, which had witnessed the genocide first hand, would remain silent for five decades. They met every 24 April to commemorate their loss, but these were not political meetings. Yervant Pamboukian remembers the commemoration of 24 April 1959, as he reached Beirut to teach in one of the Armenian schools after finishing his university studies in Belgium: 'I was invited to say a word on the occasion of April 24. It was an old house, there was a table in the centre, black curtains made the room very dark, and there was incense and candles on the table. It was a day of mourning.'[34] For half a century the generation that had survived was unable to talk openly about what it had gone through.

The Armenians in the Ottoman Empire had never been a homogenous group, and they were not a unified socio-political entity in exile either, with factionalism and in-fighting emerging within the community. The ARF was traumatised as a result of its experience of ruling the fragile Armenian Republic for three years, and the cataclysmic loss it witnessed with the entrance of the Soviet forces. For many years, ARF, or at least a significant part of its leadership, would consider the Soviet Union as its principal enemy. A curious alliance between the liberal Armenian Ramgavar Party, the Social-Democrat Hunchags and the Armenian Communists would come together and support Soviet Armenia, although this had little to do with Marxism or class struggle.

Rather, they argued that a fragile Armenia could not survive in the face of the Turkish threat and that they had no other choice but to remain loyal to Moscow.

There were also genuine Armenian internationalists. The most famous among them was Stepan Shahumyan, who was a leading Bolshevik revolutionary a close friend of Lenin, a member of the Central Committee and head of the Baku Commune. He was the leader of the '26 Baku Commissars', a mixture of multi-ethnic and left-wing revolutionaries, who had escaped after the fall of Baku Commune to advancing Ottoman troops, before crossing the Caspian Sea, only to be arrested by the White Armies and executed in Turkestan. The twenty-six commissars became part of Soviet iconography, with posters, paintings and monuments dedicated to the honour of Shahumyan and the other fallen commissars. Yeghishe Charents, the 'Armenian Mayakovski', was another Armenian internationalist. He was fighting for the revolution in Petrograd with the Bolsheviks while the Republic of Armenia was at war with the Azerbaijani forces to the east, and Turkish invaders to the west. As Stalinist repression became more intense, Charents was forbidden from publishing his poems after 1933 and a campaign was launched against him. Accused of being 'counterrevolutionary and nationalist', he fell victim to Stalin's purges. He was arrested in 1936 and sent to a Siberian prison camp, where he died in 1937.

Stalin's purges took a heavy toll on the Armenian intelligentsia in the east, just two decades after the Young Turks had decimated the Armenian intellectuals in the west. The mass arrests of intellectuals throughout the USSR was only the latest and most expansive part of the terror campaign, after several waves of arrests within party ranks and among intellectuals in the 1920s and 1930s. Tens of thousands perished in Soviet Armenia under Stalinist repression. The Armenian victims ranged from the head of the Communist Party of Armenia, Aghasi Khanjian, who was killed in Tbilisi in 1936, to the supreme Catholicos of all Armenians, Khoren I, who was killed in Echmiadzin by the NKVD in 1938, as well as scores of other Armenian Bolsheviks, politicians, teachers and writers.[35]

The Armenians suffered major losses during the Second World War, particularly in Soviet Armenia. During this period, the population of the Armenian SSR declined by 174,000 (from 1,360,000 in 1941 to 1,186,000 in 1945), while overall Armenian losses are estimated to have been around 300,000.[36] While hundreds of thousands of Armenian soldiers were enrolled in the Red Army fighting the German invasion, which threatened the survival of Armenia itself as the Nazi armies approached the North Caucasus, there were Armenian groups—although limited in magnitude—who fought under the German banner. Dro (Drastamat Kanayan), the former defence minister in the last days of the Republic of Armenia, allied himself with the Axis Powers in a desperate attempt to regain independence from Stalinist rule. He led several thousand Armenian fighters, most of whom were prisoners of war (POWs) who had been captured by the German forces.

At the end of the Second World War there was new hope that Armenian' territorial ambitions might be realised when Stalin demanded control of Turkish territory: the return of Kars, Ardvin and Ardahan provinces, which had been part of the Russian Empire between 1878 and 1917. The demands regarding this territory of 6,500 square kilometres were presented in the name of Soviet Armenia. At the same time, the Soviet authorities launched a repatriation project, calling 'home' thousands of diaspora Armenians with the aim of populating the territory claimed from Turkey. Yet this territorial transfer never took place due to US opposition to the plan. Most of the repatriates were subsequently denounced by the Soviet authorities, and instead of flourishing the Armenians were soon exiled to Siberian gulags.[37]

The polarisation of the Cold War had a devastating effect on the Middle East and the Armenian communities who lived there. The region was torn, on the one hand, between anti-colonialist and pro-Soviet forces, a mixture of Arab nationalist and left-leaning movements, and conservative pro-Western forces on the other. These tensions led to the eruption of the first civil war in Lebanon in 1958, during which the Armenian community witnessed violent acts between the ARF, which had allied itself with right-wing forces, and the socialist Hunchags, who found themselves in the other camp. Beirut River divided the community between ARF-held Bourj-Hammoud and the Hunchag-dominated Nor Hajin neighbourhoods.

1965 marked a turning point. There was an unprecedented popular mobilisation in support of the Armenian cause during the fiftieth commemoration of the genocide. In Yerevan, the capital of Soviet Armenia, a popular demonstration poured on to the streets, numbering between 100,000 and 200,000 people, an extraordinary development in the Soviet Union. The magnitude of the protest was a source of concern to the Soviet authorities, which deployed the Red Army to encircle the city.[38] Following these events, the Soviet Armenian authorities constructed the Dzidzernagapert Monument dedicated to the victims of 1915, which became a pilgrimage site each year on 24 April.

On the same day, in every major diaspora community, mass demonstrations and commemorations were also organised for the fiftieth anniversary of the genocide. However, unlike the previous commemorations, which had been restricted to mourning the dead and lost, the fiftieth anniversary was much more political in tone. The mobilisation of 1965 led to political demands being articulated, the first of which was the 'return' of Wilsonian Armenia. In 1965 Soviet Armenia had a population of 1.9 million people, while 4.5 million Armenians lived abroad. The return of Kars, Ardahan, Van and Erzerum provinces, where the population density was low, with around ten inhabitants per square kilometre, would provide enough space to regroup the Armenian refugees on their historic land. They also called on the international community to recognise the crime of 1915 in light of the 1948 UN Genocide Convention, and to bring the perpetrator to justice. Such reparations would turn the page on past wars and crimes against humanity and open up new prospects for peace in the region.

From Memory to History Writing

Richard Hovannisian is a towering figure in modern Armenian studies. Born in California to a couple that had survived the genocide, his interest in Armenian history began as a result of his research into an often neglected period of the twentieth century, the years between the collapse of the Russian Empire and the formal creation of the Soviet Union, during which time an independent Armenian Republic existed in embryonic form in Transcaucasia. At the same time the eminent historian and political scientist Ronald Grigor Suny, the grandson of a prominent Armenian composer, wrote the history of Sovietisation of the South Caucasus, as well as the history of Stalin's nationalities policies. With Marxist leanings, Suny started his career by writing the history of the Baku Commune, that moment of internationalism and cosmopolitan revolt that the powers to be prefer to forget, in favour of narratives of 'eternal' antagonism between nations and ethnic groups. Suny, on the contrary, prefers to propose a subtle narrative of identity formations, disintegration and reformation as political systems rise and fall. Suny is also the author of a seminal work on Georgian history.[39]

Hovannisian and Suny played an important role in bringing the fate of the Armenians to a broader academic audience, but neither of these two key scholars focused on the genocide initially. Scholarship on massacres was revolutionised by Vahakn Dadrian, who provided an analysis of the events of the First World War on the basis of the Ottoman archives, including German and Austro-Hungarian war correspondence and diplomatic reports. Dadrian's work was published at a critical juncture both for academia and for politics, as Turkey had launched a new campaign in the 1980s and 1990s to discredit the Armenian narrative by denying that genocide had taken place. Dadrian's writings, which were based on extensive archival sources, exposed the poverty of the official Turkish discourse.

Dadrian was well equipped to take up the challenge, and confront the Turkish official discourse. Born in Istanbul to a wealthy family in 1926, Dadrian left Turkey in 1945 to study in Europe and then the US. Having excelled in his studies in Maths and Philosophy, he went on to work in academia at Harvard University, Duke University and the State University of New York. It wasn't until the 1970s that Dadrian started researching the Armenian Genocide, a task aided by his fluency in Armenian, German, English, Turkish and his ability to read Osmanli (Turkish written in Arabic script). In 1991, thanks to a H.F. Guggenheim Foundation grant, where he was director of the Genocide Study Project for several years, he stopped his teaching activities and dedicated his time exclusively to research.

Dadrian's seminal work, *The History of the Armenian Genocide: Ethnic Conflict from the Balkans to Anatolia to the Caucasus* (1995), not only provides a comprehensive analysis of the Armenian Genocide but also seeks to place the events of 1915 in a broader historical context, beginning with the Tanzimat reforms and ending with a comparative discussion of the Armenian Genocide and the Holocaust. In order to develop this comparative discussion, Dadrian also looks at other regions such as Macedonia, Mount Lebanon, the Caucasus and beyond. The work was groundbreaking at the time, given its use of archival Ottoman–Turkish sources, as well as archival sources from states that had been allied to the Ottoman Empire such as those in Germany and Austria. In so doing, Dadrian was able to corroborate the claims made in eyewitness accounts and the archives of countries that had fought against the Ottoman Empire, which Turkey had sought to dismiss as biased and hence unreliable.

The book begins by discussing two problems in the Ottoman Empire that would subsequently escalate over time. The first of these was the legal imbalance between the empire's Muslim and Christian subjects. As a theocracy, the Ottoman Empire placed Muslims and Christians in an unequal legal position, with non-Muslims being viewed as 'tolerated infidels'. Even after the Young Turk Revolution of 1908, and a return to the constitutional system introduced by Abdul Hamid II in November 1876 but suspended just over a year later, the elite continued to believe that Muslims (increasingly Turks) formed the ruling nation (*milleti hâkime*), with policy being formulated on this basis. It is this notion of the ruling nation, the book maintains, which explains the failure to introduce modern European legal reforms and the principle of legal equality regardless of gender or race in Turkey. The second problem raised in the book concerns the intervention of the Allied powers prior to the First World War, which raised the expectations of the subjugated while increasing the level of resistance on the part of the ruling millet. When this conflict became violent, the European powers that had stated an ostensive concern with the fate of the Ottoman minorities refused to intervene to defend the victims.

It was, argues Dadrian, the Berlin Congress in 1878 that was the seminal moment in sharpening the relations between the Ottoman state and its Armenian population. The San Stefano and Berlin treaties, which demanded substantial 'reforms' to the Armenian-inhabited regions of eastern Anatolia as a prerequisite for Russian withdrawal, lead the Ottoman authorities to perceive the Armenian population for the first time as a risk factor, a pretext for foreign intervention. Consequently, over the following decades Armenians were repressed, massacred and forcibly converted to Islam. Boundaries and statistics were manipulated, while foreign powers did nothing to enforce 'reforms' or protect victims.

Dadrian puts forward a powerful case that the 'impunity that was accorded the perpetrators'[40] of the Hamidian massacres (1894–6) opened the doors to organised mass murder against the Armenians, who were subject to further organised massacres throughout the empire. He then goes on to address the Adana massacres, which took place a year after the Young Turk Revolution and led to the deaths of 25,000 Armenians. Adana was one of the few cities that had escaped the massacres in 1894–6, largely thanks to the successful uprising in nearby Zeitun, a mountainous town that had fiercely defended its semi-autonomous status throughout history. As was the case both before and after this event, the European powers were inactive: while the battleships of seven nations sailed to the shores of Adana and nearby Mersin, none was ordered to intervene in order to stop the bloodshed.

His conclusion is a pessimistic one. The UN, he argues, solely reflects the interests of its member states, and he is also sceptical with regard to the efficiency of international humanitarian intervention: 'when international actors intervene in response to persecutions in another state without firm coordination and commitment, any actions they take may actually aggravate rather than alleviate the plight of the victim population'.[41] He cites the Hamidian massacres of 1894–6, and the lack of intervention on the part of Russia, as an example of this: in the past, Russia had intervened in similar situations 'on humanitarian grounds.' Following Bulgaria's wars against the Ottoman Sultan in 1877 and the independence of the region that followed, the Russians had put a government in place. Subsequently, anti-Russian sentiment grew in Bulgaria until the government was overthrown in 1881. This was seen in Petersburg as Bulgarian 'ingratitude';[42] the Russians had had their fingers burnt, and were thus not keen to intervene again. The emergence of Armenian revolutionary parties on both sides of the Transcaucasian borders provided another reason for the tsar to avoid intervention.

As for other 'Great Powers', France was unlikely to want to damage relations with the Ottomans having made huge investments in the sultan's empire—up to 70 per cent of the empire's assets were, in fact, French investments[43]—and the Germans were also courting the sultan in order to increase their economic and political influence in the region.

For Dadrian, the trigger that led to the genocide was the re-launching of the idea of 'Armenian reforms' following the 1913 Balkan Wars, when the CUP regime felt that it was in a vulnerable position. It framed the Armenians as the next danger, as traitors.

One of the most contentious elements of Dadrian's work is the idea that a plan had been formulated in the period prior to the First World War to exterminate the Armenians. Dadrian argues that the Ittihadists had an 'operational blueprint and a plan of concealment and coverup' for the genocide.[44] He maintains that a plan had been in circulation for at least a year prior to the war that envisaged large-scale massacres, the appropriation of Armenian property and the Islamisation of women and orphaned children. In a conference held in secret in December 1914, or possibly in January 1915, the Ittihad Party Central Committee deliberated on the plan for the massacres with the participation of high-level officials: Talaat, the minister of interior and the Ittihadist strongman, and Nazim and Bahaeddin Şakir, two officials who played a vital role in planning and executing the genocide.

Ismail Canbolat, the head of public security at the Interior Ministry, and Colonel Seyfi, head of Department II Intelligence at the Ottoman General Headquarters, both of whom played a key role in the massacres, were also present at the secret meeting.

There is another dimension in Dadrian's seminal work: his continuous expectation and frustration, to see international intervention to bring justice. This is Dadrian's legal side; he does believe in international justice, but its continuous failures irritate him. The instrument of this global justice are the Western Powers. Reading Dadrian's book twenty years later, at the time of the war in Syria, makes one think about the frustrated expectations of the Syrian opposition, or the citizens taken hostage by a criminal regime, of a similar international justice, a *deus ex-machina* that would come down over Damascus and liberate them from their nightmare. But that international justice, in spite of a multiplication of bureaucratic organisations in recent times, has yet to come to fruition in Syria.

Detractors have often criticised Dadrian's work as having a teleological dimension, whereby he links the Hamidian massacres, the Adana massacre of 1909 and the 1915–16 genocide as different episodes of the same chain of events. Others have criticised Dadrian for essentialising identities, arguing that the definition of 'Turk' or 'Rumi' had been in flux in the nineteenth century. In spite of the relevance of these criticisms, the oeuvre of Dadrian continues to influence students of genocide studies today.

German Responsibility

In 1996 Dadrian published another book, entitled *German Responsibility in the Armenian Genocide: A Review of the Historical Evidence of German Complicity.*[45] This book draws on German archival sources from the First World War to highlight the role of Germany in the fate of the Ottoman Armenians.

Germany gained an increasing amount of influence over the Ottomans following the Treaty of Berlin (1878). Four years after the treaty had been signed, the first German military mission, led by

Major von der Goltz, arrived in Istanbul with the aim of organising the Ottoman armed forces, thereby opening the way for German domination over the army of the Sultan. The German company Krupp soon became the leading weapons supplier to Abdul Hamid II. German support for the sultan did not vacillate during the Hamidian massacres. Two years after the massacres, accompanying Wilhelm II on a trip to Istanbul, the liberal pastor, Friedrich Naumann, stated that Germany's national interests required maintaining 'our political indifference to the suffering of Christians in the Turkish Empire, painful as these must be to our private feelings'.[46]

Dadrian explores the intellectual responsibility of German officials for creating an enemy out of the Armenians, and for justifying their extermination on the grounds of 'military necessity'. General von der Goltz, who had spent many years in Istanbul heading the German military mission in 1878–96 and 1915–16, insisted that the Ottomans had to abandon their European provinces and turn eastward to become an Asiatic power: 'the core of Turkey is to be found not in Europe but in Asia Minor. Turkey has greater chances of military success in Transcaucasia, where Russia is militarily weak, and its ethnic and religious ties with the local Muslim populations could come in handy.'[47]

The military alliance between Germany and the Young Turk regime was strengthened in the pre-war period. The Young Turks were seeking German protection against Russia, and agreed to place all Ottoman forces under German military command in case of war. The original German military mission of 70 officers increased to some 800 officers and 12,000 soldiers during the war. As a result of this role in commanding the Ottoman armies, German officers ordered, organised, supervised and even participated in the deportation and killing of the Armenian population. One example of direct German involvement is from Urfa, where the local population revolted in legitimate self-defence and repelled the Turkish forces sent to overrun their neighbourhoods after witnessing the horrifying state of deportees passing through their town. Major Eberhard Wolffskeel of the German army and his artillery were then deployed in September/October 1915 to pulverise the Armenian quarter of Urfa before letting Turkish gendarmes finish off the surviving population.

The idea of declaring 'jihad' during the war was a German initiative that aimed to incite Muslim revolts in the British and Russian colonies. General von der Goltz, as well as General Fritz Bronsart von Schellendorf, played a key role in persuading Enver to declare jihad. However, while the declaration of jihad did not create the desired results in the British or Russian territories, it had an extremely negative impact on the Christian minorities of the Ottoman Empire, turning agitated Muslim popular masses against their Christian neighbours who were now viewed as a dangerous internal enemy.

Dadrian quotes several official Turkish memoirs indicating that Germany was insistent that the Armenian population should be deported en masse. German officers knew about the deportations and they issued strict orders to remove specific Armenian groups, such as Armenian men serving in Ottoman army labour battalions, or Armenians working for the Baghdad Railway company. Dadrian quotes an order issued by General Bronsart, the Chief of Staff of Ottoman General Headquarters, which reads: 'the deportation of the Armenian population has been decided' and that 'severe measures' should be taken against unarmed Armenian soldiers in labour battalions.[48] Few of these groups of unarmed civilians survived the deportations, and the German authorities were aware of this. Ambassador Wangenheim reported to Berlin on 17 June 1915, for instance, that the Armenian population of Diyarbakir, which had been deported to Mosul, had been slaughtered en route, while a cable to Berlin from 12 July states: 'The Armenians of the convoy from Mardin were ... slaughtered just like sheep.'[49]

Dadrian argues that the German authorities would have been able to save the lives of many of those who were deported if they had sought do so. The Christians of Smyrna, in modern-day Izmir, for instance, were saved thanks to the position adopted by General Liman von Sanders, who opposed deporting the Armenians of the city.[50]

OPEN WOUNDS

The Genocide of the Armenians and the United Nations

The end of the Second World War and the establishment of the United Nations created a new opportunity for Armenian political organisations in exile. Their attempts to revive the Sèvres Treaty—imposed by Britain and France on a defeated Ottoman Empire in 1920, leading to the empire's partition—during the San Francisco Conference (1947) had failed to create the desired results, yet the UN Genocide Convention (1948) presented a new stimulus for the Armenians seeking justice. After two world wars, after two genocides, it was time to end the impunity of the perpetrator. They identified their own experience and past suffering by the new legal term coined by the UN: 'genocide'.

In the early years of the United Nations, Turkey was able to resist attempts to define its actions against the Armenians as 'genocide' in international legal documents, despite a number of efforts to do so. On the first such occasion, in 1967, the UN sub-commission against discrimination and for the protection of minorities—which was linked to the UN Commission on Human Rights—decided to carry out a study on genocide to clarify a number of conceptual and legal questions and named a rapporteur for the task. In 1971 the UN nominated the Rwanda expert Nicomède Ruhashyankiko as its special rapporteur. An intermediary report, which was presented at the twenty-sixth session in 1973, elaborated on the concept of genocide. In paragraph thirty it notes: 'Passing to [the] contemporary epoch, we can note the existence of abundant documentation concerning the massacre of the Armenians, which leads us to consider it as "the first genocide of the 20th century".'[51]

This passing reference to the Armenian Genocide alarmed the Turkish authorities, and led the Turkish delegate, Osman Olcay, to launch a strongly worded condemnation of paragraph thirty. He ultimately succeeded in removing the relevant paragraph from the document as a majority of the delegates supported the Turkish position. However, this understandably angered the Armenians, who did not have any representation at the UN at that time. In order to counter Turkey's efforts to rewrite history, the Armenians consequently created the Committee for the Defence of the Armenian Cause, with its small working group going on to establish contacts with state representatives at the sub-commission and non-governmental organisations with representation at the UN's Geneva office, the most notable of which was the International Federation of Human Rights.

Although Turkey was able to revise the interim report, its efforts to remove any mention of an Armenian Genocide in UN documents were opposed by a number of delegates, who argued that the original wording should have remained as it was. In 1983 a new special rapporteur was appointed, the renowned British expert and former Labour MP Benjamin Whitaker, with the task of updating the report. In the updated report, entitled 'Revised and Updated Report on the Question of the Prevention and Punishment of the Crime of Genocide', presented at the thirty-eighth session of the sub-commission in 1985, paragraph twenty-four states:

> The Nazi aberration has unfortunately not been the only case of genocide in the twentieth century. Among other examples which can be cited as qualifying are the German massacre of Hereros in 1904, the Ottoman massacre of Armenians in 1915–1916, the Ukrainian pogrom of Jews in 1919, the Tutsi massacre of Hutu in Burundi in 1965 and 1972, the Paraguayan massacre of Ache Indians prior to 1974, the Khmer Rouge massacre in Kampuchea between 1975 and 1978, and the contemporary [1985] Iranian killings of Baha'is.[52]

A footnote attached to the brief mention of the Armenian massacres states: 'At least 1 million, and possibly well over half of the Armenian population, are reliably estimated to have been killed or death-marched by independent authorities and eye-witnesses.' It then goes to fill half a page with references relating to the Armenian massacres.

It was during this period that the so-called 'Armenian lobby' began to emerge in international fora such as the UN. This lobby would go on to fight for the recognition of the Armenian Genocide by international tribunals and national parliaments worldwide.

Encyclopaedic Work

Raymond Kévorkian has spent the last three decades of his life researching the Armenian Genocide, turning to every available document, and bringing the work of documentation to new levels: he has completed works of monumental magnitude with encyclopaedic exhaustion. Kévorkian was initially a specialist in the origins of the Armenian printed book in the seventeenth century rather than an expert on the genocide.[53] However, in 1986 he was appointed curator of the Bibliothèque Nubar in Paris, a post he retained until early 2013. While organising the archives in this role, he began to read a large number of eyewitness accounts of the massacres, which had been compiled from 1928 onwards, by Aram Andonian, the famous journalist and writer, and the philanthropist Boghos Nubar (the 'Naim–Andonian' archives). 'The spirit of Andonian was everywhere you turned, on everything you touched,' he said. 'Doing nothing with all this would have been criminal.'[54]

Kévorkian decided to write about the genocide. 'Historiography is a central genre in Armenian writing, … it goes back centuries. And then you find it again at the end of the war, when there were efforts to record and fix what had happened. There were three major efforts of the kind, centred around three distinct geographic locations.'[55] The three collections of genocide accounts in Syria, Armenia and Istanbul complement each other. Curiously, the grandparents of Kévorkian, themselves genocide survivors, did not leave behind their memories of those horrible events. They did not leave behind any written accounts of their ordeal. Kévorkian is currently working on the last volume of his trilogy. The first one, co-authored with Paul B. Paboudjian, *Les Arméniens dans l'Empire ottoman à la veille du génocide*, was the volume that *Agos* serialised.

In 2006, Kévorkian published his encyclopaedic history of the Armenian Genocide, entitled *Le Génocide des Arméniens*. The history begins with the emergence of the Young Turk opposition to the sultan and their relations with the Armenian revolutionaries, and ends with the Turkish Court-Martials of 1919–1920, when leading CUP members and former officials were found guilty of subversion of the constitution, wartime profiteering and the massacre of minorities, among other charges, and sentenced to death. The book reveals the network of concentration camps in the Syrian Desert, and provides an important exposition of an extermination campaign in 1916, which Kévorkian calls 'the second phase of the Genocide', where the surviving deportees in Der Ez-Zor were subjected to massacres—the Young Turks' 'final solution'.

When asked why he decided to write the book, Kévorkian states that it is a basic question of human dignity. 'When I write, I pass on knowledge and understanding that helps group healing. A century has passed, but collective healing—and healing one's own wounded soul—remains a necessity.'

'I will tell you something else', Raymond Kévorkian told me with a shrewd smile, 'Operation Nemesis was a great service to Kemal.' Operation Nemesis was a series of vengeance killings organised by the ARF (Armenian Revolutionary Federation, or Tashnaks) against key CUP leaders who played a role in the genocide. 'The Tashnaks eliminated all his major competitors for him. After the Izmir plot of 1926 [an assassination attempt against the Turkish president], Kemal himself eliminated the remaining criminals.' The uncovered Izmir plot served as an occasion for Kemal to eliminate a number of his leading political competitors—whether they were actually associated with the plot or not. 'What a massacre it was. I am sure Stalin took lessons from this on how to run show trials.'

* * *

The three-decade long struggle of the scholars discussed in this chapter ultimately bore fruit. Prior to the 1980s, those academics specialising in studies on genocide, or specialists in Ottoman studies, tended to avoid discussing the Armenian Genocide of the First World War, or simply parroted the official Turkish position on the matter. Today, however, those who seek to deny the genocide increasingly find themselves marginalised, with a growing number of non-Armenians, including ethnic Turks and Kurds, producing scholarly studies that have shed new light on this dark and tragic period of modern history.

5

DECADE OF TERRORISM

I met Alec Yenikomshian on 21 April 2014. Yenikomshian is one of the best-known figures of the Armenian terrorist movement of the 1970s and 1980s. He was the first of the militants whose identity was exposed when he accidentally set off a bomb he was preparing in his hotel room in Geneva in October 1980, causing him to lose his sight and his left hand.

Yenikomshian began our conversation by talking about the difficult political situation in Armenia and the need for a popular revolt to establish a democratic system there. He was particularly concerned by the growing numbers of Armenians who were choosing to leave the country. He was an active member of a group that organised public gatherings with the aim of encouraging Armenians to fight for their political rights. Our discussion then turned to Armenian terrorism during the 1970s.

Like many of his comrades who were involved in the armed struggle, Yenikomshian carries the scars of his experience. He graduated from Nishan Palajian Jemaran, a high school that was within the orbit of the Armenian Revolutionary Federation (ARF), before going on to study for a Master's degree in economics at the prestigious American University of Beirut. While there, he mixed with Lebanese and Palestinian militants, who were often involved in lengthy debates concerning the war in Vietnam, the best strategy to liberate Palestine and the coming Arab revolution. As with many of his predecessors, Yenikomshian's Armenian nationalism was also informed by leftist ideas, and he eventually joined the notorious Armenian Secret Army for the Liberation of Armenia (ASALA). In 1975 the organisation launched a campaign involving attacks against the Turkish state and the assassination of Turkish diplomats.

The activities and emergence of ASALA, as well as the ARF-connected Justice Commandos of the Armenian Genocide (JCAG),[1] took place in two specific contexts. The first was the general context of the time, with the rise of the Palestine Liberation Organisation (PLO) in the Middle East. ASALA emerged from the PLO camps in Lebanon, and their worldview was intrinsically related to that of the Palestinian guerrillas. The enigmatic founder of ASALA, Harutiun Takoushian, was known to the outside world by his *nom de guerre* Hagop Hagopian, and to ASALA members as the Mujahed.[2] Takoushian was born in the Iraqi city of Mosul, which he left in his teenage years to join the Palestinian resistance. He became a member of the Popular Front for the Liberation of Palestine—External Operations (PFLP—EO), which was led by Wadie Haddad, and took part in clashes between the Jordanian army and the Palestinian guerrillas during the 'Black September' of 1970, after which he escaped to Lebanon in the company of the guerrillas. According to some accounts, he played a part in the 1972 Munich terror attack. Some accounts also suggest that he was wounded in 1974 and treated in a Belgrade hospital.[3]

Haddad was a strategic thinker who sought to pursue his campaign of terrorism within the general framework of the Palestinian cause. Takoushian, on the other hand, learned how to conduct terrorist operations from Haddad, but these were never related to any broader strategy. By 1974 the PFLP—EO was exhausted and the organisation effectively fell apart when Haddad died from illness in 1978. Takoushian consequently developed an alternative plan, namely to become the Armenian Wadie Haddad by launching an Armenian version of the PFLP—EO.

In the Palestinian refugee camps throughout the Middle East, a new political culture was born, that of the modern *fedayeen* and the ideology of the armed struggle. In the 1960s and 1970s, it became the dominant political culture of opposition throughout the Middle East and influenced generations of militants from the Turkish left to the PKK, to Iranian revolutionaries as well as militant groups from Germany to Japan who graduated from the PLO camps of Saida and Bekaa. During my childhood years in Beirut, a city at war, when I thought of politics I imagined a group of bearded and armed young men positioning themselves on a street-corner behind sandbags and opening fire from their Kalashnikovs and rocket-propelled grenades on neighbouring buildings. Elections, parliaments, debates and negotiations were far from that reality. It was in this environment that an entire generation found that violence would provide answers to their existential questions.

The radicalisation of Middle Eastern politics, the rise of third-world ideologies and national liberation struggles from Latin America to Vietnam had an effect on Armenian politics too. The youth of the ARF began to adopt radical leftist ideologies, with the principal enemy in their struggle being modern Turkey.

From Bank Ottoman to Operation Nemesis

As part of the Armenian youth radicalised, many in the ranks of the ARF looked back into their own past political heritage to find references to armed struggle and even terrorism. For example, Christopher Mikaelian, one of the three founders of the ARF, was influenced by the Russian Narodnaya Volya organisation, which had assassinated Tsar Alexander II. In 1905 Mikaelian died while experimenting with a bomb that he planned to use to assassinate Abdul Hamid II. Another major reference to 'heroic' acts celebrated in many songs and poems was the attack on Ottoman central bank. On 26 August 1896, at the height of the Hamidian massacres, a group of twenty-six *fedayee* members of the ARF attacked and occupied the Ottoman Bank headquarters in Istanbul. The target was not only chosen because it was the heart of the empire's finances but also because it contained money and investments from European states and companies; occupying the bank would thus attract the attention of the great powers. The operation was planned by Papken Siuni (Bedros Parian)—who died during the attack on the bank—and Armen Garo (Karekin Pastermajian).[4] After successfully occupying the bank, the commandos that survived were granted safe passage abroad. In the streets of Istanbul, and in the provinces of the Ottoman Empire, the massacre of the Armenians continued.

At the end of the First World War, the ARF organised a clandestine operation—Operation Nemesis—led by the activists Shahan Natalie and Armen Garo in Boston, to assassinate those responsible for organising the genocide. Natalie sent a young militant called Soghomon Tehlirian to assassinate 'number one', the moniker used for Talaat Pasha, the former Ottoman grand vizier and the author of the extermination plans, who had escaped to Berlin. Tehlirian originated from Erzinjan (Garin) on the Armenian Plateau and was nineteen years old when he and his family received orders for deportation; they had hardly left town when their convoy was attacked by the gendarmes who were supposed to be protecting them. He witnessed his mother's death by bullet, the rape of his sisters and the killing of his brother of his brother as an attacker opened his skull with an axe. He himself was hit, fell unconscious, and woke up hours later in an open field littered with corpses. In March 1921, Tehlirian walked behind a couple on the streets of Berlin, touched the shoulder of the man, and after looking at his face fired from his pistol, shouting: 'This is to avenge the death of my family.'[5] Tehlirian did not try to escape and was quickly arrested by the German police and put on trial. During the court hearings, documents gathered by Aram Andonian were presented as evidence while Johannes Lepsius, a German orientalist who documented the Armenian Genocide during the war, and Otto Liman von Sanders, a German general who served as adviser and military commander for the Ottoman Empire during World War I, were called to testify. The trial turned into a political event, provoking discussions of CUP crimes and German complicity. During the trial,

Tehlirian exclaimed: 'I have killed a man, but I am not a murderer.'[6] The trial lasted only two days. On the second day, after an hour of deliberation, the jury acquitted Tehlirian although he had confessed to his crime. The crowd in the courtroom shouted: 'bravo!'[7]

Operation Nemesis also led to the assassination of the other member of the triumvirate, Jemal Pasha, as well as other leading CUP notables Said Halim Pasha, Behaeddin Shakir, Cemal Azmi, and the former Azerbaijani prime minister Fatali Khoyski and the Azerbaijani interior minister Behbud Khan Javanshir for his role in the Baku massacres. Enver Pasha, the former minister of war, was killed in Central Asia by Yakov Melkumov (Hagop Melkumian), an Armenian commander of Bolshevik troops.

Tehlirian's act attracted the attention of a twenty-one-year-old student in Lvov University, Raphael Lemkin. He asked one of his professors why Tehlirian had killed Talaat instead of having him arrested for the massacres. The professor answered that international law did not consider Talaat a criminal: 'Consider the case of a farmer who owns a flock of chickens … He kills them and this is his business. If you interfere, you are trespassing.'[8] Lemkin, a Polish Jew who would later become famous as an international lawyer who developed the legal concept of genocide, was shocked: 'It is a crime for Tehlirian to kill a man, but it is not a crime for his oppressor to kill more than a million men? This is most inconsistent.'[9]

ASALA was born out of the Palestinian experience, but JCAG was there to remind us of the long Armenian association with political violence.

* * *

In 1965, after fifty years of silence, popular anger with regard to the Armenians' plight erupted in the streets of Beirut and Paris, as well as Soviet Yerevan. The demonstrators called for justice for the victims of the 1915 genocide, and for the return of Armenian lands to their rightful owners. In the years that followed there was an intensive effort to place the Armenian cause back on the international agenda. However, when these peaceful activities failed to produce the results that were desired, the youth gradually became more radical. In 1969 a group was formed within the ARF, calling itself Vreji Yerdasartner— Youth of Vengeance. Although this group did not carry out violent acts, its members were engaged in discussions about terrorism with the aim of establishing a modern-day *fedayee* movement. *Fedayeen* were the Armenian revolutionary fighters of the Ottoman times—the word comes from Arabic and means self-sacrificing fighter.

In 1973, the seventy-eight-year-old Kurken Yanikian made head-lines by assassinating two Turkish officials in 1973 in California. Yanikian was born in 1895 in Erzerum. He was a university student in Russia when the First World War began, and he joined the Russian army in advancing towards his birthplace where he witnessed the destruction of Armenian towns and villages. He lost most of his family members to the massacres. In his final years, the memories of what he had seen began to haunt him, and in the absence of justice he decided to take matters into his own hands. Yanikian lured the two Turkish diplomats, the head of the Turkish consulate in Los Angeles and his assistant, to his hotel room in Santa Barbara to collect an old Ottoman painting and a currency bill. After presenting the items, the three men had lunch, during which a heated argument erupted, and it was at this stage that he pulled a pistol and killed them before sur-rendering himself to the police.

Two other events that took place at a similar time further radicalised some activists in the Armenian diaspora. First, as discussed in Chapter 4, in Geneva a UN sub-commission censored a 1973 report mention-ing the Armenian Genocide under pressure from Turkey, and with the support of Turkey's Western allies. For the Armenian youth politicised during the demonstrations that had accompanied the fiftieth anniver-sary of the genocide in 1965, this came as a shock, revealing a dead-end for legal, non-violent struggle for justice. The second event was the 1974 Turkish invasion of Cyprus and its occupation of the north, reviving Armenian fears of aggressive pan-Turkism.

While Justice Commandos (JCAG) operated exclusively through their own networks, ASALA was part of a larger alliance with Palestinian, Kurdish and European militants. ASALA and PKK had reached an agreement on mutual support: when one of the groups carried out a terrorist act, the other group would claim responsibility and vice versa. ASALA's terrorist operations, which lasted for a decade, started on 20 January 1975 when a bomb was placed in front of the offices of the World Council of Churches in Beirut. The Armenian terrorists generally targeted Turkish diplomatic envoys.[10] JCAG opened their campaign by assassinating Turkish diplomats in Vienna and Paris on 22 and 24 October 1975. Most of the attacks took place in Europe in order to attract international attention to their cause. As the two organisations began carrying out operations in the same year, they became engaged in what was almost a competition to commit increasingly daring acts in order to attract media and popular attention. While the Justice Commandos carried out the greatest number of assassinations, ASALA organised several spectacular operations that attracted a significant amount of media attention. In one of these attacks, the 'Van Operation', four militants overran the Turkish consulate in Paris, 24–25 September 1981, and held forty hostages for two days—the group demanded that political prisoners in Turkey, including two Armenian priests and ten non-Armenian prisoners, be freed before they would release the hostages.[11] In the summer of the following year, ASALA militants were forced to retreat in the face of the Israeli army, which was advancing northwards to crush the PLO's infrastructure in South Lebanon, and later in Beirut. The evacuation of the PLO from Beirut in 1982 was a huge blow to the militant group—as it lost its Palestinian protector, it was now forced to seek the protection of Arab states such as Baathist Syria.

The logo used by the ASALA is a map of Wilsonian Armenia, on which 'Hayasdan'—Armenia—is written in Armenian letters, with a hand holding an AK-47 depicted in the centre of the map. As the logo's crass allusion to violence would suggest, the group's political culture was poor, and did not amount to much more than a fetishism of armed struggle and criticism of the traditional Armenian parties for their passivity and inaction—an unjustified critique, given that the ARF had produced its own version of modern *fedayis*.[12] ASALA failed to ask difficult questions, such as what would happen after the initial phase of terrorism. How could a band of two-dozen militants fight effectively against a Turkish army of 600,000 soldiers and its NATO allies? Finally, and most importantly, how would it be possible to liberate Armenia, when the genocide had successfully eradicated the Armenians from their historic lands? In 1980, when the American Armenian militant Monte Melkonian,[13] who had already gained experience of fighting in Iran with the Kurds and later in Beirut with the ARF militia against the Lebanese Phalangist militias, joined ASALA, he had imagined an iron-willed and highly disciplined secret organisation. 'If there were revolutionaries behind the assassinations and press conferences,' writes his brother Markar, 'there weren't more than a dozen of them. And that was hardly an army, secret or not. To try to build a movement from this "rinky-dinky operation," as Monte later described it, would be like starting from scratch.'[14]

Prior to 1982, ASALA had primarily targeted Turkish diplomats and only caused limited 'collateral damage'. Yet this changed in July 1983 with an attack on Orly Airport in France. A bomb exploded near a Turkish airliner, killing eight people and injuring more than fifty. After being arrested, Varoujan Garabedian—a Syrian Armenian— admitted responsibility, and described how he had given a suitcase in which a bomb was placed to a passenger on a flight heading from Paris to Istanbul, with the intention of blowing-up the plane in mid-flight. On a political level, the attack was a disaster for the Armenians, as it took place only days before a major gathering on the Armenian cause in Lausanne, Switzerland. The legal activities of the ASALA were subsequently impeded by the mass arrests of its activists in France. A number of militants in Bekaa training camps were opposed to the attack and the dictatorial manner in which Takoushian ruled the group. This was followed a few days later by an attack on the Turkish embassy in Lisbon by five militants of JCAG. The operation was a failure, leading to seven deaths, including the five assailants.[15]

The Orly attack brought the internal problems with the ASALA to the surface. Monte Melkonian, along with a number of other militants, declared that he would leave ASALA and would instead create the ASALA-Revolutionary Movement.[16] Alec Yenikomshian, a close friend of Monte Melkonian, who had also left Takoushian's organisation, was in hiding to protect his life from his former comrades-in-arms. Arrests followed by assassinations decimated the organisation, leading to its eventual destruction. At the same time, the competition between the ARF and the Justice Commandos had turned into yet another bloody and senseless war. In its final years, ASALA had evolved to become a hit group for hire, receiving cash from various Middle Eastern states to 'deliver' terror attacks. Takoushian was assassinated in Athens in 1988 in an attack that was probably orchestrated by some of his former close collaborators.

However, the decade of terror had succeeded where peaceful political struggle had failed: by carrying out these acts, the Armenian Genocide and the quest for justice was now firmly back on the international agenda. Terror attacks attracted widespread media attention, which created opportunities to discuss the events of 1915 and the question of Turkish responsibility. Many Turkish intellectuals only came to learn of an Armenian cause in the late 1970s, as a result of Armenian terrorism.

Back in Yerevan, the apartment was now getting dark. 'The armed struggle died out between 1983 and 1985,' Alec Yenikomshian told me. 'Up to then, the centre of gravity was aimed at Western Armenia. By historic coincidence, a few years later, in 1988, the centre of gravity of Armenian struggle was displaced to the Eastern Armenia: the Karabakh movement started.' In Yenikomshian's view, the main goal of the diaspora—recognition of the events of 1915 as genocide by the international community—is insufficient in itself and should instead serve broader political aims: 'Without *Turkish* recognition of the genocide', Yenikomshian maintains, 'the safety of Armenians cannot be guaranteed in the future.' As the issue has increasingly been debated within Turkey, the drive to attain recognition has lost its importance. 'Turkish recognition of the genocide is not simply a recognition of a historic fact, but it is a guarantee of security for Armenia and its people.' Yenikomshian concluded: 'We need to be realistic, but we should not give up the dream of Western Armenia.'

6

A REVOLUTIONARY ACT

The Human Rights Defender

I had arranged to meet Ragıp Zarakolu, the dean of Turkish human rights activists, at café Ara in the centre of Istanbul's upmarket Beyoğlu district. Ara café is popular with Turkish artists and students, named after the famous Turkish photographer of Armenian descent, and owner of the café, Ara Güler. His black-and-white photos of old Istanbul decorate the walls of the establishment, while the old master was sitting opposite a friend of his in the centre of the crowded room. I spontaneously approached Ara Güler and shook his hand, asking 'Parev tsez, inchbes ek?': 'hello how are you' in Western Armenian. He answered me while shaking my hand: 'Ourish lezou ge khosis?'— do you speak another language?—and when I affirmed that I did he said 'then why don't you speak it?'

Why did Ara Güler ask me to speak 'another language'? Did the Armenian language evoke negative feelings, and thus he wanted to distance himself from the community, or was it interiorised fear of decades of anti-Armenian repression in Istanbul, in this haven of Turkish liberalism and multiculturalism, where speaking ones' language would be considered inappropriate?

I could not see them on the walls, I could not read them, but they were still there: 'Citizen, speak Turkish!' Those campaigns launched

133

by the Turkish state to finally subdue the minorities, to take away their language from them, to finally make them 'Turkish citizens'. Orhan Pamuk calls it 'cultural cleansing':

> The cosmopolitan Istanbul I knew as a child had disappeared by the time I reached adulthood. ... After the founding of the Republic and the violent rise of Turkification, after the state imposed sanctions on minorities—measures that some might describe as the final stage of the city's 'conquest' and others as ethnic cleansing—most of these languages disappeared. I witnessed this cultural cleansing as a child, for whenever anyone spoke Greek or Armenian too loudly in the street (you seldom heard Kurds advertising themselves in public during this period) someone would cry out, 'Citizen, please speak Turkish!' You saw signs everywhere saying the same thing.[1]

Zarakolu was late. He had just held a press conference in defence of Akram Aylisli, an Azerbaijani writer, who was renowned in his country and had once even enjoyed the title of 'People's Writer'. Aylisli had been a serving member of the Azerbaijani Milli Mejlis (parliament) between 2005 and 2010, but he now needed international support after his Russian-language novel *Daş Yuxular* (Stone Dreams) had appeared in a Russian periodical entitled *Druzhba Narodov* (Friendship of the Peoples). The novel revisits the final years of the Soviet Union and the period immediately following its collapse, and tells the story of two Azerbaijanis who try to save their Armenian neighbours and friends in the town of Sumgait, Azerbaijan, during the anti-Armenian pogroms of 1988. The novel was highly controversial in Azerbaijan because of its portrayal of the violence that was exercised against the Armenians in this period. As a result, the author was stripped of his official titles, including that of the 'People's Writer'; he also lost his state pension, and his son and his wife were sacked from their jobs. Demonstrations were organised in the streets of Baku and other towns calling for Aylisli to be stripped of his nationality. The leader of the pro-government Muasir Musavat (Modern Equality) party, Hafiz Haciyev, claimed that Aylisli had 'insulted the entire nation', and even went so far as to offer 10,000 Azerbaijani manat (the equivalent of 13,000 dollars) to anyone willing to dismember Aylisli's ear.[2]

In order to appreciate the pioneering work of Ragıp Zarakolu, it is important to understand the field of Turkish historiography. When the modern Turkish state was established, an official narrative was forced upon the population. This narrative aimed to ensure that history was only told from the perspective of the ruling authorities, with any alternative narratives, or even critical readings of the official version itself, being forcibly suppressed. In the words of Fatma Müge Göçek, this 'mythicised Turkish historiography valorised the Turkish achievements, whitewashed the crimes, blamed especially the minorities and the West for all past defeats, and silenced the violence committed against others. Between 1923 and 1975, this historiography went on to produce and reproduce itself without any interruption.'[3] The Turkish authorities employed a variety of measures in order to suppress any alternative versions of this official history, including a set of legal provisions that criminalised anyone who sought to question it or the role of Mustafa Kemal in Turkish history. One recent legal provision, for instance, Article 301 of the Turkish Penal Code, stipulates that anyone 'who publicly denigrates Turkishness, the Republic, or the Grand National Assembly of Turkey' can face a prison sentence ranging from six months to three years.[4] This and other legal instruments have been used extensively against those who have sought to shed light on the fate of the Armenians and other groups in the final years of the Ottoman Empire or their marginalisation and repression in the Turkish Republic.

* * *

I asked Ragıp Zarakolu when he had first come to learn about the Armenians and their fate during the First World War:

> From my childhood, because of the region of my family, I had an idea about what happened to the Armenians. My family is from Tokat, from the village of Niksar [Neo-Caesarea], a town that once had a significant Armenian population. I remember from family stories how the grandmother of my mother saved two Armenian girls from the deportations, who were later discovered by the state and taken away. We do not know what happened to them after that. We also did not believe the official history. I had one uncle

who was prisoner of war in Russia, and my mother's uncle was taken prisoner in Palestine by the British and taken into Egypt.[5]

He then added: 'My mother told me once that the Armenians were crying outside, and we were crying inside. We have a consciousness about what happened to the Armenians, although Turkey forgot about its past, just like a guilty criminal who wants to forget what happened.' Silence not only reigned in Turkey with regard to the Armenian Genocide, he said, but also the catastrophic mistakes committed by the Ottoman leadership during the First World War. As far as the Turkish authorities are concerned, the history of the republic begins in 1919 with Ataturk's arrival in Samsun, in which he is portrayed as a heroic, mythical figure who saved the country. 'They forgot all the mistakes, like the fact that it was Turkey who attacked Russia in 1914; it was again the Turks who attacked in Sarikamish, and were defeated. By the way, do you know that Enver Pasha thanked the Armenian soldiers after Sarikamish, because they saved him?'

Zarakolu's work in highlighting the plight of the Armenians began when he was employed as a journalist and human rights activist in the 1980s. He also worked in the publishing industry, running Belge publishing house. Zarakolu was drawn to this issue after the coup d'état of 1980, when thousands were arrested and many were executed or tortured. In the decade that followed, the central question in Turkey was the Kurdish issue, with violence erupting in the south-east:

> So, we started working on the roots of violence in Turkey, the historical basis of the Turkish state. We were facing violence in the Kurdish question, but we also recognized deeper roots of violence going back to the 1915, to the Armenian Genocide, and the roots of the deep state going back to the Teşkilât-ı Mahsusa [Special Organisation].

Zarakolu published five books written by the sociologist Ismail Beshikchi on the Kurdish question:

> When we started we were constantly harassed, until the state changed its laws and made publishing about the Kurds possible—although not without difficulties. Then, we decided to attack another taboo. When we started publishing about the Armenian Genocide in the 1990s, we understood the

issue was one of current affairs, and not just as a historic issue. At the time, we had the Balkan wars, the Genocide in Rwanda, the destruction of 4000 Kurdish villages and the deportation of 3.5 million people. Because of ASALA, there was intense anti-Armenian propaganda in Turkey.

Yet when Zarakolu published a Turkish edition of historian Yves Ternon's *Les Arméniens: histoire d'un genocide* in 1993 there was silence. Zarakolu also cooperated with *Agos* from 1996 onwards: 'There was a division of labour between us. They published our human rights information, and we published books on taboo subjects. It gave us a great opening. It is still a great opportunity for us, as we still have a major problem with the Turkish media. They continue to ignore our work.' In 1994, one year after the publication of Ternon's book, Belge published Vahakn Dadrian's *The History of the Armenian Genocide*. The book opened the door to discussions on the events of 1915. There was still an enormous gulf to cross, however, in making the topic the focus of a constructive, public discussion in Turkey.

It is interesting to compare, for example, the differences between Turkish intellectuals' responses to issues connected to the Kurdish question, and their responses to issues connected to the Armenian question. In 1995 Yaşar Kemal, a novelist of Kurdish origin, wrote against the violent campaign being waged against the Kurdish population. He was put on trial for his writings and sentenced to twenty months imprisonment for 'inciting hatred'.[6] When he was taken to court, some forty Turkish writers and intellectuals showed up to offer their support, and a broader campaign was launched by a number of Turkish intellectuals to defend him against the charges he was facing. Turkish intellectuals at the time were ready to express support to Kurds and acknowledge their victimisation, but they did not have the same standards towards the Armenians. When Belge faced a similar campaign from the state, the same intellectuals 'did not want to be associated with us, with our campaign, and the reason was that we published the Ternon book,' as Zarakolu put it. This illustrates how deep the anti-Armenian taboo was in Turkish society. 'The Turkish intellectual class only started speaking about it after the ninetieth commemoration of the Armenian Genocide.'

Throughout the 1990s, both public opinion and the Turkish intelligentsia were preoccupied with the Kurdish problem, and hence the issue of the Armenians was largely ignored in public discourse. It was only in the following decade that the Armenian question would begin to be discussed widely in the public arena:

> The state now stops saying the 'so-called' when referring to the Armenians, but refers to 1915 as 'events'. It means something did happen, but the question is what? They say: Armenians are also not angels, they also committed massacres. But they are playing with dates. Those massacres that they are referring to happened in 1917, when Armenians massacred Turks and Kurds. It was when the Russian army was withdrawing, and Armenian fighters did take their revenge. History remains taboo in Turkey … They do not explain in history books why the entire Ottoman army was concentrated in the east, in fighting the newly born Armenian state and conquering Baku, leaving its entire southern borders without defences in front of the British army.

I asked Zarakolu who, in his opinion, had played the most important roles in instigating a debate about the fate of the Ottoman Armenians nine decades later.

'Taner Akçam, he played an important role. His work with Vahakn Dadrian was a milestone.' Zarakolu views the cooperation between these two figures as symbolising the hopes and possibility of two people from the two nations engaging in a common endeavour. While Akçam is a leading Turkish scholar on the Ottoman Armenians, Dadrian, as we have seen, wrote a highly detailed work on the subject on the basis of Turkish sources, thereby enabling him to avoid accusations of bias from the Turkish authorities.

> Turkish denial of the Genocide is not just for legalistic matters, but has a social-psychological nature. Denial aims to hide the crime. It is the other side of the trauma: what happened? How did we do it? Even if it happened one hundred years ago it is still the story of our grandfathers, of our national heroes. Our national history, instead of being a heroic fight against imperialist attacks, becomes a war of occupation, of annihilation of a nation just like the annihilation of the American Indians.

Zarakolu has paid a high price for engaging in his work in the pursuit of truth and human rights. He was first arrested after the

1971 military coup, when he was working as a journalist for the left-leaning journal *Ant*. 'At that period I was arrested three times, and spent a total of two years in prison.' On the first occasion he was accused of having collaborated with Amnesty International and sentenced to five years imprisonment; in the following year he was arrested and imprisoned again, this time for publishing an article that was critical of the Vietnam War. He was released during the general amnesty of 1974. In 1982 Zarakolu was arrested once more while working for a newspaper, *Demokrat*, which had been ordered to cease publication following the 1980 military coup. The trial against Zarakolu lasted ten years; during this period he was unable to travel abroad and his passport was confiscated, only to be returned in 1991.

> My late wife was arrested in 1982 up to 1985 because of the Kurdish question. In 1994 and 1996 she was again arrested, this time for publishing on Armenian issues. On December 1994, there was a bomb attack against our offices, we lost all of our office material. It was the same day another bomb attack targeted the offices of a Kurdish paper *Ozgun Gunden*, in Ankara. The bomb attacks were organized by the same Susurluk group.

When Zarakolu was arrested again in October 2011, an international campaign was launched in order to demand that he be released.[7] A group of activists nominated him for the Nobel Peace Prize:

> The latest arrest was because I was doing a freedom of information campaign. My son is still arrested, he was giving a lecture to Peace and Democracy Party conference. There are now nine thousand political prisoners. It is like taking hostages. You see it is not easy to arrest guerrillas. They have guns, they are in the mountains.

Breaking the Taboo

Taner Akçam was invited to join the Hamburg Social Research Institute by sociology professor Hadi Ressesade. The two men first met when Akçam was studying Ressesade's course on the idea of 'progress', which examined how this idea had been conditioned by Western culture and especially by Marxism, and was not a universal concept. In the late 1980s, the Hamburg Institute launched a research programme on torture, and Ressesade, who was already researching torture in Iran (his country of origin), proposed that Akçam should do a similar study on the history of torture in Turkey. After learning of his research, the institute's director, Jan Philipp Reemtsma, who studied torture from a theoretical perspective, invited Akçam to join the research project.

Although Akçam had not done any research on torture before, he did have practical experience—he had been arrested in Turkey when engaged in activism as a twenty-year-old student. While he had been deprived of food and sleep, in addition to being subjected to physical assaults and threatened with death and physical torture during his imprisonment in a central Ankara prison, at the time he did not believe that this amounted to 'torture'.[8] 'If I would call that "torture" back in Turkey my friends would simply laugh at me.'

Yet when he began his research on torture in Turkey, Akçam was effectively starting a second life, one which would take him into uncharted territory.

Akçam recalls the librarian at the institute in the final years of his research, whose mother was an Armenian from Lebanon. The librarian had become fully assimilated into German society: 'But she had such an Armenian face, now that I think back.' She had only met the relatives of her mother on one occasion, when she visited Lebanon, yet she repeatedly asked Akçam to research the Armenian Genocide: 'You have to do something, this is such a controversial issue.' Akçam, however, wanted to avoid the subject because it was simply too complex; moreover, while he had read about the Hamidian massacres through his research on torture, he did not know a great deal about the events of 1915.

After he had completed his research, the institute launched a research project entitled 'Violence in the 20th Century', which primarily focused on the Holocaust. As part of this project, Akçam decided to work on a comparative study of German and Turkish nationalism, and one of his colleagues suggested that he should read Norbert Elias's *Studien über die Deutschen*. The book sought to locate the Holocaust within the broader context of German national history.

In 1991 Akçam planned to organise a workshop at the institute on the Istanbul Trials—the post-World War I court martials in which Turkish officials and the leadership of the CUP were tried for their wartime crimes. At that time Akçam was unable to read English, but he had seen an article on the subject by Vahakn Dadrian, and looking at the footnotes he saw that Dadrian had used a large number of primary Turkish sources and hence concluded the latter was able to read Turkish. Akçam consequently sought to invite Dadrian to attend the workshop. 'Mihran Dabag, who is from Diyarbakir and now lives in Bochum, gave me the address of Dadrian. I wrote to him. It is such a pity I did not keep his answer, the letter he wrote back. He was shocked. His answer started by something like: "This is the first time I am communicating with a Turk since I left Turkey."' A close friendship soon developed between the two men, with Dadrian becoming Akçam's mentor.

When Akçam organised the workshop there was almost no interaction between the Armenian and the Turkish community. The violence of 1915 had broken the links between the people who had previously lived on the same land; a wall of pain and ignorance separated them. 'Some Armenians who came to the workshop were very aggressive towards me.' The institute's director told him: 'Taner, you have to answer to your entire nation now.' Ultimately, however, the workshop ended in success: Vahakn Dadrian was enthusiastic and encouraged Akçam to engage in further research on the subject, as did Petra Kopert, the famous German Turkologist.

During his research on the history of torture in Turkey, Akçam came to learn of the anti-Armenian pogroms under Sultan Abdul Hamid II in 1894–6:

This was the first time I came to the subject of the Armenians, before that I did not know anything about it; it was not a subject for the Turkish left, who were suspicious of Armenians and ASALA, considering them instruments of Western imperialism. As I progressed in my readings of Abdul Hamid's massacres, I thought to myself: I know the history of the French Revolution, of Russia in 1917, of Chinese Communism, but I do not know Turkish history.

This sense of surprise at learning that they were ignorant with regard to the history of their own country is something many Turkish intellectuals have experienced. 'For me, this was like entering a no man's land,' Akçam recalled, 'it was so hard to believe what had happened, to recognise this mass killing.' Akçam went on to write his doctoral thesis on the mass killing of the Armenians, entitled 'Turkish Nationalism and the Armenian Genocide: On the Background of Military Tribunals in Istanbul between 1919 and 1922', which he successfully defended at Hanover University in 1995.

The first, and recurrent, problem Akçam faced concerned the use of the term 'genocide' in his work, and it took some time before he was able to bring himself to describe the events of 1915 in this way. He was far from alone in his hesitancy to do so—numerous Turkish intellectuals have gone through much soul-searching when confronting the deportations and massacres, as much of this history has been pushed to the margins of public and intellectual discussion, and many have consequently been reluctant to describe the fate of the Armenians as 'genocide' (or *soykirim* in Turkish). I asked Akçam why the term was so rarely used in the context of the Armenians:

> By using that term is like to be directly accused by the crime ... by qualifying it a genocide you become a member of a collective associated to a crime, not any crime but to the ultimate crime, of genocide.

> To use the Turkish term *soykirim* it took me a while. Then I wrote a whole page explaining why I was using that term. It is also a psychological issue, as using that term increases pressure on me. I had no problem using the German term—*Völker mörd*—but *soykirim* means race murder, and it was directly associated with Nazis and their Genocide, and we always thought we were not like the Nazis.

> ... When I was working on history of torture in Turkey, I came to realise how important history was and is in our everyday life. One of the conclusions I came to is that the Turkish left is nothing but an offspring of the Committee of Union and Progress. I was harshly attacked when I first published this idea, but now it is widely accepted in Turkey.

When the penal code was reformed in 1991, Akçam ceased to be targeted by the Turkish justice system and he was able to return to

Turkey without risking imprisonment. He returned in 1993, after an absence of sixteen years. In a second visit to Istanbul in 1995, a local NGO organised a public meeting with him to discuss his research, in which he would present his findings on the Armenian Genocide: 'Do you know how many people came?' he asked me:

> Less than twenty! And one of them was Hrant. It was simply a 'no' subject. People kept asking me: don't you have anything else to work on. The issue in Turkey was to convince people about how important history is. You don't need to explain that in Europe, in Germany or Switzerland for example. In France you might hear people say: 'we talk too much about history'. In Turkey you do not speak about history, and it is absolutely important to convince the Turkish public why history is important.

One of the ways in which he tried to do this was by linking the Armenian Genocide to the Kurdish question in his first published book, *The Armenian Question and Turkish National Identity* (1992). The book caused a major stir in the field of Turkish history. Prior to its appearance, a number of books by Vahakn Dadrian, Yves Ternon and others had discussed this issue and had been translated into Turkish through the efforts of Ragıp Zarakolu and his wife Ayse Nur Zarakolu. But Taner Akçam's work was the first attempt to deconstruct the Armenian Genocide by a Turkish author.

* * *

But who is Taner Akçam? What qualified him to become the first Turkish scholar to challenge the official Turkish narrative on the Armenian Genocide? What does his life story reveal about the Armenian Genocide and its place in contemporary Turkish society?

Taner Akçam is the son of Dursun Akçam, who was born to a poor peasant family in Olçek, in the Ardahan province of eastern Turkey. Dursun literally means 'it should stop'; his parents had lost three children to illness before he was born, and their next child was consequently called Durmush—meaning 'it has stopped'. Dursun Akçam was fortunate in that he was invited to enrol in the newly opened Village Institute, which sought to bring progress and Western modernity to the backward provinces of Turkey by educating the children of peasants before sending them back to the villages in which they had been born. When Dursun Akçam graduated and returned to his village as a teacher, he was committed to the secular ideology of Kemalism and a belief in progress, according to which the poverty and backwardness of the Turkish peasantry was attributable to 'superstition' (i.e. Islam). Those who had been educated in this way described themselves as '*ileriçi*', or 'progressists'.

This generation strongly identified with the state and the military. Over time, however, the *ileriçi* gradually began to embrace socialist and Marxist ideas on progress. Dursun Akçam became a trade union activist and eventually rose through the ranks to become the vice-president of the Turkish teachers' union. All his friends were members of the Turkish Social-Democratic Party, and they would often hold heated political debates when they visited his house in Ankara. Although Dursun Akçam was not a member of the party, his ideas and beliefs were very similar to those which it promoted—he even went on one of the party's visits to the Soviet Union, returning with books by Marx and Lenin, red posters and other Soviet propaganda material.

In 1971 Dursun Akçam was arrested and imprisoned for six months for his role in preparing an abortive left-wing coup on 9 March 1971. After this effort to overthrow the government had failed, there was a military coup and arrests of leftist activists and trade union members began three days later. Taner Akçam recalls how his father burnt all of his Marxist–Leninist paraphernalia in the wood oven: 'My father was restless for several months, all his friends were arrested but not him, not until June 1971.' Unlike the rank-and-file trade unionists, who were tortured while in police custody, Dursun Akçam and other trade union leaders were treated well by the authorities and were soon released.

Taner Akçam's early life was consequently spent in a context where politics was frequently discussed, with his formative years taken up by debates on armed struggle in the fight against fascism and US imperialism, among other issues. 'Some parents try to keep their children away from politics, from commitment and associated dangers. But my father encouraged me. He gave me arguments to confront nationalist teachers at school.' As a teenager, one of his icons was Deniz Gezmiş, whom Taner Akçam describes as 'our Che Guevara'. Gezmiş had been active as a militant student of the 1968 generation, and after becoming radicalised he went on to found the People's Liberation Army of Turkey (THKO). The organisation was involved in radical student circles and in demonstrations against US influence over Turkey, where members would clash with right-wing students and the police. Like many Turkish and other Middle Eastern activists of his generation, Gezmiş was heavily influenced by the Latin American guerrilla movements as well as the experience of the Palestinians. In 1969 Gezmiş was able to escape the surveillance of the Turkish authorities and travelled to Jordan, where he attended a training camp run by the Democratic Front for the Liberation of Palestine (DFLP). After he returned to Turkey, Gezmiş took part in a number of armed attacks and kidnappings, including the kidnapping of US military personnel, and was eventually arrested before being executed in 1972. When he was a university student Taner Akçam met a number of individuals who had collaborated with Gezmiş, including Mahir Çayan, who was one of the founders of the People's Salvation Party and Front of Turkey (Türkiye Halk Kurtuluş Partisi ve Cephesi, THKP—C). Mahir Çayan later became one of the student movements' leaders following the arrest or imprisonment of the earlier generation of activists.

The military coup of 1971 had severe consequences for those on the Turkish left. Yet the coup did not put an end to leftist activism, nor to the almost continuous clashes between those on the left and those belonging to nationalist, state-sponsored right-wing groups.

A few years later, student activism started again. University circles were formed that were inspired by the struggle of the previous generation in their fight against fascism and efforts to bring about a progressive left-wing revolution. These groups also had more immediate demands, such as the democratisation of higher education, which was seen as 'part of a greater revolution in Turkey, which would change power relations'.[9]

In 1975 Taner Akçam was a twenty-two-year-old student at the Middle East Technical University (METU), and was already working as a teaching assistant. His dream was to go abroad to continue his education. One night he was attending a meeting with seven or eight people who had met to discuss the newly established fortnightly journal, *Devrimci Gençlik* (Revolutionary Youth). During the meeting, those who were in attendance discussed who should serve as the journal's editor-in-chief, yet no one seemed willing to assume the role. Taner Akçam ultimately agreed to take up the position, and from that moment on he was pushed into the spotlight of Turkish political activism.

On 10 March 1976 Taner Akçam was arrested for the fifth time, and the second since becoming the journal's editor-in-chief. The arrest was made in response to his work in *Devrimci Gençlik*, which discussed the class struggle and the Kurdish issue—both of which were strictly off-limits for public or intellectual discussion.

Up to this point, Akçam had viewed being arrested and imprisoned as almost akin to taking a holiday, a break from the stresses of operating underground and trying to avoid arrest or being killed by right-wing militants or the police. Prisons were like 'universities', he says, where he and his friends had time to rest, to sleep and to read. The Ankara central prison, where he and his colleagues were incarcerated, was a former stable, with large rooms housing fifty to 100 prisoners at a given time, all of whom were political prisoners. The prison also had a large library, which contained some Marxist literature.

On this occasion, however, Akçam's imprisonment was far from being a short escape from the travails of left-wing activism. A prosecutor, whom Taner describes as 'crazy', took over responsibility for his case: 'As I was giving my statement, he physically attacked me across the table, and while shouting at me spittle flew out of his mouth.' Akçam was accused of promoting communism and of having spread Kurdish propaganda, and the prosecutor requested that he be sentenced to 750 years in jail: 'I became famous as a result.' Following an international campaign launched by Amnesty International to highlight his plight, the judge eventually sentenced him to eight years, nine months and twenty days of imprisonment. This was to be followed by a further three years in exile.[10]

Akçam would later write how his early days in prison were spent preoccupied with planning how to escape. A group started digging a tunnel; their cell was only 5 metres away from another building where the prison workshops were located, and that building had windows overlooking the outside wall from where it would possible to make a jump for freedom. After some hesitation, Akçam eventually agreed to join the group. On 12 March 1977 Taner Akçam, along with six other prisoners, managed to jump from the windows of the building. Before escaping, the group had written the words of the famous poet Nazim Hikmet, 'That wall, your wall, means nothing to us', on the walls of the carpentry workshop. Akçam was the last to jump; the guards captured the seventh member of the group, while Zäki Sherif, a member of TIKKO (Türkiye İşci ve Köylü Kurtuluş Ordusu—The Workers' and Peasants' Liberation Army of Turkey) who had organised the escape, was later killed in Izmir.

Akçam spent the next seven months in hiding in Ankara. He was constantly changing apartments, going from one student house to the other. He could not sleep at night, fearing police would break in to arrest him. Then came the decision to escape into exile, to seek refuge in Germany. A friend from Aintab, a town in southern Turkey bordering Syria, could arrange border crossings. He gave Akçam a false passport with the name 'Mehmet Ali Tekinbay'. From Aleppo Akçam took the first plane to Munich, and to what he thought would be his freedom.

However, once he arrived in West Germany, Akçam was treated as an illegal immigrant and arrested. He refused to reveal his true identity because he was scared that the German police would hand him over to the Turkish authorities, having heard about the close security collaboration between the two states. He was held in a prison in Munich for ten weeks on charges of 'trying to enter Germany through illegal means', before receiving a surprising visit from German lawyer Roswitha Wolf on 23 December 1977, who promised Akçam that she would get him released. 'Your father is here, and he says hello,' she added. He was soon released from prison and received political asylum in Germany.

On 12 September 1980, another military coup took place in Turkey, the consequences of which were even more severe for those on the left than those that followed the coup of 1971. General Kenan Evren, the head of the military General Staff, sought to put an end to left-wing activism once and for all as radical leftist ideologies and activists were gaining increasing influence among local communities and had even taken control of a number of municipalities. During this period, there was an atmosphere of terror in Turkey as right-wing organisations such as the Grey Wolves attacked left-wing militants, student movements and trade-union activists and intellectuals. Over 5,000 people were killed as a result, generating political instability and threatening to drag the country into civil war. Those involved in the coup were consequently able to portray themselves as saviours of the nation.

The coup was followed by a wave of repression in which more than 650,000 people were detained; fifty people were executed, while hundreds of others died as a result of the torture they experienced in prison, including many of Taner Akçam's friends:

> So, I came out of the German prison and became active in the solidarity movement with Turkey, with Amnesty International, with Devrimci Yol [an underground political organisation founded in 1977 by a group of university students in Turkey influenced by Maoism and the earlier generation of Turkish revolutionaries like Deniz Gezmis and Mahir Çayan]. After the 1980 coup all my friends were arrested and tortured. I was the only one left out of prison from the founding generation of Devrimci Yol.

Akçam started to be contacted by individuals from a range of disparate organisations, all of whom were looking towards him as a source of guidance. He was the natural leader of the Turkish left during this period as he was still in exile and hence beyond the reach of the Turkish authorities. Akçam worked to save his friends who were now in hiding in Turkey by arranging for them to escape to Syria. He was also involved in organising a solidarity movement in Europe that sought to expose the violence inflicted on political prisoners in Turkey.

Akçam left Germany and travelled to Syria, where he began to organise resistance to the Turkish military. However, as he had been away from Turkey for so long, he sought the advice of his comrades who had escaped to Syria from Turkey, or who had taken up arms in the mountains, with regard to the best way in which to conduct the resistance. Their answer was to create a political party prior to forming alliances with others as part of a broad, national front, and to engage in armed struggle. It was on the basis of this advice that he launched the United Resistance Front Against Fascism.

While he was in Syria, Akçam was in close contact with Abdullah Öcalan, or 'Apo', the founder of the Kurdistan Workers' Party (PKK). Akçam had first met Öcalan during his years as a student in Ankara, when both men had been active in leftist circles. Akçam remembers Öcalan as 'a timid person'. The two had similar ideological beliefs, having read classical Marxist texts, and both admired figures from the earlier generation of militants, such as Mahir Çayan. Öcalan later wrote to Akçam saying that 'Mahir Çayan's ideas can best be put in practice in Kurdistan. Let's give up on these big cities and go to Kurdistan and organise an armed struggle.'[11]

To fund their militant activities in Syria, Akçam and his group relied heavily on Turkish immigrant workers in Germany. Some of the workers who sympathised with Akçam's Devrimci Yol movement gave one month's earnings a year to the organisation, amounting to some 300,000 German Marks annually. A second source of funding came from Palestinian organisations based in Lebanon. In this period, both Devrimci Yol and the PKK were closely associated with one of the Palestinian groups. Akçam received a Fatah identification card, while the Democratic Front for the Liberation of Palestine (DFLP) sponsored the PKK. Akçam remembers meeting with Abu Ayad, Fatah's number two, but he was left distinctly unimpressed by the PLO, which he later described as 'a decadent movement, relying on hired fighters from the outside, and having lost the revolutionary dynamism'.

Akçam claims that he first encountered the Armenian question in Lebanon in 1982, when he was a political activist and the leader of Devrimci Yol:

> I do not remember myself, but this is what I have been told by a PKK
> member who was accompanying me during my visit to Beirut. Abdullah

149

Öcalan told me that they had links with ASALA, then jokingly added: 'The problem is that we claim the same territory, and I don't know how to resolve it.' Then, in 1982 I went to Beirut for political contacts, and a PKK representative who served as a local guide to me asked to introduce me to ASALA. He later told me that my reaction was violent, I cursed him and told [him]: 'don't you ever mention that name again to me.' You see, we considered ourselves fighting against imperialist powers, against the imperialist partition of the Middle East. Armenians, Greeks, they were imperialist instruments of partition. May be there were some killings from both sides, but that was the past. We saw ourselves as the second generation of national liberation movement, the first being the Kemalist movement that did not accomplish the national democratic revolution to the end. In this narrative Armenians were traitors, and we argued to forget it, we had more serious issues to address. Plus, we in the Turkish left believed that ASALA was a product of the French secret services.

Taner Akçam recalls another adventure: a day before the Israeli invasion of Lebanon started in 1982, Akçam travelled from Beirut to Damascus with Abdullah Öcalan. The three month long invasion changed the geopolitics of the Middle East. The PLO guerrillas were defeated and went into exile, and now the Turkish militants who had found safe haven in Lebanon had to seek protection in Syria. There, security officers of the notorious *mukhabarat* (intelligence) wanted to bring Turkish exiles under their protection, in order to control and use them for their own purposes. They asked Akçam whether his group was ready to launch attacks inside Turkey. 'We did not want to be a pawn in the hand of one government fighting another,' Akçam said. 'We discussed this with Apo [Öcalan] and he said he had no problem with that.' He was thinking strategically and the end result is that he succeeded in building his organisation. Apo had already started building his network at the time. 'In 1982 Apo went to Iraq and met with Barzani. After the meeting he came back very excited, saying "the history of the Kurds will change." He had received permission to settle in northern Iraq.' Apo was building his army, and his choice of Kurdistan as his cause finally became more sustainable than the choice of Turkish Leftist militants who chose to wage urban guerrilla warfare against the Turkish military.

After spending a year in the Middle East, travelling between Syria and Lebanon and trying to regroup his supporters, Akçam arrived at the conclusion that any armed struggle against the Turkish military and authorities would be utterly futile. Those on the left who arrived in Syria were blind to the true reality of the situation; the population did not want any more violence or instability, and in any case, there was almost no prospect that those on the left would be able to bring about the downfall of the military regime. Years later Akçam would describe his organisation as 'our romantic and childish movement'.

As Akçam put it, 'armed-struggle was a stupid idea ... fighting the Turkish army, with remnants of a former leftist movement! As time passed I came to the conclusion that armed struggle was an adventure. We did not have the structure for it. We did not have the necessary popular support!'

The movement was plagued by factionalism. For those militants who escaped Turkey and were now living in Europe, democracy was no longer something to be fulfilled after creating a socialist system, but a reality they were living in Germany in exile. In Akçam's words, during this period:

> I was revising my thoughts towards the relationship between socialism and democracy ... Back then, for us, democracy was something to come after we took power. Then, I started thinking that we had to exercise democracy here and now. It was the influence of Rosa Luxemburg and her criticism of Lenin. Our culture was Stalinist—we called it of course Marxist–Leninist—and opposed any debate about democracy.

The debate that subsequently emerged with regard to democracy and the party structure served to divide the movement between those who maintained that a strict hierarchy and internal discipline was necessary for the armed struggle against the Turkish authorities and those who arrived at the view that the military struggle was futile—for the latter, it would be far better to fight the military dictatorship on the grounds of human rights and political freedoms.

Taner Akçam was among those who held the second of these interpretations, and he finally decided to dissolve the movement. There are still people today, he told me, who have never forgiven him for doing so: 'For them, it was like abandoning the struggle. It was like treason. They called me "fifth column" or "agent of German imperialism".'

According to Akçam, the realisation that led him to disband the movement came about due to the different ideas he and others were exposed to after leaving Turkey. In the 1970s, the ideas of the Turkish left were heavily informed by Turkish translations of Lenin and Stalin's work, as well as literature dedicated to interpreting Marxist–Leninist ideology more broadly. Yet when he arrived in Germany, he found that these same ideas had also been subject to critiques by prominent social-democratic thinkers such as Rosa Luxembourg and Karl Kautsky. 'Basically, the idea of democracy was introduced to me by the German left.'

This shift in the dominant ideology of the Turkish intellectuals in exile had important consequences with regard to the question of the Armenian Genocide. As they began to be exposed to a wider range of ideas, the exiled Turkish intellectuals started to learn about the history of the Armenians' fate, a process that was accelerated by advances in communication technologies.

In 1983 Akçam returned to Germany from Syria, having abandoned the armed struggle and leaving many members of the resistance demoralised. When he returned to Germany, Akçam and his colleagues were also parting ways with the PKK, which had already decided to launch a guerrilla war to liberate Kurdistan: 'Since the PKK was organising a long-term armed struggle, Öcalan interpreted my taking a step "back" as betrayal.'

The PKK had been known for its aggressive methods even before the military coup of 1980, including the use of violence against other leftist movements and especially against rival Kurdish organisations. During their common exile in Syria, the two sides discussed past practices and agreed to uphold the values of democracy and freedom, both within the organisations themselves and as part of their future goals.

Despite making this agreement, in practice the PKK remained a rigid structure that was hostile to any plurality in opinions. In 1983 the PKK launched an internal purge, often targeting those militants who were close to or had contacts with members of Devrimci Yol.

After arrests within the PKK, Akçam wrote a letter to Öcalan in which he threatened to cease collaborating with the PKK and to go public about their difference unless the arrested militants were immediately released.

By this stage, Akçam's threats did not carry much weight given the internally divided nature of Devrimci Yol, and the arrests consequently continued, with many militants being taken to northern Iraq where they were imprisoned and even tortured. Those arrested included the PKK's representative in Europe, Cetin Yetkin, known as 'Semir'. Semir was going through a similar evolution to Taner Akçam and wanted to discuss democracy within the PKK. He was arrested in Cologne, but managed to escape and went to Hamburg and contacted Akçam to ask for help. With the support of various German organisations, Semir was sent to Sweden where he was granted asylum, but in 1985 he was assassinated by a member of the PKK in Stockholm. This wave of violence against members of the PKK subsequently expanded to target former militants from Devrimci Yol, such as Kürsat Timuroglu, an old friend of Akçam.

All of this took a heavy toll on Akçam; he was not only tired of hiding from the Turkish authorities and now the PKK but also of being a leader. It was at this stage that he decided to abandon his life as a militant; after working on various journalism assignments he decided to move to Hamburg where he enrolled in the university's Department of Turkology and took additional courses in sociology and philosophy. He had many questions to answer, numerous accounts to settle. Politically, he began to struggle for the rights of Turkish migrant workers inside Germany, within the reality of German politics.

During this period, Akçam came to a much broader and profound conclusion: as he began to research the history of the Ottoman Armenians, he realised that the Turkish left was merely a continuation of the Young Turks and the Kemalists, albeit in slightly different clothing. It was only by confronting history that Turkey would be able break free of its nationalist past.

Akçam viewed his scholarship as a way to change Armenian–Turkish relations. As he wrote in 2001, by understanding the way the Ottoman

Armenians had been treated he would gain a greater understanding of the obstacles to democracy and human rights in modern-day Turkey.[12] In other words, it would be impossible to reform Turkey without confronting the Turkish Republic's original sin with regard to the Armenians and other Christian minorities in the Ottoman Empire.

He quickly recognised the importance of academia as a channel through which dialogue could be promoted between Turkey and Armenia. In 1995 he went to Yerevan to take part in an international conference on the problems of genocide, where he listened to a speech by Greg Sarkissian, the president of the Zoryan Institute, which was addressed 'to the people of Turkey, to ask them to remember that though, at one time, the state was led by mass murderers, they also had their Haji Halils [who saved Sarkissian's grandmother and her family after the grandfather was executed].'[13] In the following year, Akçam returned to Yerevan in the company of Gürbüz Çapan, the mayor of Esenyurt municipality in the suburbs of Istanbul, and both men laid a wreath at the Dzidzernagapert Monument dedicated to the victims of the Armenian Genocide.

Akçam's work had a significant impact inside Turkey because it was published in Turkish and clearly posed a direct challenge to the official narrative promoted by the Turkish state and its collaborators in academia. After 2000, when Akçam moved to the United States, his work was increasingly published in English and he became known and highly regarded within US academic circles. In 2006, Akçam published his most important book to date: *A Shameful Act: The Armenian Genocide and the Question of Turkish Responsibility*.[14]

In the book, Akçam seeks to explain why the Ottomans failed to integrate the various ethnic and religious subjects that composed the empire into Ottoman society. He argues that this is largely attributable to the nature of the Ottoman system itself, where the religious rights of the Ottoman communities were upheld, but in which there were barriers in terms of national belonging, legal equality or the civic identity of its population. Akçam argues that the fate of the Ottoman Armenians at the hands of the Young Turks was not due to their having joined the Russian armies during the First World War—no more than 4,000 Armenian volunteers enlisted in the Russian imperial army. Instead, the deportations and massacres took place because the Ottoman authorities were concerned that yet another Christian land, in the historic heartland of Ottoman rule in Eastern Anatolia, would be lost. Between 1878 and the end of the First World War, the Ottoman Empire had lost 80 per cent of its territory and 75 per cent of its population. After incurring further territorial losses in 1912–13, the CUP's leadership came to the conclusion that the presence of Christian minorities within the empire posed a danger that needed to be eradicated. In February 1914, a few months before the start of the Great War, the European powers had succeeded in imposing two commissioners on the Ottomans who were to supervise the implementation of reforms in the six eastern Armenian vilayets (provinces). Although this plan was never carried out in practice, it raised the Ottoman authorities' fears of Western intervention and of losing yet more territory. It was in order to avoid this outcome that the Ottoman Empire decided to eliminate the entire Armenian population of the empire. Moreover, while many Armenians were initially able to escape this fate by converting to Islam, this ceased to be an effective strategy as the total number of converts increased to such an extent that the Ittihadist leadership was no longer able to keep track of the numbers involved. Given the fact that many members of the new administration under the Turkish Republic were personally responsible for the deportations and massacres, it was in their interest to erect a wall of silence with regard to the issue.

Akçam's most recent publication, *The Young Turks' Crime against Humanity*, takes these arguments even further.[15] In this book, Akçam evaluates the demographic policies adopted by the CUP in the period following the First Balkan War and the genocide. According to Akçam, the policies implemented with regard to the Armenians were part of a broader strategy of eliminating populations that the authorities considered disloyal, which largely entailed actions being taken against the empire's Christian minorities. This strategy involved population exchanges, deportations and/or outright massacres, and the replacement of the previous inhabitants with Muslim refugees from the Balkans following the Balkan Wars of 1912–13, thereby creating a Turkified population in Anatolia. This policy began to be implemented prior to the First World War, with the expulsion of around 300,000 Greeks from the Aegean region in 1913–14.[16] The Greek deportations became a blueprint in the expulsion of the Ottoman Armenians in the period between 1915 and 1917, with many of the CUP figures involved in this deportation later being assigned responsibility for eliminating the Armenians. Yet there were clearly differences in the policies pursued with regard to the different Christian minorities: while the Greeks were forcibly deported, the 'Armenians were targeted for outright annihilation'.[17]

Taner Akçam's work on these subjects brought him to the attention of the authorities. He was on the hit list that the Ergenekon conspirators had prepared, the same shadowy Deep State that had assassinated Hrant Dink. He was also subject to an internet campaign launched by 'Holdwater', the webmaster of a website—'Tall Armenian Tale'—that sought to deny the crimes of the Ottoman authorities, and which launched vitriolic attacks against scholars and public figures who dared to challenge the official Turkish narrative on the extermination of the Armenians. This campaign continued for three years, with Akçam being called a 'terrorist' on YouTube and Wikipedia. In February 2007, while travelling to Canada, Akçam was detained on the basis of the false allegations Holdwater had levelled against him. When Akçam ultimately revealed Holdwater's true identity, he instead became subject to a more conventional smear campaign in the Turkish media.[18]

'Some idiots send me death threats now', he told me, referring to some reactions he has encountered to his research on the Armenian Genocide. Those people threatening him seem to ignore Taner's past. And he has one. Referring to his youth in Ankara, he said: 'Doing politics in Turkey meant two things: one, you could be arrested any time. Two, you could be killed anytime. So back in the 1970s I came to accept the idea that being killed was a possible price of political activism. And this is why I could work on the Armenian Genocide.'

A REVOLUTIONARY ACT

An Intellectual Journey

In December 2012 I was passing through Istanbul when I contacted the writer and journalist Hasan Cemal, whom I planned to interview in order to learn of any recent developments in Turkish politics with regard to the Kurdish issue. I also wanted to learn more about his latest book. Cemal responded immediately, saying that he would be willing to meet me in the office of the newspaper, *Milliyet*.[19] 'But I tell you, for the moment I don't speak on my last book. OK?'

The offices of *Milliyet*, a major Turkish daily newspaper, are situated in the Şişli neighbourhood, just next to the Florence Nightingale Hospital. Hasan Cemal is a highly influential journalist and writer— his op-ed pieces were published six times per week, and he has written ten books on issues ranging from the Kurdish question to the military coups in Turkey. He is also the grandson of Ahmet Cemal Pasha, one of the members of the triumvirate of the CUP which ruled the Ottoman Empire from 1908 until the end of the First World War, and is therefore one of the key persons responsible for the genocide.

When Cemal arrived, we started our discussion by introducing ourselves to each other, as this was the first time we had met. Cemal was unaware that I was Armenian, and when he learned this our discussion became dominated by the subject of the Armenians, the genocide and his latest book. He took a copy from a shelf, signed it and passed it to me. The book, entitled *1915: Ermeni Soykirim* (1915: Armenian Genocide), contains an image on the cover showing the author at the Dzidzernagapert Memorial Monument in Yerevan, placing four white carnations to commemorate the victims.

'This is the first signature I place on my book, after those for my wife and my daughter,' he told me.

> Initially, I did not want to sign this book. It is a sad story. But people do not understand my act; they expect me to sign it, and each time I have to explain myself. The title of this book is hard, but I paid attention not to write a book that divides. I decided not to talk about the book, not to give interviews for now.

Hasan Cemal soon began to tell me about the intellectual journey that had led him to the title of his tenth book, and how, when writing about the subject in an article in 1985, he had described the events of 1915 as 'reciprocal massacres' before coming to recognise the massacres as the 'Armenian Genocide' in a talk he gave at UCLA in 2011.[20]

'The first time I talked about the 1915 genocide was in 2008, after I visited the genocide memorial in Yerevan, and after I wrote an article about it. But I did not publish that photography', he said, pointing to the picture on the cover of the book:

> I also met the grandson of a member of the gang who killed my grandfather in Tbilisi[21]—we met in Yerevan I mean. Then there was the Harvard Humanitarian Initiative, which is run by Pamela Steiner who is the granddaughter of Ambassador Henry Morgenthau, which took place in 2009, Taner was there too, it was an interesting meeting, yet I did not utter the word 'genocide'. Then I gave a lecture in Watertown, after which Richard Hovannisian invited me to give a lecture at UCLA. This was on March 31, 2011, and there I said 'I came here to share your grief', and it was then that I used the word genocide.

In the speech, Hasan Cemal stated:

> I came here to open my heart, and to open my mind to you, and be sincere this evening, not to pretend, not act, and I will try to talk from my heart as I learnt from my dear friend Hrant Dink. I shall tell you about the change that I have undergone during the years on the subject of 1915. That will give you the clues about the changes that Turkey started undergoing as well. I came here to tell you I know about your pain, your grief of genocide, your grief of Medz Yeghern. I understand that grief very well, I feel it and I share it.[22]

Cemal recalled delivering the speech and the process that led him to do so: 'It was a personal, intellectual journey which brought me to that point. It started with what I learned from my family stories, what I learned from school, and what I experienced through my profession. And then there was the assassination of Hrant Dink.'

I then asked him why Turkey needed to go back to those events.

'You cannot supress the memory. Armenians will not forget. Turks start asking questions. Then there is the alternative history with Taner Akçam. ASALA's acts brought the 1915 question on surface as well. Official historiography tried to keep Turks in darkness.' But this had ultimately failed.

Then there was the death of Hrant Dink, which had shocked everyone:

> Hrant was very sincere. He believed in democracy in a real sense. He used to defend the viewpoint that in the process of democratisation Turkey will be forced to face the past, and he sincerely wanted to contribute to the democratisation process. Still, he was very careful not to instigate polarisation in Turkish society.

We moved on to discuss the question of the Armenian diaspora. Cemal said that the diaspora did not understand Dink's approach, and that Dink was effectively struggling against the diaspora. However, I intervened at this point, having met Dink on a number of occasions, including conferences attended by members of the diaspora, where he was always given a warm welcome. The main difference between Dink and the diaspora was the former's insistence that real change could only come from within Turkish society rather than from outside Turkey. Although this approach was opposed by many within the diaspora, he was still a highly respected figure.

According to Cemal:

> The Armenian Diaspora considers Turkey as a curse. They did not create channels of contact and dialogue. This happened only after the death of Hrant Dink, only then did they start to follow the intellectual debate inside Turkey. But Turkey is changing, and the most important thing is to open the [Armenia–Turkey] border, Turkey has to take steps towards normalisation [of relations with Armenia].

'Hrants' death was a dramatic turning point, we started re-learning our history, we were living in a lie. Turkish official historiography was dictating on us to live in falsehood':

> Nobody is going to bury their grief, but the important thing is not to become captive of this past, otherwise you cannot normalise the present. It is an ugly page of history whether you call it *tehjir* [deportations], crime against humanity, genocide or massacre. You first have to accept that it is a very ugly page of history. Without facing this ugly past you cannot become mature. You cannot have peace. You cannot have democracy. In Turkey, dealing with history means to deal with today's reality.

I then asked him what he had learned as a child about his grand-father, Cemal Pasha, and whether he was aware during his early years of the fate of the Armenians:

> What I remember in the family was very much official clichés: that because of wartime conditions there was *tehjir*, that it was war, cold weather, there were diseases, and plus crimes were committed on the way. Camal Pasha was not a topic at home. My father was the oldest son born in the year 1900, but my father spent very limited time with his father, as Camal Pasha was very often away.

Cemal's tenth book was a best-seller, occupying the most promi-nent place at kiosks at Atatürk airport, Istanbul's window to the world.[23] Upon its publication, the usual claims and slander were also targeted at Cemal, who was described as being in the pocket of the Armenian 'lobby'. But this had little effect—unlike Taner Akçam, Cemal occupied a central place in the Turkish intellectual elite.

> If I had written that book only few years back I would have been brought to court. Turkey is changing but not without a price. And it was Hrant who paid that price… Armenians, like Greeks, Jews, Kurds, they do not want to share their grief with everyone, they want to keep it to themselves. It could be a kind of existential meaning, and probably they do not want to lose it.

He then told me about an incident during a lecture he was giving in Watertown, in the United States, to an Armenian diaspora audi-ence—one of the men in attendance said that his son had refused to come because he 'did not want to shake hands' with a Turk.

Cemal told me that he started to feel sympathy for the fate of the Armenians during the 1980s as a result of ASALA's activities, but that 'the real turning point for Turkey was the death of Hrant Dink. Then the work of Taner Akçam was very important, he started a debate for the first time as an academician. In 1992 he wrote his first book, at the time the word "G" was a taboo, and remained so for years. Taner Akçam was a pioneer, that is a fact.'

'I wrote an article in *Milliyet* saying: Taner Akçam opened the lock of my mind, and Hrant Dink opened the lock of my heart.'

7

RE-AWAKENING

THE STRUGGLE FOR MEMORY AND DEMOCRACY

Taner Akçam returned to Turkey in 1993 with the aim of engaging in research on the way that the Ottoman Armenians are remembered in Turkey, and how what had been a multinational, multi-ethnic empire came to be a nation state that marginalised any ethnicity or nationality that was not Turkish in the space of a generation. He intended to research the period between 1876 and 1925, or the years between Abdul Hamid II's ascension to power and the demise of the Ottoman Empire.[1]

In Istanbul, Akçam held a meeting with the director of Tarih Vakfı (the History Foundation), Orhan Silier, who was very enthusiastic about the proposed project. After being given a tour of the institute and introduced to its researchers, Akçam was given a workspace to conduct his research. The only obstacle in his way was the need to receive approval from the foundation's Board of Directors, though Silier reassured him that this was a mere formality. But this proved to be far from the case, as the members of the Board ultimately refused to approve the project. One of the Board's members later stated that he had been concerned by the use of European money to finance the study (the project was to be funded by the Hamburg Institute of Social

Studies) in view of the PKK armed struggle in the south-east of the country—he was concerned that the European powers were once again trying to revive and empower the Christian minorities with the aim of weakening and dividing modern-day Turkey.

Following the rejection from the History Foundation, in 1994 Akçam was invited to the Istanbul School of International Studies (later re-named the Istanbul Bilgi University), which had just been established. The university's founders suggested that he would be able to establish his proposed documentation centre in this newly estab-lished private university as part of a research centre attached to the sociology department that would research issues related to the Ottoman period, including culture, identity, ethnicity and violence. The conditions attached to the funding Akçam had received stipu-lated that he had to launch his project by October 1996 at the latest, and it again needed the approval of the university's Board of Trustees. However, as had been the case in the History Foundation, the Board ultimately failed to give its approval. Akçam was particularly sur-prised by their decision as he had already spoken to each of the board members individually, all of whom had told him that they supported the project. He could not avoid the conclusion that the problem, once again, was that they did not want to be involved in stirring up the ever-sensitive issue of the Armenians:

> I had learned something from my experience with both Bilgi and the History Foundation. This academic world in Istanbul, which liked to char-acterize itself as 'progressive, leftist, and democratic' didn't want me or my project, and the reason for this was the Armenian Genocide. A colleague of mine from Bilgi University succinctly summed up the problem for me: 'The Turkish academic world views any endeavour associated with the Armenian question as a risky proposition. There's no place in Turkish academia for a person who wants to take up this question in an objective manner. That is the essence of the matter.'[2]

Things Falling Apart

The reigning taboo with regard to discussing the Armenians that Akçam encountered upon his return to Turkey was enforced through a series of mechanisms. He soon discovered that many of the academics he had contacted to discuss his research project had received letters accusing Akçam of being a traitor to the Turkish nation. He first learned about these letters from Gürbüz Çapan, the mayor of Esenyurt, who was an old friend, having made a trip together to Armenia in 1995 when both men made a widely publicised visit to the Dzidzernagapert Monument. In February 1996, Çapan called Akçam and read him a letter he had intercepted by accident, with the title: 'Who is Taner Akçam?' The letter was replete with accusations against both men, who were deemed traitors to Turkey. Çapan later learned that the letter had been sent by a group of police officers in Istanbul who were associated with the Nationalist Action Party (Milliyetçi Hareket Partisi, MHP).

Another letter, sent to a professor from the Bilgi University with whom Akçam had discussed his proposed documentation centre and research project, contained veiled threats warning him to avoid becoming involved in the project. This letter went further than the previous one by not only accusing Akçam of being 'an enemy of the Turks, purchased with Armenian money' but also calling him a convert to Islam (*dönme*) 'who was descended from an Armenian orphan who had been brought into [Akçam's] grandfather's harem'.[3] Akçam ultimately decided to return to self-imposed exile in Germany; it was too early to challenge the Armenian taboo within Turkey. Akçam would later discover that the authorities had assembled an entire file on him, containing articles from German and Swiss newspapers and transcripts of his lectures in Europe, as well as articles he had published in Turkish journals and general documentation relating to his activities. The file was most likely put together by a specialised 'Armenia desk' within one of the state departments.

In 1996, however, a turning point came. On 3 November a black Mercedes-Benz travelling at 180 kilometres per hour crashed into a truck, some 140 kilometres southwest of Istanbul, killing three of its four passengers. Medical and police units that rushed to the scene discovered in the car the lifeless body of Abdullah Çatlı—a notorious drug trafficker and a contract killer, who had been arrested in France for heroin trafficking and was on Interpol's list, having later escaped from a Swiss prison. He had been wanted by the Turkish police since 1978. Next to him was Huseyin Kocadağ, the deputy chief of Istanbul police, who had been driving the car. Kocadağ had been instrumental in setting up the special units of the police force. Çatlı's girlfriend, Gonca Us, a former beauty queen, also died in the accident. A fourth person was wounded but survived: Sedat Edip Bucak, a Kurdish tribal leader and member of the Turkish parliament from Severek, and one of the heads of anti-PKK paramilitary 'Village Guards.' Police later found an arsenal in the car, including pistols and silencers.

As a result of the 'Susurluk Scandal', it came to light how the Turkish state had co-opted criminal elements to assassinate Armenian militants in the early 1980s, and later to fight the PKK guerrillas, resulting in close relations between drugs traffickers, criminal gangs, and the state. It also revealed the existence of a Deep State within the state, one increasingly resembling a criminal syndicate.[4]

Abdullah Çatlı's character is richer than any Hollywood script-writer had ever imagined: Çatlı started his political career in the 1960s as a leading figure of the Grey Wolves, a neo-fascist paramilitary known for its violent attacks against leftist activists and trade-unionists. He is also rumoured to have belonged to the Turkish organisation associated with Gladio, a NATO inspired illegal paramilitary organisation that was set up to launch resistance in case of Communist take-over. In 1978 he (with other Grey Wolf members) attacked university dormitories housing left-leaning students, and opened fire killing five, and kidnapped two others only to kill them later. This event is known as the Bahçelievler Massacre. Similar violent incidents like the one at Taksim Square on May Day in 1977, the Beyazit Massacre in Istanbul where university students were attacked and seven were killed, and the Maraş Massacre where Grey Wolf members Wolves attacked people of Alevi confession, were intended to create an atmosphere of insecurity, and prepared the way for the army's coup in 1980. Çatlı had also helped Mehmet Ali Agça escape from prison, who later became globally notorious for his assassination attempt against Pope Jean Paul II. Çatlı was later recruited by the

Turkish secret services MIT to assassinate Armenian activists, including the French-Armenian Ara Toranian.

Çatlı was behind the 1984 explosive attack against the Alfortville monument dedicated to the Armenian victims of 1915. He was condemned in France and in Switzerland for heroin trafficking, and spent time behind bars, before succeeding to escape. Back in Turkey he was involved in not only assassinations against political activists, and people suspected to be associated with the Kurdish militants, but also in racketeering, kidnapping and assassinations for financial gains.[5] A year before his death in the crash, in December 1994, he accompanied Turkish intelligence officers (MIT) on a mission to Azerbaijan in order to take part in training local OMON (interior ministry forces) officers. In fact, they were collaborating with OMON chief Rovshan Javadov to overthrow the Azerbaijani President Heydar Aliev. According to Turkish media reports, the coup was authorised by Çiller to re-install Azerbaijani nationalist politician Abulfaz Elçibey. But when information of coup preparation reached Turkish President Süleyman Demirel, he immediately contacted the Azerbaijani leadership. Loyalist troops stormed the camp, killed Javadov and put an end to the plot.

The fact that a high level police officer, a mafia hit man and a Kurdish parliamentarian who owned a private army, were all found in the same car exposed to the Turkish public the evident overlap between the state, politics, and the criminal underworld. The scandal soon ignited public uproar against the corruption of the political elite. A popular campaign was launched known as 'One minute of darkness for continuous light' where people switched off the lights in their dwellings for one minute at 9 pm, often accompanied by blowing horns and beating pans. The campaign lasted for over a month in February–March 1997.[6] The behaviour of Prime Minister Tansu Çiller did not help to calm down the public uproar, as she rushed to Abdullah Çatlı's defence. During the funeral Çiller lauded him as the 'great patriot', reflecting the warm relationship between the head of the government and the notorious criminal. Later, she tried to defend him against the parliamentary inquiry by stating: 'I do not know whether he is guilty or not, but we will always respectfully remember those who fire bullets or suffer wounds in the name of this country, this nation and this state.'[7] She came under heavy attack, being accused of corruption and complicity, and eighty members of the parliament demanded an investigation into her activities.

In spite of the public uproar, no major figure was brought to trial, and the minor officials who were brought to justice were soon cleared and released. Sedat Bucak went back to his previous career and in 1991 he was elected once again to the parliament, representing Urfa for the ruling True Path Party.

The scandal offered a momentary glimpse into the inner-workings of Turkish politics. In the polemic that followed, former Prime Minister Bülent Ecevit revealed that he had 'first discovered this illegal organisation in 1974 when I was Prime Minister. During my second term as Prime Minister I asked the military Chief of Staff to terminate this organisation.'[8] Evidently, the organisation was still there, and was going to survive and prosper many more years. But it had also existed before Ecevit came to notice it. The tradition of recruiting criminals for the service of the state goes back to the formation of *Teşkilât-i Mahsusa*—the Special Organisation—set up by the CUP on the eve of the First World War, which played a prominent role in the Armenian Genocide.[9]

But the scandal was deadly for the career of Tansu Çiller, already weakened by corruption charges.

It was this deep crisis within the Turkish Kemalist political elite, the Susurluk scandal and corruption—compounded by the ineptitude of their relief efforts following the 1999 earthquake—that opened the way to a dramatic change, and the coming to power of a new party: the AKP (Adalet ve Kalkinma Partisi, or Justice and Development Party). The Turkish political system opened up, and with this came the possibility for public discussion of the fate of the Armenians.

EU Association and AKP Coming to Power

Turkey's potential membership of the European Union has been the subject of a long and highly controversial debate both within Turkey and the EU member states. The debate began when Turkey applied to become an associate member of the European Economic Community (EEC) in 1959. In 1963 Turkey and the EEC signed the Ankara Agreement, which made Turkey an associate member of the EEC and contained provisions with regard to Turkey's full membership at some stage in the future. The aim in doing so was to bring Turkey into the Western bloc, as opposed to that of the Soviet Union. Yet whereas West Germany advocated a process whereby Turkey would be rapidly integrated into European structures, France argued that Turkey would pose an economic burden on the other member states.[10] The French government also argued that the cultural differences between Europe and Turkey militated against the latter's rapid integration and opposed full membership status.

The relationship between Turkey, the EU and its member states was further complicated by the Turkish invasion of Cyprus in 1974 and its occupation of the northern half of the island. In 1981, Greece had become a full member of the European Commission, and was also opposed to Turkish accession. Hence, when Turkey applied for full EEC membership in 1987, it was rejected on the grounds of its poor economic situation and its continued occupation of northern Cyprus, although this application ultimately led to the 1995 Customs Union Agreement, which has largely conditioned Turkish economic expansion ever since.[11]

The situation with regard to Turkey's potential membership changed significantly when the Soviet Union collapsed in 1991. In the period that followed, many questioned whether NATO was still relevant and whether Turkey still retained its former strategic significance. As a result, during the Luxembourg Summit of December 1997, the European Commission chose not to include Turkey in its enlargement plans. In addition to its declining strategic significance now the Cold War was over, many European politicians questioned whether Turkey's identity, and its geographic position as a state bordering Iran and Iraq, made it a suitable member of the EU. This was a hard blow for the Turkish authorities to take. Having established the Turkish Republic on the basis of imitating a secular state and parliamentary democracy and having sought to emulate the institutions of European civilisation, Turkey was left on the sidelines as former Communist countries were granted full membership, while its own aspirations were denied.

Despite this disappointment, the debate over EU accession had important consequences with regard to reform within Turkey itself. In order to be granted full membership status, the EU demanded that Turkey implement a series of constitutional reforms, uphold basic human rights, address the Kurdish question and limit the role of the military in political institutions. In the words of Turgut Özal, the Turkish prime minister from 1983 to 1989 and president until his death in 1993, 'If Turkey wants to be in the European Community, there has to be democracy in Turkey.'[12] Although Turkey was ultimately declared a candidate for EU accession in December 1999, it was clear that it would have to make some serious changes if this was ever to take place in practice.

The EU did not impose any explicit conditions with regard to the Armenian question as part of Turkey's accession, yet it was clear that this issue would feature at some stage prior to Turkey being granted full membership. On 13 December 2004, for instance, the French foreign minister stated that Turkey had 'a duty to remember … I believe that when time comes, Turkey should come to terms with its past, be reconciled with its own history and recognise this tragedy'. The French foreign minister had stated that France would raise the issue when the negotiations began.[13]

The party that profited the most from the reforms imposed by the EU was the Justice and Development Party (AKP). The party, which was founded in 2001, was led by Recep Tayyip Erdoğan, and a mere fourteen months later won an unprecedented victory in the 2002 general elections. Almost 90 per cent of the former parliamentarians failed to retain their seats, as a number of traditional Turkish political parties, such as Ciller's True Path Party, the National Action Party, Democratic Left and Motherland, did not receive the requisite 10 per cent of votes to retain their positions. The new parliament was dominated by the Kemalist Republican People's Party (CHP) and the

AKP, which received 35 per cent of the votes and two-thirds of the seats. This election was a watershed in Turkish politics.

Timid Dialogue

In January 1999 the US State Department assigned David Phillips, who had experience of Greek–Turkish negotiations, to the task of trying to find some common ground between the Armenians and the Turks. Phillips experimented with a number of unofficial meetings, bringing together academics, former diplomats and think tank leaders in an effort to identify how best to go about completing this task. In the event, Phillips decided that the best way to bring the two sides together was via a so-called 'track two' diplomatic process, in which negotiations would take place without the direct involvement of high-level Turkish or Armenian officials. The first of these meetings took place in Vienna on 10 June 2000, with the Armenian team being comprised of Rouben Adalian and Khachig Tölölyan, university professors and members of the Armenian diaspora, as well as Tevan Poghosyan, from Yerevan, who directed a think tank. The Turkish team was composed of Sabanci University history professor Halil Berktay, Ahmet Evin, the dean of the School of Social Sciences at Sabanci, and Ozdem Sanberk, a former diplomat who now led one of the most prominent Ankara think tanks. However, these initial talks led to little in terms of concrete agreements, and it was not until a new team of Armenians and Turks were recruited, and the Turkish Armenian Reconciliation Commission (TARC), an intiative to encourage the bridging of the gulf between the two groups, was created on 9 July 2001, that true progress began to be made. Simultaneously, the US State Department made a grant of 3 million dollars available for various exchange programmes between Armenia and Turkey.[14]

Although the group that TARC unveiled in Geneva was described as being composed of members 'from civil society',[15] in practice there were also a number of former diplomats in its ranks. On the Armenian side, these included the former foreign minister, Alexander Arzumanian, and the career diplomat and Orientalist, David Hovannissian, who had served as Armenia's ambassador in Damascus in the period prior to 1998. The Armenian team also included two influential members of the Armenian diaspora, namely Van Krikorian, a lawyer and the director of the Armenian Assembly of America, and Andranik Migranian, a former advisor to President Boris Yeltsin who had become an influential pundit in Moscow. The Turkish side was also heavily populated by former members of the Foreign Ministry, including Ilter Türkmen, a former foreign minister, Özdem Sanberk, a former ambassador and director of the Economic and Social Studies Foundation (TESEV), Gündüz Aktan, another former ambassador who had resigned in 1998 to chair an Ankara-based think-tank, and retired army general, Şadi Ergüvenç. The Turkish team also included Vamık Volkan, a professor of psychiatry from Virginia, and Üstün Ergüner, the former president of Istanbul's Boğaziçi University.

Although the commission was ostensibly a civil society initiative, Phillips had in fact chosen former officials who retained close links to their ministries in the hope that the TARC process would have a real political impact. Yet there were problems, with the Armenian team at least, from the outset: not only were the Armenian representatives outnumbered by their Turkish counterparts (there being only four members in the Armenian team as opposed to the Turkish team's six) but there were also problems with some of the individuals chosen to represent Armenia. Alexander Arzumanian, for instance, was subject to domestic criticism given his previous role in negotiating with Turkey, achieving little of note in return.

The work of the two teams was closely followed by politicians in both Armenia and Turkey. The Turkish team, for instance, faced intense pressure from the military and nationalist politicians to avoid recognising the Armenian Genocide, whereas the Armenian team were strongly urged to avoid making any concessions with regard to full recognition of the Ottoman Armenians' fate. Moreover, the Armenian team also stood accused of serving US regional interests and of becoming embroiled in a diplomatic game that was intended to work in Turkey's favour—the Turkish authorities, according to those who made these allegations, had no intention of recognising the genocide but were simply trying to satisfy the concerns of the EU as a means of gaining full member status. The dialogue process also ran contrary to Kochar-yan's policy to push for international recognition of the genocide, as Ankara could effectively argue that any outside intervention could hinder the on-going dialogue between Turks and Armenians.

External factors played an important role in the decision to launch the TARC process. During this period, and following initial opti-mism with regard to the shared interests of the West and Russia after 1991, attempts were being made to redefine their respective spheres of influence in the Caucasus and Central Asia, with the hydrocarbon deposits located under and in the area around the Caspian Sea being of major interest to all regional and international actors. The problem was that the Caspian region was landlocked, and major investments would need to be made to construct the pipelines that would be able to bring the oil to markets elsewhere. This issue was not solely an economic one—Moscow and Washington also sought to create new spheres of influence by signing deals with regional actors with regard to the supply of oil and pipeline networks.

Washington's first prerogative was to ensure that the Iranians did not become involved in any deals involving the supply of oil from Azerbaijan, Turkmenistan or Kazakhstan. The second US prerogative was to limit any Russian involvement, with the aim of preventing any reassertion of Russian influence over the Caucasus and Central Asia.

The obstacles in achieving both of these goals stemmed from the Nagorno-Karabakh War of the early 1990s. The conflict between Armenia and Azerbaijan over this disputed territory resulted from Stalin's decision to place Nagorno-Karabakh—which had a majority Armenian population—within the Azerbaijani ASSR. When the two former republics became independent states after 1991, both laid claims to this territory, leading to the war. The conflict had provided Moscow with an opportunity to continue to hold a position of influ-ence over both states: Armenia subsequently joined Russia's Collective Security Treaty Organisation (CIS) and agreed to give the Russian military a base in Gyumri as well as control over its borders with Turkey. In Azerbaijan, meanwhile, Russia was able to establish a major military installation in Gabala. As a result, one of the major foreign policy objectives of the United States during this period was to resolve the frozen Nagorno-Karabakh conflict with the aim of eradicating Russian influence over both Armenia and Azerbaijan. Indeed, upon coming to power, one of George W. Bush's first diplomatic initiatives was to host a summit between the Armenian President Rober Kocharyan and his Azerbaijani counterpart Heydar Aliev in Key West, Florida on 9 April 2001.[16]

However, the US administration quickly realised that it would be impossible to resolve the Nagorno-Karabakh conflict in the absence of major improvements in relations between Turkey and Armenia. Ankara refused to establish diplomatic relations with Yerevan, and had effectively imposed a blockade by closing its eastern borders with Armenia. From the Armenian perspective, Turkey remained a major military threat: while the Turkish troops amassed on the Armenian border were ostensibly there because of the threat posed by Kurdish guerrillas, it also served as a reminder to the Armenians of Turkish military power. Yerevan was consequently left with little choice but to ally with Russia. In other words, Armenia could not afford to remove itself from Russian influence unless the Turkish threat was neutralised. The US hoped that if significant improvements could be made in Turkish–Armenian relations, this would open the way for them to expand their own influence throughout the region.

A major change in the policy of the Armenian government with regard to Turkey occurred when Robert Kocharyan came to power in 1998. In the years prior to this, the Armenian government, under the presidency of Levon Ter-Petrossian (1991–8), had sought to lay the basis for a new relationship with Turkey that was extricated from the legacy of the past, but Yerevan's goodwill had not led to much by way of concrete results. When Kocharyan came to power, this policy was revised in such a way that Turkish recognition of the genocide became a cornerstone of Armenian foreign policy.[17] As part of this policy, Armenia began to offer more diplomatic support for groups and individuals lobbying for Turkish recognition of the genocide, which in turn increased the efficiency of these activities.

During this period, Armenian groups in the United States—namely the Armenian Assembly of America (AAA) and the Armenian National Committee of America (ANCA)—succeeded in pushing the issue of the genocide on to the agenda of the US House of Representatives, and the ensuing debate had significant consequences for US policy. The Californian Republican George Radanovich and the Michigan Democrat David Bonior co-authored House Resolution 596,[18] a non-binding resolution recognising the 'Armenian Genocide'. The resolution was initially opposed by a number of influential political figures, including the speaker of the house, but this changed as a result not only of the work of the Armenian groups but also because of the competition for Armenian votes in the future elections. When the resolution was put to a vote, there was consternation and concern in Turkish diplomatic circles.

But shortly after the resolution had been put to the vote, it was suddenly withdrawn. Hastert, the speaker, had come under intense pressure from the presidential administration: the evening before the vote President Clinton had called Hastert and asked him to withdraw the resolution on the grounds that it could have serious repercussions for US interests in the Middle East. The speaker had also come under pressure from the Joint Chief of Staff Henry H. Shelton, as well as Secretary of State Madeleine Albright and Secretary of Defence William Cohen.[19] Although this was a major setback for the Armenian American political groups, the Turkish authorities were concerned that this would not be the end of the matter. On the The following day a Turkish newspaper commented that the 'nightmare is over … but anyone who even knows a little bit about American politics is sure that the Armenian lobby won't end its efforts'. While the resolution may have had negative consequences for US interests at that time, this would not necessarily be the case in the future. Turkey had won a battle, but the war continued.[20]

The Turkish government viewed the TARC process as way of testing whether it would be able to shield itself from future attacks by the Armenian lobby. Turkey's short-term strategy was to continue a pretence of negotiating with the Armenians, in order to prevent any interference from the outside—any external pressure, they posited, would jeopardise these negotiations. They did not have any genuine, long-term strategy that would lead to greater understanding between the two. One of the Turkish members of the TARC, Ozdem Sanberk, a career diplomat who had retired from the Turkish foreign ministry in the year 2000 to join TARC in 2001, put the Turkish objectives of the process in a blunt way:

> The basic goal of our commission is to impede the initiatives put forward every year in the U.S. Congress and parliaments of Western countries on the genocide issue, which aim to weaken Turkey. The significant matter for us is that the genocide issue is not discussed by the American Congress any more. As long as we continue the dialogue, the issue won't be brought back to the agenda of the Congress.[21]

But this strategy was purely short term in nature and the Turkish government still lacked any policy that would address the Armenian problem in the long term. Turkey was simply buying time.

The fact that the Turkish authorities were acting in bad faith meant that the TARC process was viewed with suspicion by the Armenians, and especially the Armenian Revolutionary Federation (ARF) and other diaspora activists. The Armenian government consequently distanced itself from the process: David Hovannissian, the former ambassador who had joined the group while still a member of the Armenian diplomatic corps, suddenly found himself disavowed by his ministry—in September 2000 a ministry spokesman announced that he had resigned in order to take up a post at Yerevan State University.

During the initial stages of the TARC process, the groups involved visited the Van region and decided to implement a confidence-building measure by renovating the Akhtamar Church, which used to be part of a larger monastery on an island in Lake Van, and which had been destroyed by the Turkish army in the 1950s. They established a group, 'Friends of Akhtamar Church', which brought together Turkish and Armenian experts with the aim of evaluating the work and finances needed to renovate the church, and the Turkish Ministry of Culture eventually agreed to invest 2 million liras (1.4 million US dollars) to restore the church. The restoration work began in 2005 and was finished in 2006; however, rather than being opened as a church, the building was launched as a museum in 2007 without the traditional Cross on the top of the structure.[22] Ankara was clearly nervous about implementing even this small confidence-building measure.

The TARC process was consistently bogged down over the question of the genocide. The TARC mandated the New York-based legal group, the International Center for Transitional Justice (ICTJ), to study the applicability of the United Nations Convention on the Prevention and Punishment of the Crime of Genocide to the case in dispute. Yet this was opposed by the commission's Armenian participants, who did not want to be seen as being involved in a debate on whether the events of 1915 should be classed as genocide, and they consequently withdrew from participating in the ICTJ deliberations.[23] In 2002, ICTJ issued its conclusion—as the UN convention on genocide could not be applied retrospectively, those involved in events which had occurred prior to its adoption (12 January 1951) could not be subject to its legal stipulations: 'The Genocide Convention does not give rise to individual criminal or state responsibility for events which occurred during the early twentieth century or at any time prior to January 12, 1951.'[24] However, this did not change the fact, in the words of the ICTJ, that those involved had intended to destroy 'in whole or in part ... the Armenians of eastern Anatolia'. The ICTJ report concluded that 'the event, viewed collectively, can thus be said to include all of the elements of the crime of genocide as defined in the Convention, and legal scholars as well as historians, politicians, journalists and other people would be justified in continuing to so describe them'.[25]

In the words of David Phillips, the ICTJ's conclusion 'offered both sides enough to feel that their interests [had been] affirmed'.[26] From an Armenian perspective, the conclusion of the ICTJ report meant that the events of 1915 could now be described as genocide, even if the perpetrators could not be brought to justice under international law. For Turkey, conversely, the ICTJ's conclusion meant that it was unlikely to face any legal consequences for the annihilation of the Ottoman Armenians.

In Armenia, the TARC process was heavily publicised, yet in Turkey the commission's work was almost completely ignored in the mass media. In September 2001, for instance, when the commission met in Istanbul, an invitation was sent to thirty-seven journalists to attend a lunch with the commission's members, but only seven actually turned up.[27] When the TARC was dissolved in April 2004, the commission released a short document summarising its recommendations: to continue contacts, acknowledge the existing borders and begin opening them by 2004, and to encourage exchanges between civil society, media, culture and tourism, among other things.[28] In the period since the TARC process was launched, the world had changed dramatically, as had the priorities of US foreign policy.

Leaving History to Historians

Fatma Müge Göçek is a professor of sociology in the University of Michigan. When she first arrived in the United States as a student she was invited to give a public lecture about her country of origin, Turkey. At the end of her presentation, she was confronted by an elderly lady who asked her about Turkish responsibility for the Armenian massacres and why the Turks had killed her grandparents. This came as a shock to Göçek—at that time, she had no knowledge with regard to the fate of the Ottoman Armenians, and this led her to become interested in what she describes as the 'silences in our history'.

As a sociologist, she immediately wanted to study this phenomenon. She believes that the study of the dark pages of the past is as important for Turkey and Turks as it is for the Armenians. Why was the Turkish state seeking to deny what had happened? Why was the Turkish army—the most undemocratic of institutions—the guarantor of Turkish democracy? As a result of her research into these questions, Göçek came to the conclusion that the destruction of the Armenians had served to normalise state violence against ethnic and political minorities in Turkey. She also came to believe that the fate of the Armenians has had repercussions in other areas, including the institution of private property given the lack of any legal basis for the acquisition of Armenian property during and after the deportations.

In 1998, Ronald Grigor Suny was invited to Koç University in Istanbul by one of his former students who had become a faculty member there to give a talk on the Armenians. Suny was initially hesitant to do so—he knew that any discussion of the Armenians in Turkey would run the risk of him being punished under laws with regard to insulting the Turkish state or nation. Yet he ultimately decided that it would be worth the risk. At the outset of his talk, Suny stated that the Armenian massacres could not be dismissed as simply resulting from a civil war between two rival nationalities. Instead:

> the Genocide occurred when state authorities decided to remove the Armenians from what had been their historic homeland in order to realize a number of strategic goals—the elimination of a perceived Armenian threat to the war against Russia, to punish Armenians for activities which the Turkish authorities believed to be rebellious and subversive, and to realize their ambitions to create a pan-Turkic empire that would extend from Anatolia through the Caucasus to Central Asia.[29]

Although a number of those in attendance left the lecture hall, most of the attendees stayed for the duration of the talk and Suny was surprised that there was no hostility in the discussion that followed. Upon returning to the United States, Suny decided that the time was now ripe to begin encouraging academic exchange between the Armenians and the Turks.

In autumn 1998, Ronald Grigor Suny, then professor of political science at Chicago University, and Fatma Müge Göçek met and discussed the idea of bringing together Armenian, Turkish and American scholars studying late Ottoman history with the aim of initiating a dialogue.

Shortly afterwards, the two professors established the 'Workshop for Armenian/Turkish Scholarship' (WATS). They invited Kevork Bardakjian, professor of Armenian literature at the University of Michigan, to join them in launching the workshop; he was subsequently replaced by Professor Jirair (Gérard) Libaridian, also from Ann Arbor, Michigan, and a former foreign policy advisor to Armenia's President Levon Ter-Petrossian. Those involved in WATS sought to depoliticise the debate over the Ottoman Armenians by adopting an interdisciplinary perspective towards the issue, with the aim of producing a history that could not be said to reflect the interests of Armenia or Turkey. The participants believed that each side could profit from the insight of the other. The project was ambitious: to create a common Armenian and Turkish history. In Suny's words: 'Armenians have one version, Turks another. It is when you put all those voices together when you get the totality of the past.' It was also decided that the conference would be closed to the public in order to ensure that ideas could be debated freely.[30]

The activities of the workshop took place over an entire decade, with the first conference opening in Chicago in 2000. The American Armenian historian, Richard Hovannisian, who was initially sceptical about the possibility of launching such a project, presented a paper in the second meeting, which was held at the University of Michigan in 2002. His paper was about the Turks who had saved their Armenian neighbours during the genocide. Many more subsequently joined the process, with the number of participants increasing from twenty to forty people by 2005. The third workshop took place at the University of Minnesota in 2003, then at Salzburg in 2004, followed by New York University in 2005 and the University of Geneva in 2008, with its final meeting being held at the University of California in 2010.[31] Following closed discussions, WATS would hold a public lecture to which journalists and the public were invited in order to inform a broader audience about its work. A report prepared by the organisers of the workshops stated that the primary achievement of the initiative was its success in bringing marginalised voices to the centre of scholarly discussion.[32]

The Turkish participants, including none other than Hrant Dink, took considerable risks in attending the workshops, and a number of them, including Halil Berktay and Taner Akçam, who took an active part in WATS in its early phase, received threats urging them to withdraw their participation.

I personally took part in organising the sixth WATS meeting. Along with my colleagues at CIMERA, a Geneva-based non-governmental organisation working on conflict resolution, we hosted the workshop at the Graduate Institute of International Studies in Geneva over three days from 27 February to 1 March 2008. The title of the workshop was: 'Revisiting Ideologies and Revolutionary Practices in the Late Ottoman Empire'. Seventeen original papers were presented and debated. On the first day of the workshop, we organised a public event at Maison des Associations, with the title 'The Politics of Memory: A Path to Reconciliation?' Talks were given by Fatma Müge Göçek and Jirair Libaridian, as well as the Geneva-based writer Pierre Hazan and Jonathan Sisson from the Swiss Peace Foundation. The hall was crowded, and a lively debate ensued.

In contrast to other projects, WATS did not attempt to find a balanced, middle way that would satisfy all of the parties. WATS achieved much more than many similar initiatives with minimal costs: TARC is one example, but there were many others. As a result of its work, WATS was awarded the prestigious 'Freedom Prize' by the Middle East Studies Association in 2005.

The workshops did not produce a final conclusion with regard to the Armenians' fate—the edited volume that it ultimately produced, based on some of the most important papers presented during the eight meetings, does not contain one.[33] In the words of Suny and Göçek: 'While we are as yet unable to express a clear unanimity on whether or not the events of 1915 constitute a genocide, a shared sense of what happened and why has been established.'[34]

Istanbul Discusses the Genocide

In 2004–5, a number of Turkish university professors, including Halil Berktay from Sabanci University and Selim Deringil from Bogaziçi University, decided that the time had now come to organise a conference in Turkey with the aim of discussing the fate of the Ottoman Armenians given the success of similar projects in Europe and the United States. Considerable progress had already been made in Turkey with regard to other difficult subjects, such as the role of the military in Turkish politics, Turkish–Greek relations and the Kurdish question, yet the last remaining taboo, that of the Armenians, was rarely discussed. Three Turkish universities, Bogaziçi, Sabanci and Bilgi, partnered together to organise an international conference entitled 'The Ottoman Armenians during the Era of Ottoman Decline: Scientific Responsibility and Democracy Problem'. Fatma Müge Göçek from WATS was on its organising committee, which also included Halil Berktay, Murad Belge, Selim Deringil, Taner Akçam, Fikret Adanir and Mete Tuncay. The initial date for the conference was set for 25–6 May 2005, which would coincide with the ninetieth anniversary of the start of the massacres. As they wanted to present the voice of Turkish academics with regard to this issue, all of the participants had to be Turkish nationals, although Turkish scholars living abroad were also invited to attend.

At that time Aydan Aktar was working as a professor at Marmara University, and he recalls how the organisers of the conference contacted him because he had just published an academic article about the debate within the last Ottoman parliament with regard to the Armenian massacres.[35] He was invited to join the scientific committee. 'The idea of the conference was heard about in Ankara,' he told me, 'and they did not like it. They organised a parallel conference at Istanbul University, inviting, among others, German historian Hilmer Kaiser and British-Armenian historian Ara Sarafian, both of whom had written on the Armenian Genocide.'[36]

A number of Turkish historians who sought to maintain the official narrative of the events protested against the conference being held in Istanbul. Yusuf Halaçoğlu, head of the state-sponsored Turkish Historical Society, accused the conference organisers of having gone to the side of the Armenian diaspora: 'Those expressing views of the Armenian side are invited whereas I am not. If I am expressing the official opinion, then they guard the views of the diaspora.'[37]

On 24 May, the day before the conference was scheduled to open, the organisers announced that the event would no longer be taking place due to a campaign of 'pressure, threats and slander'. The former Turkish ambassador to the United States, and a parliamentarian from the Kemalist Republican People's Party (CHP), claimed that the conference had aimed to 'disseminate Armenian propaganda' and accused its participants and the academics who had organised the event of 'high treason'.[38] The Minister of Justice Cemil Çiçek claimed that those attending the conference were 'stabbing the Turkish people in the back'.[39] There were announcements that Turkish nationalist groups, the MHP youth, had prepared three busloads of activists to be shipped from Ankara to Istanbul to the conference. It was a result of this pressure that the organisers decided to cancel the conference.

However, the cancellation of the event proved to be something of an embarrassment for Turkey at the international level. At that time, Turkey was officially committed to seeking ways to improve its relations with Armenia; indeed, in April, Prime Minister Erdoğan had proposed the creation of a joint Turkish–Armenian commission of historians to study the 1915 controversy in a letter addressed to his Armenian counterpart Rober Kocharyan.

The remarks of government ministers with regard to the conference caused an uproar in Turkey. The leaders of the ruling AK Party made it clear that the declarations of the minister of justice reflected his personal views and these were not shared by the government. Three AKP members of parliament who had graduated from Bogaziçi University called the dean of the university to express their disappointment. The university's dean, Ayse Soysal, held a meeting with journalists from the West in which she explained why the conference had been cancelled, which in turn led to a wave of critical media reports. 'The German Ambassador told us: "Don't give up!" and this was the country that supported Turkish candidacy to the EU,' Aktar recalls. The message coming from the AKP was that they wanted this to happen.

The organisers consequently decided to reschedule the conference for 22–4 September at Bogaziçi (Bosporus) University. A group, the Union of Lawyers, headed by Kemal Kerinçsiz—the same nationalist lawyer who had launched attacks against Hrant Dink, Orhan Pamuk and others—instigated a court case against the university in which the scientific credentials of the organisers and the qualifications of the participants were brought into question, with the composition of the conference accused of being biased against Turkey. The Union also argued that a public university was not an appropriate venue for such a discussion to take place. An Istanbul court initiated a legal investigation into Bogaziçi University, which was announced a day before the conference was scheduled to take place.

Talks between Turkey and the EU were scheduled to take place ten days later, and the court banned the conference from taking place.[40] However, both Prime Minister Erdoğan and Foreign Minister Abdullah Gul expressed their opposition to this move—Erdoğan stated that the court decision had 'nothing to do with democracy' while the latter remarked: 'There is no one better than us when it comes to harming ourselves.'[41] The AKP leadership was clearly embarrassed and signalled its political will to accommodate the event in spite of the court verdict.

The obstacles put in front of the conference mobilised Turkish society, with the court's announcement leading to a debate over freedom of expression and the separation of powers in the Turkish political system. As Bogaziçi University was no longer able to host the conference, the organisers decided that it would take place at Bilgi University, which was a private institution and hence beyond the scope of the ban imposed by the court. The organisers also took the precaution of announcing the change in venue at a time when the court would be closed and would have no time to react.

The conference finally took place on 24–5 September. The university campus was encircled by the police, and hundreds of nationalist demonstrators who their feelings towards the participants known both vocally and by throwing eggs and other missiles. Although the participants had to pass through all of this simply in order to reach the conference building, the event itself was a huge success. The main hall, which could accommodate three hundred people, was packed. When the conference concluded at 9 p.m. on the second day, the audience stood up and gave a standing ovation. 'We were applauding, there was no end to it, as if people did not want to leave. We were so euphoric with our success,' recalls Ferhat Kentel, one of the organisers at Bilgi University.[42]

Foreign Minister Abdullah Gül had promised to attend the opening of the conference in person, yet as he was scheduled to go on an official visit to the United States he instead sent a letter welcoming the participants. The letter begins by discussing the centuries in which Armenians and Turks had been able to live together peacefully. It then states 'when we study the tragic period of Ottoman collapse, when like all the peoples of the empire Turks and Armenians also suffered great losses … The Turkish people is in concord with its history and with itself.' The allegations of genocide being committed against the Ottoman Armenians are dismissed as 'fake and … motivated by political aims'.[43]

The conference revealed that there was a whole community of Turkish scholars, intellectuals and journalists who did not subscribe to the official historical narrative, as all of its participants were Turkish citizens.

In the months prior to and following the conference, the event was widely covered and discussed in the Turkish media. The day after the conference ended, the front pages of the Turkish press were dedicated to the event: the leading article in *Radikal*, for instance, stated that 'Even the word "genocide" was uttered at the conference, but the world is still turning and Turkey is still in its place', while *Milliyet* claimed that 'Another taboo is destroyed. The conference began but the day of judgement did not come.'[44]

Apology campaign

In May 2013 I met Seyda Taluk, a former journalist. During the meeting our conversation turned to the subject of Istanbul Armenians and her Armenian school friends who had suffered discrimination as they grew up, and to Hrant Dink, whom Taluk knew well. Taluk told me that the marble stones of the Gezi Park were in fact tombstones from an Armenian cemetery that were confiscated by the state in the 1930s. She remembered how Diran Bakar, the father of her best friend, Sonia, had once told the story of the deportation of his mother with tears running from his eyes. 'On my identity card it says that I am a Turk,' she says, 'that I am a Muslim. So is our prime minister. But I have nothing in common with him. I have so much in common with

Sonia.' Taluk then became agitated and surprised me by saying: 'I want to apologise for all that! Do you accept my apology?'

I did not have an answer. I had not prepared myself to hear someone apologise to me for what had happened in the past, and I did not know whether I had the right to accept her apology. I was not ready for the task, although I should have been. Four years earlier, in December 2008, four Turkish intellectuals—Cengiz Aktar, Baskin Oran, Ahmet Insel, and Ali Bayramoğlu—had launched what became known as the 'apology campaign':

> My conscience does not accept the insensitivity showed to and the denial of the Great Catastrophe that the Ottoman Armenians were subjected to in 1915. I reject this injustice and for my share, I empathize with the feelings and pain of my Armenian brothers and sisters. I apologize to them.[45]

The text of the document was circulated as an online petition, with other Turkish citizens being invited to sign. A total of 200 Turkish and Kurdish artists and academics signed the initial declaration, with the petition gaining 1,000 signatures in the space of twenty-four hours. Cengiz Aktar, one of the organisers of the campaign, revealed that the campaign had taken two years of preparation, starting from the assassination of Hrant Dink:

> The European Union integration process has taken the genie out of the bottle: we understood the importance of solving the Kurdish and Armenian problems, as well as the political role of the army. Plus, the ordinary person, even in a far-away corner of Anatolia started understanding that a sin was committed against the Armenians.[46]

The use of the word 'conscience' (*vicdan*, in Turkish) in the online apology is reminiscent of Hrant Dink's work, which had sought to address the individual morality of Turkish citizens.

Cengiz Aktar stated he had the idea of launching an online petition apologising to the Armenians prior to Hrant Dink's death, but that this had become increasingly urgent following his assassination. 'There was a big debate [over] whether to use the world genocide or not. The other question was [whether] we should address our discourse to the public, to the state, or just us,' Aktar said,

For me it had a personal dimension to the question, to question, to demand absolution, to humility in front of this crime, and ask regret that we did not have talked about it earlier, that we were silent for so long in front of this permanent denial, in front of this anti-truth, in front of this permanent amnesia which arranged everyone. It was a call to put people in front of their responsibilities.[47]

I asked whether this feeling of responsibility also had something to do with the assassination of Hrant Dink. 'Yes, for sure. Many people share the feeling that Hrant was not protected enough. This was also expressed by the massive participation during the funeral.'

Aktar later published a manuscript entitled *L'Appel au Pardon* in which he summarised the background to the campaign and the reactions it received. The book claims that the campaign demonstrates that there are large numbers of Turkish citizens who reject the official narrative of the Turkish state. Aktar views the campaign not as an end in itself but as a process designed to educate the Turkish public. In the preceding three decades, Turkey had been undergoing a number of significant changes as it sought to join the EU and this opened up possibilities for revising the official historical narrative. Aktar adds that the killing of Hrant Dink had angered his friends and him personally: if the killing of Dink 'initially brought us down to the depth of hell, the following flight of resurrection was even stronger than the downfall'.[48]

Despite the success of the online apology campaign in attracting a substantial number of signatures, the campaign was not well received by certain sectors with Turkey. A counter-initiative, the 'I do NOT apologise' campaign, was subsequently launched which within ten days had 50,000 signatures—more than double the 22,000 collected by the apology campaign over the same period.

But Aktar is dismissive of the counter-initiative, which quickly disappeared from public view: 'Negationists parrot the same tired arguments, which no longer hold. If you ask any further question they have no answers. They have nothing to add to this debate.'

The Turkish political elite united in condemning the apology campaign. In Erdoğan's words, 'I neither accept nor support this campaign. We did not commit a crime, therefore we do not need to apologise.'[49] He added that 'if there is a crime, then those who committed it can offer an apology. My nation, my country has no such issue.' The Turkish military also made its opposition to the campaign known. General Metin Gürak, the chairman of the powerful General Staff Communication Department, remarked to the press: 'We definitely do not consider the campaign right. This apology is wrong and it may lead to harmful consequences.'[50] The most vitriolic attack on the campaign came from the Turkish Foreign Ministry. A group of retired Turkish diplomats described the apology campaign as an 'insidious plan against Turkish national interests', deeming it a 'disrespectful act towards Turkish history and its martyrs. Such a wrong and unilateral initiative is disrespectful to our history and also to our people who lost their lives in violent terrorist attacks during the history of the republic and during the last years of the Ottoman Empire.' At a time when Turkey was seeking to improve its relations with Armenia, the Turkish diplomats argued that the campaign could have 'grave consequences'. Deniz Bölükbaşi, the former ambassador and current parliamentarian for the far-right Nationalist Movement Party (MHP), was even more forthright:

> Who is apologizing for who? If there is anyone who should apologize, it should be the intellectuals and Armenians. They should apologize to the thousands of Anatolian people who suffered the Armenian atrocities. Are these intellectuals apologizing to the Armenian terrorists who killed Turkish diplomats and are still living in Armenia?[51]

The Turkish President Abdullah Gül took a more moderate stand, releasing a statement which read: 'The president's view is that the fact that the issue is discussed freely in academic and public circles is proof of the presence of democratic discussion in Turkey.' This angered some within nationalist circles. Canan Arıtman, a Republican Party deputy from Izmir, attacked the president, calling him a 'secret Armenian' and demanding he take a DNA test to prove that he did not have Armenian blood. Although the Turkish president launched a court case as a result of these accusations, they revealed how 'Armenian' remained a slur for many in mainstream Turkish society.[52]

Following the emergence of the PKK in the 1980s, Turkish public figures had often used 'Armenian' as a form of slander. In 1997, for instance, Meral Aksener, the minister of the interior and a member of the True Path Party, publically talked about '*Ermeni dölü*' (Armenian spawn) to insult the PKK chief Abdullah Öcalan, while the Turkish health minister, following the 1999 earthquake, declared that blood donations from Armenians or Greeks would not be accepted, even if these served to save the lives of the victims.[53]

The Turkish justice system opened an investigation with the aim of bringing criminal charges against the initiators of the campaign under the infamous Article 301, the legal stipulation that had led to the torture and stigmatisation of Hrant Dink for 'insulting Turkishness'. However, a month later, at the end of January 2009, the prosecutor dropped the charges without any explanation—by then the petition had attracted more than 28,000 signatures.[54]

The attempt to attack the apology campaign was counterproductive in that it only served to bring it to the attention of a broader sector of public opinion. The anti-Armenian media campaigns were now ringing hollow, and people were increasingly questioning the official version of Turkish history.

Yet there is another reason the apology campaign attracted criticism from some Armenian groups: the use of the phrase '*medz yeghern*', or the 'Great Catastrophe', to refer to the massacres, rather than the polarising label of genocide. Baskin Oran, one of the organisers of the apology campaign, for example, explained during his unsuccessful campaign as a candidate to Turkish parliament to a foreign reporter: 'You see, "Great Catastrophe", in Armenian "Medz Yeghern", was the only definition, the only expression, used until the Armenian Diaspora discovered the PR value of "Armenian Genocide" (...) Therefore, we use "Great Catastrophe".'[55] A publicity text from Oran's camp published in 2007, when he was running for a position in the Turkish parliament, elaborated "[t]he Armenian diaspora has put the term [genocide] forward for propagandistic reasons in order to pretend that this event is the same as the genocide of the Jews."[56] But for many Armenians, the use of the expression *medz yeghern* by non-

Armenians is simply another attempt to avoid using the legal term genocide. There was, therefore, a similar level of disappointment when Barak Obama, having made a promise to recognise the Armenian Genocide whilst he was a presidential candidate, used the term *medz yeghern* once he had become US president in a speech on Armenian Remembrance Day, 24 April 2009.

A number of intellectuals criticised the apology campaign for its lack of courage in choosing to use the expression 'great calamity' rather than genocide. Others, such as the historian and activist Ayşe Hür, refused to take part in the apology campaign because they did not want to be associated with the Turkish state: '"apology" is [only] meaningful when seen as a process [of] "coming to terms with the past" or "making peace with the past".'

> As a general principle, those who deal with human rights violations in the past must have the following two aims: first, to make sure that such violations and injustices do not happen again in the future; and second, to repair the damages that these injustices have caused. There was no such promise in the text. For instance, why weren't we demanding reparations for the material and moral damages that our Armenian brothers and sisters suffered after 1915? Why weren't we asking the people who appropriated Armenian properties and accounts, and destroyed their cultural inheritance, to compensate for these material and moral damages?[57]

In a chapter discussing the apology campaign, Ayda Erbal, who teaches political science at New York University, asked whether there was any difference between apology and apologia (i.e. between asking for forgiveness and explaining an event): 'the passive, unclear and negationist language of the text makes it [the campaign] more of an apologia in the old sense of the word than an apology'.[58] She argues that the apology campaign fell short not only in clearly defining who was apologising to whom but also in its use of the term '*medz yeghern*'. The Turkish government had never denied that the Armenians had suffered during the First World War; the issue was whether or not the Ottoman Armenians had been subject to a planned extermination campaign, something the Turkish authorities refused to accept. She consequently argues that the reference to Armenian 'suffering' in the campaign did not go beyond the official position of the Turkish state: 'Using denial without a qualifier itself can easily become an instrument of denialist discourse, since even the most notorious denialists … do not deny that something terrible happened … In this debate denial means genocide denial alone and not the denial of anything and everything.'[59]

Yet the campaign was generally supported by the Armenian organisations. Major Armenian American organisations, such as the Armenian National Committee of America (ANCA) and the Armenian Assembly of America (AAA), commended the campaign as a first step in encouraging Turkish society to recognise the genocide.

Image 1: Hrant Dink Funeral, Istanbul 2007. Credit: Agos

Image 2: The place of assassination of Hrant Dink, the pavement in front of Agos. Credit: Vicken Cheterian

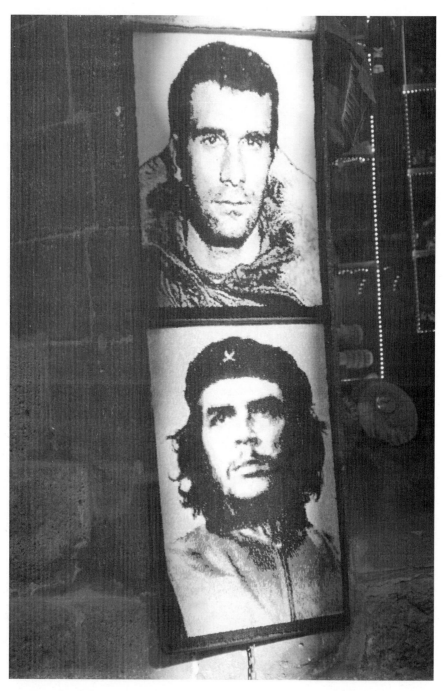

Image 3: Portraits of Deniz Gezmiş and Ernesto Guevara, Diyarbakir. Credit: Vicken Cheterian

Image 4: Heghine, the widow of Kevork Chavush. Credit: Vicken Cheterian

Image 5: Murad Uçaner in Ayntab. Credit: Vicken Cheterian

Image 6: Armenian Church Surp Astvadzadzin (Holy Virgin Mary), first converted to a prison, and now into a mosque, Aintab. Credit: Vicken Cheterian

Image 7: A Turkish flag covering the altar of Surp Astvadzadzin Church, Aintab. Credit: Vicken Cheterian

Image 8: Armen Demirciyan, reclaiming his Armenian identity in Saint Giragos Church, Diyarbakir. Credit: Vicken Cheterian

Image 9: Gathering at St. Giragos Armenian Church, Diyarbakir. Credit: Vicken Cheterian

Image 10: Khatchkars of Por, near Bitlis. Credit: Vicken Cheterian

Image 11: A picture of Varakavank (Yedi Kilise) on the walls of the ruins of monastery today, once a center of learning, print press and publication. Credit: Vicken Cheterian

Image 12: St. Bartholomew the Apostle Monastery, Turkey, near the border with Iran. It was a military stronghold until May 2013 (See before its destruction: http://www.panoramio.com/photo/72604033) Credit: Vicken Cheterian

Image 13: Surp Tovma Monastery and Lake Van. Gravediggers continue to destroy the remaining Armenian heritage in Turkey. Credit: Vicken Cheterian

Image 14: Akhtamar Monastery on Lake Van. Credit: Vicken Cheterian

Image 15: Khachkar at Akhtamar. Credit: Vicken Cheterian

Image 16: Detail of Akhtamar Monastery. Credit: Vicken Cheterian

Image 17: Ruins of a church at Ani. Credit: Vicken Cheterian

Image 18: Ani Cathedral, best example of Armenian architectural genius. Credit: Vicken Cheterian

Image 19: Armenian inscription on Ani Cathedral. Credit: Vicken Cheterian

Image 20: The last closed border of the Cold War: Turkey and Armenia. Credit: Vicken Cheterian

Image 21: View of Yerevan and Ararat on the other side of the border. Credit: Vicken Cheterian

Image 22: Karabakh Armenian fighters preparing for an attack, Hadrut, Karabakh, April 1992. Credit: Vicken Cheterian

Image 23: Karabakh Armenian fighters walking through a forest near Shushi after heavy fighting. Credit: Vicken Cheterian

Image 24: Pictures from Karabakh war, destruction in Stepanakert, 1992.
Credit: Vicken Cheterian

Image 25: Karabakh Armenian fighters. Credit: Vicken Cheterian

Image 26: Wounded civilians near Hadrut, Karabakh, 1992. Credit: Vicken Cheterian

Image 27: Echmiadzin Cathedral, Armenia. Credit: Vicken Cheterian

8

ONE HUNDRED YEARS OF WHISPERS

It was a cold day in January 2000 when Seher, the ninety-five-year-old grandmother of Fethiye Çetin, passed away. A group of women were huddled together in the mosque in Gebze, near Istanbul, where the coffin had been placed. They were crying. A man suddenly rushed in from an adjacent room, probably sent by the imam, asking for the names of the parents of the deceased. A moment of silence followed, after which Zehra, an aunt of Çetin, said that the name of the father was Hüseyn and her mother's name was Esma.

Çetin suddenly stopped sobbing and screamed: 'But that's not true! Her mother's name wasn't Esma, it was Isguhi! And her father wasn't Hüseyin, but Hovannes!'

This event was about much more than a mix-up with regard to names—it was about eighty-five years of coercion, lies, fear, violence and suffering. It was a story of a taboo suddenly surfacing amid the pain caused by the death of an old woman. Çetin's grandmother's name was not Seher either. Her name at birth was Heranush Gadarian; she was born an Armenian in what was still the Ottoman Empire. She was one among many survivors whose identity was eradicated, whose memory was supressed and who witnessed the loss of her universe. It is one case among hundreds of thousands of forced conversions where entire ethnic groups were forbidden from owning their own past, their own identity. It is a story, like so many others, that had been kept in silence.

Hours later, the imam came to pray, and said: 'May God forgive her faults! Do you give her your blessing?' Fethiye Çetin was unable to restrain herself: 'Let her give us her blessing. May she forgive us—forgive you, forgive us, forgive us all.'

Fethiye Çetin, a lawyer in Istanbul who was well known for her work in defending the rights of minority groups, had caused a sensation in 2004 when she published a book entitled *Anneannem*, which was subsequently translated into English under the title: *My Grandmother: A Memoir*. This short book records one of the stories of the thousands of young children kidnapped by Turks, Arabs and Kurds during the deportations who were forced to convert to Islam and coerced into assimilating into wider Turkish or Kurdish society.[1]

In the first half of the book, Çetin recalls her childhood in Maden, Elâzığ district (Kharpert in Armenian), a small town in mountainous south-east Turkey. The story is one of a simple life in the provincial Turkey of the 1950s and '60s. With the exception of the death of her father, when her mother was only twenty-four years old, the story is largely uneventful. After her father's death, Çetin was raised by her grandmother.

When Çetin was a law student at Ankara University, Seher, her grandmother, asked her to help her find her mother and brother, who were living in the United States. Çetin was entirely unaware that she had relatives in America: 'We had always been told that my grandmother and grandfather were cousins. This wasn't true. We'd always been told that my grandmother was from Çermik. This wasn't true either. Much of what we had thought to be true turned out to be false.'[2]

* * *

In the spring of 1915, Heranush Gadarian was a ten-year-old child living in the small village of Havav, near Palu in the district of Ergani-Maden. The village, comprised of 204 families, had two churches and a monastery. Her father, Hovannes, had left the village two years earlier with two of his brothers in order to seek work in the United States.

Heranush Gadarian helped her mother take care of her two younger brothers, Khoren and Hrayr. This peaceful village life was ruptured one hot summer day in 1915 when gendarmes burst into the village, gathered the inhabitants in the central square, and summarily executed the head of the village, Nigoghos Agha. The other villagers—the arrests and executions of the Istanbul Armenian community leaders on 24 April 1915 was now being repeated in the provinces. The gendarmes then gathered up all the men and took them to a nearby town, Palu, while the women and children were left behind.

Heranushe Gadarian's grandmother remembered how the village had been raided some two decades earlier, when its inhabitants had also been removed. This earlier event would have taken place as part of the violent Hamidian massacres of 1894–6. On that same evening, another group of armed men attacked the village kidnapping beautiful girls and women, including a young woman named Siranush, Heranushe Gadarian's aunt. It was later discovered that she had been taken by some neighbouring Kurdish tribes and had become the wife of one of her captors, a Kurd from Siverek. Following the second attack, Hranushe Gadarian's grandmother quickly gathered the remaining members of her family and left for an Armenian village which had thus far remained safe.

But it did not take long for the gendarmes to attack that village too. They rounded up the remaining population of the village and forced them to walk to Palu—once there, the men were separated from the women, the children and the elderly. The young girls in the group later saw what had happened to the men: their throats had been cut and their bodies thrown into what they used to call the Aradzani or Murat River. The grandmother describes how the river ran red for several days. Women and children were forced to walk southwards, their houses, land and property left behind, looted. She recounts what she witnessed when they reached Maden: her grandmother threw two of her grandchildren into the river. One of them immediately disappeared under the water, yet the head of the second child surfaced. She pushed the head into the water until this child also disappeared. Then she threw herself into the torrents of the River

Tigris, never to be seen again. The two children were orphaned on the way, and they could not walk anymore. By the time they reached Çermik their numbers had dwindled. Many died on the way. Years later, Heranush Gadarian told her grandchild how she still remembered how a gendarme had shoved his bayonet into her aunt; she was at the end of the *kafile*, or the convoy, unable to catch up with the rest. She was unable to walk as fast as the others. She was pregnant; her body was left on the side of the road. It was in Çermik that the head of the local gendarme by the name of Hüseyin came on horseback and snatched Heranush Gadarian from her mother and rode away. Another local man kidnapped her young brother, Khoren. The dwindling group were forced to walk further in the direction of Siverek, and later towards the Urfa Desert, where yet another massacre claimed most of those who had survived. The remaining members of the group were pushed further towards Aleppo, and later to their deaths in the desert.

For many days and nights, Heranush Gadarian would look towards the mountains of Siverek and cry. Corporal Hüseyin took Heranush to his house and gave her a new name, Seher. She was forcefully converted to Islam and became a 'servant girl'. Hidir Efendi took her brother Khoren to the village of Karamusa, where his name was changed to Ahmet. She was later married to Fikri, a relative of Corporal Hüseyin's wife.

After the war, Heranushe Gadarian's father came from New York to Aleppo to find his wife, Isguhi, who had survived the death march. He also paid a large sum of money to a smuggler who managed to bring him his son, Khoren. Heranush Gadarian received a letter via the smuggler, but by then she was a married mother and was unable to leave the family.

Throughout her life, she was constantly tormented by the other villagers, who refused to let her forget that she was a *muhtedi*, a convert. Neighbourhood children called them 'convert's spawn', while the adults referred to them as 'the leftover of the sword'. The Turkish authorities also viewed the children of converts with a great deal of suspicion. Seher's son, for instance, had planned to enrol in a military

194

school, yet despite attaining outstanding grades and being a hard-working student, his attempts to do so were always rejected. They ultimately had to bribe some civil servants to remove any reference to their being 'converts' from official documents.

* * *

Fethiye Çetin recalls how, before her grandmother told her the story of her life, she had no idea about the Armenians or their terrible fate. Her grandmother only told her about what had happened when Fethiye Çetin became politicised as a student, drawing close to leftist parties and becoming active within the teachers' union. It was her fearlessness in the face of authority which encouraged her grandmother to tell her the story: 'You took after us—she used to tell me from time to time; I was hard-working and principled.' In Maden, where Çetin grew up, there were two or three other Armenian families with whom her grandmother met regularly. Everyone knew who was who, but no one talked about it. In their conversation, they used to make references to places that no longer existed, like 'next to the church' or 'behind the monastery'.[3]

After the death of Heranoush-Seher in 2000, Fethiye Çetin decided that she wanted her grandmother's story to be published. She wrote the story in a short space of time, but found it an incredibly emotional process: 'I wrote and I cried', she said. She was unable to sleep while working on the book; she kept thinking about the children and weeping. But it was a cathartic process.

As she was not a writer by profession, she initially put her manuscript to one side as she thought that no one would be interested in publishing it. But then two events happened which led her to change her mind. The first was the scandal provoked by Hrant Dink's publication of Sabiha Gökçen's story and her Armenian origins in *Agos*. Fethiye Çetin wanted to show Turkey that Gökçen's story was not an isolated case and that this had happened to many other Ottoman Armenians as well. She also wanted to publish the story as an act of solidarity with Dink, whom she knew both as a friend and as his lawyer. The second event that led her to change her mind was the publication of an aggressively anti-Armenian article in the daily news-paper, *Radikal*, which had been written by a former ambassador, Şükrü Elekdağ Çetin.

She went to the Metis publishing house in order to talk to its co-founder, Müge Gürsoy Sökmen. Çetin knew her well, as she had earlier defended one of the publisher's book—authored by Elif Şafak—from the allegations levelled at it by the Turkish authorities. After reading the book, she told Çetin that she wanted to publish it. At the time, publishing such a book took a great deal of courage—if necessary, the publishers were prepared to go to court. Çetin also expected that she would come under attack and be taken to court for what she had written. Yet to her surprise, nothing of the sort happened: 'They attacked Pamuk and Shafak for writing novels, but not my book which was rooted in reality,' Çetin said. After the book had been published, Çetin began to receive a vast number of phone calls and letters from people who had been through similar experi-ences. The book became a best-seller in Turkey and sold over 30,000 copies. It was also successful internationally and was translated into eleven languages.

After the book had been published, she began to be contacted by the grandchildren of other victims. They told their lives, that of their families, their ancestors. Some knew the story of their families; others were just discovering them.

The stories of the grandchildren are collected in another volume, entitled *Torunlar* (The Grandchildren).[4] The twenty-four interviews collected in the book, most of which are published under pseudonyms, reveal how the suffering of their grandparents continues to affect their lives many generations after the event. Most of the interviewees only discovered their own family stories when they were adults. They recall how learning of the truth came as a shock—their grandmothers or grandfathers, and sometimes both, had an Armenian identity which the interviewees had previously associated with negative characteristics, of being the 'other', a traitor to the nation and a collaborator with European imperialist powers. It was upon learning the story when other aspects of their childhood, such as their grandparents' lack of other relatives or refusal to talk about their family history, started to become understandable.

Following the revelations published in Fethiye Çetin's work, other people began to find the courage to tell the stories of their mothers and grandmothers. Bekir Coskun, a columnist at *Hürriyet*, for instance, told the story of his grandmother, Ummuhan, who raised him and his sister in Tulmen, near Urfa, after the death of his mother. As an adult, he learned that Ummuhan was not his biological grand-mother but an Armenian girl who had been taken from among the deportees by his grandfather, who had lost his wife.[5] The rock singer Yaşar Kurt also discovered his Armenian roots, but only when he was forty years old. Upon learning of this he decided to be baptised.[6]

There were also 'Armenian mothers', as became clear in the work of Ahmet Abakay, who was the head of the Turkish journalists' asso-ciation. In his Turkish-language book, *Hoşana's Last Word* (2013), Abakay tells the story of his mother, Hoşana, who only told him the truth of what had happened to her in the weeks prior to her death. She was born to an Armenian family in the Aşkale district of Erzerum, and during the deportations of 1915 the family abandoned her on the doorstep of an Alevi Kurdish family. She had never shared her experience as a forced convert to Islam, keeping her life story hidden from close family and friends. When Abakay told his cousins that he planned to publish a book detailing her life story, their reac-tion was less than positive: 'How dare you call our aunt Armenian and insult our family's honour. You will remove the Armenian part from your book, otherwise we will pull it off the shelves.'[7]

Forced Conversions in the Ottoman Empire

There is an ongoing debate within Turkey and elsewhere with regard to the issue of forced conversions to Islam. The Sura Al-Bakara in the holy Quran says: *la ikraha fi'l din*—'Let there be no compulsion in religion.' Moreover, *ahl ul-kitab* ('the followers of the book', the non-Muslims who adhered to monotheistic religions such as Christianity or Judaism), enjoyed special protection in Islam, including under the

Ottoman millet system. In the Islamic tradition, Judaism and Christianity are not viewed as being 'incorrect', but rather as being incomplete: the Quran was revealed to the Prophet Muhammad in order to complete what was already known to other peoples. The practice of the early companions of the Prophet (al-Sah'aba) also revealed high level of religious tolerance. One story tells of Caliph Omar ibn Al-Khattab's visit to the Church of the Holy Sepulchre to receive the keys of the city from the Patriarch Sophronius, upon entering Jerusalem. It was midday and, hearing the call for prayers, he hurried to leave the church to pray outdoors. When the Patriarch invited him to pray inside, he declined, saying that if he prayed in the church Muslims after him would take that as an excuse to convert the Holy Church into a mosque.

In practice, however, the treatment of other religions under various Islamic rulers has often diverged from the ideals set out in the Quran or professed by the Prophet's early followers. This includes the mass conversion of Samaritans to Islam (as well as to Christianity under the Byzantine Empire), the conversion of Sunnis to Shiism (under Shah Ismail I, 1501–1524) once the rulers of Persia became Shiite under the Safavids, and the conversion of Oriental Christians to Islam, who would otherwise have to pay the *jizya* taxation or face outright extermination.

The conversion of Christian subjects to Islam also took place under the Ottoman Empire over many centuries. The nature of these conversions varied and served different political purposes. One form of conversion was known as *devshirme* ('collection'), and involved forcibly taking young boys (many of whom were under ten years of age) from Christian families, who would then serve as slaves to the empire once they had converted to Islam. In Armenian, this practice was referred to as *mangahavak* ('collection of children') or *aryan harg* ('blood tax'); it was primarily practised in the Balkans and the Anatolian provinces of the empire.[8] One of the most famous individuals subject to this practice was the Christian boy, Sinan, from Kayseri, who was taken to serve Sultan Selim I (1512–20) and Suleiman the Magnificent (1520–1566). After becoming a janissary (*yeni çeri*, or 'new soldierly') he learned military engineering before being appointed as the chief imperial architect, ultimately becoming the greatest of all Ottoman architects.

However, this Ottoman practice was not initially implemented with the intention of converting the non-Muslim populace of the empire, but rather to provide the sultan with loyal soldiers and bureaucrats to rule and administer the state. In the words of Dickran Kouymjian, this led to the astonishing phenomenon of the 'most powerful Muslim empire being administered and run ... by official and military men born, almost without exception, as Christians'.[9] The entire janissary corps was composed of these converts, who, after a strict military training of seven years, were selected to become the sultan's elite troops. The sons of janissaries, who were born Muslim, were not accepted into the corps. The practice was intended to act as a counterbalance to the power and influence of the tribal alliances upon which the Ottoman sultans depended for military manpower.

Although many families tried to resist their sons being taken in this way, this was not always the case. For others, the practice of *devshirme* served as a means for social mobility, and those taken in this way would at least receive regular pay. This type of conversion was last practised in 1676.[10]

Although the practice died out, the forced conversion of Christians remained a constant feature of Ottoman rule. Christians were doubly persecuted by the policies of the state on the one hand, and by Muslim nomadic tribes and local chieftains on the other. Over the ages, Christian populations found it safer to convert to Islam in order to preserve their lives and their property. Krikor Zohrab writes that all of the Armenians in Tortum, Ispir and Bayburt, in the Erzerum vilayet, as well as those in Khoyt and Silvan in the Bitlis vilayet and in the Hemshen district of Yanibol and Karadere in the vilayet of Trabizon were converted between 1800 and 1830. He adds that successive waves of Ottoman Armenians migrated to Russia in 1830, 1856 and 1878, to Marseille from 1878 until 1905, and to the United States from 1878 to 1912.[11]

There was a change in policy with regard to the forced conversions of Armenians after Abdul Hamid II came to power in 1876 and with the signing of the San Stefano and Berlin treaties. Under Hamid II, the Armenians were seen as a potential menace—a possible instrument for foreign intervention in internal Ottoman affairs—which needed to be addressed by any means available. As a result, the situation of the Armenian population deteriorated rapidly during the reign of Sultan Abdul Hamid II, and especially in the eastern provinces of the empire. This was the result both of pressure from the state and from Kurdish tribes, leading to a revolt among the Armenian population in the mountainous town of Sasoun in 1894. The revolt was eventually crushed by a combined force of the Ottoman 4th army, led by Zeki Pasha, and Kurdish Hamidiye forces. The local population was subsequently massacred, while Kurdish irregulars kidnapped large numbers of Armenian women and girls, many of whom were subject to forms of sexual abuse including rape.[12]

The Sasoun revolt triggered a wave of massacres between 1894 and 1896. To save their lives and those of their loved ones, many Armenians converted to Islam. After the wave of violence subsided, some of the Armenians who had converted tried to return to their original religious identity as Christians—European diplomatic reports show that entire families were still seeking to return to Christianity as late as 1902, many years after the Hamidian massacres had ended. Many others, however, were deterred from seeking to return to the Armenian Apostolic Church due to their fears that they would be accused of apostasy by their Muslim neighbours and sentenced to death.[13]

Forced Conversions and the Armenian Genocide

The Armenian Genocide of 1915 is unique in Ottoman history as this was the first occasion in which the authorities (in this case the CUP) had decided to destroy an entire social group. Alongside the killings and deportations, the Ottoman authorities also used forced conversion as means to destroy the Armenians, with those families who converted to Islam initially spared deportation. However, the intention of the CUP was to eradicate the Armenians in the six vilayets where the 1914 reforms were to be implemented,[14] while seeking to maintain a population of between 5 and 10 per cent in the remaining Anatolian provinces.[15] The CUP believed that the remaining Armenians could be forcibly converted to Islam.[16] Yet when it became clear that increasingly large numbers of Armenians were converting in order to save their lives, the practice of sparing those who converted from deportation was abandoned.[17]

It is not known precisely how many Armenians converted in order to escape the death marches, or the number of Armenian women and children who were forcibly abducted by Muslim families. The Turkish *jandarma*, or the Kurdish tribal fighters, sought to kidnap attractive young girls, whereupon they were branded with tattoos and served in the harems of army officers or tribal chieftains. Virginia Meghrouni, an eyewitness to the genocide, provides the following description of the Armenian women that she met in Ras ul-Ain who had escaped the harems of the captors:

> They wore long, blue, sleeveless caftans with several, very long strips of cloth, swinging from the shoulders, to shield their faces against the desert wind. Some covered their heads with turbans; some toted cushions on their heads carrying heavy loads; some had babies suspended in the cloth bags on their backs; some displayed rings in their nostrils. And all flaunted garish, dark blue tattoo marks—on their faces, bosoms, hands, arms, ankles, even knee caps.[18]

The majority of the Armenian refugees who had survived in the Syrian Desert—estimated at 100,000 people in the concentration camps at Der Ez-Zor by the end of the First World War—were forcibly converted to Islam,[19] yet many returned to their original faith when they no longer faced the threat of death at the hands of the authorities. The surviving Armenians in Syria organised committees to search for abducted children and women and buy them them from their captors. Many such children were forcibly taken away from Muslim houses by Armenians or by the post-war authorities.

The Armenian orphans resulting from the deportations and massacres were subject to a policy of forceful assimilation into Turkish society, with abducted or abandoned children being placed in Muslim houses. Kazim Karabekir, the Turkish general in charge of the Eastern Front, formed a military unit comprised primarily of 6,000 Armenian orphans, in a practice reminiscent of the janissary tradition described earlier.[20]

Survivors, Converts, Crypto-Christians

According to the Armenian Patriarchate, by early 1920 100,000 orphans were under its care, and another 100,000 women and children remained in captivity. This applies solely to those Armenians who lived outside Istanbul at the end of the First World War, as in Istanbul itself (including Ismit, Bursa and Eskishehir) 6,000 women and children were still captive at that time.[21] There is little agreement in the existing literature with regard to the number of people in Turkey who have Armenian ancestry. In the introduction to Fethiye Çetin's *My Grandmother*, Maureen Freely claims that there are 'as many as two million Turks who have at least one grandparent of Armenian extraction'.[22] Yet there were also mass conversions during and after the Hamidian massacres in the final decade of the nineteenth century. What happened to these people? How did they live through one hundred years of solitude?

The Armenians who were left behind after the genocide have, for the most part, received little attention in existing research; the outside world and the Armenians beyond Turkey's borders have largely ignored them. But this is not true of the Armenian community of Istanbul, which had organic links with the remaining Armenians in the provinces. Patriarch Shnorhk Kaloustian was one of them. Born in 1913 in the village of Ighdeh, near Yozgat, he was orphaned at an early age and raised and educated at the American missionary orphanage. He graduated from the seminary of the Armenian Patriarchate in Jerusalem, and was ordained a deacon in 1932. After serving the Armenian Church in England and the United States, he was elected patriarch of the Armenians in Turkey.[23] He has extensive knowledge of his nation's history, and he has authored numerous books about theology and the history of the Church. As he hailed from Anatolia, he knew that there were large numbers of Armenians who had been left behind in the eastern Turkish provinces, in which there was no institutional structure that could serve to preserve their identity as Armenians.

In 1965 Patriarch Shnorhk Kaloustian launched a project to find the remaining Armenians in Anatolia and to bring their children to Istanbul to provide them with an Armenian education in the schools of the former imperial capital. The secret project, which was implemented by the Kaghtaganats Hantsnakhump (Committee for Refugees) over a fifteen-year period, succeeded in bringing some 8,000 children from the provinces to be educated in Istanbul.[24]

Shnorhk Kaloustian was not the only Armenian to be concerned by the fate of those left behind after the deportations. Hrant Guzelian, the pastor of the Gedikpaşa Armenian Protestant Church, was also concerned with the issue of the remaining Armenians and with helping them to preserve their original identity. Like Shnorhk Kaloustian, Guzelian brought young Armenians from the provinces to Istanbul, where they would receive a Christian and Armenian education. It was thanks to his efforts that a group of Armenians of the Varto (or Vartan) clan in Silopi, on the border with Iraq, were identified and their children brought to Istanbul, including Rakel Yağbasan, the future spouse of Hrant Dink. As a result of these efforts, he was arrested in the aftermath of the 1980 military coup for 'kidnapping children', whereupon he was imprisoned and tortured. It was at this juncture that Hrant Dink took over the responsibility for the Tuzla Camp, which was the summer camp of the Gedikpaşa church school.

The efforts of these two priests in seeking to preserve the Armenian identity of those left behind in the provinces meant that there was internal migration away from these areas towards the more cosmopolitan Istanbul. In the provinces there were no churches or schools, and even declaring oneself to be an 'Armenian' was an invitation to receive abuse. Many survivors were forced to convert to Islam in the 1920s and 1930s; I even met people from Sasoun who had converted to Islam and changed their names in the 1960s. Once in Istanbul, many returned to the Armenian Church and sent their children to

Armenian schools. For many others, Istanbul was merely the first stop on a journey to other (usually European) countries. The majority of the Varto clan, for example, currently lives in Marseille and Brussels—the only remaining members in Turkey being Rakel Dink and her family.[25]

The discrimination against ethnic and religious minorities in Turkey is not an issue confined to the past. Turkish identity cards refer to religious denomination, and hence, in order to be able to attend Christian schools, the holder of an identity card has to be classed as Christian by the Ministry of Education. Thus the Ottoman practice of differentiating between confessions, which was central to the millet system, carried over into the nationalist and ostensibly secular Kemalist regime.[26] In August 2013, for instance, an article appeared in *Agos* revealing the existence of 'race codes' within the Turkish administration, which were used to identify minorities in official documents. Greeks received '01', Armenians '02', and Jews '03'.[27] Other Turkish newspapers later added that Assyrians were given '04', while 'others' were filed under '05'. The revelations of the weekly paper were confirmed later when the Turkish ministry of interior issued a communiqué, in which it said: 'Minority citizens' race status is given to the Education Ministry depending on the nationality or race information taken from the state register of the Ottoman period.'[28] According to official Turkish sources, this practice has continued since 1923, that is, since the establishment of the modern Turkish republic. The information has been used to discriminate against the children and grandchildren of converts, and bar them from accessing state jobs, such as teaching or a career in the army.

Hemshins, Muslim Armenian-Speakers

There are numerous anecdotes of Muslim individuals from Hemshin—a mountainous region in northeast Turkey—arriving in Istanbul and finding, to their surprise, that their dialect, Homshetsma, is understood (albeit with difficulty) by a group of Istanbul's inhabitants. And that they, similarly, can understand the language spoken by the group.

Their biggest surprise is when they learn that those people are *bolsa-hayer*—or Istanbul Armenians; the root language is Armenian.

The Hemshins (*Hamshenahay*, in Armenian) are a unique people: though they are Muslim, part of their community has preserved the Western Armenian dialect, as well as old pagan Armenian traditions, such as the *vartavar* feast, an old Armenian Pagan festival, still observed today, which serves as a tribute to Astghik, the goddess of water and fertility. Yet most of this community's members refuse to be associated with the Armenians and deny having Armenian ancestry. They were separated from mainstream Armenian culture over the course of several centuries. The mystery surrounding these Islamised Armenians has increasingly attracted the attention of scholars.[29]

The roots of the Hemshin community have been attributed to a migration led by Shabuh Amaduni and Hammam Amaduni, from the Amatuni noble family based in the Arakadzodn region, northeast of Yerevan in contemporary Armenia, in the mid- or late-eighth century. They were seeking to escape to the Byzantine-controlled territories in the north in order to free themselves from the oppression they were suffering at the hands of Arab rulers.[30] Three distinct Hemshin communities live in three different geographic locations: the Western Hemshen, who live in Rize and are known as Bash Hemshen after the region, gradually lost their Armenian dialect and became Turkish speakers. The Eastern Hemshen, who live in the Hopa and Borçka counties of Artvin, eastern Turkey, continue to speak an Armenian dialect largely due to their insular lifestyle in mountainous regions. The third community is the Christian Hemshens who left their original settlement during the seventeenth century and resisted Islamisation by moving northwards. This community currently resides in Abkhazia, or the Krasnodar region of southern Russia. Moreover, there is also large number of Islamised Hemshins who migrated westward after the 1878 Russo-Ottoman War; 10,000 of their descendants currently live in the environs of Adapazari.[31]

It is unusual to find Islamised Armenians who have retained their original Armenian dialect, and in this sense the Hopa Hemshins are a unique case. The conversion of the Hemshins to Islam began in the mid-seventeenth century, with the aim of consolidating Ottoman control over border regions neighbouring Christian states; many also converted due to the burdens of taxation imposed on non-Muslim members of the empire. Those Hemshins who remained Christian were either deported or killed—in 1860 a number of Christian Hemshins consequently migrated towards the Russian Empire, while those that remained were destroyed as a result of the genocide.

The Islamised Hemshins who lived in southern Soviet Georgia were in turn deported to Central Asia in 1944 at Stalin's order, along with other Muslim groups, such as the Meskhet Turks and Kurds. While Muslim Hemshins were settled in southern Kyrgyzstan (Osh and Jalalabat) and Kazakhstan (Chimkent), the Christian Hemshins were saved from the deportations. They numbered 1,397 people in a 1953 Soviet census of the settlers.[32] Unlike many other national and ethnic groups deported during this period, neither the Hemshins nor the Meskhets have ever been rehabilitated and they have been subject to ethnic pogroms in the years following the collapse of the Soviet Union. They are unable to live safely in their new homes, yet they are unable to return to the land of their ancestors as the Georgian government refuses to grant them citizenship. The inter-ethnic tensions between the Uzbek and Kyrgyz populations of south Kyrgyzstan, which erupted into violent pogroms in 2010, have further threatened the security of the deportees.[33]

In the officially sanctioned Turkish historiography, the Hemshins do not have an Armenian past but are of Turkic origin, belonging to tribes who have migrated to their current location from Central Asia. They are sometimes described as belonging to the Oghus–Türkmen tribes, while on other occasions they are referred to as being related to the Balkars and the Kipchak Turkic group. As Rüdiger Benninghaus has argued, this policy of seeking to deny the Hemshin–Armenian relationship should be seen as part of the Turkish state's broader policy of eradicating any Armenian presence from north-east Turkey.[34]

However, while the Turkish authorities have sought to deny the Armenian roots of the Hemshins, neighbouring ethnic groups remember them as Armenian converts. This is certainly the case with the Laz, a Caucasian people living to the north of Hamshin, on the shores of the Black Sea, and in the contemporary Turkish provinces of Rize and Artvin, as well as in neighbouring Ajaria in Georgia. This community speaks a language associated with modern Georgian, and more specifically with the Mingrelian, and they were Islamised at around the same time as the Hemshins in the mid-sixteenth century. The Laz refer to their southern, mountainous neighbours as '*Sumkhiti*', which is almost the same term used in Georgian to describe Armenians '*Somekhi*'. Moreover, the Laz also refer to the Hemshins as *ermeni dönmesi* in Turkish (Armenian converts), while the Armenians describe the Laz as *megrel dönmesi* (Mingrelian converts).[35]

Given their dispersal throughout their historic lands and in major urban centres in Turkey, as well as in Georgia and Russia, it is difficult to arrive at a precise figure for the total Hemshin population, although the figure most often cited is around 150,000.

Historically, scholars and travellers have noted that the Hemshins are fearful of being associated with the Armenians, and that they usually insisted that their origins and identity were Turkish. However, in more recent times, this trend has started to change, especially in Hopa Hemshin, where the community has retained and preserved its Armenian dialect. Hovann Simonian describes a conversation he had with an elderly Hemshin woman he met in the high mountain *yaylas* (pastures). After recounting proudly how her father was a soldier in the Turkish army, the lady surprised him by saying: 'We are converts from the Armenian … I am not afraid, what can they do to me?' Her daughter then said that 'all the *yayla* names you see in this region are Armenian. This used to be an Armenian area.'[36]

While cautious in front of foreigners, Hemshins are more relaxed when in the company of Armenians. As Yelmaz Topaloglu related to a group of journalists who had come to visit from Yerevan: 'I feel uncomfortable that we are talking to each other through a translator, we can talk that language enough but unfortunately we were subject to Islamisation, we were subject to pressures, and that is why we are not able to understand each other enough.' One of the journalists reported that his visit to various parts of Hemshin received very different reactions from the locals. When the journalists arrived in Chamlihemshin, the main centre of the Turkish-speaking Hemshin community, for instance, the locals would avoid contact when learning that the journalists were from Armenia, whereas in Hopa, the centre of the Armenian-speaking Hemshin community, the reaction was often: 'Are you from Armenia? We are also Armenians.'

Hikmet Akçiçek is an Istanbul-based academic who originates from Hemshin. During the Dink Foundation conference dedicated to Islamised Armenians, he talked about the Hemshins and the difficulties they faced. In his presentation, he argued that it was still problematic to even describe the Hemshinli language as an old form of Armenian for some among the community, and, more broadly, that the community does not wish or see any need to convert from Islam to Christianity.[37]

Dersim

Dersim—or 'Dzopk' in Armenian—has historically served as a land of refuge, populated by rebels. It is here that Armenak Bakirçyan, or Orhan Bakir, the school friend of Hrant Dink, chose to go to fight the state as a TIKKO guerrilla leader.

The Dersim population numbered 65,000 in the opening decade of the twentieth century. During the genocide, some 20,000 Armenians who had been deported from Erzincan (Yerzenga, in Armenian) were kept by the Dersim Kurdish population and thus saved from destruction.[38] They converted to the Alevi creed and abandoned their language in favour of Kurmanji, assimilating with the neighbouring Kurdish population. Others, after finding temporary refuge in the mountains of Dersim, crossed the border and reached territory controlled by Russia. A generation later, those who survived the events of 1915 were again subject to mass slaughter, this time at the hands of the Turkish republican armies in the period between 1937 and 1938.

The similarities between the Armenian Genocide of 1915 and the Dersim massacres did not escape the attention of contemporary observers. The British consul at Trabzon, for instance, detailed the massacres in Dersim in a report:

Thousands of Kurds including women and children, were slain; others, mostly children, were thrown into the Euphrates; while thousands of others in less hostile areas, who had first been deprived of their cattle and other belongings, were deported to *vilayets* in Central Anatolia. Women and children of rebellious tribes, who had escaped to the mountains, were massacre[d] without [mercy] by the military. Even tribes who did not join the rebellion suffered heavily; their leaders were arrested, tortured, and then executed, while the remaining population were deported like the case of the Kirgan tribe. Young men from Dersim serving in the Turkish army were taken away and shot. It is now stated that the Kurdish question no longer exists in Turkey.[39]

The Dersim massacres do indeed share a number of similarities with the 1915 genocide in terms of the methods that were used, yet unlike the Armenians, the Dersim deportees were allowed to return to the land of their ancestors thirty years after the massacres.

* * *

Murad Kahraman is originally from Dersim, which is now known as 'Tunceli'. Like many of his generation he became a rebel. He became an active member of TIKKO, the Maoist guerrilla group, and went into hiding in Izmir. He was arrested in 1994. When he tried to convince the officers that he was not the militant they were looking for, one of the police officers retorted: 'We know who you are, we know your name is Murad Kahraman, and you know what, we have a surprise for you: we know you are Armenian!'[40]

This is how Murad Kahraman learned of his Armenian heritage. 'I did not know that I was an Armenian, but the state knew it.' In prison, he started to put the pieces of his life together. He remembered how his clan—the Feratan—was the oldest in his village. He also remembered the ruins of the church in his ancestral land. He did not know how, and in what circumstances, they converted to become Kizilbash.[41] 'If you ask us, the genocide is not finished,' Murad told me. 'It still continues. We do not know when it will end.'

* * *

I met Miran Pirgiç on Istiklal Street near Taksim, downtown Istanbul. He was born under the name Salaheddin Gültekin. I had wanted to arrange a meeting to discuss the history of the Crypto-Armenians, about Dersim and about re-conversions. Miran Pirgiç was born in 1960 in Dersim (Tunceli), to a family with ten brothers and sisters. He did not know anything about his Armenian ancestry until he was eight years old, when, following a fight with the children of a neighbouring family, he was addressed as *ermeni piç*—'Armenian bastard'. 'We did not know the Armenian names of our ancestors, did not hear the Armenian language at home.' They only felt different because his ancestors were often craftsmen working as tailors or metalworkers. They originated from Tari village, near the Kizil Kilise (Red Church). 'In Dersim we were Alevis, but all our neighbours knew about our Armenian past.'[42]

After the assault on Dersim, the Armenians who had survived there were deported yet again. The family of Miran Pirgiç were dispersed throughout Turkey. Some relatives were sent to Harput, where they became Sunni Muslims, while other family members returned to Dersim years later and became Alevis. An aunt of Miran Pirgiç moved to Istanbul and joined the Armenian Apostolic community. In the 1960s, many of his family members travelled to Germany and France and converted back to Christianity. Pirgiç described how his ancestors had been saved from the horrors of 1915 due to the protection of the local Kurdish tribes. This was not offered simply as a result of their altruism, however: the Armenians were masters of various crafts that were needed in the mountains of Dersim. Moreover, the same tribal leaders who had offered them protection during the deportations took over their old lands. His great uncle was the leader of the clan. He dreamed of gathering the family together and migrating to Soviet Armenia, though this was never realised in practice. For many decades, these Armenians would stick together, only marrying their children within this hidden community, hoping that one day they would be able to go to Armenia.

Miran Pirgiç moved from Dersim to Istanbul in 1978, where, entirely by chance, he found a job working with Armenians. At that time he was an active member of the Alevi Union and was focused on the Kurdish struggle; he was involved in distributing the pro-Kurdish newspaper *Özgür Gündem*, and he was also active in the pro-Kurdish HADEP Party. When he was working for *Özgür Gündem*, Pirgiç remembers how his director once asked him: 'Why don't you openly reveal your Armenian identity?' During the same period, he was pressured by other members of the HADEP Party to avoid revealing his true identity, 'so that the Turks would not say the Kurds and the Armenians are together'.

Over time, as a result of his contacts with Istanbul Armenians and pressure from outside, he discovered his own Armenian heritage and decided to part ways with the Kurdish movement. During a conversation with a friend he was asked what was the meaning of a certain Armenian expression, and when he answered that he did not know, his friend reacted: 'What kind of Armenian are you that do not know how to speak Armenian!' Miran decided to learn Armenian and to study the history of the Armenians. He went to Belge, the publishing house directed by Ragıp Zarakolu, and bought all of the books related to the Armenians, including the memoirs of those who had survived the genocide. He read about Dersim and its history, and realised how much those events had touched and shaped his own region. It was then that he decided to convert to Christianity; he took a lawyer who had discovered documents at the Dersim regional administration stating that his ancestors had been Christian Armenians prior to 1923 and went to court. The judge gave his verdict by saying: 'OK, my son, now go and live the rest of your life with Miran as your name.' It was 2010; he had just turned fifty years old.

When I asked Miran Pirgiç whether Crypto-Armenians continue to have similar problems, he said that the problems were primarily with the Turkish state rather than the local population. In the 1970s, leftist political parties found rich terrain in Dersim as a result of which strict ethnic boundaries lost their earlier significance. Inter-marriages between Armenians, Alevis and other groups increased, leading to a decline in anti-Armenian sentiment.

He has since created an association for Dersim Armenians, with the aim of encouraging them to reclaim their roots.

Why did people in Dersim wait ninety-five years before someone took the step to claim their Armenian identity? 'People have interiorised this fear too long without knowing why,' he answered. 'Still in many regions in Turkey when you say I am Armenian, the immediate reaction that follows is *istaghfar Allah*! ['God's forgiveness!']'

During a journey to Dersim in 2011, Miran Pirgiç took a group of Armenians from Yerevan to a village named Yeshilyaz, the inhabitants of which, Pirgiç claimed, were all of Armenian ancestry. They met one elderly lady who kept insisting that she was an 'Alevi Muslim'. When they later met her thirty-year-old son, he said that he was Armenian, and so was his mother, but that she had long sought to keep her identity secret.[43]

'We can now start a new phase with Dersim', he said. 'Each Dersim family has a story to tell in relation with Armenians. They all have stories about grandmothers.'

The Turkish government is also aware of these Armenian grandmothers, their ancestors and their grandchildren, as well as the date at which they had converted to Islam. In 2007, Yusuf Halaçoğlu, the head of the official Turkish Historical Society (Türk Tarih Kurumu), made a statement in which he claimed that Kurdish Alevis were 'unfortunately' (*maalasaf*, in the original text) of Armenian origin, while Sunni Kurds were descendants of Turkmens. Therefore, 'Kurds' as such did not exist, at least not in Turkey. They are all converts; by origin they were either Turks or Armenians according to Yusuf Halaçoğlu. The more controversial aspect of his statement was that the Alevi Kurds living in Tunceli (Dersim) or Sivas were originally Armenian. Halaçoğlu went further to argue that members of the PKK and other left-wing guerrilla groups like TIKKO were in fact Armenian converts:

> Some Armenians settled in some areas and defined themselves as Kurdish Alevis during the forced emigration in 1915 ... Many of them, who converted from Armenian origins to Kurdish Alevism, are not really sincere. It is known that they are trying to open a church. For example when some PKK members are arrested it becomes apparent that they are not circumcised. We have to be careful about where the terror comes from.[44]

Halaçoğlu's remarks on this issue led to a debate among Turkey's liberal intellectuals, with many questioning his claims.[45] Halaçoğlu launched a counter-attack by claiming that the state had done a house-to-house survey to identify the hidden Armenians back in 1936–7. He also claimed that he had researched the converts, having compiled a list of the Armenians, and that he would be willing to publish it if the authorities allowed him to do so.[46]

Halaçoğlu was a mainstream Turkish historian. Born in 1949 in Kozan, the Armenian Sis and the historic capital of the Armenian Kingdom in Cilicia, he grew up on a land that still retained the memory of its Armenian past.

The paranoia with regard to the 'hidden Armenians' goes far beyond the intellectuals designated as guardians of official Turkish history to the guardians of Turkey's security. A 2007 US embassy report from Ankara, published by WikiLeaks, offers an insight into the Turkish gendarme officers in the south-east of the country who were receiving 'paranoid orders from Ankara to uncover "Armenian separatists"':

The Turkish State's fear of history is reflected in a steady stream of orders from Ankara to JITEM posts in the field to combat 'Armenian separatism.' Our contact's JITEM acquaintances told him that for a long time they were mystified by the insistence of the orders, given that there is literally only a handful of Armenians left in the southeast. As they worked in vain to uncover any signs of Armenian separatism, they came to realize that Ankara was basing its suspicions on the meticulous population registry (nufus kutugu) of family lineage which, among other things, shows how many citizens—especially concentrated in certain regions of the east and southeast— actually have an Armenian background underneath their forebears' voluntary or forced conversions or adoptions during the period when Armenians were being deported and murdered en masse by the Ottoman authorities and local Muslim bands. The distant and suppressed Armenian connection is so pervasive that JITEM even came across a village imam with Armenian roots, our contact relayed. In our own extensive travels throughout Anatolia, especially east of the Kizilirmak River, we have been repeatedly struck by (a) the common knowledge among ordinary citizens of what happened in 1915, a knowledge which most will readily share; and (b) the number of people with apparent Armenian features.[47]

OPEN WOUNDS

Muslim, Christian, Crypto-Armenians

During the 1920s, several attempts were made to save women and children left behind with Kurdish, Turkish or Arab families. Most of these women were freed from captivity in exchange for payment. Yet after the early 1920s, as the Kemalist regime grew in strength, and the borders between Turkey on the one side and Syria (under the French mandate) and Iraq (under British rule) were fixed, it became difficult to continue such efforts. However, the memory of those left behind did not fade away. Stories circulated about families on their historic land who kept their original identity, often hidden from their surroundings, who made the sign of a cross before cutting fresh bread, or painting eggs for Easter celebrations. The Armenians of Istanbul continuously migrated to Europe or North America over the years. Yet for decades, their numbers remained stable at around 50,000 or 60,000 in total. The reason for this was that there was an inflow of Anatolians, who, after arriving in Istanbul, went to the Armenian Church, converted 'back' to Christianity and became part of the Istanbul Armenian community.

Discussing Islamised Armenians

On 2 November 2013 a conference was held in Istanbul on Islamised Armenians, organised by the Hrant Dink Foundation. It was Hrant Dink's dream to inform the Turkish public about the past suffering and current precarious state of Islamised Armenians in their country. The foundation dedicated to his memory was going to realise this dream six years after his death.

Rakel Dink opened the conference:

> We have a saying where people who have denied their past, their identity, are bad people, but we never asked why did they deny their past. Today, we are going to do this. For three days, we will be breaking taboos, and, looking into long kept secrets. We are looking back at this turbulent past, about which [it] was not possible to talk, only to whisper. The remains of the sword are coming back and talking about their loved ones, and how they lost them, how they could not speak their own language, how they could not worship

their religion. We, as Armenians, are looking to our other half. Hrant always said: 'we should not only think about the dead, but look at the living ones as well'. Looking at you all today I see how true these words were.

We are going to open the pages of history that have so far never been questioned and hear and witness the riddles that have never been put into words. We never want to hear what they have done. We never talk about what has happened to them and how it occurred. Our conscience was only able to deny the genocide. Hrant wanted this issue to be discussed, not only for the ones who perished but for the ones who are alive.

After Rakel Dink's opening speech, a roundtable discussion was held with Fethiye Çetin and Nebahat Akkoç as participants and moderated by Sibel Asna. Asna began by talking about the story of her own family and how they had been forced to convert to Islam in 1915 in order to stay alive. Although some of her family members were later able to convert back to Christianity, many others died before they had the opportunity to do so.

Asna then asked Fethiye Çetin how she had managed to keep silent about her family's fate for so long.

Çetin recalled how she had been entirely unaware of her grandmother's story and knew little about the Armenians themselves until her grandmother suddenly told her about her past. She talked about the town of Maden, where she was born and grew up. Then Fethiye told a story to illustrate the depth of this silence: at Maden there is a fast-flowing section of the Tigris, which was visible from the balcony of the apartment where her grandmother lived. As children, Fethiye Çetin and her siblings liked to go there for picnics and play on the riverbanks, and they often asked their grandmother to organise an excursion for them. Over the many years that they visited the spot, her grandmother never mentioned the terrible significance of this place to her. It was exactly at that spot that in 1915 Fethiye's grandmother had witnessed her own grandmother throw two of her children into the waters of Tigris. The head of one resurfaced, and she pressed it down again under the water. The child again came to the surface and she pressed even harder this time. It was an act of desperation and a final act of defiance: a mother had realised that she and her family were not simply being deported, they were being lead to their extermination. She too later jumped into the waters of the Tigris to die.

Fethiye Çetin continued talking about her book and the reaction of her family members:

> The reaction of my family was very divided; one part was very supportive that I wrote this book, but there was another part that was very critical and did not like it. 'Why did you have to open all this up?' they said. But the youth in my family were very supportive.

Then she turned to the different experiences of the women who had been forced to convert to Islam. Those who were kidnapped and converted at a very young age were often not fully aware of their Armenian identity and it was easier for them to be assimilated into Turkish society. But for those who were kidnapped as adults, the entire experience was much more difficult, as some of the women would refuse to pray and their husbands would beat them repeatedly: 'At least move your lips during praying time so that people do not notice,' one was told. They felt abandoned, lonely and lost all of the confidence that comes with being part of a wider community, having a sense of belonging. In order to regain their confidence they would apply and seek to excel in a range of tasks with the aim of being accepted in their new community.

Taner Akçam was the next to speak. He said the silence that was imposed on the subject came with a price—it had made the social sciences 'bankrupt'. He then went on to explain why the policies of forced conversion had not received the attention they deserved from scholars. He argued that one of the reasons for this was that those engaged in studying Armenia and its history tended to draw comparisons between the Holocaust and the Armenian Genocide—as there was no policy of forced conversion during the Holocaust, the issue was largely ignored in studies of the Armenians' fate. In the thinking of Raphael Lemkin, the forced assimilation, the forced transfer of children form one group to another, were elements of a genocidal policy. In Akçam's words: 'I claim that assimilation was [an] inseparable part of [the] genocide from the beginning. Ottomans had demographic policies so that Christians would not be more than 5 or 10 per cent in a given province. This group was thought to be possible to assimilate.'

Vahé Tachjian talked about the efforts made by the surviving Armenian communities in post-war Syria and Lebanon with regard to the return of the Armenian women and children who had been left behind and were now living with Turkish, Kurdish or Arab families. 'Catastrophic circumstances had often left them isolated and exhausted, without family cohesion or protection. These same circumstances—in Lawrence Langer's words—had given birth to a "diminished self", which led them to perform acts that in ordinary social situations they would not have carried out.'[48] Armenian community leaders tried to eradicate all references that continued to link the Armenians to the Turkish–Ottoman environment. 'The memory of the catastrophe, as well as the feelings of hatred towards the Turks, became the main cement in the efforts of national reconstruction that began in the Middle East.' Yet a significant number of survivors, the women and children, were still in the possession of Turks, Kurds or Arabs.

The women and girls who had lost their family members and were living with Muslim men found themselves in a very different situation: 'many had been raped, and all their possessions had been stolen from them during the deportations. They had endured famine and occasionally given birth to illegitimate children.' The leaders of the Armenian community were divided with regard to how to respond to this issue. For one group, cohabitation with Muslims was the preferred option, and those who were now living with Muslim families should not be allowed to return to the Armenian community. Yet for others, these women and young girls were victims; those who adopted this view founded women's shelters to provide protection, education and training with the aim of rehabilitating those who were prepared to abandon their Turkish, Kurdish or Arab spouses and return to the Armenian community. There was only one condition: they could not bring any children that had resulted from their marriages with their Muslim captors.

Societies choose what to remember and what to forget. The conference in Istanbul reminded Turkey what it had tried to forget for so long. It was a wake-up call. On the final day of the conference, a young woman stood up in the audience and said that her grand-mother was an Armenian too. She said she had followed the first two days of the conference via the Internet, but had now decided to put her fear and shame aside in order to attend and tell her own story.

The conference was also an occasion for a public meeting between Armenians and Muslim—or Islamised—Armenians. How should Armenian institutions—the church, the schools, the foundations—treat Muslim Armenians? Do they have to convert before being full members of the community? Moreover, which criteria should deter-mine one's membership of the Armenian community?

The conference concluded with an unusual roundtable discussion, one that reminded the audience about the reality of contemporary Turkish politics. The discussion featured three panelists, Cemal Uşşak, the head of the Writers and Journalists' Union who was close to the Gülen movement,[49] the writer Hidayet Şefkatli Tuksal, and the pastor of the Gedikpaşa Armenian Protestant Church, Krikor Ağabaloğlu, and was moderated by Rober Koptaş, the editor-in-chief of *Agos*. Uşşak was the first to talk. In his presentation he urged the 400-strong audience not to 'dig too deep'—it was only possible to make incremental progress in bringing the issue to the attention of the public, and care needed to be taken to avoid shocking Turkish society. 'People in Anatolia think that there were even more Muslims killed by the Armenians, so people do not talk about their origins.' Then it was the turn of Hidayet Şefkatli Tuksal, a writer wearing a headscarf in the Islamic tradition. 'In the last three days what I felt the most was guilt. It is very difficult to be a Muslim here. We are such a traumatised society, when two people meet the first thing they ask is: "where are you from?"' She then responded to the remarks of her co-panellist:

> So many people know so much more than what is said and spoken. You have people here who were condemned to silence, and that is the heaviest of punishments. We should talk as a sign of respect to their suffering. ... The Turkish Muslims think Islamised Armenians are not sincere, their con-version was an act of opportunism, and discriminate [against] them for that.

They do not question their own insincere behaviour to impose on a group a violent identity change.

Pastor Ağabaloğlu then intervened: 'You should know the truth, and truth will liberate you.'

The conference was covered in the Turkish media, with numerous newspaper articles and televised debates being devoted to its proceedings. Vahit Erdem, a parliamentarian and member of the ruling AKP, wrote the following letter to *Radikal*:

> Mister Oral, some honourable historians are more just than you concerning this subject. Last week I was in Erzurum. Only if you could also write about the atrocities committed there by the Armenians. I would have wished that all that would have not happened, but this catastrophe started and opened the way to mutual massacres. Apparently, you accept the hypothesis of 'genocide', politically imposed, and scientifically not verified. This anti-Turkish orgy will be terminated one day.[50]

The most impressive talk at the conference was that given by Nevin Yildiz Tahincioğlu, a professor of media studies at Selcuk University:[51]

> As [with] everyone else today, I am going to tell you a story ... The stories of the atrocities are coming from two sides; from the survivors who later established themselves in Aleppo, Beirut or Los Angeles. There are also stories from the other side in Kurdish villages where perpetrators and survivors co-exist side by side.

Tahincioğlu then told the audience about the story of Sara, who was a fifteen-year-old Armenian girl from an Armenian village near Tal Jaafar in the Viransehir district in Urfa province at the time of the atrocities. Ayip Aga, a Kurdish tribesman who led a Hamidiye cavalry corps, was told by the authorities to plunder the Armenian villages and chase their inhabitants; all of the men in the village were rounded up and taken away. One day after the event, when Sara was washing some clothes in the river, she noticed a dog holding an arm in its mouth and immediately recognised the watch on the wrist as that of her uncle's; after following the dog for a short while, she eventually came to a cave where she found the corpses of all the men who had been taken away, left there to be eaten by the dogs.

When the remaining villagers decided to leave after hearing news of the massacre, they were rounded up by armed tribesmen. It was then that Ayip Agha noticed Sara. The *agha*, who already had two wives, wanted to take Sara as his third bride, but she rejected his advances. He threatened to kill her mother; when she still refused to marry him, he eventually went ahead and killed her. Then he threatened to kill her brother, who cried and asked his elder sister for help. She eventually told him that she would agree to marry him on two conditions: first, that he spare the life of her brother, and second that she would not be forced to change her name. She wanted to bear her name, like a cross, for the rest of her life.

Despite Ayip Ahga's promises, Sara's little brother died a year later in circumstances which indicated that he had been murdered. She continuously refused to convert to Islam and resisted Ayip Agha, who subjected her to physical and sexual abuse. She had fifteen children, yet none survived; it was rumoured that the agha's two other wives had poisoned the infants. At the end of the story, Nevin Yildiz Tahincioglu shocked the audience by telling them that this was in part the story of her own family; Ayip Agha was her ancestor, and she had only been able to research this story now her father had died: 'In this country everyone says he's a victim. It is time that the perpetrators come forward and tell their story. Only then we can heal our wounds.'

9

MEMORIES OF THE LAND

I got on a bus at Antakya and began to travel westward toward Samandağ. It was a sunny Sunday in February 2013, and the bus was filled with well-dressed families on their way to pass the day in their village of origin. A man behind me was engaged in an animated conversation on his mobile phone, shifting from Turkish to Arabic half way through a sentence, and then returning to Turkish again. The majority of the Samandağ population are Alawi Arabs. Its inhabitants also remember the town under its old name—Svedya—a city of 40,000 today.

Samandağ, or Svedya, is dense with history. Seleucus Nicator, one of the generals of Alexander the Great (r. 336–323 BC), built the town in 300 BC as the seaport of Antioch. The town is on the Mediterranean coast and on the mouth of the Orontes River. The area is filled with historic treasures; one can visit Titus Tunnel, an amazing piece of engineering from the first century AD that was designed to bring fresh water to the town via a lengthy tunnel dug through the mountain. The region is also one of the early Christian lands, with the Church of St Peter near the city of Antakya having been used by some of the first Christians. During the Byzantine period, the town was called Saint Symeon; it was later overrun by the Crusaders and then occupied by the Mamluks before falling into the hands of the Ottomans.

I left the bus in the city centre, close to Eski Park ('Old Park'). Once there, I phoned Cem Çapar, my contact, and in ten minutes he drove me to the village of Vakifli (Vakef Kyugh, in Armenian)—the only remaining Armenian village in Turkey. We crossed the village of Zeytuniye, a mainly Sunni Muslim village where some Armenian families also live. We also passed Çapar's house, before continuing to Vakifli, where we stopped for a cup of tea and met Berj Kartun, the mayor of the village, who was sitting next to Panos Çapar, Cem Çapar's uncle. This village, the sole remaining Armenian village in Turkey, has only 130 inhabitants.

Vakifli has a dramatic history. It was one of the six Armenian villages of Musa Dagh, famous for its resistance against Ottoman attacks during the First World War. When the orders for deportations arrived with the Ottoman troops who were sent to the region, the majority of the population refused to obey. Information about the deportation of entire populations of Zeytun, Ayntab and Kilis had reached Musa Dagh.[1] They took to the mountains and resisted. After resisting for fifty-three days and pushing back several Ottoman attacks, the rebels began to run out of ammunition and food, and their morale was at a low ebb. It was then that they noticed French warships in the sea, and raised signs saying: 'Christians in distress. Rescue.' Two French warships approached the coast, a place where the mountains fall into the warm waters of the Mediterranean, and evacuated the population. In the words of Lord Bryce and Arnold Toynbee, this was 'the single happy incident in the national tragedy of the Armenians in the Ottoman Empire'.[2] It was also one of only two incidents in which Allied intervention saved Armenian lives—the only other example being the effort made by Russian troops to rescue those who were seeking to defend Van. More than 4,200 people were saved by the Allied warships and transported to Port Said, where they lived for three years in refugee camps until the war had come to an end. They returned to their homes in 1918; the Ottomans had been defeated, and the Sanjak of Alexandretta was now under French rule as part of its Syrian mandate.

But this is not the end of the story. The French and the Turks later reached an agreement whereby the province would be passed to

Turkey. The Allied powers had made this agreement in the hope that it would encourage to Turkey to remain neutral in a future worldwide conflagration. Hence, despite opposition from the local population, a referendum was organised in 1938 and the province was declared 'independent'. Yet this independence was short-lived: after only nine months, the Turkish army entered the region and incorporated it into the Turkish Republic.

Barely twenty years had passed since they had returned in the belief that they were safe from the Turkish threat, yet they were now faced with a new danger. Although a Turkish army general visited Musa Ler and told the Armenians that they had nothing to fear because the new Turkish Republic was different from the Ottoman Empire, very few were willing to believe the Turkish promises.

Upon learning that the region would be returned to Turkish sovereignty, most of the inhabitants of Musa Ler—Vakif, Kheredbey (Indayr, in Armenian), Kapusuyu (Kabisyé), Yoghun Oluk (Keygh), Haji Habibli (Hablak) and Bitias (Bityus)—decided to leave their land with the evacuating French troops and became refugees again, the majority of whom ultimately ended up in Anjar, Lebanon, with the remainder travelling primarily to Aleppo in Syria. In 1936, the total number of Armenians in the Sanjak of Alexandretta was 24,000, yet only 68 families totalling 384 people, decided to stay. Of those, 41 families were from Vakifli, the smallest of the six villages, which subsequently became the only remaining Armenian village in Turkey. The incoming Turkish authorities confiscated most of the land that belonged to the Armenians; out of a total of 705 acres, only 60 acres currently remain in the hands of the Vakifli Armenians today.[3] This is why so many Vakifli Armenians have since left the village, as there is simply not enough land to sustain the livelihoods of the youth.

The villagers who remain speak in the local Armenian dialect; only a few can speak modern, Western Armenian. The Armenian school that served the village in 1939 was shut down when the Sanjak came under Turkish rule. Only those who have had the opportunity to study in Istanbul Armenian schools speak modern Armenian today. With the changes taking place in Turkey, the villagers have begun to petition the

Turkish Ministry of Education, referring to international as well as European conventions on human rights, to ask for their own Armenian school, despite the lack of young people who remain in the village: there are only nineteen children in the village.

The villagers are also in contact with their relatives in Anjar, Lebanon. The mukhtar (village head) told me that he went to Anjar during the Easter holidays in 2000 and spent seventeen days there. In the past, before the war in Syria, when the roads were safe, pilgrims from Anjar used to come to Vakifli on the day of the Holy Cross (*Sourp Khachi Or*). Today, as a new war is raging across Syria, there are few travellers. Even the people of Kessab—the Syrian Armenian town just across the border from the village—do not dare to travel to Vakifli. The fate of the Syrian Armenians, and specifically those in Aleppo and Kessab, is a constant source of worry for everyone in the village.

The village has other worries too. The mainstay of its economy was the citrus fruit industry, with orange groves surrounding all of the houses. However, in the 2000s the price for a kilogram of oranges fell from 1 US dollar to 45 cents, while the price of fuel doubled, further compounding the problems generated by the lack of land. According to the *mukhtar*, each family now has around 10–15 *dunam* (or *decare*) of land, but when a father has three children the land will be divided equally between them, which means that the land which is left is not sufficient to sustain a decent livelihood.

In response to these problems, this small village is trying to adapt to globalisation by creating a local cooperative, and opening shops that sell locally produced commodities. The village is also trying to encourage tourism, which was a central economic activity for the six villages during the period of French rule. One old house has recently been repaired, and when I was visiting, work was going on to renovate another old house just next to the village church, which had fallen into a state of disrepair. The renovation is advancing rapidly thanks to a 170,000 US dollar grant from the Turkish government: 'We feel the change in government attitude towards us,' Panos Çapar said: 'in the last ten years water was brought to the village, and a new road was constructed. The provincial governor comes and visits us on our holidays, he brings with him official visitors to show that we have such a village in Hatay.'

Cem Çapar took me back to Samandağ. We drove northwards, where he showed me where the Musa Lertsis had come down from the mountain to meet the French soldiers who transported them to safety. Çapar spoke fluent literary Western Armenian as well as the village *parpar*, or dialect. He had studied in Istanbul and had trained as a veterinary surgeon. I asked him if he had found it difficult to return to Vakifli after spending so many years in Istanbul. He replied in the negative, and talked about how much he loved his village and the life he had lived there: 'I was born in 1977, and my parents gave me a Turkish name, Cem. When I think about it, my conclusion is that those years should have been difficult years, that they thought it would be better for me to have a Turkish name when I went to the military service.' After seeing where Musa Mountain fell into the Mediterranean waters, we started heading south again. Next to the modern seaport of Samandağ, Çapar showed me a terrain which previously belonged to the Armenian church of Kabusia, which had been confiscated by the Turkish authorities. The Vakifli inhabitants had twice applied to the Turkish Justice Ministry to reclaim the land, but they had lost their case on each occasion—they had just put in another application in the hope that a Turkish court would finally return the land to its rightful owners. As we travelled further south, we were able to see the silhouettes of mountains on the horizon, behind which lay the Syrian border and the Armenian town of Kessab. The population in the latter town have close historic links with Musa Lertsis; they speak a similar Armenian dialect and share the same traditions.

In March 2014, Syrian Islamist rebels launched a sustained attack from the north and the east towards Kessab. This attack was very different from previous ones: it was well organised and had evidently received some support from the Turkish military. There were rumours about Turkish artillery supporting the attackers; a Syrian MiG-23 that had flown close to the battlefield was shot down by a Turkish missile. When the rebels entered Kessab, most of its inhabitants had already been evacuated towards Latakya. Those who remained, mainly the elderly, were transported first to Vakifli and then to Anjar in Lebanon. When the rebel fighters were pushed out a few months later, Kessab was desolate; houses and shops had been pillaged, the churches destroyed and the graveyards desecrated.

Anjar, the Only Armenian Village of Lebanon

When I first visited Anjar, I was already a university student. I grew up in a country enflamed by a series of wars, and we rarely adventured far from our house. During the war, Anjar was famous for two things: being the only Armenian village in Lebanon and housing the headquarters of the notorious Syrian *mukhabarat*, the much-feared secret services. Among Lebanese Armenians, Anjar is known for its specific dialect, and for being a stronghold of the Armenian Revolutionary Federation (ARF). The road from Beirut to Anjar goes up to the Lebanese Mountains, passing through Alei and Bhamdoun, then climbs up Mount Lebanon until it reaches the Dahr al-Baydar pass. As we began our descent, the lush Bekaa Valley, and on the horizon the Anti-Lebanon Mountain chain and Syria, became visible. The shop of Yesayi Havatian is on the main highway linking Beirut to Damascus, a few hundred meters from the Syrian border. He has a thin, elegant face, with his hair and moustache greying, and his skin tanned from working under the rays of the Bekaa sun. The shop was crowded; villagers were coming in for his advice as much as for buying agricultural products. 'When I studied agriculture engineering at the AUB [American University of Beirut], my problem was to exercise a profession which would allow me to live on my land.' Although he studied agriculture, and he spends his mornings helping his clients from across the Bekaa Valley to cultivate their land, his nights are dedicated to history, on the past of Musa Dagh and the present of Anjar.[4]

Armenian Diaspora foundations that received substantial contributions from Calouste Gulbenkian bought Anjar to house the Musa Dagh refugees under the authority of the French mandate. Lebanese neighbours in the nearby Majdel Anjar village took the Armenians into their homes during the winter months. Out of the 5,125 refugees, between 800 and 1,000 perished in the first two years due to the cold and diseases such as malaria. The village was slowly constructed. The six neighbourhoods of Anjar are named after the six villages in Musa Dagh. In 1946, when the Soviet Union began to encourage Armenians to repatriate, half of the refugees—primarily those who were sympathetic to the pro-Soviet Hnchagyan Party—decided to move to Soviet Armenia. They currently live in a village called Musa Ler, near Yerevan.

As one of the villagers was toiling the earth, he made a sensational discovery: the ruins of an Umayyad-era (661–750) town, one of the archaeological gems of eastern Lebanon. The city was built in the eighth century under Caliph Walid Ibn Abd al-Malak (705–715); it was on the crossroads of the trading routes stretching north–south from the plane of Homs to Palestine, and east–west linking the Umayyad capital Damascus with coastal towns such as Beirut and Sidon. The city is divided into quarters and neighbourhoods, with the palace and the mosque occupying the highest point, and the shops of the market stretching out from these buildings; the town was supplied with sewage and water distribution systems, with high city walls supported by forty towers. The town exemplifies the exquisite Arab architecture from the early period of Islam, and in 2010 these Umayyad ruins in Anjar were placed on UNESCO's list of sites of Outstanding Universal Value.

Yesayi Havatian, the shop-owner, went to Musa Dagh with his family for the first time in 2001. He was already highly familiar with the place after having read every book or report he could about the home of his ancestors, but he now wanted to see it with his own eyes. He was able to speak to the villagers of Vakifli in his own dialect. He visited the village of his grandparents, Veri Azor, adjacent to Kheder Bey, but no trace of their presence remained. Two major pilgrimages took place in 2004 and 2010, ending with a fiesta on 13 August in which the entire village of Vakifli participated. After sixty-five years, the inhabitants of Vakifli finally felt they were not alone.

OPEN WOUNDS

Aintab

My maternal grandmother was born in the town of Aintab, from which her entire family, the Nazarians, also hail. The town has since been renamed as 'Gazi-Antep' ('gazi' meaning conqueror in Arabic, or holy warrior in Turkish) due to its role in Kemalist mythology, and the battle between Turkish nationalists and the French army in the town (as well as Marash and Urfa) in the Cilician war (May 1920– October 1921).

I had travelled to Aintab in order to meet some Syrian refugees. On the first evening, I went to a café, Café Papirüs, in a large stone house with some friends when the owner approached us and asked where we were from. I answered, in my limited Turkish, that I was Armenian; he then took my hand and led me to one of the windows, where he showed me an inscription that was clearly written in the Armenian alphabet.

Hanife, the café owner, invited me to come again the next day, as he would like to give me a tour of the building. Although part of the building was being renovated, what I saw was very impressive. The building had once belonged to a powerful and wealthy Armenian family from Aintab, the Nazaretians. A black-and-white portrait of Nazaretian was placed next to the window of the visiting hall, with colourful paintings of angels and natural scenery decorating the walls. In another room there were black-and-white portraits on the wall, surrounded by beautiful frames. The names read: Mehmet Akif, Mehmetcik, Mithat Pasha, Abdulhak Hamit.

There is a building in the town, on the Ataturk Boulevard, a short distance from the café, which resembles the architecture of a Catholic church; the façade bears the scars of bullet holes from the War of Liberation. Further up the hill there is an imposing mosque known as 'Kurtulush Jami' ('Kurtulush' means 'liberated' in Turkish). I was aware that there also used to a big Armenian church here called 'Surp Asdvadzadzin', which had been built at the end of the nineteenth century, but which had been converted to a mosque after 1915. I eventually found this building in the middle of a neighbourhood with old, crumbling houses, some of which had windows in the shape of a cross. This was one of the three Armenian neighbourhoods of Aintab known as Kayajik, Kastelbashi and Hayik Hill (now Tepe Başi).

Surp Asdvadzadzin Church was closed. But there was a guardian sitting in front of it. For a few Turkish liras he opened the door and let me in. I was alone. The emptiness underlined the loneliness of the place. It is a huge building of white stones with a large imposing dome. From the street it looks imposing, as it stands on the side of a hill. A huge Turkish flag was hanging where the altar used to be. In the 1920s, this building had been used as a prison, before being converted to a mosque in the 1980s. The church's bell-tower had been converted into a minaret, while one of the other minarets that had been added to the building referred to the date of construction: 1985. There is a cultural centre on the same street, 100 metres from the church. This building also used to be an Armenian church—the Surp Bedros Armenian Catholic Church—but it is now called Omer Ersoy Kültür Merkezi. For many years it was used as a warehouse until it was 'discovered' and turned into a cultural centre.

One of the best ways to learn about the hidden history of a city is to find someone with local roots to guide you and introduce you to aspects and individuals that you would otherwise not encounter. When I was in Aintab, my guide was Murad Uçaner. Before relaying the hidden story of the city he unveiled to me, it is important to take note of his life history.

Murad's Story[5]

Murad Uçaner is an electrical engineer who was born and raised in Aintab. In 2005 he was involved in renovating an old house in the Kayacik neighbourhood, in old Aintab, near Papirüs café. While removing some wood that covered the walls in one of the rooms, he discovered a curious picture: it was of a young woman, holding a pistol in one hand and a rifle in another. She had cartridge belt around her waist and two others across her chest. The lower end of the picture contained the words 'M.H. Halladjian, Aintab Asia-Minor', which Uçaner assumed to be a reference to the photographer.

On the other side of the picture he saw some writing he did not recognise, though it may have been Arabic. It read '21', followed by something which was illegible, and then the year of 1910.

When Uçaner showed his friends the picture, he was told that the wording was neither Arabic nor Ottoman Turkish. One of his friends suspected that the wording could be Armenian. At a later date, and entirely by chance, he met a group of tourists who were visiting Aintab, and who were talking in a language he did not recognise. He approached one of them and asked them whether they could tell him what was written on the old picture. They could: it was in Armenian. It said:

> Hankutsyal heros Kevork Chavushi ayri Heghine. Mer hishadagi nvere 21 hulis 1910, Ho. Hi. Ta.

> [Heghine widower of hero Kevork Chavush. The gift to our memory. July 21, 1910, ARF.]

After researching Kevork Chavuch, Uçaner learned that he had been born near Sasoun and that he had been an Armenian *fedayee* (guerrilla fighter). He took part in the Sasoun uprising in 1894, after which he was arrested and imprisoned. When he managed to escape he took part in the second Sasoun uprising of 1904 after joining the ARF. In 1907 he was wounded in a skirmish with Ottoman army soldiers and later died.

The discovery of the picture and its story shocked Murad. He did not know that Armenians had lived in his town; nor did he know a great deal about the Armenians in general. This meant he did not know the history of Aintab, the past of his own city. It became his obsession—he even called his cat 'Kevork Chavush'. One day a group of Armenian tourists were visiting the old town when a colleague of Uçaner shouted out the name of the cat 'Kevork Chavush, come back here!' One of the visitors turned around and asked who had given that name to the cat. The man answered that it was Murad Uçaner, but that he was not currently available. The tourist, Armen Aroyan, decided to wait until he came back.

Aroyan is a Californian Armenian who has organised tourist trips to the Armenian homeland for many decades, and has an encyclopaedic knowledge of Armenia and the history of the Armenians. He has organised over sixty tours to former Armenian monasteries and has visited more than 600 mountain villages.[6] Aroyan gave Uçaner a copy of K. Sarafian's *Brief History of Aintab*.

Uçaner started learning to read and write Armenian in order to learn the true history of his city, which the authorities had tried to destroy or silence. He is currently translating *Aintabi Koyamarde* ('Aintab's Struggle for Survival', in Armenian) into Turkish.[7]

During this period he began to research the history of the house he was involved in renovating. He learned that it had once belonged to one of the wealthy Aintab Armenian families, the Danielians. It was currently owned by Ahmet Dai, a local potentate: 'Ahmet Dai is not interested in the history of the house,' Uçaner told me. 'Most wealthy people in this town are not interested in the history of our city, because if they do, they might discover the real face of their grandfathers.' Heghine, the young, armed woman in the picture, was the widow of Kevork Chavush. 'I presume Heghine visited Aintab and stayed with the Danielian family,' Murad said. Aintab had a long tradition of receiving Armenian migrants from Sasoun who were bakers by profession.

Murad Uçaner is currently working on a book to reconstruct the life of Aintab Armenians in the nineteenth century.

* * *

I first met Murad in November 2013. He was accompanied by his friend, the former journalist Alev Er, who had founded the *Taraf* daily newspaper and who was in Aintab to undertake research for a book on Sabiha Gökçen.

We first visited Surp Asdvadzadzin Church, now known as Kurtulush Camii. As we walked around the church, Uçaner lifted the big Turkish flag which was still hanging on the wall where the church altar used to be to reveal traces of two cross carvings—the flag had not only been placed in the church to indicate that it had been 'liberated' but also to hide the remnants of its Christian past. We then toured the narrow streets above the Kurtulush Camii. One of the streets was called 'Heyik Mescit Cikmaz Sokak', while a second was called 'Heyik Müslüman Sokak'. Then we came to another street where the words 'Hayik Imam Sokak' had been written, yet the first word, Hayik, had been painted over and changed to 'Heyik'. In Armenian, the Armenians call themselves 'Hay', with the plural in classic Armenian (*krapar*) being Hayk—Hayk had become Heyik in reference to the Islamised Armenians who lived in this neighbourhood whose names were used as street names. Hayk in Turkish becomes Heyik, and the mistake on the third street sounds like it was first written in Armenian, and then 'corrected' to sound more Turkish. People might forget, but the streets of Aintab remember.

In the evening, I met Murad Uçaner near the former Catholic church and he led me into an apartment where a party was being held. When I entered, Murad introduced me to Erol Akçay, a jovial man in his late forties who had previously served as a captain in the Turkish army. When I was introduced to him, since I was Armenian his instant reaction was to ask me for forgiveness—he told me that he did this every time he met an Armenian, and that it was a moral imperative to do so. He then told me his story: he had been in the army in the 1990s and was involved in the anti-PKK war, but refused to take part in the slaughter of Kurdish villagers and was imprisoned for eight months, and later stripped of his rank. I then asked him how he had come to learn about the Armenians. He told me he had learned about the Armenians as a result of his childhood: he had been born in Aintab, in the Armenian Kestelbashi neighbourhood immediately below Surp Asdvadzadzin church/Kurtulush mosque, and grew up in one of the old Armenian houses. As a teenager, he often wondered why the houses in his neighbourhood were different from those in other parts of the town, and after the ASALA terrorist attacks his interest was further kindled with regard to why the Armenians should be seeking to attack Turks. Although there were few available resources on the Armenians at this time, he eventually read Meguerdich Margosyan's *Gyavur Mahallesi* (The Infidels' Quarter), a book concerned with the Armenians of Diyarbekie. After reading this book he went on to read many more about the Armenians in a range of different cities, and learned about their fate. He said that it was then that he realised that everything he had been taught was a lie, and decided that every time he met an Armenian he would hug them and apologise.

* * *

Prior to the First World War, Aintab had 80,000 inhabitants, 36,000 of whom were Armenian.[8] All of the Armenians were artisans and merchants. The Aintab Armenians were deported and massacred in the dark years of 1915–16, during which half the population perished. After the war, the population of the city had reduced to 40,000; the surviving Armenians then returned, increasing the population to 55,000 by 1919, among whom 18,000 were Christians. When the French forces replaced the British in Aintab on 29 October 1919, the local Armenian population apparently received them with 'cries of joy'.

The French Légion arménienne used Aintab as its headquarters. The local Turkish notables held an antagonistic attitude towards the French forces from the outset, with violent incidents taking place in Aintab as well as in neighbouring Marash. In April 1920, some 150 Armenian men formed a group of volunteer fighters led by Colonel Levonian, and joined the French forces when the town was besieged by the Turks in order to defend the Armenian quarter. At the end of the Cicilian War the city had largely been destroyed—the mosques and converted churches are still peppered with bullet and cannon holes—and the population fell as low as 28,000.[9] Aintab was a shadow of its past.

When I asked my friends in Aintab how many Armenians currently lived in the town, they told me there were many thousands, but that no one would be prepared to admit this as they would lose their jobs and it would cause other problems for them too.

From Caesarea to Diyarbakir

When travelling across Turkey, it is very difficult to find traces of Armenian life without trained eyes. I took a night bus to the central

Anatolian city of Kayseri, the classic Caesarea. The city is one of the 'Anatolian tigers', the capital of the Turkish textile industry. Gregory the Illuminator (302–325), the founder of the Armenian Church, was first introduced to Christianity in Caesarea. The city is one of the few Turkish cities east of Istanbul with an Armenian church: Saint Grigor the Illuminator. The neighbourhood around the church is composed of new high-rise buildings and old crumbling houses. The latter were where the once thriving Armenian community had lived. Before the First World War there had been a large and prosperous Armenian community in Kayseri; the province had an Armenian population of over 52,000 living in thirty-one towns and villages, who owned forty churches and seven monasteries, as well as fifty-six schools with 7,019 pupils. In Kayseri itself, a total of 18,907 Armenians lived in the town, constituting 35 per cent of the population.[10] There are only three Armenian families in the town today. The other church in Kayseri, which stands near the city walls, is called 'Surp Asdvadzadzin' (Holy Virgin Mary), but it has since been converted into a sports club.

The nouveau riche are currently building mansions in Talas, a town located on the side of a mountain a few kilometres away from Kayseri. I began to wonder why the wealthy inhabitants of Kayseri were not renovating the beautiful old houses in the town. Was it because they knew that the houses did not belong to them? At the lower side of the town, the foundations of the Talas American School, a boarding school which once served Greek and Armenian children from the region, can still be found. Inside the town itself there are numerous old houses, mostly inhabited by poor families. The rich here prefer new houses, or to live in high-rise buildings. There is a structure here that is reminiscent of a Byzantine church, the Panaya Greek church, built in 1886, but it is now the 'New Talas Mosque'.

As I walked through the former Armenian quarter we found an old mansion that had been left in ruins. The local guide who was accompanying me said that it had once belonged to the Gulbenkian family, the ancestors of the legendary Armenian oil magnate. Although the Gulbenkian family wanted to renovate the house, the Turkish authorities had consistently failed to provide them with the requisite authorisation to do so. Today there is only one Armenian family left in Talas.

* * *

When I visited the Surp Giragos church in Diyarbakir I met a number of new people: there was Remzi Demir, a construction material merchant who had a strong Kurdish identity, and though he was Muslim he was very conscious of his Armenian origins. I also met Çetin Yilmaz, an ethnic Turk from Gallipoli, who had been sent to the south-east as a Turkish language teacher in order 'to make good Turks out of Kurds', in his words, but had instead converted to Christianity. A group of young people was also visiting the church, including Nesrin Güngörmüs and Hebun Polat, who had decided to visit the church after discovering their Armenian ancestry. I also met Armen Demirjian, the deacon of Surp Giragos, who, before converting 'back' to Christianity, was called Abdulrahim Zoraslan. Demirjian received me with a wide, joyful smile, saying '*parev aghparig*' (hello, little brother).

Armen Demirjian is in his mid-fifties. He was born in Lice, a town north of Diyarbakir, from where his ancestors originate. His grandfather's family was annihilated during the 1915 massacres; the only exception was a five-year-old boy, Hovsep, who was saved by the powerful Kurdish agha of the region, Haji Zubayr. When Hovsep grew up his name was changed to Abdullah, he converted to Islam and eventually married the daughter of Haji Zubayr. Abdullah became a famous baker in Lice, and while everyone remembered him as a good Muslim they also knew that he was an Armenian. Demirjian took me around the church. The seventh-century building had recently been renovated with much care. In one hall there was an exhibition of pictures representing the life of the Armenians of Diyarbakir before the great calamity.

There was a large Armenian community in Diyarbakir, which was mainly comprised of craftsmen, artisans and farmers. In 1915, when the CUP decided to eradicate the empire's religious minorities, the 120,000 Armenians who lived in the province were rounded up, taken outside the city walls or to the outskirts of their villages, and killed. The few survivors, mainly women and orphans, ended up in camps in the Syrian Desert. In the 1920s and 1930s, the Armenians who had survived in provincial towns and villages moved to Diyarbakir in order to form a new community, but they later left the town when the south-east became caught up in the conflict between the PKK and the Turkish army. Now that they have returned, the grandchildren of the survivors are trying to establish an Armenian community in this historic city.

Armen Demirjian's son, Hassan Zoraslan, had just finished his teacher training at university and was hoping to be employed as a teacher. He is fluent in English, as well as Kurdish, his mother tongue. When coffee was served Hassan refused to drink it; it was Ramadan, and Hassan was fasting—while his father was engaged in rediscovering his Armenian and Christian past, the twenty-one-year-old Hassan was finding moral righteousness through Islam. 'We are Muslims,' he told me, 'but we also know that we are Armenian.' He became a practising Muslim around 2006, when he was sent to an uncle in Bursa in western Turkey, in order to pursue his studies away from the violence that was then taking place in Diyarbakir. 'There I went through an identity crisis. It was there that I decided I should become a pious Muslim.' I asked him for his views with regard to his father's conversion to the Armenian Apostolic Church: he told me that while he was happy that his father was returning to his Armenian roots, he also feared for his safety as he might face persecution from the state and radical groups.

I also met Gafur Türkay, who played a vital role in the renovation of the church. His story is similar to many others I have heard: his grandfather was born in Sasoun, a mountainous region to the north-east of Diyarbakir, and his family name was Ohanian. The clan of which he was part was decimated during the genocide, with only three children surviving—a daughter, who became a refugee in Syria and migrated to Armenia, and two sons who remained in Turkey and converted to Islam. Türkay proudly told me how: 'From those two boys the family has grown to become five hundred members!' Gafur grew up speaking Kurdish at home, but when he was sent to school he discovered that Kurdish was a forbidden language and that he would have to learn Turkish. 'First we were forced to learn how to be Kurdish, and then we were forced to learn how to be Turkish!' he said.

Religion and language are the two markers of Armenian identity. For many centuries, the identity of the Armenians was closely inter-twined with membership of the Armenian Apostolic Church, one of the religious communities of the Ottoman Empire.

Gafur Türkay remembers the first time he visited the church of Surp Giragos in the 1980s. At the time there were thirty Armenian families living around the church, in the Sur neighbourhood of Diyarbakir in the Gyavur Mahallesi ('infidel neighbourhood', a title also used for a novel by Megerdich Margosian which describes the life of the Armenian community). It was here that Türkay met his wife. He attaches great importance to the renovation of the church, which was completed thanks to the efforts of a small number of people who expended a vast amount of effort to collect the necessary funds. Diyarbakir municipality, which is currently ruled by the Kurdish Peace and Democracy Party (BDP), provided a third of the costs involved. The church was re-opened in October 2011, with thou-sands of Armenians coming for the event from all over the world. With financial support from the Diyarbakir municipality, it is now possible to study the Armenian language here. In 2012 there were thirty-five students, a figure which rose to sixty-five in the following year. According to Türkay, 80 per cent of the students are Muslim Armenians, with the remaining minority being either Christian Armenians or Kurds.

Gafur Türkay took me on a walk around the former Armenian quarter of Diyarbakir in order to visit the ruins of Surp Sarkis church. A Kurdish family currently lives in some of the rooms there. The architectural style is similar to that of Surp Giragos, with its beautiful vaults, yet it has been left in ruins. Projects are underway to renovate this church too. At the altar there is a newly dug hole. 'They are look-ing for gold again!' Gafur angrily exclaimed. 'I was here just two weeks ago and the hole was not here.' There are similar holes in the

Armenian churches throughout eastern Anatolia: much of the local population believes that, before the deportations in 1915, Armenians living in the area buried their gold near their houses, churches and cemeteries, with the intention of unearthing them upon their return—which never happened.

Travelling through the area, one hears all kinds of tales surrounding this buried treasure: parents killing children over a discovered stash; foreigners descending upon the area and manipulating the locals in a bid to find gold; villagers investing in expensive metal detectors. As we were ascending the hills of Saint Tovmas monastery near the shores of Lake Van, we were followed by two small children. They had been sent by the villagers, our guide told us, to see if we knew where the gold was hidden.

In the past it was government orders that were bringing down the domes and the walls of millenary churches; today, treasure hunters are doing the job.

Renovation of Aghtamar

Lake Van possesses one of the jewels of Armenian architecture. It also retains stories of glory and tragedy. The name of the island originates from an Armenian legend, a tragic love story about Tamar, a princess who lived on the island and fell in love with a young man from a lower social class. Every evening the young man would swim from the mainland to the island in order to meet his beloved Tamar by following the light from a lantern she would use to guide him. Yet Tamar's father eventually learned of the relationship, and extinguished the light during one of the evenings in which the young man was swimming to the island, leaving him to die from exhaustion.

For a period of three centuries of Arab rule, church building on the Armenian plateau practically came to a standstill. However, between the tenth and eleventh centuries, as Arab influence began to wane and prior to the divisions of Armenian lands by the great powers and nomadic invaders, Armenian culture flourished. The architect Trdat Mendet, known as Manuel, built the Cathedral of the Holy Cross

238

(Surp Khach) between 915 and 921 under King Gagik I (r. 904–936/943), from the Ardzruni dynasty of Vasburagan.[11] King Gagik also constructed his palace on the island, although this building no longer survives; there is also a harbour that is celebrated for its complex structure. The basic structure of the cathedral resembles that of the Surp Hripsime Church in Echmiadzin, yet it also has some striking bas-reliefs carved into its external walls depicting biblical stories. These include images of David and Goliath and Jonas being swallowed by a whale, as well as some scenes depicting more contemporary activities like hunting and people drinking wine. The interior of the church is covered by frescos, one of which depicts Jesus entering Jerusalem. The decoration of the church and its architecture reflect the influence of Arab and Islamic art and architectural styles from Baghdad and Damascus. The construction of the cathedral marked the beginning of the Armenian cultural renaissance, which would reach its maturity in the numerous magnificent buildings in Ani, the Armenian capital. The architectural styles here would later influence Muslim and European architecture.[12]

The Holy Cross Cathedral gradually became a centre for Armenian ecclesiastic and intellectual activity. Aghtamar and its monastery were also the site of an Armenian Catholicosate which was established in 1116 and was only closed in 1895, with the death of Khachadur III, Catholicos of Aghtamar. In 1915 the monks and civilians who had found refuge on the island were massacred and the cathedral was looted. It was left to decline.

As a result of diplomatic pressure from the EU and the United States, the Turkish government decided to renovate the cathedral with the aim of using it as a showcase of its policy towards the Armenians. Yet when the cathedral was eventually opened to visitors on 19 September 2011, the Turkish authorities insisted that it was a museum rather than a place of worship, and was simply designed to encourage tourism to the area. The Turkish authorities also prevented a cross being placed over the dome of the cathedral and a bell from being added to the bell-tower. Cengiz Çandar wrote angrily: 'Whatever the intention was, it looks like a "cultural genocide." ... You restore a historical church and find absurd reasons for not putting a cross and a bell onto it?'[13]

Prior to the opening day, the Turkish prime minister's office sent invitations to the All-Armenian Catholicos in Echmiadzin in Armenia, to the Catholicosate of the Great House of Cilicia, established in Antelias in Lebanon, as well as to Armenian organisations and journalists. However, given the authorities' stance with regard to the use of Christian symbols on the building, a number of those who had been invited declined to participate in the ceremony. The Catholicos Aram of the Great House of Cilicia was the first to do so, citing the fact that more than 2,000 churches in historic Armenia had been destroyed, left to ruins or turned into mosques, and claiming that the renovation of the cathedral was simply an exercise in propaganda. The All-Armenian Catholicos in Echmiadzin also declared that it would not participate in the ceremony. In the end, only a handful of participants came from Armenia and a few hundred from the diaspora, with most of those in attendance being local Kurds and representatives of Turkish officialdom. Archbishop Aram of the Istanbul Patriarchate led the religious ceremonies. In the words of one of the few Armenian journalists who attended the event: 'It was a ceremony of collective mourning for 1915, for the innocent victims, although Aram Archbishop in his holy mess did not mention any date in any way ... It was the saddest mess I had ever witnessed.'[14]

Ani, capital of melancholia

When approaching Ani one is left with an impression of its magnificent architecture, but there is also something very melancholy about the place. The city is surrounded by walls with round rose-coloured towers built of tuff and punctured with the marks of thousands of arrows. The city itself is built on a triangular site where two rivers have carved deep ravines into the landscape: from the east and the south the Akhuryan River ravines and from the west the smaller river Tsaghkots flows across a gorge where hundreds of caves served as dwellings for the poorer classes of the past. A system of fortification walls and towers once surrounded Ani, much of which can still be seen by visitors today. On the wall above the main gate, a lion has been carved into the stone, the symbol of the Bagratuni, or Bagratid, dynasty (884–1045), which constructed this once prosperous city. Beyond the gate is a vast field with churches, temples, caravanserai and palaces, all of which have been left to ruin.

Ani's survival, despite facing repeated invasions and natural disasters, has come at quite a price. As the first tourists arriving that summer morning, we found children from neighbouring villages grazing their cows next to the foundations of King Gagik Church.

The city contains one of the finest examples of Armenian architecture, the Mother Cathedral of Ani, which was designed by Trdat the Architect (circa 940–1020) and completed in 1001. David Marshall Lang writes:

> [T]he cathedral amazes the onlooker. Technically, it is far ahead of the contemporary Anglo-Saxon and Norman architecture of western Europe. Already, pointed arches and clustered piers, whose appearance together is considered one of the hallmarks of mature Gothic architecture, are found in this remote corner of [the] Christian East. The rigorous simplicity of design, like a Mozart symphony, gives Ani Cathedral a stately and sublime quality.[15]

Ani contains many examples of the grandeur of Armenian culture, and in many ways the city symbolises its rise and fall. The city is situated between Kars in Turkey and Gyumri in Armenia, on the western banks of the Arpaçay (Turkish) or Akhuryan (Armenian) River. Ani is a vast archaeological site of the medieval Armenian capital of the Bagradite royal dynasty. At its peak, during the reign of Byzantine Emperor Michael IV (r. 1034–1041), the city had a population of more than 100,000 people; there were no European cities west of Constantinople of an equivalent size.[16] It was an important trading, cultural and religious centre. After the Bagradite kings made Ani their capital in 961, the city grew quickly, and in 992 the Catholicos of the Armenian Church moved there. The Silk Road passed through the city, linking European markets with Persia and China, and this served as the basis for its growth and prosperity.

The decline of Ani, which was equally rapid, began when the Byzantine Empire sought to subdue the 'Armenian heretics' to the east. The Byzantine Emperor Michael IV finally managed to gain control of the city in 1045; however, the city was captured by Seljuk armies led by Alp Arslan in 1064, who plundered it and killed its inhabitants. Seven years later, the Byzantine Emperor Romanos IV Diogenes was taken prisoner by the Seljuks in the battle of Manzikert, a major turning point in the fortunes of the Byzantine Empire which also marked the Seljuk conquest of Anatolia.

In the two centuries that followed, the city experienced both revival and further invasions and destruction. Under the four-decade rule of Minuchihr (or Menucher), the Shaddadid prince (r. 1072–1118), the city was relatively stable and prosperous, but his son and successor, Abul-Aswad (1118–1124), adopted a repressive policy towards the Armenian inhabitants, and eventually lost Ani to the Georgian King David Bagrationi in 1124. Ani again prospered under the rule of Georgian Queen Tamar (1184–1213). Many of the late structures in Ani, including the Church of Dikran Honents, are from this era. Yet this period of prosperity for Ani was again cut short in 1236 with the arrival of the Mongol armies under Chormaghan, who massacred the city's inhabitants. After the Mongol invasions, the city entered a period of long-term decline as the trade routes between Asia and Europe shifted away from Asia Minor. A devastating earthquake in 1319 led to waves of migrations in various directions: Persia to the south, Cilicia and Venice to the west, Crimea and Poland to the north. The invasion of Tamerlane (or Leng Timur, Timur the Lame) was the most devastating; after the passage of his armies, the region was largely depopulated—Ani was left in ruins.[17]

The inscriptions on the buildings and streets in Ani, installed by the Turkish tourism authorities, mention several of the nationalities and empires that have had a presence in the city at one time or another: there is the 'Seljuk Palace (Palace of Trader)', the 'Small Turkish Bath', the 'Big Turkish Bath', the 'Georgian Church' and so on and so forth. Yet one national reference is conspicuously absent: that of the Armenians, the civilisation that built Ani.

From Minuchihr mosque there is a majestic view over the Akhuryan River, and over Armenia on the left bank. There is an ancient bridge, originally constructed of a single vault spanning over thirty metres, which once connected Ani with towns and cities to the east, over which the caravans travelled transporting silk, spices as well as knowledge across markets and nations. According to one account the bridge was destroyed during the Tamerlane siege of the city in 1386, and never built again.[18] In the nineteenth century travellers reported that a guardhouse existed next to the bridge, but this has collapsed since.

The bridge remains in ruins and one cannot walk through it to cross to the other shore. No one will use it as the government of Turkey continues to close the border, to impose a total blockade on land-locked Armenia. This is the last fragment of the Iron Curtain that survived the Cold War.

10

THE OWNER OF THE TURKISH
PRESIDENTIAL PALACE

Silence has long reigned in Turkey with regard to the appropriation of Armenian, Greek, Assyrian and Jewish property. Turkish society subconsciously censored this aspect of its hidden guilt. However, in recent years, the truth about many of these properties has slowly begun to emerge, with shocking effect.

On 25 March 2007 Soner Yalçin published an article in the newspaper *Hürriyet* about the Turkish presidential residence, the Çankaya Palace (Çankaya Köşkü). The palace has been used for this purpose since 1921, when Mustafa Kemal ordered the local authorities to buy it from a man named Bulgurluzâde Tevfik Efendi, the owner at the time.

One piece of information, almost hidden in the article, created something of a sensation in Turkey. The article talked about how Ohannes Kasabian, a wealthy Armenian merchant from Ankara, had built the mansion and lived in it for many years prior to the war, before selling the house and all of its contents to Bulgurluzâde Efendi when he left the town during the war.[1] The article did not discuss why the Kasabians—Armenians and Christians—had to leave Ankara, so far away from any military front, while the Bulgurluzâdes—Turks and Muslims—were able to stay behind and purchase property. It was this piece of information that would subsequently generate a heated debate, with many maintaining that it must be incorrect—the 'White House' of republican Turkey must surely have never been occupied by Armenians.

Yet this could hardly be denied, as the names of the original owners are still visible in Armenian lettering on the fountain in the Çankaya, which is open to the public.[2]

Like the majority of the Armenians in the sanjak of Angora, the Kasabians were Armenian Catholics. They were well-respected merchants and artisans, Turkish-speakers and had not been involved in any political agitation.

In mid-July 1915, 5,200 non-Catholic Armenians had been arrested, before being chained together two-by-two a month later, whereupon gendarmes and officers from the Special Organisation killed all of them. At the end of August, 1,500 Armenian Catholic men were arrested and deported towards Aleppo. Only 200 hundred of them reached the city, the rest dying during the journey. A total of thirty-four survived until they reached Meskené, the final concentration camp, on the banks of the Euphrates.[3]

The family were among the more fortunate Armenians of the region that were not arrested, deported, or murdered. But they did not 'sell' the house, as the *Hürriyet* article maintained; instead it was simply confiscated by the local government and passed to Turkish notables. Edward J. Cuhaci, an architect who has lived in Ottawa since 1957 and the son of Rose Kasparian—Ohannes Kasabian's daughter—wrote a letter pointing this out to *Hürriyet*, but the newspaper refused to publish the correction.[4] Few of the Kasabian family's descendants remain in Turkey. Verkin Kasapoğlu is one of them. She remembers how her father Antoine used to take her to Ankara to visit houses without revealing past history.

In 1942 the state launched the *Varlık Vergisi*—a one off 'Wealth Tax' imposed only on religious minorities. Armenians had to pay 232 per cent of their income—compared to the 4.94 per cent tax imposed on Muslims. It specifically targeted the minority communities of Istanbul, the only location in the Ottoman Empire where minorities had survived the WWI deportations and massacres. Antoine

Kasapoğlu sold whatever property he still owned, yet could not pay the tax. He was sent to a mountainous area near Erzurum and forced to work in a concentration camp. No wonder that Antoine Kasapoğlu did not tell his daughter Verkin about the family's history, or about the properties left behind in Ankara and confiscated by their own state. It was only in 2001 when the Armenian patriarch told her the story of the family, and concluded: 'Çankaya belongs to you.'

The story of the Turkish Presidential Palace raises a number of questions about republican Turkey and the fate of Armenian property after the genocide. In the words of historian Donald Bloxham, the 'Turkish elites inherited strong personal, material rationales for refusing to recognise the origin of stolen land and property, as by extension did the state.'[5] The destruction of the Armenians had several objectives, including the elimination of a political problem (the 'Armenian Question') and the confiscation of the property of the Armenians and its transfer to Muslims with the aim of creating a 'Muslim bourgeoisie'. The confiscation of Armenian property remains at the heart of today's debate.

Ataturk's Palace is not the only famous property that was stolen from the Armenians. The 'Erzurum Congress' of August 1919, for instance, where the largely unknown army officer Mustafa Kemal gathered a group of Turkish nationalist militants, most of them former CUP members, to launch his liberation struggle, took place in Sanasarian College, an Armenian secondary school. The teachers and students of the school were massacred in 1915.

Incirlik is a major US air base in Turkey; it is situated near Adana in the south, close to the Mediterranean coast. It also serves as a base for Turkish and British warplanes. It has been used in this capacity since 1951. It served as a major asset for American force projection in the Middle East during the Cold War, and it remains an important base for NATO in this turbulent yet strategically important region.

Incirlik used to belong to the Armenians. The region was home to a sizeable Armenian population until the 1909 anti-Armenian massacres and the bigger wave of deportations and massacres in 1915. In 2010, a case was filed in a California district court by Rita Mahdessian and Anais Haroutunian from Los Angeles, and Alex Bakalian from Washington, DC, who had documents proving that the land belonged to them. They accused the Turkish Central Bank and the Ziraat (agriculture) Bank of having confiscated their assets, and of profiting from the income this generated by renting the land as an airbase. The plaintiffs demanded 63.9 million USD as compensation for their land, plus additional compensation for the loss in rent over the previous sixty years.[6]

The court case did not receive a great deal of media attention.[7] After three years, the court in California rejected their claims on the grounds that this was a political rather than a legal issue.[8]

Property Confiscation

When the deportations began in 1915, it immediately raised the question of what should be done with the vast amount of Armenian property that was left behind. The CUP authorities issued a number of laws and administrative directives with regard to this issue, and those who have sought to deny that genocide took place often point to these as evidence that the authorities merely intended to relocate the populations in question and to compensate them with housing and food. But no compensation was given.

The real intentions of the CUP leadership are revealed in a series of secret directives, which clearly show that there was no intention of protecting Armenian properties until the end of the war. On 31 May 1915, the Ottoman Council of Ministers adopted a decision on the distribution of land to the Armenian deportees in their new places of residence. It also stated that the state would construct new houses and provide the deportees with tools that would enable them to earn a living. This was followed by detailed regulation on 'Abandoned Properties' on 10 June 1915, which set out how the vast number of properties left behind should be managed. Houses were to be sealed and taken under state protection; goods were to be recorded under the name of their owners 'in a detailed way' and placed into storage; perishable goods and animals were to be sold at auction and the sum 'preserved in the name of the owner'. Thirty-three 'Liquidation Commissions' were established to manage the properties in various provincial capitals. Finally, on 26 September 1915, a temporary law was passed that removed any right of the deportees to reclaim their property in the future.[9]

None of the three temporary laws and directives specified how the Armenians would be recompensed for their property. Arthur Gwinner, the chairman of the Baghdad Railway Company, summarised these laws in a letter to the German Foreign Office:

> It could have been expressed much more simply and clearly in two paragraphs, namely:
>
> Article 1: 'All of the Armenians' goods have been confiscated.'
> Article 2: 'The government will collect the exiles' claims and reimburse (or not reimburse) their debts.'[10]

The Armenian deportees were prevented from selling their property as soon as the orders for the deportations to take place had been given, and they were also forbidden from withdrawing money from their bank accounts. The inhabitants of the towns and villages were given very little time to collect their belongings before they were pushed into convoys, often given no time at all. The inhabitants of Kayseri, a prosperous town with a large Armenian population, were ordered to abandon all of their property before departure:

> Leave all your belongings—your furniture, your beddings, your artefacts. Close your shops and businesses with everything inside. Your doors will be sealed with special stamps. On your return, you will get everything you left behind. Do not sell property or any expensive item. Buyers and sellers alike will be liable for legal action. Put your money in a bank in the name of a relative who is out of the country. Make a list of everything you own, including livestock, and give it to the specified official so that all your things can be returned to you later. You have ten days to comply with this ultimatum.[11]

When the Armenians had been deported, Muslim refugees were brought from the Caucasus and the Balkans to occupy their vacant houses. This in itself reveals that the CUP authorities did not view the deportations as a temporary measure.

The theft of Armenian property was part of a broader CUP strategy of creating a 'national economy' and a 'Muslim bourgeoisie'. This is reflected in an order issued by Talaat on 6 January 1916:

> The movable property left by the Armenians should be conserved for long-term preservation, and for the sake of an increase of Muslim businesses in our country, companies need to be established strictly made up of Muslims. Movable property should be given to them under suitable conditions that will guarantee the business' steady consolidation. The founder, the management and the representatives should be chosen from honourable leaders and the elite, and to allow tradesmen and agriculturists to participate in its dividends, the vouchers need to be half a lira or one lira and registered to their names to preclude that the capital falls in foreign hands. The growth of entrepreneurship in the minds of Muslim people needs to be monitored, and this endeavour and the results of its implementation need to be reported to the Ministry step by step.[12]

The CUP leadership also profited from the confiscation of the Armenian property. Ahmet Refik Altınay, an Ottoman officer as well as a journalist and historian, wrote the following in 1919:

> There is calm in Eskisehir ... The elegant Armenian houses around the train station are empty. This element [meaning the Armenians], with its wealth and commerce has shown superiority, obeyed the orders of the government and evacuated their houses ... and now their vacated houses with valuable carpets, elegant rooms and their shut doors, are as though they were waiting expectantly for the arrival of the fugitives.

But the 'fugitives' would never return. Much of their property had already been divided up between the CUP leadership:

> Eskişehir's most beautiful most refined houses are around the train station. Houses near the train station, suitable for residence, were assigned to Ittihad's most important officials: the German school, its exterior deprived of paint and not even plastered, to Sultan Mehmet Reşat, a huge Armenian mansion to the prince, two canary yellow coloured houses side by side in the area of Sarısu Bridge, to Talaat Bey and his assistant Canbolat Bey, a magnificent villa in the Armenian neighbourhood to Topal Ismail Hakkı.[13]

Most of the Armenian property went directly to the Turkish state. On 24 August 1915, a telegram sent by the Interior Ministry to the province of Sivas gave the following order: 'The state has decided to expropriate the immovable property and possessions of the deported Armenians, and to pay off their (outstanding) debts. Therefore, it is necessary to preserve the rights devolving upon to government and to reconcile [these actions] with the laws on the transfer of property.'[14]

Continuum

When Turkey was defeated in the First World War, the CUP leaders abandoned their country in order to save their lives. The newly established government, led by Ahmet Izzet Pasha, revised the policies of the CUP with regard to confiscated property. On 18 October 1918, the government issued an order that would allow the deported Armenians to return to their homes, and on 4 November 1918 it annulled the laws passed in 1915 concerning the confiscation of Armenian property.[15]

However, when the Armenian survivors tried to return home, they had to be accompanied by gendarmes because of the hostility they faced from their former neighbours, who had been occupying their properties in the three-year period since the deportations took place. Violence soon erupted between the two communities—many of those who now lived in these properties, having purchased them at auction, felt that their rights were being violated. The anger of those who had profited from the genocide fed into the nationalist revolt led by Mustafa Kemal.

When the army officer Mustafa Kemal came to power in 1923, it effectively marked a return to the rule of the CUP as he had been a member of the latter organisation since the 1908 revolution. Many of the people associated with the Kemalist movement, such as Rauf Orbay Bey, Kâzım Karabekir and Celal Bayar, to name but a few, had also been members of the CUP.[16]

After 1923, the nationalist Kemalist regime returned to the practices of the CUP with regard to Armenian property: all Armenian property was to be transferred to the state and the Armenians were prohibited from returning or reclaiming their belongings. This policy continued in the republican era. The Kemalists also continued the CUP tradition of dividing Armenian property between the leading members of the movement. Historians Uğur Ümit Üngör and Mehmet Polatel have compiled the following list of properties distributed between CUP-Kemalist dignitaries:

[T]he family of district governor of Muş, Servet Bey, who in 1915 had annihilated the Armenians of that city, was awarded a composite package of Armenian property. The family of Cemal Azmi, the murderous governor of Trabzon, was also assigned considerable 'reparation', specifically from Armenian properties. Hafız Abdullah Avni, a hotel owner who had collaborated in the genocide in Erzincan, was executed for his crimes in 1920 by the Istanbul tribunal. His wife, Hatice Hanım, was compensated with a house and a field from the Armenian villages of Şuhe and Kani. The fanatical district governor of Boğazlıyan, Mehmed Kemal Bey, had left behind a family in Yozgat. They received a large apartment and a house from the available Armenian property in that area. Dr. Bahaeddin Shakir Bey's family received a house in the upmarket Şişli district of Istanbul. The former district governor of Urfa, Mehmed Nusret Bey, had played a key role during the genocide and was executed in 1919 for his crimes. His wife, Hayriye Hanım, was compensated with a shop and a house in Istanbul's Beyoğlu district, on Cadde-i Kebîr [currently İstiklâl Caddesi] on numbers 264 and 266. The property was located in the Aznavur Han and originally belonged to a merchant named Bedros. Cemal Pasha's heirs and family were compensated with the property of Vicken Hokachian, a merchant in Istanbul. A shop and a strip of land in Beyoğlu across the French cemetery as large as 1,450 square metres, was assigned to his wife Senice, his daughter Kamran, his sons Ahmed Rüşdü, Hasan Necdet, Hasan Behçet, his big sister Şaziye and little sister Bakire. The list is long. The files contain details on the original owners and new recipients as well as on the nature, size and location of the property. All are signed by President Mustafa Kemal Pasha and his cabinet of veteran Young Turks, including Mustafa Abdülhalik Renda, Mahmud Celâl Bayar and Şükrü Kaya.[17]

In 1923 Kemalist Turkey and the Western Allies signed the Lausanne Peace Treaty, which laid the legal basis for the emergence of modern Turkey on the ruins of the once mighty Ottoman Empire. It replaced the Treaty of Sèvres (1920), which the Ottoman Empire had signed but not ratified.

Section III of the Treaty of Lausanne, Articles 37–45, is dedicated to the protection of minorities. The treaty states that these articles are fundamental laws (*lois fondamentales*) that cannot be altered, and which were designed to ensure the 'life and liberty to all inhabitants of Turkey without distinction of birth, nationality, language, race or religion'. According to the treaty, the right of the minorities to use and receive an education in their mother tongue must be upheld, and the Turkish authorities must respect the principle of freedom of worship. The treaty was to be enforced by the League of Nations.[18]

No mention is made in the treaty of the return of refugees or the fate of the confiscated property, as the Turkish delegation simply refused to discuss these issues, and while the Kemalists signed the treaty, they had no intention of adhering to its measures with regard to minority rights. The confiscation of property, violence against minorities and systematic discrimination continued. It has continued ever since.

The Second World War provided another occasion to attack minority properties. The government imposed what was known as the 'Wealth Tax' (*Varlik Vergisi*). The intention was to collect a one-off tax from the wealthy classes, mainly from Istanbul, Izmir and Ankara, to cover the budget deficit. City merchants were accused of being 'war profiteers', having kept products to push market prices upwards. Yet the taxes were not the same for all citizens: Muslims paid only 4.9 per cent of their revenue as Wealth Tax, while Greeks were asked to pay 156 per cent and Jews 179 per cent. But the highest percentage of all was imposed on Armenians: 232 per cent. The tax was often enforced in an arbitrary manner, with non-Muslims being given a mere fifteen days to pay their bills. Those who could not pay the tax were stripped of their property. Properties in the Beyoğlu district of Istanbul, including hotels, factories and mansions, were taken over and sold to Turks at prices well below their market value.[19]

Those who could not pay were sent to labour camps in Aşkale, west of Erzurum. Some 15,000 people were transferred to these camps, half of whom were Armenian. As a result of US and British pressure, the Wealth Tax was abandoned in March 1944 and the deportees were freed, although many did not return.

On 6–7 September 1955, a new pogrom was launched in Istanbul, the target of which was the Greek community, or what remained of it, after rumours had begun to circulate that they had burnt down Mustafa Kemal's house in Salonika. An angry mob started attacking Greek shops on Istiklal Avenue and Taksim Square. This soon escalated into a general anti-minority riot, with attacks against Greeks, Armenians, Georgians, Jews and other groups living in the once cosmopolitan Beyoğlu neighbourhood. Half a century later, a Turkish newspaper published a list of the properties that had been attacked: 'According to court records, 4,214 residences, 1,004 shops, 73 churches, one synagogue, two monasteries, 26 schools, and 5,317 other buildings including factories, hotels, bars and such were attacked in Istanbul.'[20] Similar events took place in Izmir.

The Turkish government was responsible for the pogrom, as the rumour regarding the Greeks had originally been spread by the Turkish secret services. Truckloads of rioters were brought into the city, organised and supervised by state officials. It was the official Turkish response to inter-communal tensions in Cyprus between the Greek Cypriot government and the ethnic Turkish minority there. This became even more obvious after the 1960 coup d'état, when the new military authorities accused the deposed Prime Minister Adnan Menderes of being responsible for the 1955 pogroms.

The 1955 pogroms effectively ended the Greek presence in the city once called Constantinople. The number of Greeks in Turkey has declined from 130,000 in 1923 to below 2,000 today. Fifty years after the pogroms, when a gallery in the same Beyoğlu district organised a photo exhibition dedicated to the events of 1955, a group of Turkish nationalists erupted into the hall, carrying red Turkish flags, and attacking the pictures, destroying some and throwing others out of the windows.[21]

The continuous internal conflict in Cyprus—and especially the 15 July 1974 military coup by the Cypriot National Guard, followed by the Turkish military invasion of the island five days later—provided yet another opportunity for state racketeering. In 1974 the Turkish government confiscated thousands of properties belonging to minority foundations, including churches, schools and summer camps. In 1936 the Turkish authorities had asked minority foundations to present a list of their properties. This was the period when 'secularist' state bureaucracy was carrying out a ruthless attack on Muslim foundations, confiscating their property, and nationalising the social role they played until that time. Forty years later, at the height of the Cyprus crisis as Turkish armed forces invaded the island, the Turkish parliament passed a law declaring all property owned by minority foundations outside the list presented in 1936 to be illegal and confiscated all such assets, which included some 1,400 properties belonging to Armenian foundations.[22]

Diran Bakar, a famous Istanbul lawyer and one of the founders of *Agos*, struggled for years against the injustice of the '1936 Declaration' and the confiscation of Armenian property. After he passed away in 2009, his family gave all his archives to the Hrant Dink Foundation. A research team worked on the archives for two years, and eventually published a bilingual, 478-page book filled with maps, photographs and official documents.[23]

One of the properties discussed in the book is the Bomonti Mekhitarist School. The Armenian Catholic Congregation, with its headquarters in Venice, had constructed three schools in Istanbul during the nineteenth century: the first, the Galata Saint George Latin Church, opened in 1803; the second, the Mekhitarist Armenian Primary School at Sakızağacı in Pera, opened in 1830; and the third, at Moda in Kadıköy, opened in the late 1850s. The school in Sakızağacı was consumed by fire in 1870, forcing the students to move to other facilities in order to continue their education. The school in Moda, on the other hand, was taken over by the Ottoman army and was used as dormitories for the soldiers. On 21 January 1915, as soldiers were lighting a fire in the basement of the building for laundry, it was also destroyed by fire and remained closed in the period that followed. In 1958 the Mekhitarists sold the land on which the Moda School once stood, and bought a building in Bomonti in the Şişli district of Istanbul, where they established a new school called the 'Bomonti Private Armenian Catholic School'.

In 1979, the Directorate General of Foundations (DGF)—a Turkish state institution that oversees foundation activities and manages historic buildings—filed a lawsuit against the Bomonti School under the 1936 Declaration, which claimed that the community foundation's acquisition of this property was illegal. The DFG demanded that the property be returned to its previous owner. In 1985, a Şişli court ruled in favour of the DGF. After a long battle to save the school, the foundation ultimately signed a rental agreement with the new owners of the property in 1998; having had their property confiscated and given to Muslims free of charge, the foundation was now forced to pay those who had taken it.[24]

It is not known how many properties were confiscated by the thirty-three Liquidation Commissions. As a result of EU pressure, Turkey began to digitise the Ottoman land registry and made the records available to the public. Yet on 26 August 2005, the National Security Committee of the Turkish Armed Forces issued a stern warning: 'The Ottoman records kept at the Land Register and Cadaster Surveys General Directorate offices must be sealed and not available to the public, as they have the potential to be exploited by alleged genocide claims and property claims.'[25]

Confiscated Capital

The question of Armenian capital, and more generally the economic function of the Ottoman Armenians, played a central role in the CUP decision to destroy the community. Any recognition of the crime committed against the Ottoman Armenians will consequently incur a cost for the Turkish government in terms of compensation.

Talaat, the strongman of the CUP junta and the person who bears leading responsibility for genocidal policies, was openly interested in Armenian capital. This motivation transpires on several occasions during his conversations with American Ambassador Morgenthau:

One day Talaat asked US Ambassador Morgenthau to ask American life insurance companies to send to him a "complete list of their Armenian policy holders. They are practically all dead now and have no heirs to collect the money. It of course escheats to the State. The Government is the beneficiary now. Will you do so?"[26]

Talaat even wanted to appropriate money transfers sent for humanitarian purposes to the starving Armenians. 'Here is a cablegram for you from America, sending you a lot of money for the Armenians. You ought not to use it that way; give it to us Turks, we need it as badly as they do' he told the American Ambassador, after having intercepted telegrams sent to the US embassy in Istanbul.[27] The next argument the American envoy thought of to push Talaat to stop massacring the Armenians was the losses the state treasury would bear as a result of the destruction of the leading tax-payers of the empire: 'We care nothing about the commercial losses' answered Talaat, 'We have figured all that out and we know that it will not exceed five million pounds.'[28]

In a meeting with Morgenthau, Talaat clearly articulates the reason why the CUP decided to destroy the Armenians: 'We base our objections to the Armenians on three distinct grounds. In the first place, they have enriched themselves at the expense of the Turks. In the second place, they are determined to domineer over us and to establish a separate state. In the third place, they have openly encouraged our enemies. They have assisted the Russians in the Caucasus and our failure there is largely explained by their actions.'[29]

'Massacre as a means of destroying business competition was certainly an original concept!' angrily writes Morgenthau.[30]

This was about more than eliminating a business competitor. It was the plunder of the century. In 1916, the CUP administration transferred the sum of 5,000,000 Turkish lira, the equivalent of 30,000 kilogrammes of gold, to a deposit at the German Reichsbank. This sum was likely amassed from the confiscated bank deposits of the Armenians who had been killed or deported to the Syrian Desert.[31]

It was not just the CUP leaders and other sections of Turkish and Kurdish society that profited from withholding Armenian assets. Other, ostensibly neutral, parties also profited: just as in the wake of the Second World War it came to light that Swiss banks had kept accounts belonging to Holocaust victims, in the wake of the massacres of the Armenians, banks that had provided life insurance—predominantly New York Life Insurance Company, Equitable Life Assurance Society, also located in New York, and Paris based Union-Vie—created Kafkaesque bureaucratic obstacles to avoid paying out.[32]

Destruction

Naregavank was a tenth-century monastery. It is situated to the south of Lake Van, not far from Akhtamar Island and monastery. Naregavank was a major centre of learning for 1,000 years. It is here that the tenth-century mystic monk, poet, theologian and philosopher Krikor Naregatsi studied, lived and worked, writing such masterpieces as *Song of Songs* and *Book of Lamentations*. His mausoleum was still visible until the start of the war. The monastery, which was still active at the beginning of the twentieth century, ceased to operate during the First World War when the monks and villagers were deported and killed. In 1951, the Turkish army arrived and destroyed the monastery. The few surviving stones, pieces of Khachkars, can still be seen in what is now a Kurdish village, with the newcomers having used the stones to build their own dwellings.

Hence Armenian property in Turkey was not only confiscated in the twentieth century, but in many cases it was also destroyed. According to an estimated by the Armenian Patriarchate of Constantinople, in 1914 there were 210 monasteries, 700 monastic churches and 1,639 parish churches active on Turkish territory.[33] Today there are only seven functioning Armenian churches in Turkey east of Istanbul.

The destruction of the churches progressed in waves. The destruction started with the genocide and continued in the 1920s, before resuming in the 1950s, 1970s and 1980s. The fifth-century church of Tekor, for instance, which was still standing in 1956, was destroyed when the Turkish army began to use it as a target for artillery exercises. The monastery of Saint Garabed, which had been plundered in 1915, suffered the same fate when it was used for the same purpose in 1960. The marvellous Surp Nshan Monastery in Sivas (Sebastia) was dynamited in 1978, and a military base was built in its place.

Other churches were 'converted'. In 1994, a British writer made the following notes during a visit to Urfa, the ancient Edessa:

> I passed the old Armenian cathedral. Between 1915 and last year it was a fire station; now, as I discovered, it is being converted into a mosque. The altar has been dismantled, leaving the apse empty. A *mihrab* has been punched into the south wall. A new carpet covers the floor; outside lies a pile of old ecclesiastical woodwork destined for firewood. Two labourers in baggy pantaloons were at work on the façade, balanced on a rickety lattice of scaffolding, plastering the decorative stonework over the principle arch. I wondered if they knew the history of the building, so I asked them if it was an old mosque.
>
> 'No,' one of the workmen shouted down. 'It's a church.'
>
> 'Greek?'
>
> 'No,' he said. 'Armenian.'
>
> 'Are there any Armenians left in Urfa?'
>
> 'No,' he said, smiling broadly and laughing. His friend made a throat-cutting gesture with his trowel.
>
> 'They've all gone,' said the first man, smiling.
>
> 'Where to?'
>
> The two looked at each other: 'Israel,' said the first man, after a pause. He was grinning from ear to ear.
>
> 'I thought Israel was for the Jews,' I said.
>
> 'Jews, Armenians,' he replied, shrugging his shoulders. 'Same thing.'
>
> The two men went back to work, cackling with laughter as they did so.[34]

Return of Property, One by One

The policy of confiscating minority property and expelling minorities from Turkey continued for nine decades after the First World War, without any serious objections from the international community. Turkey was admitted to the League of Nations in 1932 and to the United Nations at its founding in 1945. It also became a member of NATO in 1952 and signed an association agreement with the EEC in 1963.

However, although Turkey was able to gain membership of these institutions without major opposition to its policies, this changed when Turkey sought to become a full member of the EU. In the words of a Turkish think tank:

> In the 1930s, it became evident that pushing or directly forcing the few non-Muslims left in Turkey to abandon the country was an explicit state policy. The aim of the several discriminatory laws and practices ... was to clear the country of non-Muslims ... When Turkey became a candidate for the European Union (EU), it became clear that it was not possible to sustain this state policy towards non-Muslim communities. The real estate owner-ship problems of non-Muslim foundations were brought to the attention of the government in annual progress reports issued by the European Commission.[35]

The most immediate struggle was to reclaim the Armenian founda-tion properties that had been confiscated as a result of the 1974 Declaration. After exhausting every avenue open to them in the Turkish justice system, the Armenian foundations eventually took their cases to the European Court of Human Rights in Strasbourg.

In Diyarbakir, the Surp Giragos Armenian Church Foundation, with the Armenian Patriarchate of Istanbul, submitted an appeal to the Foundations General Directorate (FGD) to return some 190 properties belonging to the Surp Giragos Church that had been con-fiscated by the Turkish state. The FGD confirmed that seventeen of the properties located along the ancient walls of Sur—the historic town of Diyarbakir—had been confiscated and returned them to the church foundation. But the FGD refused to return the remaining properties on the grounds that the title deeds were from the period prior to 1910 and were 'antiquated and insufficient'.[36]

In 2008, in another similar case, the Turkish court gave a verdict demanding that the state compensate Samatya Surp Krikor Armenian Church with 600,000 EUR, and Surp Pergiç Armenian Hospital Foundation in Yedikule with 275,000 EUR for violating their prop-erty rights. The two Armenian Foundations go back to 1832, but their property was confiscatedat a time when Turkish courts considered that the two foundations were not entitled to acquire property.[37]

THE OWNER OF THE TURKISH PRESIDENTIAL PALACE

A new wave of conversions

While some of the confiscated property has begun to be returned to its rightful owners in Istanbul, the situation is very different elsewhere in Turkey, where there is an Islamist campaign to convert the few remaining churches used as museums into mosques. One example of this is the occupation of Hagia Sophia Church in Trabzon by Muslim religious activists. Built as a Pontic Greek church in the thirteenth century, it was changed into a mosque several centuries later. The frescos covering the church walls were whitewashed, and the mosaics on the ground were covered by carpets, thus hiding one of the surviving jewels of Byzantine art. It was used as a hospital when the Russian army entered the town during the First World War, and afterwards was once again converted into a mosque. Under the Kemalists, the church-mosque was left to its fate, becoming dilapidated, and it was in a pitiful situation until a group of archaeologists from Edinburgh University renovated it and opened its doors as a museum in 1962.

In 2012 a court in Trabzon gave a favourable judgement to a local religious foundation that wanted to turn the Hagia Sophia into a mosque. The Ministry of Culture counterattacked, declaring the act illegal, but in July 2013 the local mufti and a mass of people gathered around the site for Friday prayers during the month of Ramadan. The court decision and the taking over of the church-museum seem to have enjoyed the support of the ruling AKP and its neo-Ottoman ideological narrative.[38] This *fait accompli* followed the conversion of yet another Hagia Sophia, this time in the town of Iznik, the ancient and historic site known as Hagia Sophia of Nicea, which also had been used as a museum until that time. These two conversions of Hagia Sophia Byzantine churches did not attract much media attention, but their stories are crucial to an on-going struggle for another Hagia Sophia: the one in Istanbul.

Istanbul's Hagia Sophia is the most remarkable site in Turkey. It is a key monument in the history of art and architecture, the pinnacle of Byzantine creativity. When the cathedral was first built under Emperor Justinian in the first half of the sixth century, on the place where two previous churches were burnt down in revolts, it was the most important edifice of its time. It became a museum under Ataturk. Now, under the AKP, there is increasing pressure to turn Hagia Sophia into a mosque.

11

KURDS

FROM PERPETRATOR TO VICTIM

One of the strongest arguments put forward by those demanding that Turkey recognise the genocide is that it will serve to prevent future genocides taking place. Negation makes mass murder an acceptable instrument for conflict resolution.

Nowhere is the negation of the genocide more relevant than in the case of the Kurds. The emergence of the Kurdish question coincided with the elimination of the Christian minorities in Turkey in the twentieth century. As soon as the Armenians and Assyrians disappeared from the eastern provinces, the Kurds occupied their place: not only did they take over the property of the Christian minorities—with what was once called 'Armenia' or the 'Armenian Plateau' becoming Kurdistan—but they also became the new 'minority' in the country. In the words of Martin Van Bruinessen, 'With the disappearance of the Armenians, most of eastern Anatolia became almost exclusively Kurdish territory ... A Kurdish nation state was now feasible.'[1] Hence the Turkish state was now faced with an increasingly assertive Kurdish population.

In the first fifteen years after the establishment of the Turkish Republic, a total of eighteen revolts took place, sixteen of which occurred in Kurdish areas.[2] Starting in 1924–5, the Turkish state simply denied the existence of the Kurds, whom it instead viewed as 'Mountain Turks' that spoke a corrupted form of Turkish.

The Kurds have historically organised themselves into tribal federations. In the early nineteenth century, the modernising ambitions of the Ottoman sultans clashed with Kurdish semi-autonomous emirates in the east of its provinces and destroyed them, only to replace this system with fragmented groups of tribes competing with each other, pillaging the peasantry, and spreading insecurity. The Ottomans destroyed the tribal confederations of the Kurds but failed to replace them with the modern institutions of a centralist state, and this was one of the expressions of the failure of the Tanzimat reforms.

It is factually inaccurate to describe the conflict in east Anatolia and Armenia as one between Muslims and Christians, or Kurds and Armenians. The divisions between the two communities had as much to do with social class as they did with religion. The Armenians, like the Assyrians in the eastern provinces, were mostly urban artisan-merchants, as well as peasantry.[3] The Kurdish peasantry were dominated by Kurdish nomadic tribal lords, to whom they were forced to pay tribute; the situation of the Armenian, Assyrian or Kurdish peasants differed depending on the armed tribal formations these communities lived under. Yet these local social tensions turned into generalised confessional conflict as a result of state policies. Following the Berlin Treaty of 1878, and the international demands for reforms in the Armenian provinces that resulted (as discussed in Chapter 4), the Ottoman Sultan Abdul Hamid II increasingly considered the Armenians an internal threat to the state and encouraged their repression, including by arming Kurdish tribes.

The identity of Armenians and Kurds in the eastern provinces of the Ottoman Empire was determined by social class as well as ethnicity. The Armenians were city-dwelling artisans, merchants and agricultural workers. Their level of education and literacy was very high compared with the Muslim population of the empire, and even more so when compared with the Kurdish population. The Kurds were mainly tribal, nomadic or semi-nomadic cattle breeders. The tribal formations were also military structures led by a class of feudal over-lords, the aghas. The Armenian peasantry came under the protection of the Kurdish tribes who were the real authority in those provinces during much of the nineteenth century. Unlike the Armenians, the Kurds did not have a movement calling for reform and equality until the 1920s.

In the period between 1880 and 1900, Sultan Abdul Hamid II sought to court the Kurdish tribes by creating the Hamidiye Cavalry—the declared aim in doing so was to fight against the Russians, but the measure was also designed as a way to gain Kurdish support and to turn the Kurds against the Armenians.[4] As the state lacked the resources to pay for the tribal cavalry, the Kurds were given free rein to rob, kidnap and pillage the Armenian peasantry. The Ottoman authorities actively encouraged these atrocities. However, after the 1908 revolution, the CUP dissolved the Hamidiye Cavalry and demanded the return of previously confiscated land as well as the payment of taxes due to the state. The discontented tribal leaders then started to organise among themselves, and some even contacted Russian representatives in Tiflis. In July 1910, the authorities responded to this by resuscitating the Hamidiye Cavalry under the name 'Tribal Light Cavalry', with a new campaign subsequently being launched to divide the Armenians and Kurds.[5]

It was in these circumstances that the Armenian Plateau, as it was known until the Treaty of Berlin, suddenly became 'Kurdistan', with the authorities forbidding any mention of Armenia whatsoever. As the English traveller Isabella Lucy Bird wrote following a visit to the region:

Van may be considered the capital of that part of Kurdistan which we know as Armenia, but it must be remembered that under the present Government of Turkey Armenia is a prohibited name, and has ceased to be 'a geographical expression.' Cyclopaedias containing articles on Armenia, and school books with any allusions to Armenian history, or to the geography of an district referred to as Armenia, are not allowed to enter Asia Minor, and no foreign maps which contain the province of Armenia are allowed to be used in the foreign schools …[6]

Although the Armenians and the Kurds made some attempts to cooperate, these invariably failed. The central authorities frequently manipulated the Kurdish fear of coming under Christian rule as a means of keeping them under its control, and was able to create divisions between the two communities by simply ordering Kurdish tribal chiefs to attack Armenian villages or towns. The Muslim population in general and the Kurds in particular were concerned that Armenian demands for reforms would alter the balance of power in the eastern provinces in favour of the Christians.

The two communities were also divided over land. This applies to the Armenian agricultural land confiscated by Kurdish tribes as well as, in a more symbolic sense, whether the regions of Van, Bitlis, Mush, Kharpert and others were part of 'Armenia' or 'Kurdistan'. As far as the Kurds were concerned, the Armenian demands for autonomy or independence were illegitimate—even in regions with a considerable Armenian population, the real authority was in the hands of the Kurdish aghas and hence any demands for Armenian autonomy or independence clashed with de facto Kurdish authority. The Kurds ultimately chose to ally themselves with the Turkish nationalist movement in the defence of a common Turkish–Kurdish state. But this came at a price—at the end of the war, the Kurds would have to submit to Turkish rule.

Kurdish Role in the Genocide

The nature of Kurdish participation in the genocide remains to be researched, as there are few works dedicated to its study. In the past, Kurdish commentators had largely supported the official, state-sanctioned interpretation of this period of Ottoman history. Many Kurds who admit that atrocities were committed against Armenians in which Kurdish tribes took part argue that Kurds should not be held accountable for those acts as they were acting on the orders of the Ottoman state.[7] However, in more recent years, a number of Kurdish intellectuals have begun to describe the destruction of the Armenians as genocide, and have sought to investigate the extent of Kurdish participation in the crime.

The Kurdish historian Kamal Madhar Ahmad is one of the first Kurdish scholars to have confronted the subject. In his book, entitled *Kurdistan During the Years of the First World War*, a whole chapter is dedicated to the role of the Kurds in the genocide. Although the author notes that religious differences played a role in dividing the two peoples, he also states that:

> there was another reason that separated the two peoples from each other, and that is the progress of the Armenians in comparison with the Kurds. This people passed the social stage of slavery since long and found basis of its own civilization and independence in this stage, and passed the stage of feudalism a long time before the Kurds and had the chance to enjoy independence several times in the Middle Ages, and it had its own advanced literature and its specific alphabet.[8]

For Kamal Madhar Ahmad, the massacres that took place during the First World War were 'new' in the history of the region and in terms of their nature, as they were different from the cycles of violence that had occurred in earlier periods. In his interpretation, the massacres of the Armenian community were not caused by religious differences: people of different religions had previously lived side by side for many centuries, and it was not uncommon for Armenians to visit mosques or for Kurds to visit churches. He points out that in many regions *mullas* and religious people used to rouse the emotions of the people and excite them to kill the 'infidel' based on orders from the government. During the first massacres (Hamidian) the mufti of Palu pushed people to kill asking them not to divert their attention to plunder and looting. Community chiefs in Erzurum used to shout openly 'kill the Christians and do not fear anything' and 'death to Christians and long life to Muslims'. In Arapkir it was communicated to simple people that the killing of Armenians was 'the mission of the Muhammad's *umma.*' He then adds: 'Many simple Kurds used to regard the killing of the Armenians as if it was "jihad" in the way of Allah' (*jihad fi sabil allah*). And the proof is that they used to let live any Armenian who converted to Islam.[9]

While Ahmad is critical of the Ottoman authorities' attempts to place the blame for the treatment of the Armenians *solely* on the

Kurds, he nevertheless recognises the direct participation of many of the tribal chiefs in the atrocities, motivated by material gains. Kamal Madhar Ahmad writes that there were Kurdish *aghas* who used to buy Armenian caravans from the Turkish gendarmes, paying money for the right to pillage the helpless deportees. He adds that the only condition that the Turkish gendarmes posed was that after looting, the Kurdish tribes would kill the deportees. 'After the killing, bodies would be dismembered, bellies slashed open in search of gold coins; pity to those who used to have gold teeth, they used to see the other world with his own eyes before dying', writes Ahmad.[10]

Nevertheless, and in spite of all that the author detailed above, he concludes that the responsibility of the massacres should be placed on the state—including army and police units—and not on the Kurdish tribes, whose actions he describes as reactionary.

While Ahmad criticises the two national liberation movements for failing to unite against the Ottoman state, he comes to the core of the Armeno-Kurdish contradiction:

> By referring to a 'Greater Armenia', an 'independent Armenia' or an 'Armenian autonomous region' that would include areas in which, in the past, the majority of inhabitants were Armenian, which comprised a former Armenian state, or which were considered 'Armenian' for any other reason, the Armenian community no doubt created legitimate fears in the heart of the Kurds.

Although the author exaggerates the existence of a Kurdish 'national liberation movement' prior to the First World War, the question of land remained a dividing issue between the two communities. Finally, the author underlines Kurdish fears 'that a state would be created for the Armenians by the assistance of the Russians, British and the French, and that the Muslim Kurds would come under the rule of this Christian state.'[11]

* * *

In Armenian memoirs, the Kurdish tribes are described as bearing a great deal of responsibility for the killings. Tovmas Mgrdchian, the British vice-consul of Diyarbakir, and a respected member of that city's Armenian community, published his memoirs immediately after the war. The atrocities were particularly brutal in Diyarbakir. The CUP had formed a local association under the name of 'Intibah Shirketi', which aimed to bring the town's commercial and industrial activities—which were dominated by the Armenians prior to the First World War—under Muslim ownership. Mgrdchian describes a meeting of Muslim notables who had gathered to decide the fate of the 150,000 Armenians in Diyarbakir. Those in attendance ultimately decided that all of the Armenians, with the exception of young girls and attractive women, should be killed. The participants put their signatures to the decision and subsequently passed it to Mehmed Rashid Shahingiray, known as Dr Rashid, a Circassian military doctor and member of the Special Organisation, who was appointed *vali* (governor) of Diyarbakir province on 25 March 1915, with the explicit mission to exterminate Armenians and Assyrians of the province.[12]

CUP anti-Kurdish population policies remain largely unreported. The price for a Kurdish alliance with the CUP regime was also very high for the Kurds: 300,000 Kurds serving in the Ottoman army died in the First World War, and nearly half a million civilians died from starvation and other consequences of the war.[13] In reaction to Russian military advances on the Eastern Front, the CUP dispersed a large proportion of the Kurdish population, probably as high as 700,000, in the western provinces.[14] There, they would make up no more than 10 per cent of the total population, forcing them to assimilate. Half of the displaced Kurdish population perished in the hardships of the war years.

The war and the deportations had disrupted the economy of the country. The entire population suffered, that is true. But the nature, causes and consequence of the suffering were not equal between all the populations of the empire. While the official policy towards the Christian minorities—Armenians, Greeks, Assyrians—was to destroy or deport, the policy reserved to Muslim groups such as Kurds, Albanians, Cherkess and others was assimilation. Historians can continue to discuss the role played by the Kurds in the crime; they can also discuss the suffering of the Kurds and its conditions. But the fact remains that on those lands only Kurds live today while the Armenians are gone.

'Happy is He Who Calls Himself a Turk'

The emergence of Kurdish nationalism was a reaction to the policies of the Turkish state. After the Young Turk revolution, it was the new policies of the CUP, that is, the adoption of Turkish nationalist positions and the abandonment of Islam as the overarching ideology of the Empire, that pushed Kurdish youth, as well as Arab intellectuals, to reposition themselves: what had bound both groups to the Ottoman Empire was religion, and both Muslim Arabs and Kurds had felt they were part of the ruling nation (*millet-i hakime*). Once Islam was replaced with Turkish nationalism as the overarching ideology, each group had a choice: assimilate or revolt. The Kurds initially chose the latter, and the Kurdish nationalist movement emerged after the end of the war. After the Armistice of Mudros was signed on 30 October 1918, Allied troops occupied Istanbul and various strategic points in the empire. Mehmet Şerif Paşa, an Ottoman official of Kurdish ethnicity who lived in Paris, expressed his interest to the British in serving as the emir of an independent Kurdistan.[15]

In his attempt to win over the Kurdish tribes, Mustafa Kemal appealed to his 'brothers-in-race' to join together in the fight against the external enemy. He also argued that the project of an independent Kurdistan was a British plot designed for the benefit of the Armenians. For Mustafa Kemal, at least during the period of the war of independence, the future state was to be composed of Turks and Kurds, hence his insistence on keeping Mosul within the future state.[16] He went on to make generous promises to the Kurds: 'I am in favour of granting all manner of rights and privileges in order to ensure the attachment and the prosperity and progress of our Kurdish brothers, on condition that the Ottoman state is not split up.'[17] The Kurds participated in the war under the banner of the Ottoman caliph and Islam. Yet once the war was over and the boundaries of the new state had been agreed in the Treaty of Lausanne, none of these promises was ever fulfilled. In October 1923 the creation of the republic was officially declared and the caliph was deposed in March 1924. The victorious leadership now insisted there were no differences between Turks and Kurds—there were only Turks. Kemalism embraced the various Muslim ethnic groups as the composite elements of the republic, but adopted radical secularism as the new ideology into which they were to assimilate. To be a member of the new republic, the Muslim groups in Turkey would have to abandon their ethnic origins as well as Islam.

Kemalism established a single party system (1925–45). In the 1930s, it flirted with fascist ideas and the social engineering projects of the Third Reich and other regimes.[18] The Kemalist regime also sought to control the way in which Ottoman and Turkish history was presented. In 1930 the Turkish Historical Society (THS) was created under the patronage of Mustafa Kemal himself, who handpicked its members. This organisation was given the task of developing an official 'history' of human 'civilisation' centred on the 'Turk'. In 1930 it launched the Turkish History Thesis, publishing a 606-page work entitled 'General Themes of Turkish History' (*Türk Tarihinin Ana Hatları*), which defined the themes and variations of the official historical narrative. The Turkish History Thesis argued that the Turks originated in Central Asia where they lived in an area around an inland sea, which disappeared due to ecological changes and led to a wave of migration away from the region. It insisted on linking early Anatolian civilisations with Turkish identity as a way to legitimise the modern Turkish state and negate the existence of any other civilisation.[19] Next was the 'Sun theory of languages', which insisted that most major languages originated form the Turkish language.[20] Consequently, this showed that Turkish culture was at the origin of world civilisations.[21] The Turkish History Thesis was, in a way, the intellectual destruction of the Other, following on from its material destruction undertaken during the war. In their drive to build a centralised state, the Turkish nationalists imagined a single nation with one language and one version of history.

As soon as the Kemalists had consolidated their hold on power, ethnic Turks began to be installed as officials in place of Kurds in the local administrations in the Kurdish regions. The use of the Kurdish language was strictly prohibited in official documents and education. After completing their service in the army, Turkish officers would be sent to occupy former Armenian properties in order to increase the number of Turks in Kurdish areas. This process was completed with the abolition of the caliphate, the ideological foundation around which Turks and Kurds had been able to unite.

A series of revolts broke out in the Kurdish regions in the first two decades of the republic. The first was the Kuçgiri rebellion led by Alevi tribes in Dersim, which was crushed by the army in June 1921. This was followed by the Sheikh Said revolt, which started in the Zaza-speaking regions of Diyarbakir province and spread to other regions in the spring of 1925. Sheikh Said, a Naqshbandi sheikh, had demanded the creation of an independent Kurdistan, to be led by one of the sons of Sultan Abdul Hamid, and the restoration of the caliphate. The army quickly crushed the revolt before arresting and executing its leaders and massacring the local population, especially in the Zaza. The third revolt, the Ararat rebellion, was led by a former army officer, Ihsan Nuri, and received support from tribes across the border in Iran, as well as Kurdish nationalists who had regrouped in Bhamdoun in Lebanon in 1928. The Ararat rebellion lasted for nearly three years (1927–30), but was eventually crushed when the Turkish army dispatched 50,000 troops to the region. Thousands of Kurdish fighters and their families were massacred, and many others were deported westwards. The final uprising, the Dersim revolt, was a direct response to the Turkish government's efforts to bring the regions under its control through the laws adopted in June 1934 which gave the government the ability to use violent methods in order to assimilate regions and populations. As Dersim had retained its autonomy under the sultans and had resisted previous attempts at state centralisation, this region was one of its main targets. Thousands of Turkish soldiers were deployed and the region was subject to aerial bombing—in which the adopted daughter of Atatürk, Sabiha

Gökçen, participated—as well as the use of chemical weapons. Even after the leader of the revolt, Sayyid Reza, had surrendered in 1937 and had been executed, the brutality continued for a number of years. The Turkish state ultimately renamed the province 'Tunceli'.

Many of the inhabitants of Dersim were converted Armenians who had found refuge in the region during the 1915 deportations and massacres; many of them were now being subjected to the violence of the Turkish state for a second time.[22] Foreign diplomatic reports compared the suppression of the Dersim revolt to the Armenian massacres of 1915. According to the figures released by Turkey, 13,806 people were killed and another 12,000 people were deported.[23]

The revolts were the direct result of Kurdish disappointment with Kemalism, its dissolution of the caliphate and the regime's secular ideology. However, while those involved in the revolts had made some demands regarding a national homeland, the Kurds had yet to form an effective nationalist movement.

Kurdish Nationalism

After the Dersim revolt, the Turkish authorities believed that the Kurdish question had largely been resolved and that the Kurds would now resign themselves to their fate. Yet the Kurdish resistance did not disappear altogether. In the 1960s and 1970s, Kurdish identity would be shaped by left-wing activists rather than the feudal lords, tribal chiefs and Sufi mystics who had led the uprisings in the 1920s and 1930s. As the parties on the Turkish left were not specifically concerned with the Kurdish issue, however, the Kurds began to establish organisations for this purpose. When several left-wing parties launched an armed uprising against the government after the 1980 coup, a small Kurdish left-wing group, the Kurdish Workers' Party (Partiya Karkeren Kurdistan, or PKK) sought refuge and support among the Palestinian refugee camps in Lebanon. By the time the PKK launched its armed struggle inside Turkey, the PLO had been expelled from Beirut and the PKK was under Syrian patronage.

Heavy-handed repression by the Turkish military—500,000 people were arrested and tortured and thousands were killed in custody after the coup—only served to strengthen the Kurdish revolt. The PKK subsequently became the dominant Kurdish group under the leadership of Abdullah Öcalan, whom we encountered in Chapter 6, also known as 'Apo'. The organisation simultaneously fought against the Turkish military and Kurdish tribal system. For several years, the PKK was supported by Syria, which allowed the movement to recruit young Syrian Kurds. However, as a result of pressure from Turkey, Syria eventually expelled Öcalan from Damascus and in 1998 closed the PKK's bases in Syria and the Lebanese Bekaa. In the period that followed, the Kurdish guerrillas retreated to the Qandil Mountains and regrouped.

The Turkish government and the media attributed the violence of the PKK to foreign forces, and claimed that it was part of a broader Armenian conspiracy, as the PKK emerged during the decade in which Armenian terrorist organisations had begun to use violence against the Turkish state. The Turkish authorities even went so far as to commission a team of researchers to try and establish that Öcalan had Armenian roots. Although they were unable to do so,[24] this did not prevent the Turkish media from claiming that the PKK leader was Armenian and that his original name was 'Artin Agopyan', with the media often referring to him as 'Ermeni tohumu' ('of Armenian semen').

In the 1980s and 1990s the situation of the Kurds in Turkey was similar to that of the Armenians in the late nineteenth and early twentieth centuries. Estimates of the total number of Kurds in Turkey vary; however, they are likely to number between 10 and 12 million (out of a total Turkish population of 75 million). Half of this population lived in the south-east, with the remainder living in western Turkey and the major urban centres. When the PKK started to attack the state with the aim of establishing an independent Kurdistan, the Turkish authorities not only attacked those who were directly involved in the movement but also the Kurds as a community. 'Village guards'—loyal paramilitaries—were created to fight the PKK guerrillas, and those villagers who refused to join these paramilitary organisations were simply deported. According to the Interior Minister Abdülkadir Aksu, by 2005 a total of 57,757 village guards were employed in twenty-two provinces.[25]

The conflict between the Kurdish guerrillas and the Turkish army had devastating consequences: between 2,000 and 3,000 villages were depopulated as a result of the violence and up to 2 million people were displaced—it led to the death of 40,000 people.

* * *

A New Kurdish Policy

In November 2012 I visited northern Iraq to interview members of the PKK, where I met Nureddin Sufi, one of the Kurdish military commanders. He was originally from Syria and spoke fluent Arabic; he has fond memories of the time he spent at the Bar Elias camp in the Lebanese Bekaa, where the PKK was able to establish a base in the 1980s after making contact with the PLO.[26] According to Sufi:

> The political map of the Middle East is not natural. It was not organised according to its ethnic, cultural, religious realities. Up to the 1970s it was a classical colonisation, and in spite of various treaties like Sykes–Picot, Sevrès and Lausanne, it was divided according to the desires of Westerners. ... Americans are trying to dominate over the region while on the other side we have antiquated fascist states like Turkey, Iran, Iraq and Syria. There is the third force, the popular democratic forces [i.e. the PKK and related organisations].

We then discussed the conflict in Syria:

> Before the events we had a project for Syrian Kurds. Democratic and confederal, in which Kurds, Alawis, Christians, Assyrians, Armenians live together, which would become a model for the Middle East. ... But Bashar Asad wants to preserve the nation-state by having Alawis in power while excluding all others—but this does not work. By relying on the Alawis and the security apparatus the regime wants to maintain its power by playing on regional balance of power. For Iran, Syria is the last fortress; if the war is not in Syria it will come to Iran.

Sufi criticised the Syrian opposition for being under the influence of the Muslim Brothers and the Turkish government. He said that Turkey allowed jihadi groups to enter Ras ul-Ayn in order to fight the PYD (the PKK's Syrian sister organisation).

275

Sufi claimed that organisations like the PYD were also seeking to protect Christian minorities in Syria and elsewhere:

> It is also our own self-critique, Christian minorities were badly treated by the Kurds in history. In the last century [of] the Ottoman Empire these minorities repeatedly suffered massacres, in which Kurds, out of ignorance, played a role. Our approach is to correct this mistake and to express our sorriness. We would like the region of Kurdish autonomy to be [a] model of democracy and coexistence for all minorities.

* * *

The Kurds benefited directly from the US-led wars against Iraq, which enabled them to establish a de facto state in northern Iraq known as the Kurdistan Regional Government (KRG). Its capital, Erbil, is one the most prosperous Iraqi cities.

The 2003 US invasion of Iraq allowed the Peshmerga to advance southwards, where they were able to acquire large quantities of arms and ammunition left behind by the Iraqi army. In January 2013 the Turkish authorities declared a cease-fire agreement with the PKK. This was part of the Erdogan government's attempt to put an end to violence in the south-east, and was the result of long negotiations with the imprisoned Abdullah Öcalan. Öcalan's followers are now expanding their domination over northern Syria, increasing their manpower, and even playing with the idea of creating a second autonomous Kurdish region.

* * *

In Diyarbakir I met the mayor of the historic Sur neighbourhood, Abdullah Demirbaş. He is a member of BDP, a pro-PKK Kurdish party. He told me that he had been dismissed from office by the government in the period between 2007 and 2009, and had been imprisoned between December 2009 and May 2010 for promising the region's voters that he would serve them in their own languages, including Kurdish, Armenian, Arabic and Assyrian.

According to Demirbaş, the central government refuses to cooperate with the local authorities with regard to policy in a range of areas, including education and agriculture,[27] and instead seeks to manage the provinces through appointed governors (*vali*):

> If we do not succeed in bringing the people from the mountains to the political process ... During the last two months 3,000 young people went to the mountains. I know about 230 cases myself; parents come and tell me about it. My son is also in the mountains. We already made up our mind. We wish for a democratic Turkey, democratic autonomy, democratic Middle East. Without changing the current borders we want the people of the region to live in peace. ... Borders are not important. What we really care for is freedom.

> These lands are places where different peoples lived all through history. Kurdistan is a land where not only Kurds lived, but also Armenians, Assyrians, Arabs, Turkmens, Jews. We know that these lands had always had multi-ethnic, multi-religious identity. But the Turkish state wants to unite everyone and to enforce on all people one ethnicity, one language, and one religion. To realise its policy the Turkish government tried physical destruction, assimilation, and exile. They made one people fight the other. An example is the 1915 genocide when they used Kurds as soldiers to realise their project. They not only used Kurds against Armenians, but also Kurds against Kurds. Back then it was the Hamidyan guards, now it is the village guards. These policies were not in the benefit of the Kurds. Once the Kurds realised this, they expressed solidarity towards the minorities. In the last 30–40 years their views towards their identity changed, and now Kurds support multi-cultural and multi-ethnic policies. This is the result of the philosophy of Mr Ocalan. What Kurds wish for as freedom for themselves, they also wish for the other minorities. We support Armenians in [the] diaspora to regain their confiscated property. The government restored the Armenian Catholic Church and made a carpet making workshop out of it. We want to build a monument dedicated to the suffering of the Armenians in the genocide, as a confession. We want to call this monument common conscience [*vijdan*] so that we face the past suffering, so that it will not repeat itself in the future.

The next day I met the writer Seyhmus Diken, who apologised to me on behalf of the Kurds for the genocide of the Ottoman Armenians. I asked if there will be Armenians again in Diyarbakir. 'It depends on the success of the Kurdish movement,' he answered.

12

CONTINUOUS WAR

Mount Ararat looms over Yerevan, the capital of Armenia. According to legend, after the deluge, Noah's Arc landed on the summits of Ararat, and the mountain consequently plays an important role in Armenian tradition and mythology. Even in distant communities its image is present in various forms, symbolising Armenian land.

Ararat is barely an hour's drive from Yerevan, yet the Armenians are currently forbidden from walking or climbing on the mountain. Ararat became part of the Turkish republic with the eastward advance of the Kemalist forces in the 1920s. During the Cold War, this was the frontline between the Warsaw Pact on the one hand and NATO on the other, and once the Cold War had ended, Turkey closed the border with Armenia.

* * *

In the late 1980s two movements took shape among Soviet Armenians: the first was the 'Karabakh Movement'. The Karabakh Committee (named after the autuomous region within Soviet Azerbaijan) and their supporters sought the transfer of the Nagorno-Karabakh oblast from Soviet Azerbaijan to Soviet Armenia. The second was a social and political movement that sought to bring an end to Soviet rule.

This latter movement went against the original ideas of Armenian intellectuals about the ideological basis for Soviet power in Armenia. The majority of Soviet Armenians did not see their alliance with Moscow authorities as one forged out of a shared ideology—an alliance between workers and peasants within an international movement—but rather as one forged out of the need for protection: that Armenians faced a persistent threat from Turkey, and the only way to survive within the region was under Russian domination—whether this Russia was tsarist or Bolshevik. In other words, Soviet Armenia exchanged loyalty to Moscow in return for Russian protection against Turkey. The Karabakh Committee did not believe that Armenia needed a protector, and did not exclude the possibility of living in peace with Turkey to its west, and Azerbaijan to its east. This was a revolution in Armenian political philosophy. The leadership of the new movement, led by Levon Ter-Petrossyan and Vazgen Manukyan, were ready to risk and fight for independence.

The antagonism between Armenia and Azerbaijan can be traced to the 1905–7 Armeno-Tatar war (at that time the Azerbaijanis were often referred to as 'Tatars'), when the popular mobilisation that took place during the 1905 Russian Revolution led to inter-ethnic violence which spread throughout the Transcaucasus. Violence between the two communities also erupted in 1917 with the collapse of the Russian Empire and the emergence of Armenia and Azerbaijan as independent states. The two republics fought each other in order to define their respective frontiers in the regions of Nakhichevan, Zankezur and Karabakh. Both states eventually succumbed to outside forces—first to the advancing Ottoman armies, and then to the Soviets.[1]

In the late 1980s the disputed nature of Nagorno-Karabakh once again led to violence between Azerbaijan and Armenia when the Oblast Soviet in Nagorno-Karabakh voted to become part of Armenia on 20 February 1988. Anti-Armenian pogroms erupted in Azerbaijan, and on 27 February 1988 crowds of youth armed with knives and clubs went house-to-house searching for Armenians in Sumgait, an industrial town of 223,000 inhabitants, situated on the coast of the Caspian Sea north of Baku. They attacked people in their apartments, beating them up, violating women and plundering. They had lists of Armenian families and their addresses. The police disappeared from the streets, allowing the carnage to continue for three days, until it came to an end on the evening of 29 February when the Soviet army was deployed to the region. According to official (and likely unreliable) figures, thirty-two people died during the violence, six of whom were ethnic Azerbaijanis, and hundreds were injured.[2] The remaining Armenian population were chased out of the town.

In Azerbaijan, the victims themselves were viewed as being responsible for the violence, with 'Armenian nationalists' accused of having organised the pogroms. As the influential Azerbaijani academic and author Ziya Buniatov—who had earlier developed the theory that Armenians were newcomers to the Caucasus, and that Armenian dynasties or churches were in fact built by Caucasian Albanians—put it:

> The Sumgait tragedy was carefully prepared by the Armenian nationalists. Several hours before it began, Armenian photographers and TV journalists secretly entered the city where they waited in readiness. The first crime was committed by a certain Grigorian who pretended to be Azerbaijani, and who killed five Armenians in Sumgait. As to what follows it is no more than a technical question because there was no way to stop the enormous crowd.[3]

Buniatov's argument was not new; Sultan Abdul Hamid II, CUP nationalists and Kemalists had all claimed that the victims were responsible for their fate and the perpetrators blameless. Other massacres took place in the period that followed. On 21 November 1988, the Armenian community of Kirovabad (now Ganja), the second largest city in Azerbaijan, came under attack. The Soviet army was deployed, and a number of soldiers were killed during the ensuing clashes. Ganja Armenians gathered in the Sourp Sarkis Church in the old town in order to defend themselves. The violence lasted for a week and led to numerous Armenians being killed and wounded before the army evacuated the entire Armenian population of 45,000 to neighbouring Armenia.[4] Two years later, in 1990, a further massacre took place in Baku, after nationalist activists seized control of government buildings in Lenkoran, on the border with Iran, on 11 January. On

13 January a demonstration was organised by the Azerbaijani Popular Front, during which the orators talked about the killing of Azeris in Armenia; some orators called for the expulsion of the Armenians from Baku.[5] The crowd attacked Armenian shops and apartments, and a six-day pogrom continued without police intervention. Between sixty and ninety Armenians were killed, and over 2,000 apartments were attacked and robbed—the 200,000 Armenians of Baku were evacuated by Soviet troops to other parts of the USSR. A state of emergency was declared, with a contingent of Soviet troops dispatched to Baku on 19 January 1990; more than 100 people died as a result of the ensuing clashes between the troops and the activists. In the spring of the following year, Azeri police forces, with the support of the Red Army, launched 'Operation Kaltso' (ring), in which twenty-two Armenian towns and villages north of Nagorno-Karabakh were emptied of their former inhabitants.[6]

The next major attack was against the strategic town of Khojali, the site of Nagorno-Karabakh's sole airport. The attack on Khojali took place on 25–6 February 1992, exactly four years after the Sumgait pogrom. After the Armenian fighters overran the Azerbaijani defences, a massacre ensued as surrendering Azerbaijani fighters were killed on the spot.[7] Civilians who had supposedly been given safe passage to travel east towards Aghdam were also fired upon and killed.[8]

Turkish Responsibility

There has been little discussion of Turkish responsibility in the Nagorno-Karabakh war, despite the support and military assistance Turkey gave to Azerbaijan. Turkey sent 150 'military advisors' to Azerbaijan during the war,[9] and it also provided the Azerbaijani government with considerable amounts of weaponry. It was also at this point that Ankara closed the border with Armenia, establishing a de facto blockade on the country (even in the Soviet era, trains had been able to travel between Leninakan and Kars).

In the late 1980s and early 1990s, the Turkish government began to discuss the best policy to adopt in the Caucasus and towards an independent Armenia. Turkish President Turgut Özal was ready to consider the possibility of Turkish responsibility in the destruction of Ottoman Armenians. Like many Turks, he had come into contact with the 'Armenian problem' abroad, during his studies in the US. Following the military coup of 1980, he became prime minister in 1983 under Western pressure to normalise the situation in the country. Özal had recognised at the time that the Armenian question would remain a problem for Turkey in the international arena. After a year in office, he asked a team of advisors to learn about Armenian demands, and to study the possible political and economic price Turkey had to pay for accepting the genocide. He was also looking to negotiate with Armenian representatives in order to look for possible solutions, including the potential return of land in the Van region to the Armenians.[10] At the time Özal was also concerned about how to resolve another burning issue: the Kurdish question. His political choices and his ideas for conflict resolution came under violent attack from the Turkish nationalist parties, as well as the military. He died on 17 April 1993 from a heart attack while in his office, though rumous that his death was the result of poisoning remain popular until now.[11]

Armenian–Turkish Relations

The first president of independent Armenia, Levon Ter-Petrossian, wanted to normalise relations with Turkey. He argued that contemporary relations between the young republic of Armenia and its western neighbour should be freed from the burden of the past. However, as the Nagorno-Karabakh war quickly escalated, the prospects of this being realised grew ever more distant. In May 1992, when Armenian fighters captured Shushi, the strategic town between Stepanakert and the Armenian border, Turgut Özal threatened Turkish military intervention in order to 'scare Armenia':[12] 'What harm would it do if a few bombs were dropped on the Armenian side by Turkish troops holding manoeuvres on the border?'[13] This in turn led to the intervention of the Russians, with the commander of the CIS joint armed forces,

Marshal Shaposhnikov, warning that Turkish intervention could cause a third world war. As Turkey had clearly sided with Azerbaijan in the war, Armenia was hence left with little choice but to ally with Russia.

In May 1994 the three sides to the conflict—Armenia, Azerbaijan and Nagorno-Karabakh—agreed to a ceasefire agreement after Russian mediation. The agreement fixed the frontlines, and the conflict was subsequently transformed into a diplomatic dispute.

In the period that followed, Baku prospered as a major site of oil production. Heydar Aliev, the president of Azerbaijan, was now convinced that the combination of the Turkish–Azeri blockade of Armenia and the interest generated by Azeri oil deals would give his administration the upper hand in negotiations with regard to the Nagorno-Karabakh conflict.

Heydar Aliev, who had also served as the leader of the Azerbaijani republic in the Soviet era, created the foundations of independent Azerbaijan, before passing the presidency to his son, Ilham Aliev, in 2003. Although the young Aliev lacked the political experience of his father, the money that was now flowing into the country led the political elite to coalesce around the new president.[14] The construction of a major pipeline linking Baku that passes through Tbilisi to the Turkish port of Ceyhan was completed in May 2005, and Caspian oil started to flow to international markets in May 2006. Per capita income subsequently rose from below 850 USD in 2003 to 7,850 USD in 2013.[15] As a result of its new wealth, Azerbaijan has also increased its military spending, with the military budget rising from 163 million USD in 2003 to 3.7 billion USD in 2013.[16] The defence budget of Armenia, in contrast, is no greater than 400 million USD.

But, as money has flowed into the country, the levels of corruption and corresponding popular protest in Azerbaijan have increased dramatically, with social tensions arising from the disparity in wealth between Baku and Azerbaijan's provincial towns. In order to deflect attention away from these issues, Armenians have frequently been used as scapegoats for the democratic and economic shortcomings of the incumbent regime. Ilham Aliev, for instance, continuously labels all Armenians as enemies, and international conspirators against Azerbaijan:

> Our political influence and economic power are growing. This is seen by those who like us and those who don't. There are quite a lot of those who rejoice in our successes. But there are forces that don't like us, our detractors. They can be divided into several groups. First, our main enemies are Armenians of the world and the hypocritical and corrupt politicians under their control. The politicians who don't wish to see the truth and are engaged in denigrating Azerbaijan in different parts of the world. Members of some parliaments, certain political figures, etc. who live on the money of the Armenian lobby. We know them all. There is no need to name them.[17]

This anti-Armenian discourse in Azerbaijan appears to be widespread, as was suggested by the reaction of Azeri society to the murder of an Armenian officer (Gurgen Margaryan) by an Azeri, Ramil Safarov, in Hungary in 2004. During the trial, Safarov discussed the motivation behind the crime:

> I regret that I hadn't killed any Armenian before this. The army sent me to this training and here I learnt that two Armenians were taking the same course with us. I must say that hatred against Armenians grew inside me. In the beginning we were greeting each other, or rather they said 'hi' to me but I didn't respond. The reason why I committed the murder was that they passed by and smiled in our face. At that moment I decided to kill them, i.e. to saw their heads off.[18]

A Hungarian court found Safarov guilty of premeditated murder and sentenced him to life imprisonment, with a thirty-year minimum term before any parole hearings. Although some within Azerbaijan condemned the killing,[19] many others, including Azeri officials, described Safarov as a 'hero'; the Azerbaijani 'Human Rights Ombudsman' Elmira Suleimanova even went so far as to call him a 'model of patriotism for Azerbaijani youth'. On 31 August 2012, Safarov was extradited to Azerbaijan on the condition that he would serve the remainder of his sentence once he had arrived in the country. Yet on his arrival in Baku airport, Safarov was received as a hero—he was taken to Martyr's Lane where he laid flowers at the tomb of the former president, Heydar Aliev. After Ilham Aliev issued a pardon, the Defence Minister Safar Abiyev promoted him to the rank of major and paid all of the salary he would have received while he was imprisoned; he was also given a free apartment in Baku.

Azerbaijani Identity and State Ideology

When Heydar Aliev came to power in the early 1990s, a campaign was launched with the aim of establishing a single interpretation of Azerbaijan's identity and history, according to which all of the peoples living in Azerbaijan, both in the past and the present, were Azerbaijani.

This official, ahistorical narrative is imposed on the youth through history textbooks. In their effort to 'prove' the autochthonous nature of the Azeri people, some Azeri historians have even claimed that an 'Azeri' prototype existed in antiquity. In the words of one author:

> The key premise of the Azerbaijani myth of origin is that the Azerbaijani people are the indigenous people of the Caucasus. The history of Azerbaijan, as depicted in the fifth- and sixth-year textbooks, begins from very early times, 300,000 to 400,000 years ago, with the men of antiquity called Azix adami, the ancestors of contemporary Azerbaijanis. The books assert that Azerbaijanis currently live on the same territory and that they have inhabited it since time immemorial and this fact is proved by the examination of fossils, cave illustrations, and other monuments. Correspondingly, 'Azerbaijan was among the oldest civilizations in Europe.' The sixth-grade book utilizes more scientific language and merely states that 'the land of Azerbaijan was one of the places where ancient men originated.'[20]

The same history textbooks also claim that 'the acceptance of Islam as a religion united all the Turks and non-Turks of Azerbaijan. The non-Turks as new Muslims eventually accepted the traditions and moral values of the Oghuz Turks.'[21]

The sociologist Ceylan Tokluoğlu conducted interviews with the Azerbaijani political elite about their views on the Nagorno-Karabakh conflict in 2001 and April 2009. Her research reveals that the leading figures in Azeri politics continue to view Armenians in stereotypical ways, and this is likely to serve as an obstacle to the normalisation of relations and the resolution of the now frozen conflict. The interviewees stated that the Armenians were newcomers who were settled in

the Caucasus by the Russians in the eighteenth and nineteenth centuries, and, as such, their claims to Nagorno-Karabakh are invalid.[22]
In the words of one of the interviewees, a historian who is also a
member of the Azerbaijani parliament: 'All these Armenian lies are
planned against the Greater Turkish World, against Great Turkey.
Today these lies still continue. The Armenians kill each other and say
that Azerbaijanis did the killings. They do this to create conflicts
between different nations.'[23] Another academic stated:

> Armenians polish the shoes of those who are powerful. However, if the
> powerful ones grow weak, they stab them from behind and then ally with
> other powerful states. This is what they have always done. In the Ottoman
> society they were once known as *millet-i sadika*, meaning the most loyal
> nation of the Ottoman state. What did they do? They joined hands with
> Russians and stabbed the Ottomans from behind.[24]

Overall, what emerges from the interviews is the sense that acts of
Armenian aggression against Azerbaijan are the continuation of the
events of 1915—as the Armenians were unable to fight against
Turkey, they instead chose to attack the weaker and more vulnerable
Azerbaijan. As far as the Azeri political elite is concerned, countries
that recognise the Armenian Genocide are enemies of Azerbaijan, and
are taking sides in the Nagorno-Karabakh conflict.[25]

Tokluoğlu argues that contemporary Azerbaijani national identity
is constructed on the belief that the Armenians were predestined to
create conflicts by occupying Turkic lands:

> Azerbaijanis also attribute a 'unique destiny' to the Armenians: a destiny to
> be deported from all countries they once lived in. In this context, remem-
> bering the past becomes important for the Azerbaijanis since 'national des-
> tiny' presupposes a well remembered past. ... the Turks of Anatolia are
> accused for not remembering their past well. It is claimed that if they had
> remembered the Armenian aggressions against the Anatolian Turks, they
> would willingly support the Azerbaijanis against the Armenians.[26]

On 26 March 1998, Heydar Aliev declared that 31 March would
now be a 'Day of Genocide of Azerbaijanis' to commemorate the
genocides the Azeri community had supposedly suffered over the
course of two centuries. The decree in which this announcement was

made begins by referring to the transfer of the Transcaucasus to Russia as a result of the Russian–Persian treaties of Gulistan (1813) and Turkmenchai (1828). According to the document, this was followed by a 'massive resettlement of Armenians on Azerbaijani lands. A policy of genocide was to become an essential element in that occupation of Azerbaijani territory.' It then refers to the inter-communal clashes between 1905 and 1907, which the decree attributes to Armenian efforts to establish a 'Greater Armenia'. The decree also alleges that the Armenians consistently sought to exterminate the Azeris throughout the Soviet period, before turning to the massacres at Khojali: 'This bloody tragedy, which has entered our history as the Khojaly Genocide, ended with the annihilation of thousands of Azerbaijanis, with others taken prisoner and the city erased from the face of the earth.'[27] In reality, hundreds rather than thousands were killed: the Azerbaijani government had previously claimed that 613 people were killed, while other sources have arrived at the figure of 161.[28]

The latter event also has its own day of commemoration each year on 23 February in Azerbaijan, with state-financed ceremonies and gatherings taking place both in Azerbaijan and abroad. The commemoration on 23 February has also served as a date on which extreme nationalist groups have mobilised in Istanbul. On the twentieth commemoration in 2012, for instance, thousands of supporters of right-wing parties, such as the Nationalist Movement Party (MHP) and the Islamist Great Unity Party (BBP), carried Azeri and Turkish flags through the streets of Istanbul, screaming 'revenge' and 'We are all Turks, what about you?' in reference to the shout of 'We are all Armenians' at Hrant Dink's funeral.[29] On the same day in 2014, Turkish ultra-nationalists marched from the Armenian-inhabited Şişli district in Istanbul towards Taksim Square, carrying Azerbaijani and Turkish flags along with a banner saying: 'Hooray for Ogün Samast! Down with Hrant Dink! Salute Azerbaijan and keep on fighting.'[30]

Destruction of Armenian Monuments in Azerbaijan

In the spring of 1603 the Persian emperor, Shah Abbas I, led his troops north to attack the Ottomans to regain lands he had earlier lost. He rapidly took Tabriz, and advanced towards Nakhichevan, occupying Julfa without resistance. Julfa was a prosperous city of some 15,000 on the left bank of Arax River, populated entirely by Armenians. It grew to prominence due to its role in the Iranian–European silk trade. However, the Persians eventually lost the city to the Ottomans, and ordered the deportation of 300,000 people in the region, including 150,000 Armenians. Shah Abbas subsequently agreed to provide the Julfa Armenians with land near the Zayandarud River to build a new town next to the imperial capital, Isfahan. This in turn became New Julfa.[31]

In Old Julfa a magnificent cemetery with enormous historic, cultural and religious signifcance was left behind. The cemetery of Old Julfa, located in today's Nakhichevan Autonomous Republic of Azerbaijan, originally boasted around 10,000 khachkars, or tombstones decorated with cross carvings. Most of them were from the fifteenth and sixteenth centuries.

After 1917, when the city became part of Soviet Azerbaijan, the authorities not only failed to protect the Julfa cemetery, they systematically destroyed the site and used the stones for construction. According to historian Arkam Ayvazian, by the 1970s only 3,000 khachkars had survived. In 1998, the Azerbaijani authorities in Nakhichevan sent workers with heavy equipment to destroy the cemetery entirely, which continued until early 2003. Several ancient Armenian Apostolic and Catholic churches in Nakhichevan were also destroyed. In December 2005, more than 100 Azeri soldiers were dispatched to destroy the remaining khachkars with sledgehammers. The site of the former cemetery is now used by the Azerbaijani army as a firing range and military camp.[32]

The Protocols

Two weeks before the ninetieth commemoration of the genocide, Turkish Prime Minister Erdoğan sent a letter to the Armenian President Robert Kocharyan. The Turkish letter proposed setting up a joint history commission to discuss 'diverging interpretations of events that took place during a particular period of our common history':

> [W]e are extending an invitation to your country to establish a joint group consisting of historians and other experts from our two countries to study the developments and events of 1915 not only in the archives of Turkey and Armenia but also in the archives of all relevant third countries and to share their findings with the international public. I believe that such an initiative would shed light on a disputed period of history and also constitute a step towards contributing to the normalization of relations between our countries.[33]

Kocharyan replied on 25 April 2005 by suggesting that the first step in any such initiative should involve the full normalisation of Turkish–Armenian diplomatic relations:

> Your suggestion to address the past cannot be effective if it deflects from addressing the present and the future. In order to engage in a useful dialog, we need to create the appropriate and conducive political environment. It is the responsibility of governments to develop bilateral relations and we do not have the right to delegate that responsibility to historians. That is why we have proposed and propose again that, without pre-conditions, we establish normal relations between our two countries. In that context, an intergovernmental commission can meet to discuss any and all outstanding issues between our two nations, with the aim of resolving them and coming to an understanding.[34]

This exchange of letters was part of a broader diplomatic opening in relations between the two countries. The United States had been placing pressure on Turkey to normalise its relations with Armenia, and the Swiss had offered to facilitate any negotiations. A series of meetings took place near the Swiss capital Berne between an Armenian delegation led by Deputy Foreign Minister Arman Giragosyan and a Turkish delegation led by Undersecretary of Foreign Affairs Ertuğrul Apakan.

* * *

The August 2008 war between Georgia and Russia led Turkey to revise its policies vis-à-vis the Caucasus, and especially its relations with Armenia'. In the weeks after the war, Ankara announced a diplomatic initiative entitled the 'Caucasus Stability and Cooperation Platform', with the aim of reformulating its policy towards its eastern neighbours, and part of this initiative envisaged the normalisation of relations with Armenia. In Yerevan, meanwhile, the war in Georgia had affected Armenia's ability to communicate with the outside world, and when the new president, Serzh Sargsyan, came to power in March 2008 he sought to bring his country out of isolation. Under Sargsyan, the Armenian government no longer pushed for Ankara to recognise the events of 1915 as 'genocide'. During a visit to meet with Russian president, Dmitri Medvedev, in Moscow in June 2008, Sargsyan made a surprising announcement: he had invited Turkey's President Abdullah Gül to Yerevan to watch a football match.[35]

Sargsyan received Russian support for his initiative, and Turkey was also under increasing pressure to alter its policy with regard to Armenia as the new US president, Barack Obama, had previously stated that the United States would publicly recognise the events of 1915 as 'genocide'. Abdullah Gül visited Yerevan to watch the football match on 6 September 2008, and though he only stayed for a few hours, after his departure a team of high-level diplomats, including Foreign Minister Ali Babacan, remained in Armenia to discuss a range of issues with their Armenian counterparts.

This in effect marked a shift in Turkey's previous policy, according to which the normalisation of relations with Armenia would depend on Armenia making concessions in the Nagorno-Karabakh conflict: two diplomatic protocols resulted from the visit—neither of which mentions Nagorno-Karabakh—thereby separating the two issues. According to David Phillips, 'Gül publicly reiterated that normalisation of relations between Turkey and Armenia would not precede resolution of NK [Nagorno-Karabakh]'.[36] In 2008 Ankara was ready to normalise its relations with Armenia, lift the blockade it had imposed since Armenia became independent and to assemble a sub-commission of historians to debate what had happened in the past.

However, only a year later external pressure on Turkey to normalise relations with Armenia had reduced. In February 2009, the Turkish media revealed that in a telephone conversation between Obama, Gül and Erdoğan, the American president had promised 'not to hurt' Turkey on the question of genocide.[37] On 23 April 2009, the foreign ministries of Armenia, Turkey, and mediating Switzerland, announced that the parties had agreed to a 'road map' to normalise their relations: the Obama administration was already making concessions to Turkey, in spite of previous promises made during his election campaign to American-Armenians. For those to whom Turkish recognition of the genocide was of fundamental importance, the timing was painful: the announcement came only a day before April 24, the day of mourning for the Armenian victims of the genocide.

The Swiss diplomat Michael Ambühl had been engaged in shuttle diplomacy between the two capitals and, in the first days of April 2009, managed to get the agreement of both parties on the Protocols outlining steps to establish diplomatic relations and open the common border. On 10 October 2009 the Protocols were signed by the Armenian and Turkish foreign ministers. After the two protocols had been signed, Turkey began to shift its position with regard to normalising relations with Yerevan: for the Turkish leadership the two documents themselves were the achievement, and they had no interest in actually implementing them. The Protocols had already served their purpose: to alleviate foreign pressure on Turkey concerning its relations with Armenia. Meanwhile, Turkey was coming under immense Azerbaijani pressure. For Baku, the football diplomacy was nothing less than betrayal. Baku openly threatened Turkey with increased hydrocarbon prices, and approached Russia for future natural gas export projects. Azerbaijan feared that by unrolling the Turkish blockade against Armenia it would lose a major leverage in the Karabakh dispute. In the end, Azerbaijani blackmail was successful. The Protocols were the project of the Turkish President Abdullah Gül, while Erdoğan and Davutoğlu wanted to revise them. The latter two travelled to Baku on May 12–13, in order to assure the Azerbaijanis. Both the public and private messages of Erdoğan were the same: 'Turkey will not finalise the roadmap on reconciliation with Armenia unless Azerbaijan and Armenia come to terms on the occupied territories and Nagorno-Karabakh.'[38] He added that the cause of closing its borders with Armenia was the Karabakh conflict: 'The Turkey-Armenia border has been closed due to Nagorno-Karabakh's occupation and will not be solved until it is liberated,' he said.[39] In his enthusiasm, Erdoğan had gone even further than the framework of Karabakh negotiations that were taking place within OSCE's Minsk Group: to ask for the complete withdrawal of Armenian forces from both the occupied territories and from Mountainous Karabakh.

The protocols were signed in Zurich on 10 October 2009. However, the controversy over the ceremony in which they were to be signed clearly indicated that much of the goodwill accumulated between the two sides had now started to dissipate. The ceremony was to be attended by the Armenian Foreign Minister Eduard Nalbandyan and the Turkish Foreign Minister Ahmet Davutoğlu, as well as US Secretary of State Hillary Clinton. Nalbandyan and Davutoğlu had earlier agreed that they would refrain from mentioning sensitive issues in their speeches at the ceremony, such as the genocide or the Nagorno-Karabakh conflict. Yet just before the ceremony was scheduled to take place, the members of the Armenian delegation received a copy of Davutoğlu's speech, which explicitly referred to the resolution of the Nagorno-Karabakh conflict as a condition for normalising Turkish–Armenian relations. The Armenian delegation refused to sign the protocols and departed to their hotel. After a delay of three hours, a last minute compromise was reached whereby neither the Armenian nor the Turkish side would give a speech, and the protocols were signed. But tensions clearly remained in relations between the two states and even at the time it was clear they were doomed to failure. To come to force they needed the ratification of the two parliaments, and Turkish Prime Minister Erdogan made a declaration immediately after the signing ceremony linking the fate of the protocols to progress in the resolution of the Karabakh conflict. Diplomacy had come full circle and was back to square one.

* * *

The failure of the protocols came with a price. In Yerevan, there was a sense among the political elite that Turkey was again acting in bad faith, and had simply used the protocols as a means to deflect international pressure rather than being sincere in normalising relations with Armenia. The normalisation of relations with Armenia could also have eased tensions over Nagorno-Karabakh, as the opening of the Turkish–Armenian border would have sent a clear message to Baku and perhaps encouraged Azerbaijan to adopt a more conciliatory approach. In the event, the failure of the protocols only served to embolden the nationalistic and anti-Armenian stance of the Azeri government.

In the period that followed, the Armenian government stepped up its rhetoric with regard to Turkey and the treatment of the Ottoman Armenians. In March 2010, for instance, Sargsyan, along with a delegation of officials, visited the eastern Syrian town of Deir ez-Zor, which had served as s concentration camp in which large numbers of Armenians had been killed. In doing so, the Armenian leadership were indicating to Turkey that its recognition of the genocide was very much back on the table. In his speech at the conclusion of the trip, Sargsyan declared that 'Auschwitz is the Deir ez-Zor of the Jews.'[40]

On 24 April 2013, two Armenian Catholicoi demanded that Turkey return property belonging to the Armenian Church which had been confiscated in the aftermath of the genocide. The statement was issued by the Catholicos of All Armenians Karekin II and the Catholicos of the Great House of Cilicia Aram I. The properties involved included churches, monasteries and holy places, as well as real estate belonging to the Church, including educational and humanitarian centres, and cultural and religious objects of great value such as khachkars, manuscripts and icons. The document concludes by demanding that Turkey recognise the genocide and compensate the Armenian people for all they had lost.

The Gordian Knot between Ankara and Yerevan

Relations between Armenia and Turkey further deteriorated when the Armenian prosecutor-general, Aghvan Hovsepyan, stated that the descendants of those who had died in the genocide should receive compensation and that the Armenian Church should reclaim its stolen property. Moreover, Hovsepyan even went so far as to argue that the Armenian state should seek to recover any territory it had lost to Turkey.[41] This was the first time that an Armenian official had made territorial demands of Turkey. The Turkish reaction was swift and unequivocal: the Foreign Ministry described the demands as being the 'product of delirium'.

The territorial problem had long been the elephant in the room when discussing relations between Armenia and Turkey. One of the central points discussed during the negotiations leading to the protocols was the recognition of the current border. David Phillips writes:

> Discussing Armenian issues meant addressing the Armenian genocide, and Ankara rejected territorial or financial claims arising thereof. Kocharian tried to assuage these concerns in an interview with Turkey's well-respected journalist, Mehmet Ali Birand, stating: 'Genocide recognition by Turkey will not lead to legal consequences for territorial claims.'[42]

Giro Manoyan, a leading member of the ARF and the head of its Armenian Cause Office, remarks that there are three major problems in contemporary Turkish–Armenian relations, all of which stem from the Turkish conditions for normalising bilateral relations:

> Turkey made three demands of Armenia as a prerequisite for normalising relations. The first was that Armenia should not put forward territorial claims. The second was that Armenia should give up its efforts of Genocide recognition, and the third point, which was added later in 1993, was the demand that the conflict of Karabakh should be resolved according to Azerbaijani position.[43]

For Armenia, the priorities were is very different: first to establish diplomatic relations between the two countries and end the Turkish blockade, and later to address issues of recognition of the 1915 genocide and related compensation.

Ankara is specifically worried about one of the articles contained in the 1991 Declaration of Independence of the Republic of Armenia. Article 11 states: 'The Republic of Armenia stands in support of the task of achieving international recognition of the 1915 Genocide in Ottoman Turkey and Western Armenia.' The term 'Western Armenia' possesses a legal ambiguity: The Ottoman delegation signed the Treaty of Sèvres on 10 August 1920, but Turkish nationalists led by Mustafa Kemal rejected the treaty and started their rebellion against the Ottoman authorities and allied occupation forces. Following Turkish victories in the War of Independence (1919–1922) the new authorities in Ankara signed a number of new treaties, first with the Bolsheviks in Kars (1921) establishing the contemporary border between Turkey and the South Caucasus, and later with the Allies in Lausanne (1923) the founding treaty of modern Turkey. The term 'Western Armenia' denotes the provinces that belonged to Armenia according to the Wilsonian line, but not according to the new treaties. By referring to 'Western Armenia', Article 11 highlights that the border dispute between the two remains unresolved.

Legal expert and former Armenian diplomat Ara Papian argues that the Treaty of Lausanne did not eclipse that of Sèvres, and that the arbitration of Wilson is not forgotten. Armenia and Turkey, as well as American diplomats continue to acknowledge its effects, revealing that the Armenian-Turkish borders are not definitively settled. For example, during the intense rounds of Armeno-Turkish diplomatic negotiations, high-level American diplomat, Assistant Secretary of State for European and Eurasian affairs Dan Fried declared that 'Armenia must be ready to ... disavow any claim on the territory of modern Turkey.' Just like the question of extermination of Ottoman Armenians and the expropriation of their property, the land issue remains unresolved and the two parties have a significant task ahead if they are to find a diplomatic, negotiated solution.

Erdoğan's Condolences

On 23 April 2014, a day before the commemoration of the genocide was scheduled to take place, Erdoğan addressed a message to the Armenians:

> It is our hope and belief that the peoples of an ancient and unique geography, who share similar customs and manners will be able to talk to each other about the past with maturity and to remember together their losses in

a decent manner. And it is with this hope and belief that we wish that the Armenians who lost their lives in the context of the early twentieth century rest in peace, and we convey our condolences to their grandchildren.[44]

This was highly significant: after ninety-nine years, it was the first occasion on which a leading Turkish politician had explicitly equated the Armenian losses in the First World War with those of the Muslims of the empire. How long will we have to wait for officials to distinguish between the victims of the genocide and its perpetrators?

13

CONSEQUENCES

When I think about the Armenian genocide, it is not images that come to my mind—there are few pictures of the concentration camps established Der Ez-Zor or the massacres that took place there. The horrors of the Armenian genocide have instead been revealed almost entirely through books; writing has become a means of resistance.

But this poses a problem in an age where much information is conveyed through imagery. Although some efforts have been made to portray the suffering of the Armenians in Hollywood films—notably the adaptation of Arshaluys (Aurora) Mardiganian's autobiographical novel *Ravished Armenia* in the film *Auction of Souls* (1919)—very few attempts have been made to do so in more recent times. The controversy surrounding Franz Werfel's *The Forty Days of Musa Dagh*, discussed earlier, is only one example of the kind of problems such efforts can generate.

* * *

In Susan Sontag's words, 'The memory of war ... like all memory, is mostly local ... Armenians, the majority in diaspora, keep alive the memory of the Armenian genocide of 1915.'[1] While writing this book, I have often wondered why the fate of the Armenians has remained largely confined to and discussed by only the Armenians themselves. For a whole century, the events of 1915 were seen as an Armenian issue, which precluded the world from learning the lessons of that terrible time and preventing the same from happening again. It is only in the last decade that the Armenian Genocide has become mainstream in Genocide Studies and Ottoman Studies, and it still remains marginal in other fields of academic history, such as the study of the First World War.

Denial, Historic Research and Freedom of Expression

In 2001, the United Kingdom officially created a 'Holocaust Memorial Day', which is remembered on 27 January each year, the day Soviet forces entered Auschwitz. On this day, the victims of the Nazi genocide, as well as the victims of the Cambodian, Rwandan, Bosnian and Darfur genocides, are commemorated. Thousands of events take place under a specific theme chosen throughout the UK: in 2001, for example, the theme was 'Remembering Genocides: Lessons for the Future'. However, when the day was announced, a controversy erupted with regard to the Armenians. The organisers had initially left the Armenians out of the programme for the event, but at the last moment—two days before—two Armenian genocide survivors were suddenly invited to attend.[2] But this in turn proved controversial with other organisations. The Muslim Council of Britain, for instance, issued a press release in which it condemned the Nazi Holocaust and offered sympathy to the families of its victims, but which also expressed the organisation's dismay at the inclusion of 'the controversial question of alleged Armenian genocide as well as the so-called gay genocide' in the programme for the event.[3]

On 11 October 2006, the lower house of the French parliament passed a bill which criminalised the denial of the Armenian Genocide. The move ignited a debate in France and elsewhere in Europe about historic memory, freedom of expression, and denialism. 'What a magnificent blow for truth, justice and humanity the French national assembly has struck' wrote historian Timothy Garton Ash, arguing against the criminalisation of denialism in France. The problem, he believes, is the potential for laws against denial of massive violations of human rights to escalate to an unreasonable scale. He argues that prosecuting someone for genocide denial is akin to prosecuting someone on grounds of 'thought crimes', and accuses French-Armenian lobbyists of having forced such a decision on the French parliament, under the weight of half a million French-Armenian voters. For the sake of free speech, there should be no legal or political intervention in holocaust denial. He concludes: 'No one can legislate historical truth.'[4]

French historians, too, resisted political intervention in their affairs. A group of nineteen prominent French historians, who became known as the 'Liberté pour l'histoire' association, opposed what they call *les lois mémorielles* ('memory laws') and published an open letter in *Libération* expressing their opposition to the interference of politics in their profession, which each of them signed. History is not religion, they wrote, it does not accept dogma, it does not respect prohibition, it does not know taboos. History is not a juridical object. From the initial 19, the open letter went on to attract more than 600 signatures.[5] The influential historian Pierre Nora, a member of the French academy, heads the association, and demands the abrogation of Gayssot Act of 1990.[6]

A different group of French historians answered the declaration of 'Liberté pour l'histoire' by arguing that there is a clear distinction between scholarly research and state-sponsored denialism, that the 'right to dignity' does not contradict freedom of expression. They argued that the legislation did not invade historians' territory, but addressed specific historical cases, which have a criminal dimension.[7] The question is: can we make the distinction between historical research and state-sponsored denialist campaigns?

In 2011, when the Assemblée Nationale (parliament) discussed the penalisation of the denial of the genocide, Pierre Nora made yet another call to defend history. He argued that the alignment of the Armenian Genocide to the Holocaust was the creation of a false parallel. His argument was based on the fact that in the case of the Holocaust, Vichy France had been a collaborator, while in the case of the Armenian Genocide, France had been an external actor.

Nora also argues that if the French government were to now put pressure on Turkey, it would be counterproductive; it would only excite Turkish nationalism. Moreover, Nora argues, Turkey had proposed a commission in 2005 and that 'the Armenians had rejected [it] in the name of their certainty: there was a genocide and there is nothing more to add.'[8] However, in 2005, Turkish Prime Minister Erdoğan proposed a second historic commission and the Armenian response was not outright rejection. Armenian President Robert Kocharyan wrote back immediately, expressing his readiness to discuss all bilateral issues, but only after Ankara agreed to establish diplomatic relations between the two countries. There was no answer to Kocharyan's letter. Erdoğan simply continued to use the idea of a 'commission of historians' for PR purposes.

The scholars and historians quoted above are some of the most prestigious public thinkers of our times, and one cannot disregard their concerns without serious scrutiny. The intervention of parliamentarians, concerned with winning votes and elections, is not something that any writer or freethinker would welcome. Past political interventions in determining the contours of historical research have been catastrophic, and French support for the criminalisation of Armenian Genocide denial has an anti-Muslim dimension, argues Martin Shaw.[9]

Historians and intellectuals cannot simply insist on freedom of speech and ignore the fact that the discussion is about a genocide which never had its Nuremberg, and which after one hundred years is still denied. Intellectuals entering the debate must also consider how we are to explain indifference towards the Armenian Genocide during the First World War, and the consequences of this for contemporary denialism in Turkey.

In Turkey, too, there has been a debate, although limited at the time for fear of state repression, where intellectuals such as Hrant Dink and Orhan Pamuk opposed the legal repression of denial of the genocide as one against freedom of expression. Others, such as Taner Akçam and Mehmet Ali Birand, supported initiatives from the outside to open up a debate within Turkey itself, which was non-existant a decade back.[10]

The expression 'leave history to historians' presupposes that we can trust the historian to conduct impartial research and defend the victim even in the face of powerful opposition. It presupposes that the free thinking historian, the intellectual, the journalist, the filmmaker, the photographer, and the curator of the Holocaust Memorial Day can freely inform us about the 'historical truth.' The problem is that in this case historians do not seem to have broken taboos, to have challenged the 'certainties' of the powerful any more than politicians.

Marc Nichanian raises another problem: the limitation of historic research based on archival evidence. His is the expression of desperation of an intellectual facing the immensity of genocidal destruction of the twentieth century, including the destruction and distortion of memory.[11] Total destruction leaves no trace behind for the researcher to study. The CUP destruction of the party archives in 1919 disarms the historian from both its instruments and its means. The archives are non-existent, says Nichanian. The error of historians is to think that a historic debate is possible. Unlike the case of Stalinist crimes, where the victims were forced to confess and notes of the accusations were kept in KGB archives, the CUP did not preserve any memory of its crimes, erasing it and all references to its victim. The executioner equally rejects the eyewitness accounts of the survivors, insisting that the last survivor is proof against the intention of total destruction, against genocide. Didn't the Turkish Prime Minister say that the fact that Armenians continue to live in Turkey is proof that no genocide had taken place?[12]

Freedom of Expression

Doğu Perinçek is a Turkish politician. Formerly an extreme-left activist, he was arrested after the 1980 military coup and spent time in the notorious Diyarbakir prison. In 1992 he founded the Workers' Party (İşçi Partisi), the ideology of which is a mixture of Maoism and Kemalism, although the party is more concerned with nationalism than defending the rights of Turkish workers. Perinçek has strong connections with the Turkish Deep State, as the Ergenekon conspiracy, discussed in more detail later in this chapter, revealed. He was one of the leading characters.

In 2003 the Swiss Federal Assembly adopted a text that recognised the genocide of the Armenians. The Turkish authorities were furious, as a wave of similar acts of recognition was taking place throughout Europe and beyond. The Turkish authorities wanted to challenge this trend, and Switzerland was chosen as an easy target. In July 2005, Perinçek travelled to Switzerland and gave several provocative denial-ist speeches, including one in Lausanne. Nationalist networks close to Turkish embassies in Europe mobilised their supporters and bussed them to Lausanne. Perinçek gave a vitriolic 'anti-imperialist' speech in which he described the Armenian genocide as 'an international ... [and] imperialist lie'.[13]

The Association Suisse–Arménie filed a complaint against Perinçek in a Swiss court, condemning the Turkish politician for genocide denial and incitement to hatred. The association won the case, and the decision was subsequently upheld by the criminal court of cassa-tion of the Canton de Vaud and again by a Federal Tribunal.

When the court opened in Lausanne, Perinçek did not show up alone. He travelled with a delegation of 160 people, including 'acade-micians, historians, retired military officials, and politicians from Turkey, who left Istanbul on a specially chartered Turkish Airlines flight for Geneva'.[14] Among the delegation was Rauf Denktaş, the former president of Northern Cyprus, occupied by the Turkish army. This was clearly about more than Perinçek's right to freedom of expression.

Perinçek accused the Swiss judiciary of 'racist hatred' towards Turkey and said he would appeal to the European Court of Human Rights. 'I defend my right to freedom of expression,' he declared. 'There was no genocide; therefore this law cannot apply to my remarks.' In this, Perinçek received the support of the Turkish Foreign Ministry, which criticised the Swiss court for failing to uphold Perinçek's right to freedom of expression.[15]

Perinçek and the Turkish authorities took the fight to the European Court of Human Rights (ECHR) in Strasbourg. The verdict of the ECHR was issued on 17 December 2013. In the verdict, the court condemns the Swiss justice system on the grounds that it had violated the principle of freedom of expression. The court also argued that there was a lack of 'general consensus' on the Armenian Genocide.[16] However, this did not mean that it was permissible to deny other genocides:

> the present case is clearly distinguishable from the cases that dealt with the denial of the crimes of the Holocaust. ... It also agrees with the Turkish government that the denial of the Holocaust is now the main driver of anti-Semitism. Indeed, it considers that this is a phenomenon that is still relevant and against which the international community must stand firm and vigilant. It cannot be said that the rejection of the legal definition of 'genocide' for the tragic events that occurred in 1915 and in subsequent years can have the same impact.[17]

The Turkish Human Rights Association wrote to the Swiss justice minister, Simonetta Sommaruga, expressing its 'disappointment' at the peculiar logic of the court's decision. The letter continues:

> As human rights defenders in Turkey, we are the most immediate, most direct witnesses of how the denial of the genocide against Armenians and other Christian ethnic groups of Asia Minor has right from the start generate[d an] anti-democratic system, allowing racist hatred, hate crimes and violation of the freedom of expression and the human rights in general.[18]

Lost in a Deep State

Turkey never acknowledged its responsibility for the destruction and deportation of Armenians, Assyrians and Greeks, and this fact has consequences for its political culture and the nature of state institutions. The clandestine state structures that were set up immediately before the First World War, namely the Special Organization (Teşkilât-ı Mahsusa)—the secret paramilitary organisation within the state—was never dismantled. On the contrary, it was celebrated and continued to dominate over the state. This clandestine structure was the main instrument in the implementation of the Armenian Genocide, and played a role in the various military coups and crimes against humanity under the republic. When the Kemalist movement came to power, the old CUP structures were not dismantled; Mustafa Kemal used the same network to lead his fight, reinventing the Special Organisation under new names, such as Karakol, which in 1927 became the Milli İstihbarat Teşkilatı (MIT, or the Turkish intelligence services). There is an extra-legal structure within the state that has acted without legal checks and balances, from the time of the Special Organization to the more recent 'Deep State.' The Susurluk scandal in 1996, outlined in Chapter 7, brought to light the reality of the Deep State and its links with the death squads in Kurdistan, organised crime and international heroin trafficking. Even before the scandal, there had been murmurings about such a secret structure within the state, with numerous whistle-blowers warning of the existence of such an organisatio, As early as 1997, Erol Mütercimler, a former navy officer, spoke to the media of the existence of a secret organisation that was 'above the General Staff, the MIT and the prime minister'.[19] However, it was another incident ten years later that brought this home. In 2007—a few weeks after the assassination of Hrant Dink—the Turkish government declared that it had uncovered a plot by a secret organisation known as Ergenekon to overthrow the elected government, and a number of arrests were made. When the trial opened in May 2009, 142 people including army generals and officers, politicians, judgers, lawyers and journalists were brought to trial. What the trial once again revealed was the existence of a network within the state that behaved as the supreme power in the country, obeyed no laws, and used criminal methods to shape the political space—and that those involved in Ergenekon scandal were only a part it.

Among those indicted during the trials, several are relevant to us: Brigadier General Veli Küçük, the founder of JITEM, who had taken personal interest in the trials of Hrant Dink; Kemal Kerinçsiz, the ultranationalist lawyer and author of the attacks against Hrant Dink and other intellectuals; and Doğu Perinçek, the famous leader of the Workers' Party. In 2007, Turkish media revealed links between the Ergenekon conspirators and the murder of Hrant Dink. If one considers the key figures in Ergenekon such as Veli Küçük and Kemal

Kerinçsiz, both instrumental in the smear campaign against Dink, then the link between the conspiratorial network and the Dink murder is evident. An Istanbul police report revealed telephone conversations between six Ergenekon suspects and defendants in the.[20] Yet soon afterwards the prosecutors excluded any connection between the two cases. As a result, the case of Hrant Dink, instead of being investigated as a murder ordered by the Deep State, was transformed into a crime committed by a small gang of ultra-nationalists.

'There was a struggle between the army and [the] AKP, and Hrant's killing was part of this struggle,' Fethiye Çetin, the Dink family's lawyer told me. 'Erdoğan at the time declared that the assassination was against him as well, and he was sincere in this.'[21] Çetin argues that Erdoğan effectively used the case of Hrant Dink and finally made a compromise with the army to obtain what he and his party needed, and then abandoned the Dink case.

> There was a meeting between Erdoğan and head of the Turkish Army General Staff Yaşar Büyükanıt in Dolmabahçe Palace, in June 2007. We do not know exactly what they discussed, but the Ergenekon investigation started after that: the heads of the Army General Staff before Büyükanıt were arrested, but he was not arrested, nor questioned. In the Dolmabahçe meeting they decided the limit of Dink investigation, and there was no step forward taken on the case since then. In order to strengthen its power, the AKP made an agreement with part of the government and the army against its enemies by using the Dink file.

On 28 August 2007 the parliament elected Abdullah Gül as the first Islamist president of Turkey. Court-ordered arrests of the Ergenekon conspirators were made in January 2008.

The charge levelled against the Ergenekon conspirators was carrying out illicit activities, including assassinations, to create instability in the country as a first step towards an army coup and overthrow the Erdoğan government. Through Ergenekon, Erdoğan managed to domesticate the Turkish military and take it under his wing. At the height of the struggle between the AKP and the military, Erdoğan said the Deep State 'had always been there' and was a phenomenon carried over from the Ottomans.[22] A US diplomatic cable sent from

Ankara to Washington, later released by Wikileaks, starts with the following remark: 'The Ergenekon investigation marks a swing of the power pendulum away from an entrenched, rigid urban elite to an Anatolian elite more representative of the Turkish populace.'[23] The ruling elite might have changed, but the state structure, the Deep State, survived.

The Turkish Deep State and the denial of the Armenian Genocide are intimately linked. Unless those structures and mechanisms are dismantled, they will continue to function within the state. The official recognition of the Armenian Genocide by Turkey will discredit the Deep State and its illegal activities, and open the way to dismantling it. Only then will Turkey be ready for rule of law and democracy.

* * *

In early summer 2014 fighters carrying the black banners of the Islamic State of Iraq and Syria (ISIS or *Daesh* in Arabic) launched a daring attack in northern Iraq. In a matter of a few days they had overrun Mosul, the second largest city in the country, and then occupied Tikrit, the birthplace of the country's former ruler Saddam Hussein. As fighting continued on the frontlines, the Christian population of Mosul and the villages in the Nineveh Valley—many of them Assyrians, the oldest inhabitants of the region—received the following order: convert to Islam or pay the *jizya* (the tax Islamic regimes have imposed on Christian minorities). The Christian population fled Mosul. ISIS confiscated houses and property and distributed it amongst its fighters and the local Muslim population. Christian Churches—as well as Muslim shrines—were destroyed.

On 3 August 2014 Islamist fighters broke the resistance of Kurdish Peshmerga forces and reached the outskirts of Sinjar, a town in the northwest corner of Iraq, near the Syrian border. As soon as news of advancing ISIS fighters spread through Sinjar, the entire local population, composed largely of Yazidis, took to the mountains, leaving all they owned behind them. Images of entire families scattered across barren mountains revealed the tragedy of a people being decimated by violent attack. Many were trapped in the desolate mountains for weeks, searching for shadow during the day and suffering from hunger and thirst. The Yazidis who did not manage to escape before the arrival of Islamist fighters were immediately captured. The men were murdered in several mass killings; the rest were forced to convert to Islam. Many of the women and girls were enslaved, others passed around as war booty and distributed between ISIS commanders. Many Yazidi women committed suicide to avoid capture.

ISIS fighters systematically targeted Assyrians, Yazidis, and Shiites, both Arab and Turcoman. Sunni Muslims who opposed ISIS policies were equally targeted, whether tribal groups, rival rebel fighters, or intellectuals in cities like Mosul and Raqqa. As a result of their violence, 830,000 people were forced to flee their homes in a matter of few weeks.[24]

The political system in the Middle East is crumbling again, unleashing limitless violence. In Syria, the regime opposed initially peaceful protests with brutal force, arrests, torture, and outright massacres. It has brought villages and urban centres under siege and indiscriminate shelling, turning entire neighbourhoods into Stalingrad-like piles of debris. The rebels did not show any greater deference to moral standards and behaviour, in their turn using mass violence including torture, executions, and indiscriminate attacks on civilian targets. The images of Yazidis suffering in desert lands were reminiscent of the Armenian deportees sent southwards towards the Syrian Desert a hundred years ago. And images of Syrian prisoners killed by torture in the prisons of the Syrian regime reminds us of the concentration camps of 20th century totalitarian regimes. [25]

The Armenian Genocide, largely put aside in international relations, remains politically relevant in an acute way. In Turkey, there was strong organic continuity between the CUP and Kemalism, and in the policies to 'purify' and harmonise the political space through an imposed Turkish national identity which continued several decades after the end of the First World War. The discrimination against religious minorities, sporadic pogroms, confiscation of their property, continued throughout Republican Turkey. When there were no more religious minorities left, especially in historic Armenia, the state began to treat Muslim Kurds as a minority, with similar indiscriminate violence, deportations and massacres.

The official Turkish denial of the Armenian Genocide led to both the polarisation and limitation of the debate. Much intellectual effort has been put into proving—or denying—the intention of the Ottoman state to exterminate the Armenian population. But social scientists are yet to study the consequences of the genocide on international relations. There are only a handful of studies looking at the impact of Ottomans policies during the First World War—their impunity—on Nazi thought and action.[26] In the Middle East, Turkish and Arab nationalisms and their heroic, positivist historiography have been oblivious of Ottoman history. Nobody was interested in those defeated, massacred remnants that hardly survived the dark pages of the war. Those populations and civilisations—Armenians, Greeks, Assyrians—who for millennia made up an organic part of Asia Minor, the Near East, and beyond, had become ghosts in the new political order; at best exotic strangers. Until recently the Kurds did not even have official existence in Turkey, and were barely tolerated in Syria and Iraq. Only recently have the continuities between the CUP and Kemalist systems been discussed in Turkey, while the impact of the CUP, Kemalism and late Ottoman experience on Arab nationalism and Baathism remain to be studied.

The international community fought against Nazism, and its genocidal crimes were brought to Nuremberg and identified as such: as crimes against humanity. This has not happened for the heads of the CUP responsible for earlier crimes, and their legacy survives in the Middle East. There is no 'Adolf Hitler Secondary School' in Berlin, but there are streets and schools in Istanbul dedicated to the 'glorious' memory of Talaat, Enver, and other perpetrators of genocide. The result is a moral order with shifting parameters: if crimes are committed 'against us' then they are condemned, but if it is 'our boys' committing the same crimes against 'others', then it is acceptable.

For Islamic political groups the abolition of the Ottoman Empire in 1922 is the starting point of modern history. When the Muslim Brotherhood, Hizb ut-Tahrir and other salafi-jihadi groups talk about restoring the Caliphate, they use vague references to glorious periods of Islamic civilisation, while their practical reference is the dark decades of the decline of the Ottoman Empire. Abu Bakr al-Baghdadi's declaration of a caliphate is the latest expression of this longing to the lost Ottoman Empire.

* * *

Today in academic circles the denialist thesis is largely discredited. Public opinion in many countries is sensitive to the Armenian issue. But when we reach high politics, international relations and diplomacy, the Armenian Genocide is largely absent, left in the dark. In this book I have argued that the 1915 genocide is not just about history, ad that the debate is not just about what happened in the past: it is relevant to the politics of today. By censoring the Armenian Genocide, its impact, traces and consequences do not simply disappear. It continues in various forms: the repression of Armenian and other Christian minorities and their destruction as organised communities within Turkey; anti-Kurdish violence; and the aggressive stance taken towards the Armenians by Azerbaijan. But most of all, the extra-legal organisation that was so instrumental in orchestrating the genocide survives in the depths of the Turkish state.

The Armenian struggle for justice has taken different shapes in the last five decades; it was awoken in 1965 by the eruption of popular demonstrations around the globe and for a decade demanded justice from those claiming to represent international political order. Disappointed, a new generation plunged into violence, inspired by the Armenian guerrilla fighters in the old land, and by the Palestinian resistance of the 1970s. The result was a decade of senseless and often self-destructive violence. What followed was a new period of political and legal struggle aiming to achieve international recognition of the Genocide and the criminalisation of its denial as instruments to fight against official Turkish negation. Although four decades of struggle have arguably brought an end to Turkish silence, it has also failed to change the Turkish attitude.

It was the courage of Hrant Dink that transformed this struggle into an internal debate within Turkey. For a decade he engaged

Turkish public opinion and the intellectual class, questioning their silence. He paid the highest price for his daring; he was threatened, harassed, and eventually murdered. Yet, he won. He succeeded in making the Armenian Genocide a Turkish issue, a debate necessary for freedom of expression, of justice and democratisation inside Turkey.

Much of this change was possible because of internal power struggles in Turkey. With the emergence of the AKP, political Islam in Turkey started taking a new colour, that of reform. Stimulated by the prospect of joining the EU, the AKP clashed with the guardians of the Turkish Deep State, promising justice, freedom of speech, an end to corruption and a more just social distribution. A new Turkey started emerging which enflamed the imagination of Turkish liberals and Arab Islamists alike. Could Islam and democracy unite under one roof? The promise of the AKP was that this was possible.

It was under these circumstances that the military's grip on political life weakened and taboos started to fall. For the first time it was possible to discuss the real problems of the Kurds. It also became possible to take a few, timid steps towards undoing the consequences of the Armenian Genocide: in the last few years we saw steps towards restoration of churches and monasteries, some land confiscated from Armenian foundations was returned, and a handful of people marked as 'Islamised Armenians' expressed their right to claim their own identity after several generations of coercion. Will these positive trends continue and become new norms of justice and equality in the Middle East?

New risks are on the horizon, revealing once again the dangers that often stem from oblivion. The Arab Spring that inspired so much hope in its early months has turned into a nightmare. The Turkish leadership, already accused of flirting with radical Islamist groups in Syria, has refused assistance to Kurdish fighters encircled in the border town of Kobane/Ain al-Arab. President Erdoğan's declaration equating the PKK with ISIS has caused much frustration among Kurdish populations, and led to clashes and deeper polarisation.[27] Are democracy, reform and justice still compatible with political Islam in modern Turkey? The choices made by the AKP, now fully in power, will answer this question.

* * *

I think it unlikely that the Turkish government will denounce the crimes against humanity committed by the founders of the Republic anytime soon. Nor do I expect that the Turkish leadership will begin taking the necessary steps in order to correct this historic injustice in the near future. Turkey is not ready for it.

But I know that in the future Turkey will recognise the genocide, and it will be a beautiful country.

NOTES

1. 'WE ARE ALL HRANT DINK, WE ARE ALL ARMENIAN': THE SACRIFICE

1. 'Hrant Dink Funeral Today in Istanbul; 8 Kilometre Protest March Planned', *Hurriyet*, 23 Jan. 2007, http://www.hurriyet.com.tr/english/5823459. asp?gid=74.
2. Author interview with Karin Karakaşli, Istanbul, 7 May 2013.
3. Yavuz Baydar, 'Family Boycotts Retrial for Murder Of Turkish–Armenian Journalist', *Al-Monitor*, 20 Sep. 2013, http://www.al-monitor.com/pulse/ originals/2013/09/family-slain-journalist-boycotts-trial.html.
4. Ian Fisher, 'Turkish Writers Say Efforts to Stifle Speech May Backfire', *New York Times*, 6 Oct. 2006, http://www.nytimes.com/2006/10/06/world/ europe/06turkey.html.
5. Vercihan Ziflioğlu, 'Varto Armenian Clan Makes Long Trip from Turkey to France', *Hürriyet Daily News*, 14 Jan. 2011, http://www.hurriyetdailynews. com/default.aspx?pageid=438&n=armenian-clan-vartos-long-trip-to-marseille-2011-01-14.
6. Dilek Kurban and Kezban Hatemi, *The Story of an Alien(ation): Real Estate Ownership Problems of Non-Muslim Foundations and Communities in Turkey*, Istanbul: TESEV, 2009, p. 16.
7. Author interview with Zakarya Mildanoğlu, Istanbul, 7 May 2013.
8. Laure Marchand and Guillaume Perrier, *La Turquie et le Fantôme Arménien*, Arles: Solin-Actes Sud, 2013, p. 166. The two French journalists add that several former TKP/ML militants have told them that Kaypakkaya himself was of Armenian origin.
9. Author interview with Rakel Dink, Istanbul, 20 May 2013.

10. Author interview with Tuba Çandar, Istanbul, 18 Dec. 2013.

11. Huberta von Voss, 'A Seedbed of Words: Hrant Dink, Editor-in-chief of the Armenian Newspaper *Agos* (Istanbul)', in Huberta von Voss (ed.), *Portraits of Hope: Armenians in the Contemporary World*, New York: Berghahn Books, 2007, p. 105.

12. 'Turgut Özal Period in Turkish Foreign Policy, Özalism', *The Journal of Turkish Weekly*, 9 Mar. 2009, http://www.turkishweekly.net/article/333/turgut-ozal-period-in-turkish-foreign-policy-ozalism.html.

13. Hrant Dink, *Deux peuples proches, deux voisins lointains, Arménie–Turquie*, Paris: Actes Sud, 2009, p. 85.

14. Tessa Hofmann, *Armenians in Turkey Today*, Brussels: Forum of Armenian Associations in Europe, 2002, p. 21.

15. Author interview with Istanbul Armenian community member who wanted to remain anonymous, Istanbul, Mar. 2013.

16. This picture of the PKK leader Abdullah Öcalan with the 'Armenian' priest is still circulating on Turkish websites and discussion blogs as proof of Öcalan's Armenian origins, while some discussion forums go as far as to claim that the PKK is nothing more than the continuation of the Armenian Secret Army for the Liberation of Armenia (ASALA).

17. Hofmann, *Armenians in Turkey Today*, p. 20.

18. Quoted in Hratch Tchilingirian, 'Hrant Dink and Armenians in Turkey', Open Democracy, 23 Feb. 2007, http://www.opendemocracy.net/democracy-turkey/dink_armenian_4378.jsp.

19. Author interview with Luiz Bakar, Istanbul, 7 May 2013.

20. Stepan Partamian, 'Hrant Dink's Interview November 2006', Pari Luys programme, 1 Nov. 2006, Horizon TV, http://www.youtube.com/watch?v=oAwDPfkuqEI.

21. Notes from author's interview with Hrant Dink, Istanbul, 20 Mar. 2000.

22. Hrant Dink, 'Being Armenian in Turkey', *Agos*, 23 Jan. 2004. French translation in: *Être Arménien en Turquie*, Reims: Fradet, 2007, p. 23.

23. Nouritza Matossian, 'Commemorating Hrant Dink: "Let's Talk about the Living"', Index on Censorship, 2004, http://www.indexoncensorship.org/2010/01/hrant-dink-turkey-armenia-agos/.

24. Raymon Kévorkian, *Le Génocide des Arméniens*, Paris: Odile Jacob, 2006, p. 929.

25. Dorian Jones, 'Armenian Quest for Orphans', BBC World Service, 1 Aug. 2005, http://news.bbc.co.uk/2/hi/europe/4735171.stm.

26. Boghos Levon Zekiyan, 'Hrant Dink's Innovative Approach to Armenian–Turkish Relations, its Context, Challenge, and Prospects', *Society for Armenian Studies Newsletter*, XXXII, 1 (71) (Summer 2008), p. 11.

27. Von Voss, *Portraits of Hope*, p. 106.

28. Ibid., p. 107.

29. Tatul Hakobyan, 'Hrant Dink. "Im Pezhishge Turkne"' (Armenian: 'Hrant Dink. "My Doctor is the Turk"'), *Azg*, 29 June 2001, http://www.azg.am/AM/2001062818.

30. Nilüfer Zengin, 'A Portrait of a Nationalist Lawyer: Kemal Kerincisiz', *Bianet*, 24 Jan. 2008, http://www.bianet.org/english/english/104374-a-portrait-of-a-nationalist-lawyer-kemal-kerincsiz.

31. Ergenekon is allegedly a secular ultra-nationalist organisation with ties to military and security forces. Around 275 members have been put on trial since 2007 for plotting against the government. This is discussed in more detail in Chapter 13.

32. Maureen Freely, 'Why they killed Hrant Dink', Index on Censorship, 6 June 2007, available at: http://www.eurozine.com/articles/2007-06-06-freely-en.html.

33. Fatma Ulgen, 'Sabiha Gökçen's 80-Year-Old Secret: Kemalist Nation Formation and the Ottoman Armenians', Doctoral Dissertation, University of California, San Diego, 2010, p. 118.

34. See the article by Simon Simonian, 'Ataturki Aghchige' (The Daughter of Ataturk), *Spyurk*, 23 Aug. 1970.

35. Ersin Kalkan, 'Sabiha Gökçen mi Hatun Sebilciyan mi', *Hurriyet*, 21 Feb. 2004, http://arama.hurriyet.com.tr/arsivnews.aspx?id=204257.

36. 'Gökçen Ermeni'ydi' (Turkish: 'Gökçen is Armenian'), *Hürriyet*, 22 Feb. 2004, http://webarsiv.hurriyet.com.tr/2004/02/22/416897.asp.

37. Ulgen, 'Sabiha Gökçen's 80-Year-Old Secret', p. 112.

38. 'Furor over Ataturk's Daughter's Armenian Ancestry Exposes Turkish Racism', WikiLeaks, 10 Mar. 2004, Cable ID 04ISTANBUL374_a, https://wikileaks.org/plusd/cables/04ISTANBUL374_a.html.

39. Celal Şengör, 'Sabiha Gökçen, Earthquakes and Critical Newsmaking in the Press', *Cumhuriyet*, 28 Feb. 2004. In Ulgen, 'Sabiha Gökçen's 80-Year-Old Secret', p. 121.

40. Ulgen, 'Sabiha Gökçen's 80-Year-Old Secret', p. 123.

41. Hrant Dink, 'Why Am I Chosen as a Target?' article published on 12 Jan. 2007, quoted in *Chroniques d'un Journaliste Assassiné*, Paris: Galaade Editions, 2010, p. 179.

42. 'Furor over Ataturk's Daughter's Armenian Ancestry Exposes Turkish Racism', US Consulate Istanbul, WikiLeaks, 10 Mar. 2004, Cable ID 04ISTAN BUL374_a, http://wikileaks.org/cable/2004/03/04ISTANBUL374.html.

43. See the letter of the Dink family lawyers addressed to the chief of justice of the fourteenth High Criminal Court of Istanbul, Hrant Dink Foundation, 5 Dec. 2011, http://www.hrantdink.org/picture_library/Hrant%20Dink% 20Murder%20Case%20-%20Opinion%20of%20the%20intervening%20 attorneys.pdf.

44. Quoted in 'Hrant Dink (1954–2007)', Hrant Dink Foundation website, http://www.hrantdink.org/?HrantDink=10&Lang=en.

45. Ibid.

46. Author interview with Arat Dink, Istanbul, 17 May 2013.

47. Peer Teuwsen, 'Der meistgehasste Türke', *Das Magazin*, 5 Feb. 2005, http:// archive.is/7FCD.

48. Nick Birch, 'Judge Throws Out Charges Against Turkish Novelist', *The Guardian*, 22 Sep. 2006, http://www.guardian.co.uk/world/2006/sep/22/ turkey.books.

49. A French translation of this article is available in Hrant Dink, *Être Arménien en Turquie, Fradet*, 2007, pp. 89–94.

50. Author interview with Karin Karakaşlı, Istanbul, 18 May 2013.

51. Author interview with Rakel Dink, Istanbul, 20 May 2013.

52. An English translation of the article can be found in 'Hrant Dink, A Pigeon-Like Unease of Spirit', Open Democracy, 22 Jan. 2007, http://www.open-democracy.net/democracy-turkey/pigeon_4271.jsp.

53. See the French translation in: *Être Arménien en Turquie*, Reims: Fradet, 2007, pp. 95–119.

54. Author interview with Pakrad Esdoukian, Istanbul, 7 May 2013.

55. Author interview with Rakel Dink, Istanbul, 20 May 2013.

2. CRIME WITHOUT PUNISHMENT

1. Hrant Dink, 'Why Am I Chosen as a Target?' 12 Jan. 2007, quoted in *Chroniques d'un Journaliste Assassiné*, Paris: Galaade Editions, 2010, pp. 177–8.

2. Armenakan (founded in 1885 in Van), the Social-Democrat Hnchagyans (founded in Geneva in 1887) and Armenian Revolutionary Federation (ARF, founded in Tbilisi in 1890).

3. Raymond Kévorkian, 'Facing Responsibility for the Armenian Genocide? At the Roots of a Discourse that Legitimizes Mass Violence', in Hans-Lukas Kieser (ed.), *Turkey Beyond Nationalism: Towards Post-Nationalist Identities*, London: I.B. Tauris, 2013 (first published 2006), pp. 104–5.

4. Author's notes, Van, July 2013.

5. Kévorkian, *Le Génocide des Arméniens*, p. 343.

6. The name of the monastery in Armenian is: Surp Khachi Vank, or Saint-Cross Monastery.

7. Gözde Burcu Ege, 'Remembering Armenians in Van, Turkey', unpublished MA thesis, Sabanci University, Autumn 2011.

8. There are several excellent books on the history of Armenia and Armenians. See: René Grousset, *Histoire de l'Arménie, des origines à 1071*, Lausanne: Payot, 1995; George A. Bournoutian, *A Concise History of the Armenian People: From Ancient Times to the Present*, Mazda Publishers, 2002; Richard G. Hovannisian (ed.), *Armenian People from Ancient to Modern Times*, New York: St. Martin's Press, two volumes, 2000 and 2004; Razmik Panossian, *The Armenians, From Kings and Priests to Merchants and Commissars*, London: Hurst, 2006; Simon Payaslian, *The History of Armenia, From the Origins to the Present*, Basingstoke: Palgrave Macmillan, 2007.

9. Fatma Müge Göçek, 'Defining the Parameters of a Post-Nationalist Turkish Historiography through the Case of the Anatolian Armenians', in Hans-Lukas Kieser (ed.), *Turkey Beyond Nationalism: Towards Post-Nationalist Identities*, London: I.B. Tauris, 2013 (first published 2006), pp. 92–3.

10. Under Islam, other monotheist religions were provided protection and permitted to practice their own religion in return for a protection tax *al-jizya*. These protected 'others' were called *dhimmis*.

11. Ronald Grigor Suny, 'Truth in Telling: Reconciling Realities in the Genocide of the Ottoman Armenians', *American Historical Review* (Oct. 2009), p. 933.

12. See 'The History of the Emblems', ICRC webpage, 14 Jan. 2007, http://www.icrc.org/eng/resources/documents/misc/emblem-history.htm.

13. Erik J. Zürcher, *Turkey: A Modern History*, London: I.B. Tauris, pp. 14–17.

14. André Mandelstam, *La Société des Nations et les Puissances devant le Problème Arménien*, Paris: Pédone, 1926, p. 11.

15. Zürcher, *Turkey, A Modern History*, pp. 50–1, 56–66; Alan Palmer, *The Decline and Fall of the Ottoman Empire*, London: John Murray, 1993, pp. 110–12.

16. Çağlar Keyder, *State and Class in Turkey: A Study in Capitalist Development*, London: Verso, 1987, p. 16.

17. Zürcher, *Turkey, A Modern History*, p. 67.

18. Kemal H. Karpat, 'The Transformation of the Ottoman State, 1789–1908', *International Journal of Middle East Studies*, 3 (1972), p. 244.

19. Suna Kili, *Kemalism*, Istanbul: Robert College, 1969, p. 128.

20. Hovann H. Simonian, 'History and Identity among the Hemshin', *Central Asian Survey*, 25, 1–2 (Mar.–June 2006), p. 171.

21. Pascal Carmont, *Les Amiras, Seigneurs de l'Arménie ottoman*, Paris: Editions Salvator, 1999, pp. 95, 106. Anahid Ter Minassian, 'Une Famille d'Amiras Arméniens: Les Dadian', in Daniel Panzac (ed.), *Histoire Economique et Sociale de l'Empire ottoman et de la Turquie (1326–1960)*, Paris: Peeters, 1995, pp. 506–19.

22. Philip Mansel, *Constantinople: City of the World's Desire, 1453–1924*, London: John Murray, 2006 (first published 1995), pp. 254–5, 298; Carmont, *Les Amiras*, p. 114.

23. Feroz Ahmad, 'The Late Ottoman Empire', in Marian Kent (ed.), *The Great Powers and the End of the Ottoman Empire*, London: Frank Cass, 1996, p. 7.

24. There is a debate about the ethnic and religious origins of Sinan, with some sources referring to his Greek origins, while others refer to him as having Armenian roots.

25. Sarkis Balmanoukian, 'The Balian Dynasty of Architects', in Richard G. Hovannisian and Simon Payaslian (eds), *Armenian Constantinople*, Costa Mesa, CA: Mazda Publishers, 2010, p. 266.

26. See Mansel, *Constantinople*, pp. 240–4.

27. Asa Briggs and Peter Burke, *A Social History of the Media: From Gutenberg to the Internet*, 3rd edn, Cambridge: Polity, 2009, pp. 14–15; Suraiya Faroqhi, *The Ottoman Empire and the World Around It*, London: I.B. Tauris, 2004, p. 199.

28. Sina Akşin, *Turkey: From Empire to Revolutionary Republic*, London: Hurst, 2007, p. 44.

29. Christopher J. Walker, *Armenia: The Survival of a Nation*, 2nd edn, London: Routledge, 1990, p. 12.

30. Stephan Astourian, 'The Silence of the Land', in Ronald Grigor Suny, Fatma Müge Göçek and Norman M. Naimark (eds), *A Question of Genocide: Armenians and Turks at the End of the Ottoman Empire*, Oxford: Oxford University Press, 2011, p. 59.

31. Ibid., p. 58.

32. Dikran Mesrob Kaligian, *Armenian Organization and Ideology under Ottoman Rule 1908–1914*, New Brunswick, NJ: Transaction Publishers, 2009, p. 121.

33. Tovmas C. Megerdichian, *Dikranagerdi Nahanki Chartere yev Kyurderu Kazanutyunnere* (The Massacres of Diyarbakir Province and Kurdish Beastiality), Cairo: Krikor Jihanian Printer, 1919, p. 16.

34. See Merrill D. Peterson, *'Starving Armenians': America and the Armenian Genocide, 1915–1930 and After*, Charlottesville, VA: University of Virginia Press, 2004, p. 17.

35. Marcel Léart (pseudonym of Krikor Zohrab), *La Question Arménienne, A La Lumière des Documents*, Paris: Augustin Challamel, 1913, pp. 5–6. Zohrab also states that the Armenian Patriarchate opposed the sultan's policy during the Berlin Conference by demanding administrative autonomy in the eastern provinces, which was eventually disregarded by the great powers.

36. Jelle Verheij, '"Les frères de terre et d'eau"': Sur le rôle des Kurdes dans les massacres arméniens de 1894–1896', *Les Cahiers de l'autre Islam*, 5 (1999), pp. 225–76.

37. Norman M. Naimark, *Fires of Hatred: Ethnic Cleansing in Twentieth-Century Europe*, Cambridge, MA: Harvard University Press, 2001, p. 22.

38. Şükrü Hanioğlu, *A Brief History of the Late Ottoman Empire*, Princeton, NJ: Princeton University Press, 2010, p. 131.

39. Quoted in Selim Deringil, '"The Armenian Question Is Finally Closed": Mass Conversions of Armenians in Anatolia during the Hamidian Massacres of 1895–1897', *Comparative Studies in Society and History*, 5, 2 (2009), p. 369.

40. Raymond Kévorkian, *Le Génocide des Arméniens*, Paris: Odile Jacob, 2006, pp. 39–41; Şükrü Hanioğlu, *Preparation for a Revolution: The Young Turks, 1902–1908*, Oxford: Oxford University Press, 2001, p. 131.

41. Anahide Ter Minassian, *Nationalism and Socialism in the Armenian Revolutionary Movement (1887–1912)*, Cambridge, MA: Zoryan Institute, 1984.

42. Zabel Yesaian, *Averagneru Mech* (Among the Ruins), Istanbul: Aras, 2010 (first published in Istanbul, 1911), p. 34.

43. Dikran Mesrob Kaligian, *Armenian Organization and Ideology under Ottoman Rule 1908–1914*, Piscataway, NJ: Transaction Publishers, 2011, pp. 201–13.

44. Sina Akşin, *Turkey: From Empire to Revolutionary Republic*, London: Hurst, 2007, p. 91.

45. Ibid., pp. 92–3.

46. Raymond Kévorkian, 'Krikor Zohrab et les Jeunes-Turcs: La Trahison de l'Idéal Ottoman', *Armenological Issues Bulletin*, 1, Yerevan State University Press (2014), pp. 20–33.

47. Hagop Jololian Siruni, *Inknagensakragan Noter* (Autobiographic Notes), Yerevan: Sarkis Khachents Publishers, 2006, p. 194. As editor of the ARF publication *Azadamard* in the capital, and a close friend of a number of key Armenian intellectuals there including Daniel Varoujan, Siamanto, Gomidas and others, H.J. Siruni reflects well the positive atmosphere that reigned among Istanbul Armenians in the months before the start of the war.

48. An eyewitness to the event, Hovanness Manoogian, described the evening in a letter to H.J. Siruni. See Rita Soulahian Kuyumjian, *Archaeology of Madness: Komitas, Portrait of an Armenian Icon*, 2nd edn, London: Gomidas Institute, 2002, p. 115.

3. OBLIVION

1. Jennifer M. Dixon, 'Education and National Narratives: Changing Representations of the Armenian Genocide in History Textbooks in Turkey', *The International Journal of Education Law and Policy*, Special Issue, 'Legitimation and Stability of Political Systems: The Contribution of National Narratives' (2010), p. 110.

2. Lusine Sahakyan, *Turkification of the Toponyms in the Ottoman Empire and the Republic of Turkey*, Montreal: Arod Books, 2010.

3. Ibid., p. 14.

4. Ibid., pp. 18–19.

5. Varoujan Attarian, *Le Génocide des Arméniens devant L'ONU*, Brussels: Editions Complexe, 1997, p. 61.

6. Surp Krikor Lusavorich in Kayseri is one of the few remaining Armenian churches in Anatolia that continues to function as a church.

7. Kamuran Gürün, *The Armenian File: The Myth of Innocence Exposed*, London: K. Rustem and Brothers, 1985, p. 216.

8. Michael Provence, *The Great Syrian Revolt and the Rise of Arab Nationalism*, Austin, TX: University of Texas Press, 2005, Chapter 1.

9. Hasan Kayali, *Arabs and Young Turks, Ottomanism, Arabism, and Islamism in the Ottoman Empire 1908–1918*, Berkeley, CA: California University Press, 1997, pp. 108–9.

10. While stressing here the continuity between the CUP and the Kemalists, it does not mean that there were no essential breaks in a number of fields. For example, the former insisted on saving the empire, even building a new one with an eye on new territories in the Caucasus and Central Asia, while the latter struggled to build a nation-state with fixed frontiers. Another major break was the attempt of CUP to build a new identity in which Islam still played a role, while Kemalists suppressed it.

11. Taner Akçam, *A Shameful Act: The Armenian Genocide and the Question of Turkish Responsibility*, New York, NY: Metropolitan Books, 2006, p. 303.

12. This includes the speech he delivered to the Ottoman Parliament in 1919 and the speech that would subsequently form the foundation for modern Turkish historiography, the '*nutuk*'.

13. From Ulgen, '"Sabiha Gökçen's 80-Year-Old Secret": Kemalist Nation Formation and the Ottoman Armenians', Doctoral Dissertation, University of California, San Diego, 2010, pp. 276–7. Italics added by the author.

14. See Hülya Adak, 'National Myths and Self-Na(rra)tions: Mustafa Kemal's *Nutuk* and Halide Edib's *Memoirs* and *The Turkish Ordeal*', *The South Atlantic Quarterly*, 102, 2/3 (Spring/Summer 2003), pp. 509–10.

15. Fatma Ulgen, 'Reading Mustafa Kemal Atatürk on the Armenian Genocide of 1915', *Patterns of Prejudice*, 44, 4 (2010), p. 385.

16. Translation by Fatma Ulgen, in 'Reading Mustafa Kemal Atatürk', pp. 387–8.

17. Ulgen, 'Reading Mustafa Kemal Atatürk', p. 290.

18. Sabrina Tavernise, 'On the Bosporus, a Scholar Tells of Sultans, Washerwomen and Snakes', *New York Times*, 24 Oct. 2008, http://www.nytimes.com/2008/10/25/world/europe/25istanbul.html?partner=permalink&exprod=permalink&_r=0.

19. Taner Akçam, *The Young Turks' Crime against Humanity: The Armenian Genocide and Ethnic Cleansing in the Ottoman Empire*, Princeton, NJ: Princeton University Press, 2012, p. 13.

20. Gürün, *The Armenian File*, p. 16. The author also confesses that he did not find any sources from the 'first half of the sixteenth century [that] make any mention of the Armenian millet'. See p. 19.

21. Esat Uras, *The Armenians in History and the Armenian Question*, Ankara: Documentary Publications, 1988, p. 370.

22. Gürün, *The Armenian File*, p. 60.

23. Gürün curiously states that it was the Catholicos based in Echmiadzin, in Russian Armenia, which came under 'increasing Russification policy' that incited the Istanbul Armenian Patriarchate to establish 'an Autonomous Armenia in the Ottoman Empire' (p. 65). The logic here is difficult to follow: Armenians came under increasing pressure in tsarist Russia, and as a reaction they allied with it to organise a rebellion inside the Ottoman lands where they had been treated well.

24. Gürün, *The Armenian File*, p. 411.

25. Ibid., pp. 161–2.

26. Gürün, *The Armenian File*, p. 216.

27. Ibid., p. 193.

28. Ibid., p. 195.

29. Ibid., p. 203.

30. Ibid., p. 207.

31. Ibid., p. 208.

32. Ibid., p. 217.

33. Uras, *The Armenians in History*, p. 868.

34. See Ara Sanjian, 'Oke's *Armenian Question* re-Examined', *Middle Eastern Studies*, 42, 5 (Sep. 2006), pp. 831–9.

35. Suna Kili, *Kemalism*, Istanbul: Robert College, School of Business Administration and Economics, 1969, pp. 4, 5.

36. Çağlar Keyder, *State and Class in Turkey: A Study in Capitalist Development*, London: Verso, 1987, p. 22.

37. Léart, *La Question Arménienne*, p. 12.

38. When he was in exile in Leipzig, working for *Bizim Radyo*—the Soviet equivalent of Radio Liberty—he was surrounded by Armenian comrades: Hayk Acikgöz and his wife Anjel, while the editor-in-chief was the Istanbul-Armenian communist militant Aram Pehlivanian; in Moscow he was in close contact with another Armenian-Turkish Communist Vartan Ihmalian. He also knew well the Lebanese-Armenian writer and leftist intellectual Armen Darian (Alphonse Attarian). Yeghishe Tcharents—the Armenian Mayakovski, they say, or the Armenian Nazim Hikmet we could say, translated some of his poems into Armenian back in 1929, that is eight years before Tcharents was assassinated in a Stalinist camp. Hikmet even wrote an introduction to Kevork Emin's translation of his poems, published in Yerevan in 1953. Khatchatur I. Pilikian, Nazim Hikmet, A Turkish Poet's

Armenian Connections, Lecture at Socialist History Society, Marx House, February 11, 2006: http://norkhosq.net/wp-content/uploads/N.Hikmet-a-türkish-Poet1.pdf.

39. Mutlu Konuk Blasing, *Nazim Hikmet: The Life and Times of Turkey's Poet*, New York, NY: W. W. Norton & Company, 2013, p. 191.

40. Elias Khoury, 'The novel of ambiguity', *al-Ahram Weekly*, October 19–25, 2006, Issue No. 817, http://weekly.ahram.org.eg/2006/817/cu4.htm.

41. Mehmet Necef, 'Turkish Media Debate on the Armenian Massacre', in Steven L.B. Jensen (ed.), *Genocide: Cases, Comparisons and Contemporary Debates*, Copenhagen: Danish Center for Holocaust and Genocide Studies, 2003, p. 227.

42. Translation from Wikipedia, 'The Obersalzberg Speech', http://en.wikipedia.org/wiki/The_Obersalzberg_Speech. The German original of the L-3 speech can be found here: http://library.fes.de/library/netzquelle/zwangsmigration/32ansprache.html.

43. Hannibal Travis, 'Did the Armenian Genocide Inspire Hitler?' *Middle East Quarterly* (Winter 2013), pp. 27–35.

44. Ibid.

45. Arnold Reisman, 'Could the US Holocaust Memorial Museum have Erred in a Major Exhibit?' Social Science Research Network, Working Papers Series, 31 Dec. 2010.

46. Heath W. Lowry, 'The U.S. Congress and Adolf Hitler on the Armenians', *Political Communications and Persuasion*, 3, 2 (1985), available on the web portal of the Assembly of Turkish American Associations: http://www.ataa.org/reference/hitler-lowry.html.

47. Kevork Bardakjian, *Hitler and the Armenian Genocide*, Cambridge, MA: Zoryan Institute, Special Report no. 3, 1985, p. 15.

48. Ibid., pp. 19 and 20.

49. Ibid., p. 21. Bardakjian bases this fact by referring to Helmuth Groschurth, an Abwehr officer, and Hans Bernd Gisevius who was a member of the German Resistance.

50. Richard Albrecht, 'Cutting the Gordian Knot—Research Report on So-Called "Armenian Quote" (Hitler's Second Secret Speech, August 22, 1939)', 6 Feb. 2008, English summary of research report published by Shaker Verlag: http://www.h-net.org/announce/show.cgi?ID=160809.

51. Bardakjian, *Hitler and the Armenian Genocide*, p. 28; see also Travis, 'Did the Armenian Genocide Inspire Hitler?' p. 32. Alfred Rosenberg was a leading Nazi ideologist.

52. Dadrian, *German Responsibility*, pp. 200–1.

53. Margaret Lavinia Anderson, 'Who Still Talked about the Extermination of the Armenians: German Talk and German Silences' in *A Question of Genocide: Armenians and Turks at the End of the Ottoman Empire*, R. Suny (ed.), Oxford: Oxford University Press, 2010, p. 199

54. Edward Minasian, '*The Forty Years of Musa Dagh*: The Film That Was Denied', *Journal of Armenian Studies*, 3, 1–2 (1986–7), pp. 121–32.

55. Yair Auron, *Banality of Denial: Israel and the Armenian Genocide*, New Piscataway, NJ: Transaction Publishers, 2004, p. 221.

56. 'Israelis Said to Oppose Parley After Threat to Turkish Jews', *New York Times*, 3 June 1982, http://www.nytimes.com/1982/06/03/world/israelis-said-to-oppose-parley-after-threat-to-turkish-jews.html.

57. For the Heath Lowry letter see Roger Smith, Eric Markusen and Robert Jay Lifton, 'Professional Ethics and the Denial of Armenian Genocide', *Holocaust and Genocide Studies*, 9, 1 (Spring 1995), pp. 1–22; and Peter Balakian, *The Burning Tigris: The Armenian Genocide and American Response*, New York: Harper Collins, 2003, pp. 383–5.

58. William H. Honan, 'Princeton is Accused of Fronting for the Turkish Government', *New York Times*, 22 May 1996, http://www.nytimes.com/1996/05/22/nyregion/princeton-is-accused-of-fronting-for-the-turkish-government.html?pagewanted=all&src=pm.

59. The 'memorandum' is reprinted in Roger Smith, Eric Markusen and Robert Jay Lifton, 'Professional Ethics and the Denial of Armenian Genocide', *Holocaust and Genocide Studies*, 9, 1 (Spring 1995), pp. 6–8.

60. See 'Attention Members of the U.S. House of Representatives', a letter published in the *New York Times* and *Washington Post*, 19 May 1995, available online at http://4.bp.blogspot.com/_9rjK1yXqTJc/SkKXdZzu45I/AAAAAAAADL8/XlcILiZJsFo/s1600-h/attentionus.jpg. See also Yves Ternon, 'Freedom and Responsibility of the Historian: The "Lewis Affair"', in Richard G. Hovannisian (ed.), *Remembrance and Denial: The Case of the Armenian Genocide*, Detroit, MI: Wayne State University Press, 1999, pp. 240–1.

61. See Donald Quataert, 'The Massacres of Ottoman Armenians and the Writing of Ottoman History', *Journal of Interdisciplinary History*, XXXVII, 2 (Autumn 2006), pp. 249–59.

62. Donald Quataert, 'The Massacres of Ottoman Armenians and the Writing of Ottoman History', *Journal of Interdisciplinary History*, XXXVII, 2 (Autumn 2006), p. 251.

63. Scott Jaschik, 'Is Turkey Muzzling U.S. Scholars?' *Inside Higher Ed*, 1 July 2008, http://www.insidehighered.com/news/2008/07/01/turkey; see also Susan Kinzie, 'Board Members Resign to Protest Chair's Ousting', *Washington Post*, 5 July 2008, http://www.washingtonpost.com/wp-dyn/content/article/2008/07/04/AR2008070402408.html.

64. Lou Ann Matosian, 'Politics, Scholarship and the Armenian Genocide: Perspectives on the ITS Scandal', *The Armenian Reporter*, 19 July 2008, http://www.reporter.am/go/article/2008-07-19-politics-scholarship-and-the-armenian-genocide.

65. Taner Akçam, 'Guenter Lewy's The Armenian massacres in Ottoman Turkey', *Genocide Studies and Prevention*, Volume 3, Issue 1, April 2008, page 120.

66. Quoted in David Phillips, *Unsilencing the Past: Track Two Diplomacy and Turkish–Armenian Reconciliation*, New York, NY: Berghahn Books, 2005, p. 48.

67. Ibid., p. 44.

4. WRITING AS RESISTANCE

1. Bedros Der Matossian, 'The Genocide Archives of the Armenian Patriarchate of Jerusalem', *Armenian Review*, 52, 3–4 (Fall–Winter 2011), pp. 17–39.

2. Aram Andonian and Medz Vojire, *Haygagan Verchin Godoradznere yev Talat Pasha* (The Great Crime: The Latest Armenian Massacres and Talaat Pasha), Boston, MA: Bahag Printers, 1921, pp. 7–8.

3. Ibid., p. 152.

4. Ibid., p. 179.

5. Şinasi Orel and Süreyya Yuca, 'Talat Pasha "telegrams": Historical fact or Armenian fiction?' Lefkosa, 1986, available online: http://www.eraren.org/index.php?Lisan=en&Page=YayinIcerik&SayiNo=15.

6. Vahakn N. Dadrian, 'The Naim-Andonian Documents on the World War I Destruction of Ottoman Armenians: The Anatomy of a Genocide', *International Journal of Middle East Studies*, Vol. 18, No. 3 (August 1986), pp. 311–360.

7. *Ibid.* p. 338.

8. Arnold Toynbee, *The Treatment of Armenians in the Ottoman Empire 1915–16, Documents Presented to Viscount Grey of Fallodon, Secretary of State for Foreign Affairs, with a Preface by Viscount Bryce*, London, 1916.

9. Ibid., Preface, p. xxi.

10. See *Key to Names of Persons and Places Withheld from Publication in the Original Edition of 'The Treatment of Armenians in the Ottoman Empire, 1915–16'*, 1916.

11. Ara Sarafian, 'The Archival Trail: Authentication of *The Treatment of Armenians in the Ottoman Empire, 1915–16'*, in Richard Hovannisian (ed.), *Remembrance and Denial: The Case of the Armenian Genocide*, Detroit, MI: Wayne State University Press, 1998, pp. 51–65.

12. Henry Morgenthau, *Ambassador Morgenthau's Story*, New York, NY: Doubleday, Page & Company, 1919, pp. 296–7.

13. Ibid., p. 298.

14. Ibid., p. 300.

15. Merrill D. Peterson, *'Starving Armenians': America and the Armenian Genocide, 1915–1930 and After*, Charlottesville, VA: University of Virginia Press, 2004, p. 6.

16. Morgenthau, *Ambassador Morgenthau's Story*, p. 309.

17. Ibid., p. 337.

18. Ibid., p. 339.

19. Ibid., pp. 337–8.

20. For a detailed discussion on the destruction of the Assyrians during the First World War, see David Gaunt, *Massacres, Resistance, Protectors, Muslim-Christian Relations in Eastern Anatolia during World War I*, Piscataway, NJ: Gorgias Press, 2006. See also: Jacques Rhétoré, « *Les Chrétiens aux bêtes* », Paris: CERF, 2005.

21. See the bibliography compiled by Mihran Minassian, 'Tracking Down the Past: The Memory Book ('Houshamadyan') Genre—A Preliminary Bibliography', *Houshamadyan*, 17 Jan. 2014, http://www.houshamadyan.org/en/themes/bibliography.html.

22. Marc Nichanian, *La Révolution Nationale, Entre L'Art et le Témoignage, Littératures arméniennes au XXe siècle*, vol. I, Geneva: Métis Presses, 2006, p. 137.

23. Ibid., p. 54.

24. Ibid., p. 55.

25. See Vahakn D. Dadrian and Taner Akçam, *Judgement at Istanbul: The Armenian Genocide Trials*, New York, NY: Berghahn Books, 2011.

26. Mark Malkasian, 'The Disintegration of the Armenian Cause in the United States, 1918–1927', *International Journal of Middle East Studies*, 16 (1984), pp. 349–65.

27. Ronald Grigor Suny, 'Soviet Armenia', in Richard G. Hovannisian (ed.), *Armenian People from Ancient to Modern Times*, vol. II, New York, NY: St. Martin's Press, 2004, p. 347.

28. André Mandelstam, *La Société des Nations et les Puissances devant le Problème Arménien*, Paris: Pédone, 1926, p. 90.

29. Ara Sanjian estimates the survivors at 240,000, see: 'The Armenian Minority Experience in the Modern Arab World', *Bulletin of the Royal Institute for Inter-Faith Studies*, 3, 1 (2001), p. 152. See also Nicola Migliorino, *(Re) Constructing Armenia in Lebanon and Syria, Ethno-Cultural Diversity and the State in the Aftermath of a Refugee Crisis*, New York, NY: Berghahn Books, 2008, pp. 31–3.

30. Vahé Tachjian, 'Gender, Nationalism, Exclusion: The Reintegration Process of Female Survivors of the Armenian Genocide', *Nations and Nationalism*, 15, 1 (2009), p. 66.

31. Author interview with Meguerditch Meguerditchian, member of ARF Bureau, Beirut, 30 Jan. 2014.

32. Walker, *Armenia*, p. 348.

33. Vahé Tachjian, 'Expulsion of the Armenian Survivors of Diarbekir and Urfa, 1923–1930', in Richard G. Hovannisian (ed.), *Armenian Tigranakert/Diarbekir and Edessa/Urfa*, Costa Mesa: Mazda, 2006, pp. 519–38.

34. Author interview with Yervant Pambukjian, Beirut, 30 Jan. 2014.

35. Mary Kilbourne Matossian, *The Impact of Soviet Policies in Armenia*, Leiden: Brill, 1962, pp. 155–62.

36. Grigor Y. Avakyan, *Hayasdane 1920–1990 Tt, Dndesaashkharakragan Agnarg* (In the Years 1020–1990, Geo-Economic View), Yerevan: Yerevani Hamalsarani Debaran (Armenian University Press), 1997, p. 52.

37. Ronald Grigor Suny, *Looking toward Ararat: Armenia in Modern History*, Bloomington, IN: Indiana University Press, 1993, p. 175; Zaven Meserlian, *Haygagan Hartsi Holovuyte 1939–2010* (Evolution of the Armenian Question, 1939–2010), Beirut: Sipan, 2012, p. 36.

38. Claire Mouradian, *De Staline à Gorbatchev histoire d'une république soviet-ique: l'Arménie*, Paris: Ramsay, 1990, p. 285.

39. See Ronald Grigor Suny, *The Baku Commune, 1917–1918: Class and Nationality in the Russian Revolution*, Princeton, NJ: Princeton University Press, 1972; and *The Making of the Georgian Nation*, Bloomington, IN: Indiana University Press, 1988.

40. Ibid., p. 116.

41. Dadrian, *The History of the Armenian Genocide*, p. xxii.

42. Ibid., p. 72.

43. Ibid., p. 76.

44. Vahakn Dadrian, 'The Secret Young-Turk Ittihadist Conference and the Decision for the World War I Genocide of the Armenians', *Holocaust and Genocide Studies*, 7, 2 (Fall 1993), pp. 173–201.

45. Dadrian, *German Responsibility in the Armenian Genocide: A Review of the Historical Evidence of German Complicity*, Watertown, MA: Blue Crane Books, 1996, 304 pp.

46. Ibid., p. 10.

47. Ibid., p. 114.

48. Ibid., p. 17.

49. Ibid., pp 21–2.

50. David Marshall Lang, *The Armenians: A People in Exile*, London: Unwin, 1988 (1st edn 1980), p. 36. The governor of Smyrna (Izmir) Rahmi Bey also played a central role in shielding the Armenian population as well as other minorities from deportations and executions. The Armenians and the Greeks of Smyrna/Izmir who were saved during the war were later destroyed in the Great Fire of Smyrna, when Kemalist forces entered the city in September 1922. See Giles Milton, *Paradise Lost, Smyrna 1922: The Destruction of Islam's City of Tolerance*, London: Scepter, 2008, pp. 65–6.

51. Varoujan Attarian, *Le Génocide des Arméniens devant L'ONU*, Brussels: Editions Complexe, 1997, p. 58.

52. Doc. E/CN.4/Sub.2/1984/SR.3 pp. 8, 9.

53. The doctoral thesis of Raymond Kévorkian was published under the title *Catalogue des 'incunables' arméniens, 1511–1695 ou Chronique de l'imprimerie arménienne*, Geneva: P. Cramer, 1986.

54. Author interview with Raymond Kévorkian, Paris, 11 Apr. 2014.

55. Ibid.

5. DECADE OF TERRORISM

1. On the relationship between the ARF and the Justice Commandos, see Gaïdz Minassian, *Guerre et terrorisme arméniens*, Paris: Presses Universitaires de France, 2002, pp. 29–32.

2. The name mujahed was given to Takoushian by Palestinian militants, as *al-mujahid al-armani* or 'the Armenian militant'.

3. Author interview with Sarkis Hatsbanian, Yerevan, 20 Apr. 2014.

4. Armen Garo later became an Ottoman parliamentary deputy, and his crossing to the Russian side in 1914, and later taking the leadership of Armenian volunteer fighters in the Russian ranks, is often quoted as a proof of 'Armenian treason'.

5. Balakian, *The Burning Tigris*, p. 345.

6. Soghomon Tehlirian, 'Yes mart em sbanel, payts martasban chem' (I Killed a Man, but I am not a Man-Killer), *Aysor*, 15 Mar. 2014, http://www.aysor. am/am/news/2014/03/15/tehleryan/.

7. Michael Bobelian, *Children of Armenia: A Forgotten Genocide and the Century-Long Struggle for Justice*, London: Simon and Schuster, 2012, p. 64.

8. Quoted in Samantha Power, *A Problem from Hell: America and the Age of Genocide*, New York, NY: Basic Books, 2002, p. 17.

9. Ibid.

10. The Turkish Foreign Ministry has compiled a list of attacks, which starts with Yanikian murdering the Turkish Consul General Mehmet Baydar, and the Consul Bahadir Demir, on 27 Jan. 1973. The last operation on this list is an explosion in Melbourne on 23 Nov. 1986, in front of the Turkish consulate, killing one and injuring another. See: 'Armenian Allegations and Historical Facts', Centre for Strategic Research, Ankara, 2007, pp. 49–62, http://www.mfa.gov.tr/data/DISPOLITIKA/ErmeniI ddialari/Ermeni_ingilizce_Soru_CevapKitapcigi.pdf.

11. The two Armenian priests were Hrant Guzelian, who was active in bringing Armenian children from the provinces to Istanbul to receive Armenian and Christian education, and Manuel Yergatian who was arrested at Istanbul airport for possessing old books making reference to the Armenian Genocide, and a nineteenth-century book with a map where eastern Turkey was indicated as Armenia. See Armand Gaspard, *Le combat arménien: entre terrorisme et utopie*, Lausanne: L'Âge d'homme, 1984, p. 85.

12. *Fedayis* were nineteenth- and early-twentieth-century Armenian guerrilla fighters.

13. Monte Melkonian would become famous in the mountains of Karabakh for commanding the forces of Mardouni—the eastern province of Karabakh. After leading his fighters during the difficult years of the war, he was ultimately killed by shrapnel as the Karabakhi fighters were attacking Aghdam, the headquarters of the Azerbaijani army, on 12 June 1993.

14. Markar Melkonian, *My Brother's Road: An American's Faithful Journey to Armenia*, London: I.B. Tauris, 2005, p. 80.

15. For more details on the Orly and Lisbon attacks, see Gaïdz Minassian, *Guerre et terrorisme arméniens*, pp. 88–96.

16. The picturesque life of Monte Melkonian is recounted by his brother in Melkonian in *My Brother's Road: An American's Faithful Journey to Armenia*.

6. A REVOLUTIONARY ACT

1. Orham Pamuk, *Istanbul: Memories of a City*, London: Faber and Faber, 2006 (1st edn 2005), pp. 215–16.

2. Damien McGuiness, 'Azeri Writer Akram Aylisli Hounded for "Pro-Armenian" Book', BBC News, 15 Feb. 2013, http://www.bbc.co.uk/news/world-europe-21459091.

3. Fatma Müge Göçek, 'Reading Genocide: Turkish Historiography on 1915', in Ronald Grigor Suny, Fatma Müge Göçek and Norman M. Naimark (eds), *A Question of Genocide: Armenians and Turks at the End of the Ottoman Empire*, Oxford: Oxford University Press, 2011, p. 42.

4. See EUR 44/003/2006, 'Turkey: Article 301: How the law on "denigrating Turkishness" is an insult to free expression', March 2006, available at: http://www.amnesty.org/en/library/asset/EUR44/003/2006/en/1a24fcc9-d44b-11dd-8743-d305bea2b2c7/eur440032006en.pdf. See also Kerem Öktem, Angry Nation: Turkey Since 1989, London: Z Books, 2011, pp. 147–48.

5. Author interview with Ragıp Zarakolu, Istanbul, February 2013.

6. John Darton, 'Istanbul Journal; A Prophet Tests the Honor of His Own Country', *New York Times*, 14 Mar. 1995, http://www.nytimes.com/1995/03/14/world/istanbul-journal-a-prophet-tests-the-honor-of-his-own-country.html, and 'From the Archives: On the Trial of Yasar Kemal', *Pen Canada*, 10 June 2013, http://pencanada.ca/archives/from-the-archives-2/.

7. Alison Flood, 'Outcry over Turkish Publisher's Arrest and Detention', *The Guardian*, 2 Nov. 2011, http://www.guardian.co.uk/books/2011/nov/02/turkish-publisher-arrest-ragip-zarakolu.

8. This biography is constructed from three interviews with Taner Akçam held in Geneva in May and June 2012.

9. Taner Akçam, 'A Slice of My Life', 1995, p. 1. I would like to thank Akçam for providing me with a copy of this article.

10. Ibid., p. 3.

11. Ibid., p. 11.

12. Taner Akçam, *Dialogue Across an International Divide: Essays Towards a Turkish–Armenian Dialogue*, Cambridge, MA: Zoryan Institute, 2001, p. ix.

13. Ibid., pp. x–xi.

14. Taner Akçam, *A Shameful Act: The Armenian Genocide and the Question of Turkish Responsibility*, New York, NY: Metropolitan Books, 2006.

15. Taner Akçam, *The Young Turk's Crime against Humanity: The Armenian Genocide and Ethnic Cleansing in the Ottoman Empire*, Princeton, NJ: Princeton University Press, 2012.

16. Ibid., p. 61.

17. Ibid., p. 125.

18. Taner Akçam, 'Turkey and History: Shoot the Messenger', Open Democracy, 16 Aug. 2007, http://www.opendemocracy.net/article/turkey_and_history_shoot_the_messenger.

19. A few months after our meeting, Hasan Cemal was fired from *Milliyet* under pressure from Turkish Prime Minister Erdogan. The probable cause for Erdogan's wrath was Cemal's revelations regarding a discussion between a Turkish parliamentary delegation and the imprisoned PKK leader, Abdullah Öcalan. See 'Author Hasan Cemal Fired from *Milliyet* Newspaper', *The Armenian Mirror-Spectator*, 20 Mar. 2013, http://www.mirrorspectator.com/2013/03/20/author-hasan-cemal-fired-from-milliyet-newspaper/.

20. Sahin Alpay, 'Neither Denial nor Recognition First, but Cognition', *Today's Zaman*, 28 Oct. 2012, http://www.todayszaman.com/columnist-296418-neither-denial-nor-recognition-first-but-cognition.html.

21. Cemal Pasha was assassinated by Stepan Dzaghigian, an Armenian Tashnak activist and member of 'Operation Nemesis' in 1922 in Tbilisi.

22. Available at: http://www.youtube.com/watch?v=fgJ35-UcmAk.

23. Orhan Kemal Cengiz, '1915 and Terrorists on Mountains', *Today's Zaman*, 11 Oct. 2012, http://www.todayszaman.com/columnist-295073–1915-and-terrorists-on-mountains.html.

7. RE-AWAKENING: THE STRUGGLE FOR MEMORY AND DEMOCRACY

1. This section is drawn from Taner Akçam, 'To Study the Armenian Genocide in Turkey, Or: Caught Between a Conspiracy of Silence and Murderous Hatred', a paper presented at Sabanci University. I thank the author for sharing this paper with me.

2. Ibid., p. 12.

3. Ibid., p. 13. Here 'my' is a self-reference by Akçam.

4. Martin A. Lee, 'Les liaisons dangereuses de la police turque', *Le Monde Diplomatique*, Mar. 1997.

5. Kendal Nezan, 'La Turquie, plaque tournante du trafic de drogue', *Le Monde Diplomatique*, July 1998. On MIT responsibility in the Alfortville bomb attack, see 'Ergenekon Document Reveals MIT's Assassination Secrets', *Today's Zaman*, 19 Aug. 2008, http://www.todayszaman.com/newsDetail_ getNewsById.action?load=detay&link=150621.

6. Sina Akşin, *Turkey: From Empire to Revolutionary Republic*, London: Hurst, 2007, pp. 305–6.

7. Stephen Kinzer, 'Scandal Links Turkish Aides to Deaths, Drugs and Terror', *New York Times*, 10 Dec. 1996, http://www.nytimes.com/1996/12/10/ world/scandal-links-turkish-aides-to-deaths-drugs-and-terror.html.

8. Quoted in Frank Bovenkerk and Yücel Yeşilgöz, 'The Turkish Mafia and the State', in Cyrill Fijnaut and Leitizia Paoli (eds), *Organized Crime in Europe: Concepts, Patterns and Control Policies in the European Union and Beyond*, Norwell, MA: Springer, 2004, pp. 585–602.

9. Ibid., p. 594.

10. Eugene Krieger, 'Turkey's Fragile EU Perspectives since the 1960s', in Hans-Lukas Kieser (ed.), *Turkey Beyond Nationalism*, London: I.B. Tauris, 2006, pp. 167–74.

11. The Agreement included the removal of customs duties, which has stimulated Turkish foreign trade with EU countries, leading to an estimated four-fold increase in growth 1996–2009. See http://www.worldbank.org/ content/dam/Worldbank/document/eca/turkey/tr-eu-customs-union-eng. pdf.

12. Quoted in Meltem Müftüler-Bac, 'The Never-Ending Story: Turkey and the European Union', *Middle Eastern Studies*, 34, 4 (1998), p. 246.

13. 'Turkey "Must Admit Armenian Dead"', BBC News, 13 Dec. 2004, http:// news.bbc.co.uk/2/hi/europe/4092933.stm.

14. David L. Phillips, *Unsilencing the Past: Track Two Diplomacy and Turkish–Armenian Reconciliation*, New York, NY: Berghahn Books, 2005, p. 75. The 3 million USD was to be managed by the American University's Centre for Global Peace.

15. See TARC's terms of reference: http://www1.american.edu/cgp/TARC/tor. htm.

16. Jean-Christophe Peuch, 'Armenia/Azerbaijan: International Mediators Report Progress on Karabakh Dispute', *Radio Free Europe/Radio Liberty*, 10 Apr. 2001, http://www.rferl.org/content/article/1096184.html. See also the remarks of the President of Armenia, Kocharyan, and the President of Azerbaijan, Aliev, at the opening of the talks on the site of US State Department, http://2001–2009.state.gov/secretary/former/powell/remarks/2001/1931.htm.

17. Vicken Cheterian, 'House Inaction Reinforces Armenian Community's Resolve to Seek Recognition of Genocide', *Eurasianet*, 22 Oct. 2000, http://www.eurasianet.org/departments/insight/articles/eav102300.shtml.

18. The text of House Resolution 596 can be found at http://groong.usc.edu/hres398/hres596.html.

19. Richard Simon, 'House GOP Kills Measure on Armenian Genocide', *Los Angeles Times*, 20 Oct. 2000, http://articles.latimes.com/2000/oct/20/news/mn-39477 and 'Speaker Hastert Kills Armenian Genocide Resolution', *Asbarez*, 20 Oct. 2000, http://asbarez.com/43880/speaker-hastert-kills-armenian-genocide-resolution/.

20. Selcuk Gultasli, 'A Relief for Turkey, for Now', *Hurriyet/Turkish Daily News*, 21 Oct. 2000, http://www.hurriyetdailynews.com/default.aspx?pageid=438&n=a-relief-for-turkey-for-now-2000–10–21.

21. Quoted in Phillips, *Unsilencing the Past*, p. 62.

22. Vercihan Ziflioğlu, 'Koç: Turkey has Undertaken its Cultural, Historical Responsibility', *Turkish Daily News*, 30 Mar. 2007, http://www.hurriyet-dailynews.com/default.aspx?pageid=438&n=koc-turkey-has-undertaken-its-cultural-historical-responsibility-2007–03–30.

23. 'TARC Armenian Commissioners Issue Statement', *Azg Daily*, 13 Dec. 2001, http://www.azg.am/EN/2001121301.

24. See 'The Applicability of the United Nations Convention on the Prevention and Punishment of the Crime of Genocide to Events which Occurred during the Early Twentieth Century', Legal Analysis Prepared for the International Center for Transitional Justice, p. 8. The document can be consulted here: http://www1.american.edu/cgp/track2/data/ICTJreport English.pdf.

25. Ibid., p. 17.

26. Phillips, *Unsilencing the Past*, p. 4.

27. Kamer Kasim, 'Turkish–Armenian Reconciliation Commission: Missed Opportunity', *Journal of Turkish Weekly*, 13 Oct. 2004, http://www.turkishweekly.net/article/12/.

28. See 'Turkish Armenian Reconciliation Commission Recommendations to Concerned Governments Regarding Improvement of Turkish Armenian Relations', 14 Apr. 2004, http://www1.american.edu/cgp/TARC/TARC Recommendations.pdf.

29. Ronal Grigor Suny, '"Truth in Telling": Reconciling Realities in the Genocide of the Ottoman Armenians', *American Historical Review* (Oct. 2009), p. 936.

30. Author interview with Ronald Grigor Suny, Geneva, 27 Mar. 2008.

31. See Suny, '"Truth in Telling"', p. 939.

32. Jirair Libaridian, 'A Report on the Workshop for Armenian/Turkish Scholarship', 24 Sept. 2006.

33. This volume was published under the title *A Question of Genocide: Armenians and Turks at the End of the Ottoman Empire*, and was edited by Ronald Grigor Suny, Fatma Müge Göçek and Norman M. Naimark Oxford: Oxford University Press, 2011.

34. Ronald Grigor Suny and Fatma Müge Göçek, 'Introduction: Leave it to the Historians', in Suny, Göçek and Naimark, *A Question of Genocide*, p. 9.

35. Ayhan Aktar, 'Debating the Armenian Massacres in the Last Ottoman Parliament, November–December 1918', *History Workshop Journal*, 64 (Autumn 2007), pp. 240–70, http://www.ayhanaktar.com/wp-content/uploads/pdf/eng/2.pdf.

36. Author interview with Aydan Aktar, Istanbul, 3 Nov. 2013.

37. Hakob Chakrian, 'Osmanyan Hayere Gaysrutyan Angman Shrchanum. Kidagan Badaskhanadvutyun yev Zhoghvrtavarutyuan Hartser' Kidazhoghove Hrker e Porpokum Turkyayum' (Ottoman Armenians during the Decline of the Empire: Issues of Scientific Responsibility and Democracy, Scientific Workshop Stirs up Excitement in Turkey), *Azg*, 25 May 2005, http://www.azg.am/AM/2005052507.

38. Igor Torbakov, 'Postponement of History Conference Sparks Controversy in Turkey', Eurasianet, 13 June 2005, http://www.eurasianet.org/departments/insight/articles/eav061405a.shtml.

39. 'Justice Minister Cicek: "Conference on Armenians like a Stab in the Back to Turkish People"', *Hurriyet*, 25 May 2005, http://www.hurriyetdailynews.com/default.aspx?pageid=438&n=justice-minister-cicek-conference-on-armenians-like-a-stab-in-the-back-to-turkish-people-2005–05–25.

40. Sarah Rainsford, 'Turkey Bans "Genocide" Conference', BBC News, 22 Sep. 2005, http://news.bbc.co.uk/2/hi/europe/4273602.stm.

41. Quoted in 'Turkish Court's Ban of Armenian Conference is Circumvented', *New York Times*, 24 Sep. 2005, http://www.nytimes.com/2005/09/23/world/africa/23iht-turkey.html?_r=0.

42. Author interview with Ferhat Kentel, Istanbul, 5 Nov. 2013. See also Scott Paterson, 'In Turkey, a First-Ever Debate about Armenian Mass Killings', *The Christian Science Monitor*, 26 Sep. 2005, http://www.csmonitor.com/2005/0926/p07s02-woeu.html.

43. Tatul Hakobyan, *Hayer yev Turker* (Armenians and Turks), Yerevan: Self Published, 2012, p. 423.

44. 'Turkey: Armenia Forum Goes Ahead', Al-Jazeera English, 25 Sep. 2005, http://www.aljazeera.com/archive/2005/09/2008491507571796.html.

45. See the website of the campaign: http://www.ozurdiliyoruz.com.

46. Ragip Duran, 'Des intellectuels turcs demandent "pardon"', *Libération*, 16 Dec. 2008, http://www.liberation.fr/monde/2008/12/16/des-intellectuels-turcs-demandent-pardon_296505.

47. Author interview with Cengiz Aktar, Istanbul, 3 Nov. 2013.

48. Cengiz Aktar, *Goch Nerumi, Turkere Timum yen Hayerin* (Armenian text translated from the French: *L'Appel au pardon, Des Turcs s'adressent aux Arméniens*), Yerevan: Actual Art, 2011.

49. 'Turkish PM Says Apology Campaign to Armenians Unacceptable', *Hurriyet*, 17 Dec. 2008: http://www.hurriyet.com.tr/english/domestic/10587736.asp.

50. 'General Staff Disapproves "Apology Campaign"', *Today's Zaman*, 19 Dec. 2008, http://www.todayszaman.com/news-161707-general-staff-disap-proves-apology-campaign.html.

51. Ayşe Karabat, 'Apology Campaign Triggers Fierce Debate', *Today's Zaman*, 18 Dec. 2008, http://www.todayszaman.com/newsDetail.action;jsessionid=0vmn8Gv5rd1NbtJGvgnhdHsx?newsId=161475&columnistId=0.

52. 'Gül Files Suit against Artiman', *Hurriyet*, 23 Dec. 2008, http://www.hurriyet.com.tr/english/domestic/10624092_p.asp.

53. Chris Morris, *The New Turkey: The Quiet Revolution on the Edge of Europe*, 2nd edn, London: Granta Books, 2006, p. 55.

54. 'Turkey Drops Probe into Armenian Apology Campaign', *Asbarez*, 26 Jan. 2009, http://asbarez.com/60001/turkey-drops-probe-into-armenian-apology-campaign/.

55. Lou Ann Matossian, 'Armenians Started using the Word "Genocide" in 1945, Khatchig Mouradian Shows', *The Armenian Reporter*, 26 June 2009,

http://www.reporter.am/index.cfm?furl=/go/article/2009-06-26-armenians-started-using-the-word—genocide—in-1945-khatchig-mouradian-shows&pg=2.

56. Quoted in Marc Mamigonian, 'Commentary on the Turkish Apology Campaign', *Armenian Weekly*, 21 Apr. 2009, http://www.armenianweekly.com/2009/04/21/commentary-on-the-turkish-apology-campaign/.

57. Ayşe Hur, 'I Apologize for Not Apologizing', *Armenian Weekly*, 20 Apr. 2009, http://www.armenianweekly.com/2009/04/20/i-apologize-for-not-apologizing/.

58. Ayda Erbal, 'Mea Culpa, Negotiations, Apologias, Revisiting the "Apology" of Turkish Intellectuals', in Birgit Schwelling (ed.), *Reconciliation, Civil Society, and the Politics of Memory, Transnational Initiatives in the 20th and 21st Century*, Bielefeld: Transcript-Verlag, 2012, p. 54.

59. Ibid., pp. 88–9.

8. ONE HUNDRED YEARS OF WHISPERS

1. Fethiye Çetin, *My Grandmother: A Memoir*, London: Verso, 2008.

2. Ibid., pp. 61–2.

3. This section is based on the author's interview with Fethiye Çetin, Istanbul, 4 Nov. 2013.

4. Fethiye Çetin and Ayşe Gül Altınay, *Les Petits-Enfants*, Arles: Actes Sud, 2011.

5. Bekir Coskun, 'My Armenian Matter', *Hürriyet Daily News*, 27 Sep. 2005, http://www.hurriyetdailynews.com/default.aspx?pageid=438&n=bekir-coskun-my-armenian-matter-2005-09-27.

6. Vercihan Zilfioğlu, 'Rocker Discovers his Origins', *Hürriyet Daily News*, 20 Oct. 2011, http://www.hurriyetdailynews.com/default.aspx?pageid=438&n=rocker-discovers-his-origins-2011-10-20.

7. Vercihan Zilfioğlu, 'My Mother was Armenian, Journalist Group Chair Reveals', *Hürriyet Daily News*, 12 Oct. 2013, http://www.hurriyetdailynews.com/my-mother-was-armenian-journalist-group-chair-reveals.aspx?pageID=238&nID=56125&NewsCatID=339.

8. Ruben Melkonian, *Islamatsvadz Hayeri Khntirneri Shurj* (On the Problems of Islamised Armenians), Noravank, 2009, p. 8.

9. Dickran Kouymjian, 'Armenia from the Fall of Cilician Kingdom (1375) to the Forced Emigration under Shah Abbas (1604)', in Richard G. Hovannisian (ed.), *Armenian People: From Ancient to Modern Times*, vol. II, Basingstoke: Palgrave Macmillan, 2004, p. 12.

10. Alan Palmer, *The Decline and Fall of the Ottoman Empire*, London: John Murray, 1993, p. 23.

11. Marcel Léart (pseudonym of Krikor Zohrab), *La Question Arménienne, A La Lumière des Documents*, Paris: Augustin Challamel, 1913, p. 5.

12. V.A. Barsamyan and Sh. R. Harutyunyan, *Hay Zhoghovrti Badmutyun, 1801–1978 TT.* (History of the Armenian People, 1801–1978), Yerevan: Luys, 1979, p. 261.

13. Selim Deringil quotes a British diplomatic report from 26 Apr. 1902, which states that in Çatal, a village in Aleppo province, seventy-five people who were forcibly converted to Islam wished to return back to the Armenian Church but were prohibited from doing so by the local authorities. See '"The Armenian Question is Finally Closed": Mass Conversions of Armenians in Anatolia during the Hamidian Massacres of 1895–1897', *Comparative Studies in Society and History*, 5, 2 (2009), pp. 344–71; the quote is from p. 367.

14. Following on from the reforms first envisioned in the San Stefano and Berlin treaties in 1878, intended to bring equality and security to the Armenians of the eastern provinces of the Empire, in 1914 there was yet another attempt to introduce reforms to the area. These were to be implemented by creating two large provinces, one with Erzurum as a centre, and the other with Van, administered by two European 'inspectors', the Dutchman Louis C. Westenenk and the Norwegian Nicolai Hoff. The Turkish leaders, who had accepted the 'package' in early 1914—a time they were weak due to their defeat in the Balkan Wars a year earlier—thought the outbreak of First World War later that year a warranted reversing their submission.

15. Fuat Dundar, *Crime of Numbers: The Role of Statistics in the Armenian Question (1878–1918)*, New Brunswick, NJ: Transaction Publishers, 2010.

16. See Akçam, *A Shameful Act*, p. 178. See also Fuat Dundar, 'The Settlement Policy of the Committee of Union and Progress 1913–1918, in *Turkey Beyond Nationalism*, pp. 37–42.

17. Akçam, *A Shameful Act*, p. 175.

18. Mae M. Derdarian, *Vergeen: A Survivor of the Armenian Genocide*, pp. 65–6. Quoted in Balakian, *Burning Tigris*, p. 258.

19. Razmik Panossian, *The Armenians, op. cit.*, p. 232, fn. 83.

20. Ruben Melkonian, *Islamatsvadz Hayeri Khntirneri Shurj*, p. 23.

21. Raymon Kévorkian, *Le Génocide des Arméniens*, Paris: Odile Jacob, 2006, p. 929.

22. See the introduction in Fethiye Çetin, *My Grandmother: A Memoir*, London: Verso, 2008, p. ix. According to historian Yervant Manoug, the overall number of the Muslim descendants of Armenian origin could be as high as 20 million, the descendants of Islamised Armenians following the genocide number between 1 and 2 million, and that of crypto-Armenians between 300,000 and 1 million. See '"Islamatsouadz yev Kakhdni Hayere Miyadar Chen", Esd Yervant Manugi' ('Islamised and Crypto-Armenians Are Not Homogenious', according to Yervant Manoug), *Hairenik Weekly*, 6 Jan. 2011, http://www.hairenikweekly.com/archives/5930.

23. 'Obituaries: Shnork Kaloustian, 76, An Armenian Prelate', *New York Times*, 8 Mar. 1990, http://www.nytimes.com/1990/03/08/obituaries/shnork-kaloustian-76-an-armenian-prelate.html.

24. Laurence Ritter and Max Sivaslian, *Les reste de l'épée*, Paris: Thaddée, 2012, pp. 37–8.

25. Vercihan Ziflioğlu, 'Varto Armenian Clan Makes Long Trip from Turkey to France', *Hürriyet Daily News*, 14 Jan. 2011, http://www.hurriyetdailynews.com/default.aspx?pageid=438&n=armenian-clan-vartos-long-trip-to-marseille-2011–01–14.

26. Vicken Cheterian, 'Turkey's "Race Codes" and the Ottoman Legacy', Open Democracy, 20 Aug. 2013, http://www.opendemocracy.net/vicken-cheterian/turkey's-race-codes-and-ottoman-legacy.

27. Orhan Kemal Cengit, 'Türkiye'nin şifreleri: 1, 2, 3', *Agos*, 2 Aug. 2013, http://www.agos.com.tr/haber.php?seo=turkiyenin-sifreleri-1–2–3& haberid=5493.

28. 'Turkish Interior Ministry Confirms "Race Codes for Minorities"', *Hürriyet Daily News*, 2 Aug. 2013, http://www.hurriyetdailynews.com/turkish-interior-ministry-confirms-race-codes-for-minorities.aspx?pageID=238&nID =51898&NewsCatID=339.

29. Hovann H. Simonian, 'History and Identity among the Hemshin', *Central Asian Survey*, 25, 1–2 (Mar.–June 2006), pp. 157–78; Hovann H. Simonian, *The Hemshin: History, Society and Identity in the Highlands of Northeast Turkey*, London: Routledge, 2007.

30. Anne Elizabeth Redgate, 'Morale, Cohesion and Power in the First Centuries of Amatuni Hamsehn', in Simonian, *The Hemshin*, pp. 3–13.

31. Vahan Ishkhanyan, 'Ovker en nrank? Musulman hayakhos Hemshintsiner' (Who Are They? Muslim Armenian-Speaking Hemshins), *Hetq*, 7 Mar. 2012, http://hetq.am/arm/articles/11632/ovqer-en-nranq-musulman-hay-akhos-hamshencinery.html.

32. Hovann H. Simonian, 'The Vanished Khemshins: Return from the Brink', *Journal of Genocide Research*, 4, 3 (2001), pp. 375–85, p. 380.

33. On inter-ethnic violence in south Kyrgzstan see Vicken Cheterian, 'Kyrgyzstan: Central Asia's Island of Instability', *Survival*, 52, 5 (2010), pp. 21–7.

34. Rüdiger Benninghaus, 'Turks and Hemshinli, Manipulating Ethnic Origins and Identity', in Simonian, *The Hemshin*, pp. 354–88.

35. Ibid., p. 169. See also Benninghaus, 'Turks and Hemshinli', p. 362.

36. Ibid., p. 169, and Bert Vaux, 'Hemshinli: "The Forgotten Black Sea Armenians"', Harvard University, p. 4; accessible at http://citeseerx.ist.psu.edu/viewdoc/download?doi=10.1.1.18.1893&rep=rep1&type=pdf.

37. Author's notes, Istanbul, 4 Nov. 2013.

38. Donald E. Miller and Lorna Touryan Miller, *Survivors: An Oral History of the Armenian Genocide*, Berkeley, CA: University of California Press, 1999, pp. 217–18, fn. 18.

39. Martin van Bruinessen, 'Genocide in Kurdistan? The Suppression of the Dersim Rebellion in Turkey (1937–38)', in George J. Anderopoulos (ed.), *Conceptual and Historical Dimensions of Genocide*, Philadelphia, PA: University of Pennsylvania Press, 1994, pp. 141–2.

40. Author interview with Murad Kahraman, Geneva, 29 May 2012.

41. The Kizilbash are Anatolian Shiites known as 'Red Heads' due to the distinctive turbans they wear.

42. This part is based on an interview with Miran Pirgiç, Istanbul, 18 May 2013.

43. Diran Lokmagyozian, 'Vets Or Dersimum' (Armenian: Six Days in Dersim), *Akunq*, 6 Sep. 2011, http://akunq.net/am/?p=12582.

44. 'Historian Halaçoğlu Accused of Racism', *Hürriyet Daily News*, 21 Aug. 2007, http://www.hurriyetdailynews.com/historian-halacoglu-accused-of-racism.aspx?pageID=438&n=historian-halacoglu-accused-of-racism-2007-08-21.

45. Şahin Alpay, 'Halaçoğlu is Practicing Racism', *Today's Zaman*, 27 Aug. 2007, http://www.todayszaman.com/columnists/sahin-alpay_120488-halacoglu-is-practicing-racism.html.

46. Hakob Chakrian, 'Armenians Converted Not Only to Kurds or Alevis, but also to Arabs', *Azg*, 4 Sep. 2007, http://www.azg.am/EN/2007090401.

47. 'A Rare Glimpse into Turkish Military Intel: IRAQ', WikiLeaks, Cable Reference ID: 04ANKARA7106, 12 Dec. 2004, http://wikileaks.ch/cable/2004/12/04ANKARA7106.html.

48. I thank Vahé Tachjian for sharing his conference paper with me.

49. The Gülen movement, also known as *Hizmet* (Service), is a transnational religious movement that originalted in Turkey, led by preacher Fethullah Gülen. The movement allied itself with Erdogan's AKP, and had enormous influence over the education establishment, police and judiciary, until Gülen and AKP fell out in December 2013.

50. See Oral Çalışlar, '"Ermeniler de Türkleri kesmişti" diyerek …' (Turkish: 'Armenians too Massacred Turks', they Say…), *Radikal*, 11 Nov. 2013, http://www.radikal.com.tr/yazarlar/oral_calislar/ermeniler_de_turkleri_kesmisti_diyerek-1160095.

51. Author's notes, Istanbul, 3 Nov. 2013. See also the video recording of the panel: http://www.youtube.com/watch?v=F4MOI9DSmkU.

9. MEMORIES OF THE LAND

1. Hapet M. Isgenderian, *Svedyo Abesdamputyune* (Armenian: The Revolt of Svedya), Cairo: Zareh Berberian Printers, 1915, p. 10.

2. Arnold Toynbee, *The Treatment of Armenians in the Ottoman Empire 1915–16, Documents Presented to Viscount Grey of Fallodon, Secretary of State for Foreign Affairs, with a Preface by Viscount Bryce*, London, 1916, p. 511.

3. Vahram Shemmassian, 'Musa Dagh in the 19th and Early 20th Century', http://www.arf1890.com/Armenian%20History/MusaDagh.htm.

4. Author interview with Yesayi Havatian, Anjar, 1 Feb. 2014.

5. Murad's story is based on two interviews with Murad Uçaner, in Istanbul, on 4 Nov. 2013, and in Gaziantep on 11 Nov. 2013. See also Vahe Habeshian, 'The Woman in the Wall: A Story of People, Places, and Things', *The Armenian Weekly*, 11 Dec. 2013, http://www.armenianweekly.com/2013/12/11/the-woman-in-the-wall/#prettyPhoto.

6. Tom Vartabedian, 'Adventurist Armen Aroyan: 20 Years and Winding Down', *Armenian Weekly*, 9 Dec. 2011.

7. A. Gesar, *Aintabi Koyamarde*, Boston, MA: Hayrenik Press, 1945.

8. Ibid., p. 10.

9. Br. M. Abadie, *Les Quatres Sièges d'Aintab (1920–1921)*, Paris: Charles-Lavauzelle & Cie, 1922, pp. 18–20.

10. Raymond Kévorkian, *Le Génocide des Arméniens*, p. 640.

11. Vasburagan (in West Armenian), or Vaspurakan (in East Armenian), is one of the historic provinces of Armenia, located in Greater Armenia, around

Lake Van. It was ruled by the Ardzruni dynasty, and it became an independent Armenian kingdom under Gagik I (904–43).

12. David Marshall Lang, *Armenia: Cradle of Civilization*, London: George Allen & Unwin, 1970, pp. 216–18.

13. Cengiz Çandar, 'The So-Called "Akdamar museum"', *Hürriyet Daily News*, 30 Mar. 2007.

14. Tatul Hakobyan, *Hayatsk Araraden: Hayer yev Turker* (Armenian: Looking from Ararat: Armenians and Turks), Antelias: Self Published, 2012, p. 10.

15. See Lang, *Armenia: Cradle of Civilization*, p. 223.

16. Robert H. Hewsen, "The Historic Georgraphy of Ani and Kars, in Richard G. Hovannisian (ed.), *Armenian Kars and Ani*, Costa Mesa, CA: Mazda Publishers, 2011, p. 32.

17. Claude Mutafian, 'Ani After Ani, Eleventh to Seventeenth Century', in *Armenian Kars and Ani*, pp. 155–65. Mutafian is sceptical about the devastating impact of the earthquake, considering it a later interpretation about the decline of Ani.

18. M. Brosset, *Les Ruins d'Ani, Capital de l'Arménie*, Imprimerie de l'Académie Impériale des sciences, St.-Pétersbourg, 1860, page 10.

10. THE OWNER OF THE TURKISH PRESIDENTIAL PALACE

1. See http://www.hurriyet.com.tr/yazarlar/6196954.asp.

2. Zeynep Kezer, 'Of Forgotten People and Forgotten Places: Nation-Building and the Dismantling of Ankara's Non-Muslim Landscapes', in D. Fairchild Ruggles (ed.), *On Location: Heritage Cities and Sites*, New York: Springer, 2012, p. 171.

3. Raymond Kévorkian, *Le Génocide des Arméniens*, pp. 619–22.

4. Laure Marchand and Guillaume Perrier, *La Turquie et le Fantôme Arménien*, pp. 148, 174.

5. Donald Bloxham, *The Great Game of Genocide*, p. 207.

6. Harut Sassounian, 'Armenians Sue Turkey Claiming U.S. Air Base Land', Huffington Post, 23 Dec. 2010, http://www.huffingtonpost.com/harut-sassounian/armenians-sue-turkey-clai_b_800003.html.

7. The only exception was the *Los Angeles Times*, with two short reports on its 'local' page. See Carol J. Williams, 'Descendants of Armenian Genocide Victims Seek $65 Million from Turkey for Seized Land', 15 Dec. 2010, http://latimesblogs.latimes.com/lanow/2010/12/descendants-of-armenian-genocide-victims-sue-turkey-over-seized-property.html.

8. http://www.panarmenian.net/eng/news/156361/.

9. Kevork K. Baghdjian, *The Confiscation of Armenian Properties by the Turkish Government Said to be Abandoned*, Antelias: Printing House of the Armenian Catholicosate of Cilicia, 2010, pp. 84–6. Taner Akçam, *The Young Turk's Crime against Humanity*, pp. 341–5.

10. Wolfgang Gust (ed.), *The Armenian Genocide: Evidence from the German Foreign Office Archives, 1915–1916*, New York, NY: Berghahn, 2014, p. 413.

11. Quoted in Uğur Ümit Üngör and Mehmet Polatel, *Confiscation and Destruction: The Young Turk Seizure of Armenian Property*, New York, NY: Continuum, 2011, p. 69.

12. Quoted in ibid., p. 79.

13. Ahmet Refik, *Two Committees, Two Massacres*, trans. with Preface by Racho Donef, London: Firodil Publishing House, 2006 (first published in Ottoman Turkish, Istanbul, 1919), pp. 11–12.

14. Quoted in Akçam, *The Young Turks' Crime against Humanity*, p. 349.

15. Uğur Ümit Üngör and Mehmet Polatel, *Confiscation and Destruction: The Young Turk Seizure of Armenian Property*, Bloomsbury Academic, London, 2011, p. 48.

16. Erik J. Zürcher, *Turkey: A Modern History*, pp. 141–2; Akçam, *A Shameful Act*, pp. 303–10.

17. Üngör and Polatel, *Confiscation and Destruction*, pp. 100–1.

18. See 'Recueil des Traités', *Société des Nations*, 701 (1924).

19. John M. VanderLippe, *The Politics of Turkish Democracy: Ismet Inönü and the Formation of the Multi-Party System, 1938–1950*, Albany, NY: State University of New York Press, 2005, pp. 83–4.

20. Hüseyin Keles, '"Adnan Menderes not Initiator of 1955 Pogrom"', *Today's Zaman*, 4 Nov. 2012.

21. Steven Kettmann, 'A Photo Show on a Pogrom 50 Years Ago is Itself Attacked by a Mob', *New York Times*, 24 Sep. 2005, http://www.nytimes.com/2005/09/24/arts/extra/24pogr.html.

22. Swiss jurist Hans Leeman was invited to Turkey in 1929 to prepare the draft Law on Foundations.

23. Mehmet Polatel, Nora Mildanoglu, Ozgur Leman Eren, and Mehmet Atilgan, *2012 Declaration: The Seized Properties of Armenian Foundations in Istanbul*, Istanbul: Hrant Dink Foundation, 2012.

24. Ibid., pp. 119–23.

25. Raffi Bedrosyan, 'Revisiting the Turkification of Confiscated Armenian Assets', *Armenian Weekly*, 17 Apr. 2012, http://www.armenianweekly.com/2012/04/17/revisiting-the-turkification-of-confiscated-armenian-assets/. For Turkish sources, see Ibrahim Halil Er, 'Ermenilerin mallari ve cumhuriyetin zenginleri' (Armenian Property and the Rich of the Republic), *Milli Gazete*, 18 Aug. 2013, http://www.milligazete.com.tr/koseyazisi/Ermenilerin_mallari_ve_cumhuriyetin_zenginleri_2/16188#.UySHFhbMFGg.

26. Morgenthau, *Ambassador Morgenthau's Story*, p. 339.

27. Ibid., p. 332.

28. Ibid., p. 338.

29. Ibid., p. 337

30. Ibid., p. 337.

31. See André Mandelstam, quoted in Üngör and Polatel, *Confiscation and Destruction*, p. 66.

32. Ibid., p. 24. According to US State Department archives, New York Life had sold life insurances of ten million dollars at the eve of the First World War, mostly to Ottoman Armenians.

33. Dickran Kouymjian, 'The Destruction of Armenian Historical Monuments as a Continuation of the Turkish Policy of Genocide', in Gérard Libaridian (ed.), *A Crime of Silence: The Armenian Genocide*, London: Permanent Peoples' Tribunal/Zed Books, 1985, p. 174.

34. William Dalrymple, *From the Holy Mountain: A Journey in the Shadow of Byzantium*, London: Flamingo, 1998, p. 78.

35. Dilek Kurban and Kezban Hatemi, *The Story of an Alien(ation): Real Estate Ownership Problems of Non-Muslim Foundations and Communities in Turkey*, Istanbul: TESEV, 2009, p. 7.

36. 'AK Party Government Returns Property to Armenians', *Sabah*, 15 July 2013, http://www.dailysabah.com/nation/2013/07/15/ak-party-government-returns-property-to-armenians.

37. 'ECHR Rules against Turkey in Armenian Property Ownership Case', *Hürriyet Daily News*, 16 Dec. 2008, http://www.hurriyet.com.tr/english/domestic/10580596_p.asp.

38. Amberin Zaman, 'Another Byzantine Church Becomes Mosque in Turkey', al-Monitor, 7 Aug. 2013, http://www.al-monitor.com/pulse/originals/2013/08/another-byzantine-church-becomes-a-mosque.html.

11. KURDS: FROM PERPETRATOR TO VICTIM

1. Martin Van Bruinessen, *Agha, Sheikh and State: The Social and Political Structures of Kurdistan*, London: Zed Books, 1992, p. 277.
2. Hamit Bozarslan, 'Les Révoltes Kurdes en Turquie Kémaliste (Quelques aspects)', *Guerres mondiales et conflits contemporains* (1988), pp. 121–36.
3. Assyrian semi-nomadic tribal structures existed, which had patterns and codes similar to the Kurds in the Hakkari or Şırnak provinces.
4. Jelle Verheij, 'Les freres de terre et d'eau: Sur le rôle des Kurdes dans les massacres arméniens de 1894–1896,' *Les Cahiers de l'autre Islam*, 5 (1999), p. 238.
5. David McDowell, *A Modern History of The Kurds*, 3rd edn, London: I.B. Tauris, 2005, pp. 98–9.
6. Isabella L. Bird, *Journeys in Persia and Kurdistan*, vol. 2, London: John Murray, 1891, p. 334.
7. Özcan Yilmaz, *La formation de la nation Kurde en Turquie*, Paris: Presses Universitaires de France, 2013, p. 35, 39.
8. Kamal Madhar Ahmad, *Krdistan, fi sanawat al-h'arb al-'alamiya al-oula* (Arabic: Kurdistan in the Years of the First World War), 3rd edn, Beirut: al-Farabi, Beirut, 2013 (1st edn 1984), p. 247.
9. Ibid., pp. 269–70.
10. Kamal Madhar Ahmad, *Krdistan, fi sanawat al-h'arb al-'alamiya al-oula* (Arabic: Kurdistan in the Years of the First World War), p. 266.
11. Ibid., p. 279.
12. Tovmas Mgrdchian, *Dikranagerdi Nahanki Chartere yev Kurderu Kazanutyunnere, Aganades Badmutyun*, (Armenian: The Massacres of Diyarbakir Province and the Beastiality of the Kurds, an Eye-Witness Account), Cairo: Krikor Jihanian Printer, 1919, p. 63.
13. Maria T. O'Shea, *Trapped between the Map and Reality: Geography and Perceptions of Kurdistan*, London: Routledge, 2004, p. 90; McDowell, *A Modern History*, p. 109.
14. McDowall, *A Modern History*, p. 106.
15. Özcan Yilmaz, *La formation de la nation Kurde en Turquie*, Paris: Presses Universitaires de France, 2013, p. 49.
16. Hakan Özoğlu, *Kurdish Notables and the Ottoman State*, Albany, NY: State University of New York Press, 2004, p. 3.
17. Quoted in Andrew Mango, 'Atatürk and the Kurds', *Middle Eastern Studies*, 35, 4 (1999), pp. 6–7.

18. Stefan Ihrig, *Atatürk in the Nazi Imagination*, Cambridge, MA: Harvard University Press, 2014.

19. Soner Cagaptay, 'Race, Assimilation and Kemalism: Turkish Nationalism and the Minorities in the 1930s', *Middle Eastern Studies*, 40, 3 (2004), pp. 86–101.

20. Erik J. Zürcher, *Turkey: A Modern History*, pp. 190–191. See also Clive Foss, 'Kemal Atatürk: Giving a New Nation a New History', *Middle Eastern Studies*, Vol. 50, Issue 5, 2014, pp. 826–847.

21. Şükrü Hanioğlu, *Ataturk: An Intellectual Biography*, Princeton, NJ: Princeton University Press, 2011, pp. 176–7.

22. Martin van Bruinessen, 'The Suppression of the Dersim Rebellion in Turkey (1937–38)', in George J. Andreopoulos (ed.), *Conceptual and Historical Dimensions of Genocide*, Philadelphia, PA: University of Pennsylvania Press, 1994, p. 142, fn. 5, http://www.hum.uu.nl/medewerkers/m.vanbruines-sen/publications/Bruinessen_Genocide_in_Kurdistan.pdf.

23. 'Dersim Massacre Monument to Open Next Month', *Today's Zaman*, 24 Oct. 2012, http://www.todayszaman.com/news-296283-dersim-massacre-monument-to-open-next-month.html.

24. Dogu Ergil, 'Knowledge is a Potent Instrument for Change', *European Journal of Turkish Studies*, 5 (2006), p. 24. Baskin Oran, 'The Reconstruction of Armenian Identity in Turkey and the Weekly *Agos*', *The Turkish Yearbook of International Relations*, XXXVII (2006), p. 129.

25. 'Human Rights Report of Turkey 2005', Human Rights Foundation of Turkey, Ankara, 2006, p. 15.

26. Author interview with Nurredin Sufi (also spelled as Nurettin Sofi), Northern Iraq, Nov. 2012.

27. Author interview with Abdullah Demirbaş, Diyarbakir, 23 July 2013.

12. CONTINUOUS WAR

1. On the 'Armenian–Tatar' wars, see Anahide Ter Minassian, 'The Revolution of 1905 in Transcaucasia', *Armenian Review*, 42, 2/166 (Summer 1989), pp. 1–23; see also Alex Marshal, *The Caucasus Under Soviet Rule*, London: Routledge, 2010, pp. 35–41.

2. For eyewitness accounts see Samuel Shahmuratian (ed.), *The Sumgait Tragedy: Pogroms against Armenians in Soviet Azerbaijan*, Cambridge, MA: Zoryan Institute, 1990.

3. Ziya Buniatov, 'Why Sumgait?' *Elm*, Baku, 13 May 1989, p. 175. See the English translation: Levon Chorbajian, Patrick Donabedian and Claude Mutafian, *The Caucasian Knot: The History and Geo-Politics of Nagorno-Karabakh*, London: Zed Books, 1994, pp. 188–9. Buniatov's article was re-published in Visions of Azerbaijan, Mar./Apr. 2010, http://www.visions.az/history,37/#cite-note_12.

4. Grigory Oganesov, 'Participant of Self-Defense Operations in Kirovabad: In Critical Situations, We Always Win if We are United', *Panorama*, 28 Nov. 2011, http://www.panorama.am/en/comments/2011/11/28/gandzak-kirovabad-self-defence/.

5. Human Rights Watch/The Inter-Republic Memorial Society, 'Conflict in the Soviet Union: Black January in Azerbaidzhan', New York, 1991, pp. 6–7.

6. Ohannes Geukjian, *Ethnicity, Nationalism and Conflict in the South Caucasus: Nagorno-Karabakh and the Legacy of Soviet Nationalities Policy*, Farnham: Ashgate, 2012, pp. 185–6.

7. See Vicken Cheterian, *War and Peace in the Caucasus*, London: Hurst, 2008, p. 128.

8. For more on Khojali, see Michael Croissant, *The Armenia–Azerbaijan Conflict: Causes and Implications*, Westpoint, NY: Praeger, 1998, pp. 78–80; Thomas de Waal, *Black Garden: Armenia and Azerbaijan through Peace and War*, New York, NY: New York University Press, 2003, pp. 170–2.

9. Croissant, *The Armenia–Azerbaijan Conflict*, p. 96.

10. Mesut Çevikalp, 'Late President Turgut Özal Worked to Solve "Armenian Genocide" Dispute', *Today's Zaman*, 23 Apr. 2012, http://www.todayszaman.com/news-278371-late-president-turgut-ozal-worked-to-solve-armenian-genocide-dispute.html.

11. Rasim Ozan Kutahyali, 'Who Poisoned Former Turkish President Ozal?' Al-Monitor, 22 Aug. 2013, http://www.al-monitor.com/pulse/originals/2013/08/turkey-president-ozal-poisoned.html.

12. Alice Kelikian, 'Nagorno-Karabakh: Azerbaijan's Colonial Rule has no Place in the Post-Soviet Era', *Los Angeles Times*, 15 May 1992, http://articles.latimes.com/1992–05–15/local/me-1998_1_armenian-population.

13. Jerry L. Johnson, *Crossing Borders—Confronting History: Intercultural Adjustment in a Post-Cold War World*, Boston, MA: University Press of America, 1999, p. 137.

14. See Alec Rasizade, 'Azerbaijan after Heydar Aliev', *Nationalities Papers*, 32,

1 (Mar. 2004), pp. 137–64; Farid Guliyev, 'Political Elites in Azerbaijan', in Andreas Heinrich and Heiko Pleines (eds), *Challenges of the Caspian Resources Boom: Domestic Elites and Policy-Making*, Basingstoke: Palgrave Macmillan, 2012, pp. 117–30.

15. Thomas Grove and Afet Mehdiyeva, 'Aliyev Wins Third Term as President of Azerbaijan', Reuters, 9 Oct. 2013, http://www.reuters.com/article/2013/10/09/us-azerbaijan-election-idUSBRE99812Z20131009.

16. Eric Eissler, 'Does Declining Oil Revenue Equal Less Security for Azerbaijan?' International Security Network, 25 Mar. 2014, http://www.isn.ethz.ch/Digital-Library/Articles/Detail/?id=178075.

17. 'Closing Speech by Ilham Aliyev at the Conference on the Results of the Third Year into the "State Program on the Socioeconomic Development of Districts for 2009–2013"', available on the official website of the President of Azerbaijan, 'Speeches', 28 Feb. 2012, http://en.president.az/articles/4423.

18. http://budapest.sumgait.info/safarov-interrogation.htm.

19. Marina Grigorian and Rauf Orujev, 'Murder Case Judgement Reverberates Around Caucasus', Institute for War and Peace Reporting, 2 Apr. 2006, http://iwpr.net/report-news/murder-case-judgement-reverberates-around-caucasus.

20. Yasemin Kilit Aklar, 'Nation and History in Azerbaijani School Textbooks', *Ab Imperio*, 2 (2005), p. 479.

21. Ibid., p. 484.

22. Ceylan Tokluoğlu, 'The Political Discourse of the Azerbaijani Elite on the Nagorno-Karabakh Conflict (1991–2009)', *Europe-Asia Studies*, 63, 7 (Sep. 2011), p. 1235.

23. Ibid., p. 1236. This is the same argument as the one put forward by Bunyatov following the anti-Armenian pogrom in Sumgait in 1988.

24. Ibid., p. 1239.

25. Ara Sanjian, 'Armenia and Genocide: The Growing Engagement of Azerbaijan', *Armenian Weekly*, 26 Apr. 2008, pp. 28–33.

26. Tokluoğlu, 'The Political Discourse', p. 1225.

27. See, 'Decree of the President of the Republic of Azerbaijan on the Genocide of the Azerbaijani People', Baku, 26 Mar. 1998, http://www.human.gov.az/?sehife=etrafli&sid=MTMyMjMzMTA4MTMyNjE1Mw==&dil=en.

28. Human Rights Watch/Helsinki, 'Azerbaijan, Seven Years of Conflict in Nagorno-Karabakh', 1994, http://www.hrw.org/reports/pdfs/a/azerbjn/azerbaij94d.pdf.

29. 'Azeris Mark 20th Anniversary of Khojaly Massacre in Istanbul', *Hürriyet Daily News*, 26 Feb. 2012, http://www.hurriyetdailynews.com/azeris-mark-20th-anniversary-of-khojaly-massacre-in-istanbul.aspx?pageID=23 8&nID=14673&NewsCatID=355.

30. 'Nationalists Unfurl Banner Hailing Assassin of Hrant Dink at Khojaly Massacre Commemoration', *Hürriyet Daily News*, 24 Feb. 2014, http://www.hurriyetdailynews.com/nationalists-unfurl-banner-hailing-assassin-of-hrant-dink-at-khojaly-massacre-commemoration.aspx?pageID=238&n ID=62849&NewsCatID=341.

31. On the role of New Julfa trade networks, see Sebouh David Aslanian, *From the Indian Ocean to the Mediterranean: The Global Trade Networks of Armenian Merchants from New Julfa*, Berkeley, CA: University of California Press, 2011.

32. For a thorough report, see: Parliamentary Group Switzerland-Armenia, 'The Destruction of Jugha and the Entire Armenian Cultural Heritage in Nakhijevan', Berne, 2006, p. 98.

33. Letter from Recep Tayyip Erdoğan to Robert Kocharyan, 10 Apr. 2005, available on the Turkish Foreign Ministry website, http://www.mfa.gov.tr/data/DISPOLITIKA/text-of-the-letter-of-h_e_-prime-minister-recep-tayyip-erdogan-addressed-to-h_e_-robert-kocharian.pdf.

34. 'WikiLeaks Publishes Armenian President's Letter to Premier Erdoğan', The Global Intelligence Files, 25 Aug. 2011, ID 1450020: https://wikileaks.org/gifiles/docs/14/1450020_-os-windows-1252-q-_armenia-turkey_.html.

35. On the official site of the Armenian president, 'President Serzh Sargsyan's Official Visit to the Russian Federation, 23.06.2008–25.06.2008', http://www.president.am/en/foreign-visits/item/2008/06/23/news-27/.

36. David L. Phillips, 'Diplomatic History: The Turkey–Armenia Protocols', Institute for the Study of Human Rights, Columbia University, Working Paper, 2012, p. 43.

37. Zaven Messerlian, *Haygagan Hartsi Holovuyte 1939–2010* (Armenian: The Declination of the Armenian Question 1939–2010), Beirut, 2012, p. 302.

38. 'Azerbaijan: Apparat, MFA, Socar, Turkish Embassy Cite Progress on Erdogan Visit, Energy Issues', WikiLeaks, Cable ID 09BAKU401_a, 15 May 2009, https://www.wikileaks.org/plusd/cables/09BAKU401_a.html.

39. Shamkhal Abilov, 'Turkish Prime Minister Recep Tayyip Erdogan's Baku

Visit: Relations Back on the Track', *Journal of Turkish Weekly*, 13 May 2009, http://www.turkishweekly.net/news/76650/turkish-prime-minister-recep-tayyip-erdogan-39-s-baku-visit-relations-back-on-the-track.html.

40. Remarks by President Serzh Sargsyan in Deir Ez Zor, 24 Mar. 2010, http://www.president.am/en/statements-and-messages/item/2010/03/24/news-58/.

41. Naira Hayrumyan, 'Armenia and Year 2015: From Genocide Recognition Demand to Demand for Eliminating its Consequences', *ArmeniaNow*, 7 July 2013, http://armenianow.com/genocide/47534/armenia_turkey_genocide_recognition_aghvan_hovsepyan.

42. Phillips, *Diplomatic History*, p. 16.

43. Author interview with Giro Manoyan, ARF leader and head of Armenian Cause Office, Yerevan, 22 Apr. 2014.

44. 'The Message of the Prime Minister of the Republic of Turkey, Recep Tayyip Erdoğan on the Events of 1915', *Hürriyet Daily News*, 23 Apr. 2014, http://www.hurriyetdailynews.com/turkish-pm-erdogans-april-23-statement-on-armenian-issue-in-english.aspx?pageID=238&nID=65454&NewsCatID=359.

13. CONSEQUENCES

1. Susan Sontag, *Regarding the Pain of Others*, New York, NY: Picador, 2003, p 35.

2. Ya'ir Auron, *The Pain of Knowledge: Holocaust and Genocide Issues in Education*, New Brunswick, NJ: Transaction Publishers, 2005, p. 100.

3. The Muslim Council of Britain, 'News Release: Holocaust Memorial Ceremony—MCB Regrets Exclusion of Palestinian Tragedy', 26 Jan. 2001, http://web.archive.org/web/20010309212038/http://www.mcb.org.uk/news260101.html.

4. Timothy Garton Ash, 'This is the Moment for Europe to Dismantle Taboos, Not Erect Them', *The Guardian*, 19 Oct. 2006, http://www.theguardian.com/commentisfree/2006/oct/19/comment.france. See also a second article by Timothy Garton Ash, 'In France, Genocide has Become a Political Brickbat', *The Guardian*, 18 Jan. 2012, http://www.theguardian.com/commentisfree/2012/jan/18/france-genocide-political-brickbat.

5. See: 'Liberté pour l'histoire', *Libération*, 13 Dec. 2005, http://www.liberation.fr/societe/2005/12/13/liberte-pour-l-histoire_541669.

6. Communist parliamentarian Jean-Claude Gayssot is the author of anti-discrimination French law no. 90–615 of 13 July 1990, which criminalises racist, anti-Semitic and xenophobic acts. It is worth noting also that Martin Shaw argues that support of the law making denial of the Armenian Genocide illegal has an anti-Muslim dimension. Martin Shaw, 'The Holocaust and Genocide: Loose Talk, Bad Action', Open Democracy, 21 Mar. 2012, http://www.opendemocracy.net/martin-shaw/holocaust-and-genocide-loose-talk-bad-action.

7. See Comité de Défense de la Cause Arménienne, 'Colonisation et liberté pour l'histoire: 31 personnalités contre la pétition des 19', 21 Dec. 2005, http://www.cdca.asso.fr/s/detail.php?r=0&id=381.

8. Pierre Nora, 'Lois mémorielles: pour en finir avec ce sport législatif purement français', Le Monde, 27 Dec. 2011, http://www.lemonde.fr/idees/article/2011/12/27/lois-memorielles-pour-en-finir-avec-ce-sport-legislatif-purement-francais_1623091_3232.html.

9. Martin Shaw, 'The Holocaust and Genocide: Loose Talk, Bad Action', Open Democracy, 21 Mar. 2012, http://www.opendemocracy.net/martin-shaw/holocaust-and-genocide-loose-talk-bad-action.

10. Mehmet Ali Birand, 'Now, the Armenians are Making us Walk the "Deportation March"', Hürriyet Daily News, 27 Dec. 2011, http://www.hurriyetdailynews.com/now-the-armenians-are-making-us-walk-the-deportation-march—.aspx?pageID=449&nID=10054&NewsCatID=405.

11. Marc Nichanian, La Révolution Nationale, Entre L'Art et le Témoignage, Littératures arméniennes au XXe siècle, vol. I, Geneva: Métis Presses, 2006, pp. 24–6.

12. See 'Turkish PM says Armenians Living in Turkey Proves there was no "Genocide"', Hürriyet Daily News, 29 Apr. 2014, http://www.hurriyetdailynews.com/turkish-pm-says-armenians-living-in-turkey-proves-there-was-no-genocide.aspx?PageID=238&NID=65734&NewsCatID=510.

13. Hürriyet, March 6, 2007: http://www.hurriyet.com.tr/english/6069762_p.asp; Swissinfo, March 9, 2007: http://www.swissinfo.ch/eng/turkish-politician-fined-over-genocide-denial/977094

14. 'In Lausanne, Dogu Perincek Goes on Trial for Denying Armenian Genocide Claims', Hürriyet, 6 Mar. 2007, http://www.hurriyet.com.tr/english/6069762_p.asp.

15. 'Swiss Court Convicts Turkish Politician of Genocide Denial', New York Times, 9 Mar. 2007, http://www.nytimes.com/2007/03/09/world/europe/09iht-turkey.4860145.html?_r=0.

16. European Court of Human Rights, 'Affaire Perinçek c. Suisse' (Requête no 27510/08), Strasbourg, 17 Dec. 2013 (§ 115), http://hudoc.echr.coe.int/sites/eng/pages/search.aspx?i=001–139276#%7B%22itemid%22:%5B%22001–139276%22%5D%7D.

17. Ibid., §117, 119.

18. Öztürk Türkdoğan, Human Rights Association, letter addressed to Mrs. Simonetta Sommaruga, Ref: 207/2014/11–46, 24 Feb. 2014. Copy obtained thanks to posting of Ayse Gunaysu on 'Reconcile', the electronic list service, 24 Feb. 2014.

19. Kamil Maman, 'Ergenekon is Above General Staff, MIT', *Today's Zaman*, 7 July 2008, http://web.archive.org/web/20080709061153/http://www.todayszaman.com/tz-web/detaylar.do?load=detay&link=146843.

20. 'Ergenekon Crossed Dink's Path Many Times before Murder', *Today's Zaman*, 13 May 2010, http://www.todayszaman.com/newsDetail_open-PrintPage.action?newsId=210064.

21. Author interview with Fethiye Çetin, Istanbul, 4 Nov. 2014.

22. Gingeras, *Heroin, Organized Crime*, p. 244. See also Gareth H. Jenkins, 'Between Fact and Fiction: Turkey's Ergenekon Investigation', Silk Road Paper, Aug. 2009, http://www.silkroadstudies.org/new/docs/silkroad-papers/0908Ergenekon.pdf.

23. 'Ergenekon: As the Power Pendulum Swings', WikiLeaks, Cable ID 09ANKARA368_a, 12 Mar. 2009, https://wikileaks.org/plusd/cables/09ANKARA368_a.html.

24. Amnesty International, *Ethnic Cleansing on a Historic Scale: Islamic State's Systematic Targeting of Minorities in Northern Iraq*, London, 2014.

25. A military photographer is known to have smuggled 55,000 photography of 11,000 individuals killed by torture in Syrian prisons. See Ben Hubbard and David D. Kirkpatrick, 'Photo Archive Is Said to Show Widespread Torture in Syria', *New York Times*, January 21, 2014: http://www.nytimes.com/2014/01/22/world/middleeast/photo-archive-is-said-to-show-wide-spread-torture-in-syria.html?_r=0.

26. Notable exceptions include Robert Melson, *Revolution and Genocide: On the Origins of the Armenian Genocide and the Holocaust*, Chicago, IL: University of Chicago Press, 1992; and more recently, Stefan Ihrig, *Atatürk in the Nazi Imagination*, Cambridge, MA: Harvard University Press, 2014.

27. Daily Sabah, 'Erdoğan: PKK, ISIS same for Turkey', October 16, 2014: http://www.dailysabah.com/politics/2014/10/04/erdogan-pkk-isis-same-for-turkey.

SELECTED BIBLIOGRAPHY

Abadie, Br. M., *Les Quatres Sièges d'Aintab (1920–1921)*, Paris: Charles-Lavauzelle & Cie, 1922.

Ahmad, Kamal, *Krdistan fi sanawat al-h'arb al-'alamiya al-oula*, (Arabic: Kurdistan in the Years of the First World War), 3rd edn, Beirut: al-Farabi, Beirut, 2013 (1st edn 1984).

Akçam, Taner, *A Shameful Act: The Armenian Genocide and the Question of Turkish Responsibility*, New York: Metropolitan Books, 2006.

Akçam, Taner, *Young Turks' Crime against Humanity: The Armenian Genocide and Ethnic Cleansing in the Ottoman Empire*, Princeton: Princeton University Press, 2012.

Akçam, Taner, "Guenter Lewy's The Armenian massacres in Ottoman Turkey", *Genocide Studies and Prevention*, Volume 3, Issue 1, April 2008, pp. 111–145.

Akşin, Sina, *Turkey: From Empire to Revolutionary Republic*, London: Hurst, 2007.

Aktar, Ayhan, 'Debating the Armenian Massacres in the Last Ottoman Parliament, November–December 1918', *History Workshop Journal*, 64, (Autumn 2007) pp. 240–70.

Aktar, Cengiz, *Goch Nerumi, Turkere Timum yen Hayerin* (Armenian text translated from the French: *L'Appel au pardon, Des Turcs s'adressent aux Arméniens)*, Yerevan: Actual Art, 2001.

Anderopoulos George J. (ed.), *Conceptual and Historical Dimensions of Genocide*, Philadelphia: University of Pennsylvania Press, 1994.

Aslanian, Sebouh David, *From the Indian Ocean to the Mediterranean: The Global Trade Networks of Armenian Merchants from New Julfa*, Berkeley: University of California Press, 2011.

Attarian, Varoujan, *Le Génocide des Arméniens devant L'ONU*, Brussels: Editions Complexe, 1997.

SELECTED BIBLIOGRAPHY

Andonian, Aram, *Medz Vojire, Haygagan Verchin Godoradznere yev Talat Pasha* (The Great Crime: The Latest Armenian Massacres and Talaat Pasha), Boston: Bahag Printers, 1921.

Auron, Yair, *Banality of Denial: Israel and the Armenian Genocide*, New Brunswick, NJ: Transaction Publishers, 2004.

Auron, Yair, *The Pain of Knowledge: Holocaust and Genocide Issues in Education*, New Brunswick, NJ: Transaction Publishers, 2005.

Avakyan, Grigor Y., *Hayasdane 1920–1990 Tt., Dndesaashkharakragan Agnarg*, (Armenian: In the Years 1920–1990, Geo-Economic View), Yerevan: Yerevani Hamalsarani Debaran (Armenian University Press), 1997.

Baghdjian, Kevork K., *The Confiscation of Armenian Properties by the Turkish Government Said to be Abandoned*, Antelias: Printing House of the Armenian Catholicosate of Cilicia, 2010.

Balakian, Peter, *The Burning Tigris: The Armenian Genocide and American Response*, New York: Harper Collins, 2003.

Bardakjian, Kevork, *Hitler and the Armenian Genocide*, Cambridge, MA: Zoryan Institute, Special Report no. 3, 1985.

Barsamyan V. A. and Sh. R. Harutyunyan, *Hay Zhoghovrti Badmutyun, 1801–1978 TT.* (Armenian: History of the Armenian People, 1801–1978), Yerevan: Luys, 1979.

Bird, Isabella L., *Journeys in Persia and Kurdistan*, vol. 2, London: John Murray, 1891.

Bloxham, Donald, *The Great Game of Genocide*, New York: Oxford University Press, 2009 (first published in 2005).

Bobelian, Michael, *Children of Armenia: A Forgotten Genocide and the Century-Long Struggle for Justice*, London: Simon and Schuster, 2012.

Bournoutian, George A., *A Concise History of the Armenian People: From Ancient Times to the Present*, Mazda Publishers, 2002

Hamit Bozarslan, 'Les Révoltes Kurdes en Turquie Kémaliste (Quelques aspects)', *Guerres mondiales et conflits contemporains* (1988) pp. 121–36.

Briggs, Asa and Peter Burke, *A Social History of the Media: From Gutenberg to the Internet*, 3rd edn, Cambridge: Polity, 2009.

Brosset, M., *Les Ruins d'Ani, Capital de l'Arménie, Imprimerie de l'Académie Impériale des sciences, St.-Pétersbourg, 1860*.

Cagaptay, Soner, 'Race, Assimilation and Kemalism: Turkish Nationalism and the Minorities in the 1930s', *Middle Eastern Studies*, 40, 3 (2004), pp. 86–101.

Carmont, Pascal, *Les Amiras, Seigneurs de l'Arménie ottoman*, Paris: Editions Salvator, 1999.

Çetin, Fethiye, *My Grandmother: A Memoir*, London: Verso, 2008.

SELECTED BIBLIOGRAPHY

Çetin, Fethiye, and Ayşe Gül Altınay, *Les Petits-Enfants*, Arles: Actes Sud, 2011.

Cheterian, Vicken, *War and Peace in the Caucasus*, Russia's Troubled Frontier, London: Hurst, 2008.

Cheterian, Vicken, 'Kyrgyzstan: Central Asia's Island of Instability', Survival, 52,5 (2010), pp. 21–7.

Cheterian, Vicken, "Karabakh conflict after Kosovo: no way out?" *Nationalities Papers* 40,5 (2012): 703–720.

Chorbajian, Levon, Patrick Donabedian and Claude Mutafian, *The Caucasian Knot: The History and Geo-Politics of Nagorno-Karabakh*, London: Zed Books, 1994.

Croissant, Michael, *The Armenian-Azerbaijani Conflict: Causes and Implications*. Westpoint: Praeger, 1998.

Dadrian, Vahakn N., "The Naim-Andonian Documents on the World War I Destruction of Ottoman Armenians: The Anatomy of a Genocide", *International Journal of Middle East Studies*, Vol. 18, No. 3 (August 1986), pp. 311–360.

Dadrian, Vahakn N., 'The Secret Young-Turk Ittihadist Conference and the Decision for the World War I Genocide of the Armenians', *Holocaust and Genocide Studies*, 7, 2 (Fall 1993), pp. 173–201.

Dadrian, Vahakn N., *German Responsibility in the Armenian Genocide: a review of the historical evidence of German complicity*, Watertown, MA: Blue Crane Books, 1996.

Dadrian, Vahakn N., *The history of the Armenian genocide: ethnic conflict from the Balkans to Anatolia to the Caucasus*, Berghahn Books, 2003.

Dadrian, Vahakn N. and Taner Akçam, *Judgement at Istanbul: The Armenian Genocide Trials*, New York: Berghahn Books, 2011.

Dalrymple, William, *From the Holy Mountain: A Journey in the Shadow of Byzantium*, London: Flamingo, 1998.

Deringil, Selim, "'The Armenian Question Is Finally Closed": Mass Conversions of Armenians in Anatolia during the Hamidian Massacres of 1895–1897', *Comparative Studies in Society and History*, 5, 2 (2009), 344–371.

Der Matossian, Bedross, 'The Genocide Archives of the Armenian Patriarchate of Jerusalem', *Armenian Review*, 52, 3–4 (Fall-Winter 2011), pp. 17–39.

De Waal, Thomas, *Black Garden: Armenia and Azerbaijan through Peace and War*, New York: New York University Press, 2003.

Dink, Hrant, *Être Arménien en Turquie*, Reims: Fradet, 2007.

Dixon, Jennifer M., 'Education and National Narratives: Changing Representations of the Armenian Genocide in History Textbooks in Turkey', *The International Journal of Education Law and Policy*, (2010), pp. 103–126.

SELECTED BIBLIOGRAPHY

Dundar, Fuat, *Crime of Numbers: The Role of Statistics in the Armenian Question (1878–1918)*, New Brunswick, NJ: Transaction Publishers, 2010.

Ergil, Dogu, 'Knowledge is a Potent Instrument for Change', *European Journal of Turkish Studies*, 5 (2006), pp. 1–32.

Faroqhi, Suraiya, *The Ottoman Empire and the World Around It*, London: I.B. Tauris, 2004.

Fijnaut, Cyrill and Leitizia Paoli (eds), *Organized Crime in Europe: Concepts, Patterns and Control Policies in the European Union and Beyond*, Norwell, MA: Springer, 2004.

Foss, Clive, "Kemal Atatürk: Giving a New Nation a New History", *Middle Eastern Studies*, Vol. 50, Issue 5, 2014, pp. 826–847.

Gaspard, Armand, *Le combat arménien: entre terrorisme et utopie*, Lausanne: L'Âge d'homme, 1984.

Gaunt, David, *Massacres, Resistance, Protectors, Muslim-Christian Relations in Eastern Anatolia during World War I*, Gorgias Press, New Jersey, 2006.

Geukjian, Ohannes, *Ethnicity, Nationalism and Conflict in the South Caucasus: Nagorno-Karabakh and the Legacy of Soviet Nationalities Policy*, Farnham: Ashgate, 2012.

Gingeras, Ryan, *Heroin, Organized Crime, and the Making of Modern Turkey*, New York: Oxford University Press, 2014.

Grousset, René, *Histoire de l'Arménie, des origins à 1071*, Payot, 1995.

Gürün, Kamuran, *The Armenian File: The Myth of Innocence Exposed*, London: K. Rustem and Brothers, and Weidenfeld and Nicolson, 1985.

Gust, Wolfgang (ed.), *The Armenian Genocide: Evidence from the German Foreign Office Archives, 1915–1916*, New York: Berghahn, 2014.

Hakobyan, Tatul, *Hayatsk Araraden: Hayer yev Turker* (Armenian: Looking from Ararat: Armenians and Turks), Antelias, 2012.

Hanioğlu Sükrü, *A Brief History of the Late Ottoman Empire*, Princeton: Princeton University Press, 2010.

Hanioğlu Sükrü, *Ataturk: An Intellectual Biography*, Princeton: Princeton University Press, 2011.

Heinrich, Andreas, and Heiko Pleines (eds), *Challenges of the Caspian Resources Boom: Domestic Elites and Policy-Making*, Basingstoke: Palgrave Macmillan, 2012.

Hovannisian, Richard G. (ed.), *Remembrance and Denial: The Case of the Armenian Genocide*, Detroit: Wayne State University Press, 1999.

Hovannisian, Richard G. (ed.), *Armenian People from Ancient to Modern Times*, St. Martin's Press, New York, two volumes, 2000 and 2004.

Hovannisian, Richard G. and Simon Payaslian (eds), *Armenian Constantinople*, Costa Mesa, CA: Mazda Publishers, 2010.

SELECTED BIBLIOGRAPHY

Hovannisian, Richard G. (ed.), *Armenian Kars and Ani*, Costa Mesa, CA: Mazda Publisher, 2011.

Ihrig, Stefan, *Atatürk in the Nazi Imagination*, Harvard University Press, 2014.

Isgenderian, Hapet M., *Svedyo Abesdamputyune* (Armenian: The Revolt of Svedya), Cairo: Zareh Berberian Printers, 1915.

Jenkins, Gareth H., 'Between Fact and Fiction: Turkey's Ergenekon Investigation', Central Asia-Caucasus Institute and Silk Road Studies Program, Stockholm-Nacka, August 2009.

Jensen, Steven L.B. (ed.), *Genocide: Cases, Comparisons and Contemporary Debates*, Copenhagen: Danish Center for Holocaust and Genocide Studies, 2003.

Jerry L. Johnson, *Crossing Borders—Confronting History: Intercultural Adjustment in a Post-Cold War World*, Boston: University Press of America, 1999.

Kaligian, Dikran M., *Armenian Organization and Ideology under Ottoman Rule 1908–1914*, New Brunswick, NJ: Transaction Publishers, 2009.

Karpat, Kemal H., 'The Transformation of the Ottoman State, 1789–1908', *International Journal of Middle East Studies*, 3 (1972), pp. 243–281.

Kayali, Hasan, *Arabs and Young Turks, Ottomanism, Arabism, and Islamism in the Ottoman Empire 1908–1918*, Berkeley: California University Press, 1997.

Kent, Marian (ed.), *The Great Powers and the End of the Ottoman Empire*, London: Frank Cass, 1996.

Kévorkian, Raymond, *Le Génocide des Arméniens*, Paris: Odile Jacob, 2006.

Kévorkian, Raymond, 'Krikor Zohrab et les Jeunes-Turcs: La Trahison de l'Idéal Ottoman', *Armenological Issues Bulletin*, 1, Yerevan State University Press (2014), pp. 20–33.

Keyder, Çağlar, *State and Class in Turkey: A Study in Capitalist Development*, London: Verso, 1987.

Kieser, Hans-Lukas (ed.), *Turkey Beyond Nationalism: Towards Post-Nationalist Identities*, London: I.B. Tauris, 2013.

Kili, Suna, *Kemalism*, School of Business Administration and Economics, Robert College, 1969.

Konuk Blasing, Mutlu, *Nazim Hikmet: The Life and Times of Turkey's Poet*, W. W. Norton & Company, 2013.

Kurban, Dilek, and Kezban Hatemi, *The Story of an Alien(ation): Real Estate Ownership Problems of Non-Muslim Foundations and Communities in Turkey*, Istanbul: TESEV, 2009.

Lang, David Marshall, *Armenia: Cradle of Civilization*, London: George Allen & Unwin, 1970.

Lang, David Marshall, *The Armenians: A People in Exile*, London: Unwin, 1988 (1st edn 1980).

SELECTED BIBLIOGRAPHY

Léart, Marcel, *La Question Arménienne, A La Lumière des Documents*, Paris: Augustin Challamel, 1913.

Libaridian, Gérard (ed.), *A Crime of Silence: The Armenian Genocide*, London: Permanent Peoples' Tribunal, London: Zed Books, 1985.

Lowry, Heath W. 'The U.S. Congress and Adolf Hitler on the Armenians', *Political Communications and Persuasion*, 3, 2 (1985), pp. 111–140.

Malkasian, Mark, 'The Disintegration of the Armenian Cause in the United States, 1918–1927', *International Journal of Middle East Studies*, 16 (1984), pp. 349–65.

Mandelstam, André, La Société des Nations et les Puissances devant le Problème Arménien, Paris: Pédone, 1926.

Mango, Andrew, 'Atatürk and the Kurds', *Middle Eastern Studies*, 35, 4 (1999), pp. 1–25.

Mansel, Philip, *Constantinople: City of the World's Desire, 1453–1924*, London: John Murray, 2006.

Marchand, Laure and Guillaume Perrier, *La Turquie et le Fântome Arménien: Sur les traces du genocide*, Paris: *Actes Sud, 2013.*

Marshal, Alex, *The Caucasus Under Soviet Rule*, London: Routledge, 2010.

Matossian, Mary Kilbourne, *The Impact of Soviet Policies in Armenia*, Leiden: Brill, 1962.

McDowell, David, *A Modern History of The Kurds*, 3rd edn, London: I.B. Tauris, 2005.

Megerdichian, Tovmas C., *Dikranagerdi Nahanki Chartere yev Kyurderu Kazanutyunnere* (Armenian: The Massacres of Diyarbakir Province and Kurdish Beastiality), Cairo: Krikor Jihanian Printer, 1919.

Melkonian, Markar, *My Brother's Road: An American's Faithful Journey to Armenia*, London: I.B. Tauris, 2005.

Melkonian, Ruben, *Islamatsvadz Hayeri Khntirneri Shurj* (Armenian: On the Problems of Islamised Armenians), Noravank, 2009.

Melson, Robert, *Revolution and Genocide: On the Origins of the Armenian Genocide and the Holocaust*, University of Chicago Press, 1992.

Meserlian, *Haygagan Hartsi Holovuyte 1939–2010* (Armenian: Evolution of the Armenian Question, 1939–2010), Beirut: Sipan, 2012.

Mgrdchian, Tovmas, *Dikranagerdi Nahanki Chartere yev Kurderu Kazanutyunnere, Aganades Badmutyun*, (Armenian: The Massacres of Diyarbakir Province and the Beastiality of the Kurds, an Eye-Witness Account), Cairo: Krikor Jihanian Printer, 1919.

Miller Donald E. and Lorna Touryan Miller, *Survivors: An Oral History of the Armenian Genocide*, Berkeley: University of California Press, 1999.

Milton, Giles, *Paradise Lost, Smyrna 1922: The Destruction of Islam's City of Tolerance*, London: Sceptre, 2008.

SELECTED BIBLIOGRAPHY

Minasian, Edward, '*The Forty Years of Musa Dagh*: The Film That Was Denied', *Journal of Armenian Studies*, 3, 1–2 (1986–7) pp. 121–32.

Minassian, Gaïdz, *Guerre et terrorisme arméniens* Paris: Presses Universitaires de France, 2002.

Morgenthau, Henry, *Ambassador Morgenthau's Story*, New York: Doubleday, Page & Company, 1919.

Morris, Chris, *The New Turkey: The Quiet Revolution on the Edge of Europe*, 2nd edn, London: Granta Books, 2006.

Mouradian, Claire, *De Staline à Gorbatchev histoire d'une république sovietique: l'Arménie*, Paris: Ramsay, 1990.

Müftülar-Bac, Meltem, 'The Never-Ending Story: Turkey and the European Union', *Middle Eastern Studies*, 34, 4 (1998).

Nichanian, Marc, *La Révolution Nationale, Entre L'Art et le Témoignage, Littératures arméniennes au XXe siècle*, vol. I, Geneva: Métis Presses, 2006.

Oran, Baskin, 'The Reconstruction of Armenian Identity in Turkey and the Weekly *Agos*', *The Turkish Yearbook of International Relations*, XXXVII (2006), pp. 123–138.

Orel, Şinasi, and Süreyya Yuca, *'Talat Pasha "telegrams": Historical fact or Armenian fiction?'* Lefkosa, 1986.

O'Shea, Maria T. *Trapped between the Map and Reality: Geography and Perceptions of Kurdistan*, London: Routledge, 2004.

Özoğlu, Hakan, *Kurdish Notables and the Ottoman State*, Albany: State University of New York Press, 2004.

Palmer, Alan, *The Decline and Fall of the Ottoman Empire*, London: John Murray, 1993.

Pamuk, Orhan, *Istanbul Memories of a City*, London: Faber and Faber, 2006 (1st edn 2005).

Panossian, Razmik, *The Armenians, From Kings and Priests to Merchants and Commissars*, Hurst, 2006.

Panzac, Daniel (ed.), *Histoire Economique et Sociale de l'Empire ottoman et de la Turquie (1326–1960), Paris: Peeters, 1995, pp. 506–19.*

Payaslian, Simon, *The History of Armenia, From the Origins to the Present*, Palgrave Macmillan, 2007.

Peterson, Merrill D., *'Starving Armenians': America and the Armenian Genocide, 1915–1930 and After*, Charlottesville: University of Virginia Press, 2004.

Phillips, David, *Unsilencing the Past: Track Two Diplomacy and Armenian-Turkish Reconciliation*, New York: Berghahn Books, 2005.

Phillips, David, 'Diplomatic History: The Turkey–Armenia Protocols', Institute for the Study of Human Rights, Columbia University, Working Paper, 2012.

Polatel, Mehmet, Nora Mildanoglu, Ozgur Leman Eren, and Mehmet Atilgan,

SELECTED BIBLIOGRAPHY

2012 Declaration: The Seized Properties of Armenian Foundations in Istanbul, Istanbul: Hrant Dink Foundation, 2012.

Power, Samantha, *A Problem from Hell: America and the Age of Genocide*, New York: Basic Books, 2002.

Provence, Michael, *The Great Syrian Revolt and the Rise of Arab Nationalism*, Austin, TX: University of Texas Press, 2005.

Quataert, Donald, 'The Massacres of Ottoman Armenians and the Writing of Ottoman History', *Journal of Interdisciplinary History*, XXXVII, 2, (Autumn 2006), pp. 249–59.

Rasizade, Alec, 'Azerbaijan after Heydar Aliev', *Nationalities Papers*, 32, 1 (Mar. 2004), pp. 137–64.

Refik, Ahmet, *Two Committees, Two Massacres*, trans. with Preface by Racho Donef, Firodil Publishing House, 2006 (first published in Ottoman Turkish, Istanbul, 1919).

Rhétoré, Jacques, *"Les Chrétiens aux bêtes", Souvenir de la guerre sainte proclamée par les Turcs contre les chrétiens en 1915*, Paris: CERF, 2005.

Ritter, Laurence and Max Sivaslian, *Les reste de l'épée*, Paris: Thadée, 2012.

Ruggles, Fairchild (ed.), *On Location: Heritage Cities and Sites*, New York: Springer, 2012.

Sanjian, Ara, 'The Armenian Minority Experience in the Modern Arab World' *Bulletin of the Royal Institute for Inter-Faith Studies, 3, 1 (2001), pp. 149–179.*

Sanjian, Ara, 'Oke's Armenian Question re-Examined', *Middle Eastern Studies*, 42, 5 (Sep. 2006), pp. 831–9.

Sahakyan, Lusine, *Turkification of the Toponyms in the Ottoman Empire and the Republic of Turkey*, Montreal: Arod Books, 2010.

Schwelling Birgit (ed.), *Reconciliation, Civil Society, and the Politics of Memory, Transnational Initiatives in the 20th and 21st Century*, Bielefeld: Transcript-Verlag, 2012.

Shahmuratian, Samuel, (ed.), *The Sumgait Tragedy: Pogroms against Armenians in Soviet Azerbaijan*, Cambridge, MA: Zoryan Institute, 1990.

Simonian, Hovann H., 'The Vanished Khemshins: Return from the Brink', *Journal of Genocide Research*, 4, 3 (2001), pp. 375–85, p. 380.

Simonian, Hovann H., 'History and Identity among the Hemshin', *Central Asian Survey*, 25, 1–2 (Mar.–June 2006), pp. 157–178.

Simonian, Hovann H., *The Hemshin: History, Society and Identity in the Highlands of Northeast Turkey*, London: Routledge, 2007.

Siruni, Hagop Jololian *Inknagensakragan Noter* (Autobiographic Notes), Yerevan: Sarkis Khachents Publishers, 2006.

Smith, Robert, Eric Markusen and Robert Jay Lifton, 'Professional Ethics and the Denial of Armenian Genocide', *Holocaust and Genocide Studies*, 9, 1, (Spring 1995), pp. 1–22.

Sontag, Susan, *Regarding the Pain of Others*, New York: Picador, 2003.

Soulahian Kuyumjian, Rita, *Archaeology of Madness: Komitas, Portrait of an Armenian Icon*, 2nd edn, London: Gomidas Institute, 2002.

Suny, Ronald Grigor, *The Baku Commune, 1917–1918: Class and Nationality in the Russian Revolution*, Princeton: Princeton University Press, 1972.

Suny, Ronald Grigor, *The Making of the Georgian Nation*, Bloomington: Indiana University Press, 1988.

Suny, Ronald Grigor, *Looking toward Ararat: Armenia in Modern History*, Bloomington: Indiana University Press, 1993.

Suny, Ronald Grigor, 'Truth in Telling: Reconciling Realities in the Genocide of the Ottoman Armenians', 114.4, *American Historical Review* (Oct. 2009), pp. 930–946.

Suny, Ronald Grigor, Fatma Müge Göçek and Norman M. Naimark (eds), *A Question of Genocide: Armenians and Turks at the End of the Ottoman Empire*, Oxford: Oxford University Press, 2011.

Tachjian, Vahé, 'Gender, Nationalism, Exclusion: The Reintegration Process of Female Survivors of the Armenian Genocide', *Nations and Nationalism*, 15, 1 (2009), pp. 60–80.

Ter Minassian, Anahide, *Nationalism and Socialism in the Armenian Revolutionary Movement (1887–1912)*, Cambridge, MA: Zoryan Institute, 1984.

Ter Minassian, Anahide, 'The Revolution of 1905 in Transcaucasia', *Armenian Review*, 42, 2/166 (Summer 1989), pp. 1–23.

Tokluoğlu, Ceylan, "Definitions of national identity, nationalism and ethnicity in post-Soviet Azerbaijan in the 1990s", *Ethnic and Racial Studies*, Vol. 28, No. 4, July 2005, pp. 722–758.

Tokluoğlu, Ceylan, "The Political Discourse of the Azerbaijani Elite on the Nagorno-Karabakh Conflict (1991–2009)", *Europe-Asia Studies*, Vol. 63, Issue 7, pp. 1223–1252.

Toynbee, Arnold, *The Treatment of Armenians in the Ottoman Empire 1915–16, Documents Presented to Viscount Grey of Fallodon, Secretary of State for Foreign Affairs, with a Preface by Viscount Bryce*, London, 1916.

Travis, Hannibal, 'Did the Armenian Genocide Inspire Hitler?' *Middle East Quarterly* (Winter 2013), pp. 27–35.

Ulgen, Fatma, "'Sabiha Gökçen's 80-Year-Old Secret": Kemalist Nation Formation and the Ottoman Armenians', Doctoral Dissertation, University of California, San Diego, 2010.

Üngör, Ugur Ümit, *The making of modern Turkey: nation and state in Eastern Anatolia, 1913–1950*. Oxford: Oxford University Press, 2012.

SELECTED BIBLIOGRAPHY

Üngör, Ugur Ümit, and Mehmet Polatel, *Confiscation and Destruction: The Young Turk Seizure of Armenian Property*, London: Bloomsbury Publishing, 2011.

Uras, Esat, *The Armenians in History and the Armenian Question*, Ankara: Documentary Publications, 1988.

Van Bruinessen, Martin, *Agha, Sheikh and State: The Social and Political Structures of Kurdistan*, London: Zed Books, 1992.

VanderLippe, John M., *The Politics of Turkish Democracy: Ismet Inönü and the Formation of the Multi-Party System, 1938–1950*, Albany: State University of New York Press, 2005.

Verheij, Jelle, "'Les frères de terre et d'eau'": Sur le role des Kurdes dans les massacres arméniens de 1894–1896, *Les Cahiers de l'autre Islam, 5 (1999), pp. 225–76.*

Von Voss, Huberta (ed.), *Portraits of Hope: Armenians in the Contemporary World*, New York: Berghahn Books, 2007.

Walker, Christopher J., *Armenia: The Survival of a Nation*, 2nd edn, London: Routledge, 1990.

Yesaian, Zabel, *Averagneru Mech* (Armenian: Among the Ruins), Istanbul: Aras, 2010 (first published in Istanbul, 1911).

Yilmaz, Özcan, *La formation de la nation Kurde en Turquie*, Presses Universitaires de France, Paris, 2013.

Zürcher, Eric J., *Turkey: A Modern History*, London: I.B. Tauris, 2004 (first published 1993).

INDEX

INDEX